A New Star-Rating System & Other Exciting News from Frommer's!

In our continuing effort to publish the savviest, most up-to-date, and most appealing travel guides available, we've added some great new features.

Frommer's guides now include a new **star-rating system.** Every hotel, restaurant, and attraction is rated from 0 to 3 stars to help you set priorities and organize your time.

We've also added **seven brand-new features** that point you to the great deals, in-the-know advice, and unique experiences that separate travelers from tourists. Throughout the guide, look for:

Finds Special finds—those places only insiders know about

Fun Fact Fun facts—details that make travelers more informed and their trips more fun

Kids Best bets for kids—advice for the whole family

Moments Special moments—those experiences that memories are made of

Overrated Places or experiences not worth your time or money

Tips Insider tips—some great ways to save time and money

Value Great values—where to get the best deals

We've also added a **"What's New"** section in every guide—a timely crash course in what's hot and what's not in every destination we cover.

Here's what the critics say about Frommer's:

Frommer's®

Puerto Rico
6th Edition

by Darwin Porter & Danforth Prince

Wiley Publishing, Inc.

About the Authors

A native of North Carolina, **Darwin Porter** was a bureau chief for the *Miami Herald* when he was 21 and later worked in TV advertising. This veteran travel writer is the author of numerous best-selling Frommer's guides, including *Frommer's Caribbean,* the most candid and up-to-date guide to island vacations on the market. He is assisted by **Danforth Prince,** formerly of the Paris bureau of the *New York Times.* Both writers have traveled widely in the Caribbean for years and happily share their secrets and discoveries with you.

Published by:

Wiley Publishing, Inc.

909 Third Ave.
New York, NY 10022

ISBN 0-7645-6645-8
ISSN 1062-4775

Editor: Kitty Wilson Jarrett
Production Editor: Bethany André
Cartographer: Roberta Stockwell
Photo Editor: Richard Fox
Production by Wiley Indianapolis Composition Services

Front cover photo: Cerromar Beach, Dorado
Back cover photo: La Fortaleza and city walls, San Juan

For information on our other products and services or to obtain technical support, please contact our Customer Care Department within the U.S. at 800-762-2974, outside the U.S. at 317-572-3993 or fax 317-572-4002.

Wiley also publishes its books in a variety of electronic formats. Some content that appears in print may not be available in electronic formats.

Manufactured in the United States of America

5   4   3   2   1

Contents

List of Maps

An Invitation to the Reader

In researching this book, we discovered many wonderful places—hotels, restaurants, shops, and more. We're sure you'll find others. Please tell us about them, so we can share the information with your fellow travelers in upcoming editions. If you were disappointed with a recommendation, we'd love to know that, too. Please write to:

Frommer's Puerto Rico, 6th Edition
Wiley Publishing, Inc. • 909 Third Ave. • New York, NY 10022

An Additional Note

Please be advised that travel information is subject to change at any time—and this is especially true of prices. We therefore suggest that you write or call ahead for confirmation when making your travel plans. The authors, editors, and publisher cannot be held responsible for the experiences of readers while traveling. Your safety is important to us, however, so we encourage you to stay alert and be aware of your surroundings. Keep a close eye on cameras, purses, and wallets, all favorite targets of thieves and pickpockets.

New! Frommer's Star Ratings & Icons

Every hotel, restaurant, and attraction listing in this guide has been ranked for quality, value, service, amenities, and special features using a star-rating scale. In country, state, and regional guides, we also rate towns and regions to help you narrow down your choices and budget your time accordingly. Hotels and restaurants in the Very Expensive and Expensive categories are rated on a scale of one (highly recommended) to three stars (exceptional). Those in the Moderate and Inexpensive categories rate from zero (recommended) to two stars (very highly recommended). Attractions, towns, and regions are rated according to the following scale: zero stars (recommended), one star (highly recommended), two stars (very highly recommended), and three stars (must-see).

In addition to the rating system, we also use seven icons to highlight insider information, useful tips, special bargains, hidden gems, memorable experiences, kid-friendly venues, places to avoid, and other useful information:

Finds	*Fun Fact*	*Kids*	*Moments*	*Overrated*	*Tips*	*Value*

The following abbreviations are used for credit cards:

AE	American Express	DISC	Discover	V	Visa
DC	Diners Club	MC	MasterCard		

FROMMERS.COM

Now that you have the guidebook to a great trip, visit our website at **www.frommers.com** for travel information on nearly 2,500 destinations. With features updated regularly, we give you instant access to the most current trip-planning information available. At Frommers.com, you'll also find the best prices on airfares, accommodations, and car rentals—and you can even book travel online through our travel booking partners. At Frommers.com, you'll also find the following:

- Online updates to our most popular guidebooks
- Vacation sweepstakes and contest giveaways
- Newsletter highlighting the hottest travel trends
- Online travel message boards with featured travel discussions

What's New in Puerto Rico

This dynamic island explodes with change year after year. Today's grand resort might be swept away in a hurricane, or last winter's hot restaurant dining choice might be a sea of empty tables this season. Even beaches come and go. Here are some of the latest developments.

SAN JUAN ACCOMMODATIONS The big news on the hotel front is the opening of **The Water Club** (℡ **888/265-6699** or 787/253-0100), the first truly authentic boutique hotel along San Juan's beachfront. It's chic and hip, with artful glass-enclosed "waterfalls" and inventive theatrical lighting contributing to its posh atmosphere. Its exotic panoramic bar boasts the Caribbean's only rooftop fireplace.

The former San Juan Grand Beach Resort & Casino has been massively restored, thanks to an output of over $15 million, and it now enjoys a better-than-ever life as the **Inter-Continental San Juan Resort & Casino** (℡ **800/443-2009** or 787/791-6100). From sushi to the best steaks on Isla Verde, dining facilities at the Inter-Continental now rank among the best in Puerto Rico.

The oldest Hilton in the Caribbean, the **Caribe Hilton** (℡ **800/HILTONS** or 787/721-0303), was growing a bit stale until an infusion of millions of dollars brought it back to life. Its oceanfront spa and fitness center—the only beachside spa in Puerto Rico—is almost reason enough to stay here, but the casino, the beach, and the beautifully restored rooms are other "excuses."

SAN JUAN RESTAURANTS There's been an explosion of top-rated restaurants in San Juan. In Old San Juan, there's a buzz about **Dragonfly** (℡ **787/977-3886**). Even though its decor has been compared to that of a Barbary Coast bordello, this Latin and Asian restaurant is a hot reservation. The cookery here has been called "sexy," and clever use is made of regional ingredients.

Right outside the entrance to Old Town, Puerta de Tierra has a bright dining picture. Most of the excitement is generated by **Invernino** (℡ **787/724-2166**), which presents a tempting array of cuisines from the major culinary zones of Italy, especially Tuscany. At the Caribe Hilton, **Morton's of Chicago** (℡ **787/977-6262**) brings succulent steaks and other choice meats to San Juan.

On the Condado, **La Belle Epoque** (℡ **787/977-1765**) is the showcase for master chef Jeremie Cruz, hailed as Caribbean chef of the year in 2001. His French fusion cuisine is a delight, and he creates delectably inventive dishes.

The Museo de Arte (see below) is now the most visited attraction in San Juan. Taking advantage of this popularity, the restaurant **Pikayo** (℡ **787/721-6194**) has been installed here, and it's a fine showcases of Puerto Rican cookery, with a Cajun inspiration. For spice and zest, this is the place.

SAN JUAN SIGHTS At its opening, the **Museo de Arte** (℡ **787/977-6277**), in Santurce, has become the most important gallery in the history of Puerto Rico. Constructed at a cost of $55 million, the museum reflects the island nation's rich cultural heritage and features a galaxy of Puerto Rico's most celebrated artists.

RINCON   Yanks are flocking in such great numbers to Rincón, the windsurfing capital of the Caribbean, that it's now nicknamed "gringoland." Regal travelers have long patronized the tony Horned Dorset Primavera, and the opening of **Lemontree Waterfront Cottages** (© 787/823-6452) has made top-rate accommodations available to those with modest purses. You can prepare some of your meals in the complex's new kitchenettes.

ISABELA   An equally good choice to Lemontree (see above) lies up the coast near the pastel-colored town of Isabela, close to some excellent beaches. Here you'll find a family-friendly *parador* (inn) **Villas del Mar Hau** (© 787/872-2045), a series of West Indian–style cottages that offer some of the best shelter for those who need an inexpensive anchor along the northwestern coast.

PALMAS DEL MAR   One of the best dive centers in Puerto Rico, **Palmas Dive Center** (© 787/633-7314) has opened at the eastern Puerto Rican holiday complex Palmas del Mar. Bill Winnie offers some of the best scuba lessons on the island and takes divers and snorkelers to fauna-rich reefs and Monkey Island.

The dining picture in the Palmas del Mar area has brightened considerably with the opening of **Barracuda Bistro** (© 787/850-4441), located on the grounds of Palmas del Mar. Puerto Rican and international cuisines are featured, and you can order everything from excellent T-bone steaks to Mexican and Creole specialties.

FAJARDO   Western Puerto Rico no longer dominates the parador scene in Puerto Rico: These country-style inns are opening on the east coast as well,

giving visitors an alternative to high-priced resorts. Chief among these is **The Fajardo Inn** (© 787/860-6000), which is a good base for exploring the El Yunque rainforest. An hour's drive east of San Juan, it stands on a hilltop overlooking the colorful port of Fajardo.

You can also stay south of Fajardo at **Hotel Parador Palmas de Lucía** (© 787/893-4423), which is a worthy goal for those driving the Ruta Panorámica, a network of scenic roads that stretch from Mayagüez in the west to Yabucoa in the east.

VIEQUES   The home of a U.S. naval station, Vieques is becoming increasingly fashionable for both its inns and restaurants. Excitement is currently focused on **Café Media Luna** (© 787/741-2594), a charming eatery known for its new Latin and Asian cuisines. Everything is freshly prepared, and many evenings you can hear jazz concerts.

CULEBRA   Numerous tiny inns and cottages have opened on this island, which lies off Puerto Rico's eastern coast. Chief among these is **Tamarindo Estates** (© 787/742-3343), which lies on 60 lush acres beside a private bay and rents kitchen-equipped cottages. Another choice is **Casa Ensenada Waterfront Guesthouse** (© 800/484-9659 or 787/742-3559), a B&B with clean, comfortable rooms at bargain prices.

Culebra has also seen the opening of many dining options. **Dinghy Dock** (© 787/742-0233), outside Dewey, is a choice hangout that attracts because of its combined American and Caribbean cuisine. **Mamacita's** (© 787/742-0090) not only has the island's best bar but also offers the finest cuisine on the island, a culinary blend of the Caribbean with the regional specialties of Puerto Rico. For pizza, the winner is **Oasis Pizzeria** (© 787/742-3175), which also serves the best sandwiches around.

The Best of Puerto Rico

Whatever you want to do on a tropical vacation or business trip—play on the beach with the kids (or gamble away their college funds), enjoy a romantic honeymoon, or have a little fun after a grueling negotiating session—you'll find it in Puerto Rico. But you don't want to waste precious hours once you get here searching for the best deals and the best experiences. We've done that work for you. During our years of traveling through the islands that form the Commonwealth of Puerto Rico, we've tested the beaches, toured the sights, reviewed countless restaurants, inspected hotels, and sampled the best scuba diving, hikes, and other outdoor activities. We've even learned where to get away from it all when it's time to escape the crowds.

Here's what we consider to be the best that Puerto Rico has to offer.

1 The Best Beaches

White sandy beaches put Puerto Rico and its offshore islands on tourist maps in the first place. Many other Caribbean destinations have only jagged coral outcroppings or black volcanic-sand beaches that get very hot in the noonday sun. The best beaches are labeled on the "Puerto Rico" map on p. 20.

- **Best for Singles (Straight & Gay):** Sandwiched between the Condado and Isla Verde beaches along San Juan's beachfront, **Ocean Park Beach** attracts more adults and less of the family trade. Only Isla Verde beach to the east matches Ocean Park for its broad beach and good swimming. The people watching here is nothing compared to the well-stuffed bikinis (both male and female) found on South Miami Beach or Rio de Janeiro. However, for the Caribbean, Ocean Park is as good as it gets. Because many gay boarding houses lie in Ocean Park, a lot of the beach here is frequented by gay young men,

mainly from New York. However, straight people looking to meet someone while wearing swimwear will find plenty of lookers (and perhaps takers). See "Diving, Fishing, Tennis & Other Outdoor Pursuits" in chapter 6.

- **Best Beach for Families:** Winning without contest, **Luquillo Beach,** 30 miles (48km) east of San Juan, attracts both local families, mainly from San Juan, and visitors from Condado and Isla Verde beaches in San Juan. Beach buffs heading for Luquillo know they will get better sands and clearer waters there than in San Juan. The vast sandy beach opens onto a crescent-shaped bay edged by a coconut grove. Coral reefs protect the crystal-clear lagoon from the often rough Atlantic waters that can buffet the northern coast, making Luquillo a good place for young children to swim. Much-photographed because of its white sands, Luquillo also has tent sites and other facilities, including picnic areas with changing rooms, lockers, and showers. See "Luquillo Beach" in chapter 7.

• **Best for Teenagers:** More families with teenagers check into the Hyatt resorts west of San Juan—the Hyatt Dorado Beach Resort & Country Club and the Hyatt Regency Cerromar Beach Hotel—than into any other competitor in Puerto Rico, including the resorts along the San Juan beach strip. Six beaches border the Hyatt resorts, each a strip of white sand fronting the north coast. Because the Dorado features many activities for kids of all ages, its beaches over the years have become family favorites. The **Hyatt beaches** originally opened onto a grapefruit-and-coconut plantation, but today these 1,000 landscaped acres are devoted to fun, ranging from jogging and biking trails to swimming in the longest pool on the island. Young people find it easy to meet other teenagers here, not only on the beach but while participating in the resorts' myriad of activities. See the Hyatt resort listings under "Dorado" in chapter 7.

• **Best for Swimming:** Whereas on much of the northwest coast of Puerto Rico, rough Atlantic waters often deter bathers but attract surfers (see below), the south coast waters are calmer. On the south coast, **Playa de Ponce,** outside Ponce, Puerto Rico's second-largest city, consists of a long strip of beautiful white sand that opens onto the tranquil waters of the Caribbean. Less crowded than Condado and Luquillo, Playa de Ponce is an ideal place to swim year-round in clearer, less polluted waters than those along the more heavily populated northern coastline. See "Ponce" in chapter 8.

• **Best for Scenery:** In the southwestern corner of Puerto Rico, **Boquerón Beach** lies in a section of the island called the Cape Cod of Puerto Rico. The beach town of Boquerón itself, filled with colorful scenery, stands at the heart of a 3-mile (5km) bay, with palm-fringed white sand curving away on both sides. In addition to this panoramic vista, you can also sample vignettes of local life. Fisherfolk, sailors, and scuba divers are also attracted to this beach, where fresh oysters are shucked on the spot and doused with Tabasco and sold at various ramshackle shacks, each of which is ideal for a photo op. While enjoying the scenery and the sands, you can take a break and order a regional ice cream at one of the stands. It's made with sweet corn and dusted with paprika. Sound awful? Try it: It's good. See "The Southwest Coast" in chapter 9.

• **Best for Windsurfing:** Rincón's winter surf, especially at **Playa Higüero,** puts Malibu to shame. Today surfers from all over the world are attracted to Rincón, which they have dubbed "Little Malibu." From Borinquén Point south to Rincón, nearly all the beaches along the western coast are ideal for surfing from November to April. As the windsurfing capital of the Caribbean, the Rincón area was put on the map when it was the site of the 1968 world surfing championships. Some of the 16-foot breakers here equal those on the north shore of Oahu. See "Rincón" in chapter 9.

• **Best Beaches for Being Alone:** The main island is filled with isolated sandy coves that only the locals seem to know about. The best, all guaranteed to delight the escapist in you, stretch between

Cabo Rojo (the southwesterly tip of Puerto Rico) all the way east to Ponce. Beginning in the west, directly east of Cabo Rojo, you'll discover **Rosado Beach, Santa Beach, Caña Gorda Beach,** and **Tamarindo Beach.** Access to many of these is limited because of poor roads, but the effort is worth it. Be sure to bring the necessary supplies. See "Puerto Rico's Secret Beaches" in chapter 9.

- **Best for Snorkeling:** For snorkeling, we prefer to escape from the Puerto Rican mainland altogether, heading for the isolated beaches of the offshore islands of **Vieques** and **Culebra,** part of the Spanish Virgin Islands. In Vieques alone there are some 40 beaches, most of them officially unnamed even though U.S. sailors stationed on the island have nicknamed their favorites— everything from Green Beach to Orchid. The best beach for snorkeling on Vieques is **Playa Esperanza,** especially that spot in front of the Trade Winds Guesthouse. Another favorite location, which we discovered when directed there by a Navy SEAL, is across the little harbor at **Cayo de Afuera.** This site gives you the best preview of dramatic (and living) antler coral. Nurse sharks and the occasional manatee also hang out here. See "Vieques" in chapter 11.

On the neighboring island of Culebra, the beaches are less visited by snorkelers, even though they open onto coral reefs and clear waters. The snorkeling is not so hot at the island's most frequented beach, Flamenco Beach. But all you have to do is take a 15- to 20-minute hike from the parking lot at Flamenco over the hill to **Playa Carlos Rosario,** which offers some of the best snorkeling in Puerto Rico. A barrier reef virtually envelops the beach, and you can snorkel all day. For other great snorkeling, you can walk along the cliffs south of here for about a quarter mile (.5km) to a place called **"The Wall,"** which has 40-foot drop-offs, rainbow-hued fish, and other delights. See "Culebra" in chapter 11.

2 The Best Hotel Beaches

- **Condado Plaza Hotel & Casino** (San Juan; © **800/468-8588** or 787/721-1000) stands on a strip of tasty beachfront that marks the beginning of the Condado, arguably the most famous beach in the Caribbean. This beach also enjoys the most popularity because of its closeness to Old San Juan. Once the stamping ground of the rich, including the Vanderbilts and the Rockefellers, this 2-mile (3km) band of white sand winds its way between a blue lagoon and some of the island's major resort hotels. Starting in the 1970s, the beach's popularity mushroomed, as fast-food joints, watersports concessions, restaurants, and high-rise condos lined the beach. But the Condado Plaza's wide strip of sands remains more pristine, and you can also enjoy the facilities of this deluxe hotel. See p. 91.

- **Wyndham El San Juan Hotel & Casino** (San Juan; © **800/WYN-DHAM** or 787/791-1000): This posh resort occupies the choicest beachfront real estate at Isla Verde Beach, one of the finest in Puerto Rico. Ideal for swimming, the golden sands near the airport evoke South Miami Beach. Picnic tables are found here, and the beach is also good for snorkeling. But it is mostly the sands themselves that provide the attraction—that and all the many facilities of El San Juan resort itself. See p. 101.

- **Hyatt Resorts at Dorado** (Hyatt Dorado Beach Resort & Country Club: **©** **800/233-1234** or 787/ 796-1234; Hyatt Regency Cerromar Beach Hotel: **800/233-1234** or 787/796-1234): Lying 18 miles (29km) west of San Juan, these two plush resorts were carved out of a plantation. Today they open onto several miles of white sandy beaches at the mouth of the Río de la Plata. Since the turn of the 20th century, Dorado, which means "golden," has attracted U.S. presidents and rich folks like the Rockefellers. Today families can be seen romping along its sands. See p. 180.

3 The Best Scuba Diving

With the continental shelf surrounding it on three sides, Puerto Rico has an abundance of coral reefs, caves, sea walls, and trenches for divers of all experience levels to explore. See "The Active Vacation Planner" in chapter 2 for detailed information.

- **Metropolitan San Juan:** This easy **beach dive off the Condado district** in San Juan is not as spectacular as other dives mentioned here, but it's certainly more convenient. Lava reefs sculptured with caverns, tunnels, and overhangs provide hiding areas for schools of snapper, grunts, and copper sweepers. In the active breeding grounds of the inner and outer reefs, divers of all levels can mingle with an impressive array of small tropical fish— French angels, jacks, bluehead wrasse, butterfly fish, and sergeant majors, among them—along with sea horses, arrow crabs, coral shrimp, octopuses, batfish, and flying gunards. Visibility is about 10 to 20 feet. The Condado reef is also ideal for resort courses, certification courses, and night dives. See "Diving, Fishing, Tennis & Other Outdoor Pursuits" in chapter 6.
- **Mona Island:** Mona Island, 40 miles (64km) west of the city of Mayagüez in western Puerto Rico, is the Caribbean version of the Galápagos Islands. Renowned for its pirate tales, cave-pocked cliffs, 3-foot-long iguanas, and other natural wonders, its waters are among the cleanest in Puerto Rico, with horizontal visibility at times exceeding 200 feet. More than 270 species of fish have been found in Mona waters, including more than 60 reef-dwelling species. Larger marine animals, such as sea turtles, whales, dolphins, and marlins, visit the region during migrations. Various types of coral reefs, underwater caverns, drop-offs, and deep vertical walls ring the island. The most accessible reef dives are along the southern and western shores. Getting there is a pain, however. You must brave a 5-hour boat ride across the often rough Mona Passage. See "Mona Island: The Galápagos of Puerto Rico" in chapter 8.
- **Southern Puerto Rico:** The continental shelf drops off precipitously several miles off the southern coast, producing a dramatic wall 20 miles (32km) long and teeming with marine life. Compared favorably to the wall in the Cayman Islands, this Puerto Rican version has become the Caribbean's newest world-class dive destination. Paralleling the coast from the seaside village of La Parguera to the city of Ponce, the wall descends in slopes and sheer drops from 60 to 120 feet before disappearing into 1,500 feet of

sea. Scored with valleys and deep trenches, it is cloaked in immense gardens of staghorn and elkhorn coral, deep-water gorgonians, and other exquisite coral formations. Visibility can exceed 100 feet. There are more than 50 dive sites around Parguera alone. See "The Southwest Coast" in chapter 9.

- **Fajardo:** This coastal town in eastern Puerto Rico offers divers the opportunity to explore reefs, caverns, miniwalls, and channels near a string of palm-tufted islets. The reefs are decked in an array of corals ranging from delicate gorgonians to immense coral heads. Visibility usually exceeds 50 feet. You can hand-feed many of the reef fish that inhabit the corals. Sand channels and a unique double-barrier reef surround Palomino Island, where band-tailed puffers and parrotfish harems are frequently sighted. Cayo Diablo, farther to the east, provides a treasure box of corals and marine animals, from green moray eels and barracudas to octopuses and occasional manatees. See "Las Croabas" in chapter 10.

- **Humacao Region:** South of Fajardo are some 24 dive sites in a 5-mile (8km) radius off the shore. Overhangs, caves, and tunnels perch in 60 feet of water along mile-long (1.5km) Basslet Reef, where dolphins visit in spring. The Cracks, a jigsaw of caves, alleyways, and boulders, hosts an abundance of goby-cleaning stations and a number of lobsters. With visibility often exceeding 100 feet, the Reserve offers a clear look at corals. At the Drift, divers float along with nurse sharks and angelfish into a valley of swim-throughs and ledges. For the experienced diver, Red Hog is the newest site in the area, with a panoramic wall that drops from 80 to 1,160 feet. See "Palmas del Mar" in chapter 10.

4 The Best Snorkeling

Puerto Rico offers top-notch snorkeling even though freshwater run-offs from tropical outbursts feeding into the sea can momentarily cloud the ocean's waters. In most places, when conditions are right, visibility extends from 50 to 75 feet.

- **Mona Island:** This remote island off the west coast of Puerto Rico (refer to "The Best Scuba Diving," above) also offers the best snorkeling possibilities. The reefs here, the most pristine in Puerto Rico, are home to a wide variety of rainbow-hued fish, turtles, octopuses, moray eels, rays, puffers, and clownfish: the single largest concentration of reef fish life in Puerto Rico. You must bring your snorkeling equipment to the island, however, as there are no rentals available once you are here.

See "Mona Island: The Galápagos of Puerto Rico" in chapter 8.

- **Caja de Muertos:** The best snorkeling off the coast of Ponce is on the uninhabited coast island of Caja de Muertos ("Coffin Island"). This isla got its name from an 18th-century French writer who noted that the island's shape resembled a cadaver in a coffin. Over the years there have been fanciful legends about the island, including tales of necrophilia, star-crossed lovers, and, of course, piracy. Island Adventures will take you to this remote spot for a full day's outing, with plenty of snorkeling. See "Ponce" in chapter 8.

- **Fajardo's Playa Escondido & La Cordillera:** On the eastern coast of Puerto Rico, the clear waters along the beachfront are the best on mainland Puerto Rico for snorkeling. The best beach here for snorkeling is Playa Escondido, although the marine wildlife refuge known as La Cordillera right off the coast is even more alluring. See "Las Croabas" in chapter 10.

- **Vieques & Culebra:** For a quick preview of the underwater possibilities, refer to "The Best Beaches," above. For more information, refer to chapter 11, "Vieques & Culebra."

5 The Best Golf & Tennis

- **Westin Rio Mar Golf Course** (Palmer; © **787/888-6000**): A 45-minute drive from San Juan on the northeast coast, the 6,145-yard Rio Mar Golf Course is shorter than those at both Palmas del Mar and Dorado East. One avid golfer recommended it to "those whose games and egos have been bruised by the other two courses." Wind here can seriously influence the outcome of your game. The greens fees are a lot lower than those of its two major competitors. See "Diving, Fishing, Tennis & Other Outdoor Pursuits" in chapter 6.

- **Hyatt Resorts at Dorado** (Hyatt Dorado Beach Resort & Country Club: © **800/233-1234** or 787/796-1234; Hyatt Regency Cerromar Beach Hotel: © **800/233-1234** or 787/796-1234): With 72 holes, Dorado has the highest concentration of golf on the island. Two courses—east and west—belong to the Hyatt Regency Cerromar and the Hyatt Dorado Beach resorts. Dorado East is our favorite. Designed by Robert Trent Jones, Sr., it was the site of the Senior PGA Tournament of Champions throughout the 1990s.

  True tennis buffs head here, too. The Dorado courts are the best on the island, and both hotels sponsor tennis weeks and offer special tennis packages. The Hyatt Regency Cerromar has 14 Laykold courts alone, two of them lit for night play. The Hyatt Dorado Beach Resort & Country Club weighs in with seven Laykold courts, two of them lighted. See "Dorado" in chapter 7.

- **Wyndham El Conquistador Resort & Country Club** (Las Croabas; © **800/468-5228** or 787/863-1000): This sprawling resort east of San Juan is one of the island's finest tennis retreats, with seven Har-Tru courts and a pro on hand to offer guidance and advice. If you don't have a partner, the hotel will find one for you. Only guests of the hotel are allowed to play here. See "Las Croabas" in chapter 10.

- **Palmas del Mar Golf Club** (Humacao; © **787/285-2256**): Lying on the southeast coast on the grounds of a former coconut plantation, the Palmas del Mar resort boasts the second-leading course in Puerto Rico—a par-72, 6,803-yard layout designed by Gary Player. Crack golfers consider holes 11 through 15 the toughest five successive holes in the Caribbean. See chapter "Palmas del Mar" in 10.

- **Tennis Center at Palmas del Mar** (Humacao; © **787/852-6000**, ext. 15): On the eastern coastline, this resort complex on the grounds of a former coconut plantation has 20 courts, 5 of which are Har-Tru and 15 are Tenne-flex (a harder surface). Seven of the courts are lighted. The resort offers tennis packages, and an on-site pro conducts private lessons. See "Palmas del Mar" in chapter 10.

6 The Best Hikes

Bring your boots. Puerto Rico's mountainous interior offers ample opportunity for hiking and climbing, with many trails presenting spectacular panoramas at the least-expected moments. See "The Active Vacation Planner" in chapter 2 for detailed information.

- **El Yunque** (© 787/888-1880 for information): Containing the only rain forest on U.S. soil, this Caribbean National Forest east of San Juan offers a number of walking and hiking trails. The rugged El Toro trail passes through four different forest systems en route to the 3,523-foot Pico El Toro, the highest peak in the forest. The El Yunque trail leads to three of the recreation area's most panoramic lookouts, and the Big Tree Trail is an easy walk to La Mina Falls. Just off the main road is La Coca Falls, a sheet of water cascading down mossy cliffs. See "El Yunque" in chapter 7.

- **Guánica State Forest** (© 787/724-3724 for information): At the opposite extreme of El Yunque's lush and wet rain forest, Guánica State Forest's climate is dry and arid, the Arizona-like landscape riddled with cacti. The area, cut off from the Cordillera Central mountain range, gets little rainfall. Yet it's home to some 50% of all the island's terrestrial bird species, including the rare Puerto Rican nightjar, once thought to be extinct. The forest has 36 miles (58km) of trails through four forest types. We prefer the mile-long (1.5km) Cueva Trail, where hikers look for the endangered bufo lemur toad, another species once thought to be extinct but still jumping in this area. Within the forest, El Portal Tropical Forest Center offers 10,000 square feet of exhibition space and provides information. See "Ponce" in chapter 8.

- **Mona Island:** Off the western coast of Puerto Rico, this fascinating island noted for its scuba-diving sites provides hiking opportunities found nowhere else in the Caribbean. Called the "Galápagos of Puerto Rico" because of its unique wildlife, Mona is home to giant iguanas and three species of endangered sea turtles. Some 20 endangered animals also have been spotted here. Ecotourists like to hike among Mona's mangrove forests, coral reefs, cliffs, and complex honeycomb of caves, ever on the alert for the diversity of both plant and animal life, including 417 plant and tree species, some of which are unique and 78 of which are rare or endangered. More than 100 bird species (2 unique) have been documented. Hikers can camp at Mona for $1 per night. Contact the **Puerto Rico Department of Natural Resources** (© 787/721-5495) for more information. See "Mona Island: The Galápagos of Puerto Rico" in chapter 8.

7 The Best Natural Wonders

- **El Yunque** (© 787/888-1880 for information): Forty-five minutes by road east of San Juan in the Luquillo Mountains, and protected by the U.S. Forest Service, El Yunque is Puerto Rico's greatest natural attraction. Some 100 billion gallons of rain fall annually on this home to four forest types containing 240 species of tropical trees. Families can walk one of the dozens of trails that wind past waterfalls, dwarf vegetation, and miniature flowers, while the island's colorful parrots fly overhead. You can hear the sound of Puerto Rico's mascot, the *coquí,* a small frog. See "El Yunque" in chapter 7.

- **Río Camuy Caves** (© **787/898-3100**): Some 2½ hours west of San Juan, visitors board a tram to descend into this forest-filled sinkhole at the mouth of the Clara Cave. They walk the footpaths of a 170-foot-high cave to a deeper sinkhole. Once they're inside, a 45-minute tour helps everyone, including kids, learn to differentiate stalactites from stalagmites. At the Pueblos sinkhole, a platform overlooks the Camuy River, passing through a network of cave tunnels. See "Arecibo & Camuy" in chapter 7.
- **Las Cabezas de San Juan Nature Reserve** (© **787/722-5882**): This 316-acre nature reserve about 45 minutes from San Juan encompasses seven different ecological systems, including forestland, mangroves, lagoons, beaches, cliffs, and offshore coral reefs. Five days a week (Wed–Sun), the park staff conducts tours in Spanish and English, the latter at 2pm only. Each tour lasts 2½ hours and is conducted with electric trolleys that traverse most of the park. Tours end with a climb to the top of the still-working 19th-century lighthouse for views over Puerto Rico's eastern coast and nearby Caribbean islands. Call to reserve space before going, as bookings are based on stringent restrictions as to the number of persons who can tour the park without damage to its landscape or ecology. The cost is a relative bargain, $5 for adults, $2 for children under 13, and $2.50 for seniors. See "To the Lighthouse: Exploring Las Cabezas de San Juan Nature Reserve" in chapter 10.

8 The Best Family Resorts

Puerto Rico has a bounty of attractions, natural wonders, and resorts that welcome families who choose to play together. Here are some of the best.

- **Condado Plaza Hotel & Casino** (San Juan; © **800/468-8588** or 787/721-1000): This resort offers Camp Taíno, a regular program of activities and special events for children ages 5 to 12. The cost of $25 per child includes lunch. The main pool has a kids' water slide that starts in a Spanish castle turret, plus a toddler pool. For teenagers, the hotel has a video game room, tennis courts, and various organized activities. For the whole family, the resort offers two pools and opens onto a public beach. It also has the best collection of restaurants of any hotel on the Condado. See p. 91.
- **Wyndham El San Juan Hotel & Casino** (San Juan; © **800/WYNDHAM** or 787/791-1000): The grandest hotel in Puerto Rico lies on Isla Verde, the less-famous strip of beach connected to the Condado. Its Kids Klub features trained counselors and group activities for the 5-to-13-year-old set. A daily fee of $28 buys lunch and an array of activities. The hotel opens onto a good beachfront and has some of the best restaurants in San Juan. See p. 101.
- **Hyatt Resorts at Dorado** (Hyatt Dorado Beach Resort & Country Club: © **800/233-1234** or 787/796-1234; Hyatt Regency Cerromar Beach Hotel: **800/233-1234**

or 787/796-1234): Sitting 18 miles (29km) west of San Juan, the Hyatt Regency Cerromar Beach Resort & Casino and the Hyatt Dorado Beach Resort & Country Club share a Camp Coquí program available for guests ages 3 to 12. Certified counselors direct programs of educational, environmental, and cultural activities. In the evening, movies, talent shows, and video games occupy the agenda. All this costs $40 a day per kid. Parents find one of the largest beaches and resort complexes in the Caribbean, including the world's longest freshwater river pool. See p. 180.

- **Wyndham El Conquistador Resort & Country Club** (Las Croabas; ✆ **800/468-5228** or 787/863-1000): Located 31 miles (50km) east of San Juan, this resort offers Camp Coquí on Palomino Island for children 3 to 12 years of age. The hotel's free water taxi takes kids to the island for a half or full day of watersports, and nature hikes. This resort has some of the best facilities and restaurants in eastern Puerto Rico. See p. 232.

- **Doral Palmas del Mar Resort** (Humacao; ✆ **800/725-6273** or 787/852-6000): The major rival in the east to El Conquistador, this sprawling resort has an Adventure Club for children ages 3 to 13. Supervised activities include arts, crafts, and sports, plus horseback riding for those old enough. For nonguests, the cost is $30 per half day or $35 per day, including lunch; guests are free. The resort is one of the most extensive in the Caribbean, with beaches, restaurants, and lots of watersports. See p. 236.

9 The Best Honeymoon Resorts

- **Wyndham El San Juan Hotel & Casino** (San Juan; ✆ **800/WYN-DHAM** or 787/791-1000): If you want Vegas-style shows, gambling, nightlife, great restaurants, and the most famous beach in Puerto Rico, El San Juan is at your disposal. It has the most glamorous lobby in the Caribbean and is set on 12 acres of Isla Verde, a strip of beach connected to the Condado. Options include a suite in the main tower with a whirlpool or your own private casita with a sunken Roman bath. The best deal is a package, costing from $337 per night for 3 nights. A lot of freebies are thrown in, including champagne and tropical fruit, daily tennis, one dinner, continental breakfast, and two massages. See p. 101.

- **Hyatt Dorado Beach Resort & Country Club** (Dorado; ✆ **800/ 233-1234** or 787/796-1234): This resort offers a more tranquil atmosphere than the nearby Hyatt Regency Cerromar, yet guests can use all the facilities and attractions of the neighboring hotel. You can book one of the elegantly furnished upper-level rooms in the Oceanview Houses and enjoy romantic vistas of two crescent-shaped beaches. There's casino and disco action, plus a spa, a health club, jogging trails, and 14 tennis courts. In low season packages range from $1,750 to $3,261 for two for the week, including one breakfast, champagne, T-shirts, $25 in casino chips, two massages, one dinner with wine, and transfers to and from the airport. In high season the tab rises by $1,000 a week per honeymooning couple, but breakfast and dinner are included. See p. 180

- **Ponce Hilton & Casino** (Ponce; 𝄋 **800/HILTONS** or 787/259-7676): A first-class act at Puerto Rico's "second city" on the south coast, this sprawling resort is set in an 80-acre garden. On-site amenities include a casino and disco, plus a whirlpool, tennis courts, and a fitness room. The two restaurants serve the best food on the south coast. Five suites are ideal for honeymoons. A $195 per night package includes a bottle of champagne, truffles, chocolates, and fresh strawberries, as well as breakfast daily, plus $25 in casino chips. You also receive a coupon granting 50% off on your next visit. See p. 197.

- **Horned Dorset Primavera Hotel** (Rincón; 𝄋 **800/633-1857** or 787/823-4030): The most romantic place for a honeymoon on the island, unless you stay in a private villa somewhere, this small, tranquil estate lies on the Mona Passage in western Puerto Rico, a pocket of posh where privacy is almost guaranteed. Accommodations are luxurious in the Spanish neocolonial style. The property opens onto a long, secluded beach of white sand. There are no phones, TVs, or radios in the rooms to interfere with the soft sounds of pillow talk. This is a retreat for adults only, with no facilities for children. Seven-night packages, including a bottle of champagne, breakfast, and dinner, range from $3,350 to $4,880 per couple, depending on the season. See p. 212.

- **Wyndham El Conquistador Resort & Country Club** (Las Croabas; 𝄋 **800/468-5228** or 787/863-1000): If you're looking for good food and diversions rather than a tranquil retreat, El Conquistador is the best big-time resort on the island. Atop a 300-foot bluff in eastern Puerto Rico, it has virtually everything for outdoor play, including golf and tennis, but when you want seclusion, you can post the PRIVADO sign and the world is yours. Honeymoon packages, based on 3 nights and 4 days, cost $562 per person in winter or $365 off-season, and include a fruit basket and champagne, two dinners in the room, two massages, and all breakfasts. See p. 232.

- **Doral Palmas del Mar Resort** (Humacao; 𝄋 **800/725-6273** or 787/852-6000): This luxury resort complex sits on 2,750 acres of a former coconut plantation on Puerto Rico's southeast coast. Only an hour's drive from San Juan, this sheltered spot is like another world, with Mediterranean villas, cobblestone plazas, condos, and Spanish-style fountains. You get some of the best golf on the island here, along with 20 tennis courts, a spa and health club, and miles of hiking and jogging trails. The Palmas Inn suites are best for honeymooners, unless you want to rent a private villa. Honeymoon packages for two people cost from $1,355 to $2,085 for a double room for two people to $1,484 to $2,200 for a suite for 7 nights and 8 days. Included in the package are such frills as daily breakfasts, one lunch, one dinner, and baskets of fruit and bottles of champagne. This particular arrangement is offered only between April and December, but other cost-conscious packages are available during high season (Dec–Apr) as well, on slightly different terms. See p. 236.

10 The Best Big Resort Hotels

- **Wyndham El San Juan Hotel & Casino** (San Juan; ℂ **800/WYNDHAM** or 787/791-1000): An opulent circular lobby sets the haute style at the Caribbean's most elegant resort. From its location along Isla Verde Beach, it houses some of the capital's finest restaurants and is the city's major entertainment venue. Guest rooms are tropically designed and maintained in state-of-the-art condition. See p. 101.

- **Ritz-Carlton San Juan Hotel, Spa & Casino** (San Juan; ℂ **800/241-3333** or 787/253-1700): At last Puerto Rico has a Ritz-Carlton, and this truly deluxe, oceanfront property is one of the island's most spectacular resorts. Guests are pampered in a setting of elegance and beautifully furnished guest rooms. Hotel dining is second only to that at El San Juan, and a European-style spa features 11 treatments "for body and beauty." See p. 100.

- **Hyatt Dorado Beach Resort & Country Club** (Dorado; ℂ **800/233-1234** or 787/796-1234): Lying on the former stamping grounds of the Rockefellers, these low-rise buildings blend into the lush surroundings of a grapefruit-and-coconut plantation. Spacious rooms open onto a long stretch of secluded beach, and grounds include an 18-hole championship golf course designed by Robert Trent Jones, Sr. Tennis, windsurfing, swimming, and dozens of watersports are available, as is the most elegant dining in Dorado. See p. 180.

- **Westin Rio Mar Beach Resort, Country Club & Ocean Villas** (Rio Grande; ℂ **800/WESTIN-1** or 787/888-6000): This $180 million 481-acre resort, 19 miles (31km) east of the San Juan airport, is one of the three largest hotels in Puerto Rico. Despite its size, personal service and style are hallmarks of the property. Twelve restaurants and lounges boast an array of cuisines. Along with its proximity to two golf courses, entertainment, such as an extensive program of live music, is a key ingredient in the hotel's success. See p. 186.

- **Wyndham El Conquistador Resort & Country Club** (Las Croabas; ℂ **800/468-5228** or 787/863-1000): The finest resort in Puerto Rico, this is a world-class destination—a sybaritic haven for golfers, honeymooners, families, and anyone else. Three intimate "villages" combine with one grand hotel, draped along 300-foot bluffs overlooking both the Atlantic and the Caribbean at Puerto Rico's northeastern tip. The 500 land-scaped acres include tennis courts, an 18-hole Arthur Hills–designed championship golf course, and a marina filled with yachts and charter boats. See p. 232.

- **Doral Palmas del Mar Resort** (Humacao; ℂ **800/725-6273** or 787/852-6000): Although not as impressive as El Conquistador, this sprawling complex evokes a Mediterranean village, opening onto over 3 miles (5km) of beach on the east coast of Puerto Rico. Palm trees grow everywhere. The complex boasts the largest tennis center in the Caribbean and an 18-hole Gary Player championship golf course. Additional amenities include a horseback-riding center for beach rides, watersports galore, an outstanding scuba-diving program, and deep-sea fishing charters. There's even a casino and nine restaurants. See p. 236.

11 The Best Moderately Priced Hotels

- **Gallery Inn at Galería San Juan** (San Juan; © **787/722-1808**): The most whimsically bohemian hotel in the Caribbean sits in the heart of the historic city. Once the home of an aristocratic Spanish family, it is today filled with verdant courtyards and adorned with sculptures, silk screens, and original paintings. Staying in one of the comfortable rooms here is like living in an art gallery. See p. 88.

- **At Wind Chimes Inn** (San Juan; © **800/946-3244** or 787/727-4153): This renovated and restored Spanish manor house is one of the best guesthouses in the Condado district. It lies only a short block from Puerto Rico's most famous beach. A favorite with families, the inn offers spacious rooms with kitchens and has recently added a swimming pool. See p. 95.

- **Copamarina Beach Resort** (Caña Gorda; © **800/468-4553** or 787/821-0505): Near Ponce, this resort was once the private vacation retreat of local cement barons the de Castro family.

Today it's been converted into one of the best beach hotels along Puerto Rico's southern shore. In fact, its beach is one of the best in the area. Set in a palm grove, the resort is handsomely decorated and comfortably furnished, with a swimming pool and two tennis courts. See p. 224.

- **Lemontree Waterfront Cottages** (Rincón; © **787/823-6452**): On a sandy beach at the windsurfing capital of the Caribbean, this colony offers large apartments with kitchenettes, ideal for families who like to prepare some of their own meals. See p. 214.

- **Hacienda Tamarindo** (Vieques; © **787/741-8525**): On the site of a 1990s nightclub, this expanded inn has style, flair, and charm, and a desirable location—just inland from a great white sandy beach. Built around a massive 2-century-old tamarind tree and operated by a couple from Vermont, the inn has comfortable and appealing accommodations, which are often furnished with antiques. The welcome is warm. See p. 244.

12 The Best Attractions

- **The Historic District of Old San Juan:** There's nothing like it in the Caribbean. Partially enclosed by old walls dating from the 17th century, Old San Juan was designated a U.S. National Historic Zone in 1950. Some 400 beautifully restored buildings fill this district, which is chockablock with tree-shaded squares, monuments, and open-air cafes, as well as shops, restaurants, and bars. If you're interested in history, there is no better stroll in the West Indies. See "Exploring San Jaun" in chapter 6.

- **Castillo de San Felipe del Morro** (Old San Juan): In Old San Juan and nicknamed El Morro, this fort was originally built in 1540. It guards the bay from a rocky promontory on the northwestern tip of the old city. Rich in history and legend, the site covers enough territory to accommodate a nine-hole golf course. See p. 134.

- **The Historic District of Ponce:** Second only to Old San Juan in terms of historic significance, the central district of Ponce is a blend of Ponce Créole and Art Deco building styles, dating mainly from the 1890s to the 1930s. One street, Calle Isabel, offers an array of Ponceño architectural styles, which often incorporate neoclassic details. The city underwent a massive restoration preceding the celebration of its 300th anniversary in 1996. See "Ponce" in chapter 8.

- **Museo de Arte de Ponce** (Ponce): This museum has the finest collection of European and Latin American art in the Caribbean. The building was designed by Edward Durell Stone, who also designed the Museum of Modern Art in New York City. Contemporary works by Puerto Ricans are displayed, as well as works by an array of old masters, including Renaissance and baroque pieces from Italy. See p. 191.

- **Tropical Agriculture Research Station:** These tropical gardens contain one of the largest collections of tropical species intended for practical use. These include cacao, fruit trees, spices, timbers, and ornamentals. Adjacent to the Mayagüez campus of the University of Puerto Rico, the site attracts botanists from around the world. See "Mayagüez" in chapter 8.

- **The City of San Germán:** In the southwestern corner of Puerto Rico, and founded in 1512, this small town is Puerto Rico's second-oldest city. Thanks to a breadth of architectural styles, San Germán is also the second Puerto Rican city (after San Juan) to be included in the National Register of Historic Places. Buildings, monuments, and plazas fill a 36-acre historic zone. Today's residents descend from the smugglers, poets, priests, and politicians who once lived here in "the city of hills," so-called because of the mountainous location. See "San Germán" in chapter 8.

- **Iglesia Porta Coeli** (San Germán): The main attraction of this ancient town is the oldest church in the New World. It was originally built by Dominican friars in 1606. The church resembles a working chapel, although mass is held here only three times a year. Along the sides of the church are treasures gathered from all over the world. See "San Germán" in chapter 8.

13 The Best Restaurants

- **Chef Marisoll** (San Juan; ℭ 787/ 725-7454): One of Puerto Rico's best chefs, Marisoll Hernández, prepares Old Town's finest cuisine in this Spanish colonial building in the heart of the historic district. With a strong background in classic cooking, she has expanded her repertoire to include innovative and memorable dishes, including curried chicken with fried sweet bananas, homemade mango chutney, and saffron risotto. Or try her grilled swordfish with Calamata olives. See p. 111.

- **Parrot Club** (San Juan; ℭ 787/ 725-7370): This recent addition to the San Juan scene has already been acclaimed as one of the finest and most innovative restaurants on the island. Its chef serves a Nuevo Latino cuisine that is a happy medley of Puerto Rican delights, drawing upon the Spanish, African, and even Taíno influences of the island. Menu items are based on updated interpretations of old-fashioned regional dishes—everything from *criola*-styled flank steak to a pan-seared tuna served with a sauce of dark rum and essence of oranges. See p. 112.

- **La Belle Epoque** (San Juan; ℭ 787/977-1765): Jeremie Cruz is being celebrated as the finest chef of the Caribbean. From his elegant Condado setting, he serves a combined fusion and French cuisine that is about as close to perfection as it gets on the Condado. The cuisine is exquisitely prepared, and the selections of vintage wines are dazzling. See p. 121.

- **Ramiro's** (San Juan; © 787/ 721-9049): Chef Jesús Ramiro has some of the most innovative cookery along the Condado beachfront strip, along with the city's best wine list. Ramiro has made his culinary reputation with such dishes as quail stuffed with lamb in a port sauce and lamb loin in a tamarind coriander sauce, both equally delectable. His dessert menu is two pages long, including the town's best soufflés. His death-by-chocolate mousse on a green grape leaf is equaled only by his caramelized fresh mango napoleon. See p. 122.

- **Ajili Mójili** (San Juan; © 787/ 725-9195): On the Condado beachfront, Ajili Mójili provides the most refined interpretation of classic Puerto Rican cookery on the island. Locals find it evocative of the food they enjoyed at their mother's table, one example being *mofongos*—green plantains stuffed with veal, chicken, shrimp, or pork. The chefs take that cliché dish *arroz con pollo* (stewed chicken with saffron rice) and raise it to celestial levels. The restaurant takes its name from the lemon-garlic sweet chili salsa that's traditionally served here with fish or meat. See p. 120.

- **Mark's at the Meliá** (Ponce; © 787/284-6275): Mark French has elevated Puerto Rican dishes to a new high at this endearing restaurant that also serves an impeccable international cuisine. He took over what was a backwater and turned the place into an enclave of refined dining with such imaginative and good-tasting dishes as tamarind barbecued lamb with yucca mojo. See p. 199.

- **La Cava** (in the Ponce Hilton, Ponce; © 787/259-7676): The stellar restaurant of this first-class hotel, La Cava was designed to resemble a 19th-century coffee plantation. It's the most elegant restaurant along the southern tier, and it serves delectable international cuisine. From the ever-changing menu, you are likely to be served everything from grilled lamb sausage on a bed of couscous to tuna loin seared with sesame oil. See p. 199.

- **The Landing** (Barrios Puntas/ Playa Antonio; © 787/823-3112): One of the best dining spots along the western coast of Puerto Rico, this restaurant has a setting like a stylish private home. Its international cuisine draws hundreds of patrons nightly who enjoy jerk chicken and lobster kebabs, among other dishes, while taking in a view of the legendary Rincón surf. See p. 216.

14 The Best Offbeat Travel Experiences

- **Attending a Cockfight:** Although a brutal sport that many find distasteful, cockfighting is legal in Puerto Rico and has its devotees. The most authentic cockfights are in the town of Salinas in the southeast. But it's not necessary to go that far to witness one of these bouts. Three fights a week are held at the **Coliseo Gallistico,** Route 37 (© 787/791-6005), in San Juan. Betting is heavy when these roosters take to the ring. See "San Juan After Dark" in chapter 6.

- **Diving off Mona Island** (Mayagüez): Surrounded by some of the most beautiful coral reefs in the Caribbean, Mona Island has the most pristine, extensive, and well-developed reefs in Puerto Rican waters. In fact, they have been nominated as a U.S. National Marine Sanctuary. The tropical marine ecosystem around Mona includes patch reefs, black coral, spore and groove systems, underwater caverns, deep-water sponges, fringing reefs, and algal reefs. The lush environment attracts octopuses, lobster, queen conch, rays, barracuda, snapper, jack, grunt, angelfish, trunkfish, filefish, butterfly fish, dolphin, parrotfish, tuna, flying fish, and more. The crystal waters afford exceptional horizontal vision from 150 to 200 feet, as well as good views down to the shipwrecks that mark the site—including some Hispanic galleons. Five species of whales visit the island's offshore waters. See "Mona Island: The Galápagos of Puerto Rico" chapter 8.

- **Visiting Vieques & Culebra:** Puerto Rico's offshore islands— still relatively undiscovered by the modern world—remain an offbeat adventure, and they've got great beaches, too. The most developed is Vieques, which attracts visitors with its gorgeous stretches of sand with picnic facilities and shade trees. It is an ideal retreat for snorkelers and tranquillity seekers. The beaches are nearly always deserted, even though they are among the Caribbean's loveliest. Although nearly three-quarters of the island is owned by the U.S. Navy, you'll never know you're visiting a military complex. The even less developed Culebra has a wildlife refuge, coral reefs, and Playa Flamenco, another of the Caribbean's finest beaches.

And is it ever sleepy here! See chapter 11.

- **Spending the Evening at Mosquito (Phosphorescent) Bay** (Vieques Island): At any time except when there's a full moon, you can swim in glowing waters lit by dinoflagellates called *pyrodiniums* (whirling fire). These creatures light up the waters like fireflies, and swimming among them is one of the most unusual things to do anywhere—truly a magical, almost psychedelic experience. It's estimated that a gallon of bay water might contain about three-quarters of a million of these little glowing creatures. See "Vieques" in chapter 11.

- **Sampling the Island's Nosh Pits:** Think of Puerto Rico as one gigantic fast-food joint, for no other island in the Caribbean offers such a delectable array of roadside eats. Snack food lies around virtually every turn in the road. As you drive throughout the island, stop and take your pick of the roadside dives. They may look junky, even trashy, but the food is often a delight—and cheap, too.

You'll find succulent barbecued pig, *pastelillos* (pastry turnovers filled with meat, cheese, or seafood), *surullitos* (deep-fried cornmeal sticks), *alcapurrias* (a filling of fish or meat in a deep-fried casing of finely grated green plantains and taro root), *bacalaitos* (deep-fried codfish fritters), *papas rellenas* (stuffed potatoes), and *arañitas* ("little spiders"—actually, deep-fried clusters of shredded green plantains).

You don't have to go far for barbecued pig—just head to the roadside food stands in Luquillo Beach, to the east of San Juan. It makes for a great picnic at the beach.

A truck stop, **Café Restaurant La Nueva Union,** 35 miles (56km) west of San Juan at the junction of Carretera 2 and Highway 22 between Arecibo and Hatillo, serves the most succulent traditional fare. Sample its fresh octopus salad, its meaty goat stew, and definitely its *guisados* (beef stew). Don't leave without an order of coconut flan.

If you make it all the way around the island to La Parguera, stop at **El Quenepo,** a lunch wagon parked under a towering *quenepa* (tropical fruit tree) on Route 116 between routes 304 and 324. You can usually spot it by a line of cars letting passengers out to sample the delights from its crowded postage-stamp kitchen. El Quenepo offers a vast array of Puerto Rican specialties, many of which you may never have sampled before: cold codfish soup, even a green-bean omelet, and *piononos* (a "mountain" composed of fried eggs, plantain strips, and seasoned meat filling).

2

Planning Your Trip to Puerto Rico

This chapter discusses the where, when, and how of your trip to Puerto Rico—everything required to plan your trip and get it on the road. Here we've concentrated on what you need to do *before* you go.

1 The Regions in Brief

Although the many geological divisions of Puerto Rico might not be immediately apparent to the ordinary visitor, its people take great pride in the island's diversity. The most important geological and political divisions are detailed below.

SAN JUAN

The largest and best-preserved complex of Spanish colonial architecture in the Caribbean, Old San Juan (founded in 1521) is the oldest capital city under the U.S. flag. Once a linchpin of Spanish dominance in the Caribbean, it has three major fortresses, miles of solidly built stone ramparts, a charming collection of antique buildings, and a modern business center. The city's economy is the most stable and solid in all of Latin America.

San Juan is the site of the official home and office of the governor of Puerto Rico (La Fortaleza), the 16th-century residence of Ponce de León's family, and several of the oldest places of Christian worship in the Western Hemisphere. Its bars, restaurants, shops, and nightclubs attract an animated group of fans. In recent years, the old city has become surrounded by densely populated modern buildings, including an ultramodern airport, which makes San Juan one of the most dynamic cities in the West Indies.

THE NORTHWEST: ARECIBO, RIO CAMUY, RINCON & MORE

A fertile area with many rivers bringing valuable water for irrigation from the high mountains of the Cordillera, the northwest also offers abundant opportunities for sightseeing. The region's districts include the following:

AGUADILLA   Christopher Columbus landed near Aguadilla during his second voyage to the New World in 1493. Today the town has a busy airport, fine beaches, and a growing tourism-based infrastructure. It is also the center of Puerto Rico's lace-making industry, a craft imported here many centuries ago by immigrants from Spain, Holland, and Belgium.

ARECIBO   Located on the northern coastline a 2-hour drive west of San Juan, Arecibo was originally founded in 1556. Although little remains of its original architecture, the town is well known to physicists and astronomers around the world because of the radar/radio-telescope that fills a concave depression between six of the region's hills. Equal in size to 13 football fields and operated jointly by the National Science Foundation and Cornell University, it studies the shape and formation of the galaxies by deciphering radio waves from space.

Puerto Rico

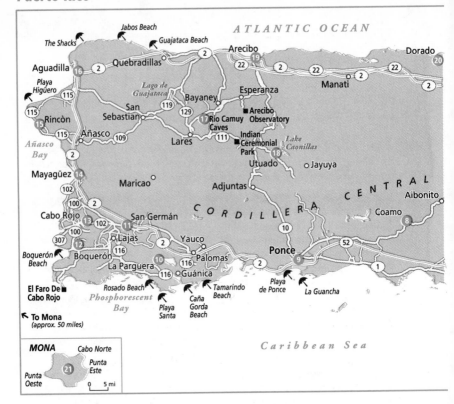

RINCON Named after the 16th-century landowner Don Gonzalo Rincón, who donated its site to the poor of his district, the tiny town of Rincón is famous throughout Puerto Rico for its world-class surfing and beautiful beaches. The lighthouse that warns ships and boats away from dangerous offshore reefs is one of the most powerful on Puerto Rico.

RIO CAMUY CAVE PARK

Located near Arecibo, this park's greatest attraction is underground, where a network of rivers and caves provides some of the most enjoyable spelunking in the world. At its heart lies one of the largest known underground rivers. Aboveground, the park covers 300 acres.

UTUADO Small and nestled amid the hills of the interior, Utuado is famous as the center of the hillbilly culture of Puerto Rico. Some of Puerto Rico's finest mountain musicians have come from Utuado and mention the town in many of their ballads. The surrounding landscape is sculpted with caves and lushly covered with a variety of tropical plants and trees.

DORADO & THE NORTH COAST

Playa Dorado, directly east of San Juan at Dorado, is actually a term for a total of six white-sand beaches along the northern coast, reached by a series of winding roads. Dorado is the island's oldest resort town, the center of golf, casinos, and two major Hyatt resorts

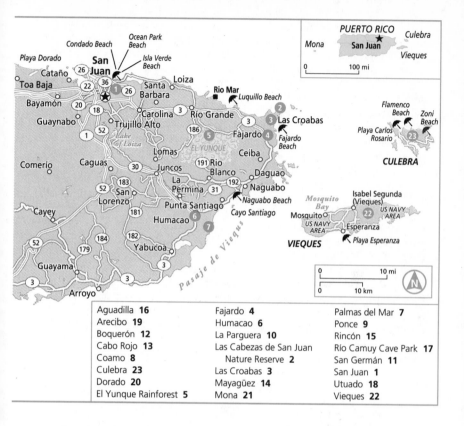

PUERTO RICO

Aguadilla **16**
Arecibo **19**
Boquerón **12**
Cabo Rojo **13**
Coamo **8**
Culebra **23**
Dorado **20**
El Yunque Rainforest **5**

Fajardo **4**
Humacao **6**
La Parguera **10**
Las Cabezas de San Juan
 Nature Reserve **2**
Las Croabas **3**
Mayagüez **14**
Mona **21**

Palmas del Mar **7**
Ponce **9**
Rincón **15**
Río Camuy Cave Park **17**
San Germán **11**
San Juan **1**
Utuado **18**
Vieques **22**

(see p. 180). At the Hyatt resorts at Dorado, you'll find 72 holes of golf, the greatest concentration in the Caribbean—all designed by Robert Trent Jones, Sr. The complex is quite family-friendly, with its Camp Coquí, which offers programs for children ages 3 to 15. There is also a water playground at the Hyatt Regency Cerromar Beach Hotel, with a 1,776-foot-long fantasy pool—the world's longest freshwater swimming pool.

Another resort of increasing importance is also found along the north coast: Wyndham El Conquistador Resort & Country Club at Palomino Island, a private island paradise with sandy beaches and recreational facilities. This resort lies near Las Croabas, a fishing village on the northeastern-most tip of Puerto Rico's north coast.

Challenging both the Hyatt resorts and El Conquistador is the Westin Rio Mar Beach Resort, Country Club & Ocean Villas, which lies 19 miles (31km) to the east of the San Juan international airport.

THE NORTHEAST: EL YUNQUE, A NATURE RESERVE & FAJARDO

The capital city of San Juan (see above) dominates Puerto Rico's northeast. Despite the region's congestion, there are still many remote areas, including some of the island's most important nature reserves. Among the region's most popular towns, parks, and attractions are the following:

EL YUNQUE   The rain forest in the Luquillo Mountains, 25 miles (40km) east of San Juan, El Yunque is a favorite escape from the capital. Teeming with plant and animal life, it is a sprawling tropical forest (actually a national forest) whose ecosystems are strictly protected. Some 100 billion gallons of rainwater fall here each year, allowing about 250 species of trees and flowers to flourish.

FAJARDO   Small and sleepy, this town was originally established as a supply depot for the many pirates who plied the nearby waters. Today, a host of private yachts bob at anchor in its harbor, and the many offshore cays provide visitors with secluded beaches. From Fajardo, ferryboats make choppy but frequent runs to the offshore islands of Vieques and Culebra.

LAS CABEZAS DE SAN JUAN NATURE RESERVE   About an hour's drive from San Juan, this is one of the island's newest ecological refuges. It was established in 1991 on 316 acres of forest, mangrove swamp, offshore cays, coral reefs, and freshwater lagoons—a representative sampling of virtually every ecosystem on Puerto Rico. There is a visitor center, a 19th-century lighthouse (El Faro) that still works, and ample opportunity to forget the pressures of urban life.

THE SOUTHWEST: PONCE, MAYAGÜEZ, SAN GERMAN & MORE

One of Puerto Rico's most beautiful regions, the southwest is rich in local lore, civic pride, and natural wonders.

BOQUERON   Famous for the beauty of its beach and the abundant birds and wildlife in the nearby Boquerón Forest Reserve, this sleepy village is now ripe for large-scale tourism-related development. During the early 19th century, the island's most-feared pirate, Roberto Cofresi, terrorized the Puerto Rican coastline from a secret lair in a cave nearby.

CABO ROJO   Established in 1772, Cabo Rojo reached the peak of its prosperity during the 19th century, when immigrants from around the Mediterranean, fleeing revolutions in their own countries, arrived to establish sugarcane plantations. Today, cattle graze peacefully on land originally devoted almost exclusively to sugarcane, and the area's many varieties of exotic birds draw birdwatchers from throughout North America. Even the offshore waters are fertile; it's estimated that nearly half of all the fish consumed on Puerto Rico are caught in waters near Cabo Rojo.

LA PARGUERA   Named after a breed of snapper (*pargos*) that abounds in the waters nearby, La Parguera is a quiet coastal town best known for the phosphorescent waters of La Bahía Fosforescente (Phosphorescent Bay). Here, sheltered from the waves of the sea, billions of plankton (luminescent dinoflagellates) glow dimly when they are disturbed by movements of the water. The town comes alive on weekends, when crowds of young people from San Juan arrive to party the nights away. Filling modest rooming houses, they temporarily change the texture of the town as bands produce loud sessions of salsa music.

MAYAGÜEZ   The third-largest city on Puerto Rico, Mayagüez is named after the *majagua,* the Amerindian word for a tree that grows abundantly in the area. Because of an earthquake that destroyed almost everything in town in 1917, few old buildings remain. The town is known as the commercial and industrial capital of Puerto Rico's western sector. Its botanical garden is among the finest on the island.

PONCE   Puerto Rico's second-largest city, Ponce has always prided itself on its independence from the Spanish-derived laws and taxes that governed San Juan and the rest of the island. Long-ago home of some of the island's shrewdest traders, merchants, and smugglers, it is enjoying a renaissance as citizens and visitors rediscover its unique cultural and architectural charms. Located on Puerto Rico's southern coast, about 90 minutes by car from the capital, Ponce contains a handful of superb museums, one of the most charming main squares in the Caribbean, an ancient cathedral, dozens of authentically restored colonial-era buildings, and a number of outlying mansions and villas that, at the time of their construction, were among the most opulent on the island.

SAN GERMAN Located on the island's southwestern corner, small, sleepy, and historic San Germán was named after the second wife of Ferdinand of Spain, Germaine de Foix, whom he married in 1503. San Germán's central church, Iglesia Porta Coeli, was built in 1606. At one time, much of the populace was engaged in piracy, pillaging the ships that sailed off the nearby coastline. The central area of this village is still sought out for its many reminders of the island's Spanish heritage and colonial charm.

THE SOUTHEAST: PALMAS DEL MAR & MORE

The southeastern quadrant of Puerto Rico has some of the most heavily developed, as well as some of the least developed, sections of the island.

COAMO Although today Coamo is a bedroom community for San Juan, originally it was the site of two different Taíno communities. Founded in 1579, it now has a main square draped with bougainvillea and one of the best-known Catholic churches on Puerto Rico. Even more famous, however, are the mineral springs whose therapeutic warm waters helped President Franklin D. Roosevelt during his recovery from polio. (Some historians claim that these springs inspired the legend of the Fountain of Youth, which in turn set Ponce de León off on his vain search for Florida.)

HUMACAO Because of its easy access to San Juan, this small, verdant inland town has increasingly become one of the capital's residential suburbs.

PALMAS DEL MAR This sprawling vacation and residential resort community is located near Humacao. A splendid golf course covers some of the grounds. Palmas del Mar is at the center of what has been called the "New American Riviera"—3 miles (5km) of white-sand beaches on the eastern coast of the island. Palmas del Mar is the largest resort in Puerto Rico, lying to the south of Humacao on 2,800 acres of a former coconut plantation—now devoted to luxury living and the sporting life.

The Equestrian Center at Palmas is the finest riding headquarters in Puerto Rico, with trails cutting through an old plantation and jungle along the beach. The resort is ideal for families and has a supervised summer activities program for children ages 5 to 12.

THE OFFSHORE ISLANDS: CULEBRA, VIEQUES & MORE

Few *norteamericanos* realize that Puerto Rico has at least four well-known islands and a multitude of tiny cays lying offshore. The most famous of these are:

CAYO SANTIAGO Lying off the southeastern coast is the small island of Cayo Santiago. Home to a group of about two dozen scientists and a community of rhesus monkeys originally imported from India, the island is a medical experimentation center run by the U.S. Public Health Service. Monkeys are studied in a "wild" but controlled environment both for insights into the behavioral sciences and for possible cures for such maladies as diabetes and arthritis. Casual visitors are not permitted on Cayo Santiago, but they can cruise along the shore and watch the monkeys.

CULEBRA & VIEQUES Located off the eastern coast, these two islands are among the most unsullied and untrammeled areas in the West Indies, even though Vieques is being belatedly discovered. Come here for sun, almost no scheduled activities, fresh seafood, clear waters, sandy beaches, and teeming coral reefs. Vieques is especially proud of its phosphorescent bay, Mosquito Bay.

MONA Remote, uninhabited, and teeming with bird life, this barren island off the western coast is ringed by soaring cliffs and finely textured white-sand beaches. The island has almost no facilities, so visitors seldom stay for more than a day of swimming and picnicking. The surrounding waters are legendary for their dangerous eddies, undertows, and sharks.

2 Visitor Information

For information before you leave home, visit **www.prtourism.com** or contact one of the following **Puerto Rico Tourism Company** offices: 666 Fifth Ave., New York, NY 10103 (© **800/223-6530** or 212/586-6262); 3575 W. Cahuenga Blvd., Suite 405, Los Angeles, CA 90068 (© **800/ 874-1230** or 213/874-5991); or 901 Ponce de León Blvd., Suite 604, Coral Gables, FL 33134 (© **800/815-7391** or 305/445-9112).

In Canada contact the company at 230 Richmond St. W., Suite 902, Toronto, ON M5V 1V6 (© **416/ 368-2680**).

If you have Internet access, visit **CityNet** (www.citynet.com), which has links, organized by location and then by subject, to sites with information about many destinations. To find Puerto Rico, click on the "Caribbean" heading; when a map of the region appears, click on the island. Here you will find a number of links pertaining to Puerto Rico.

One of the best Caribbean websites is **Caribbean-On-Line** (www.webcom. com/earleltd), a series of virtual guidebooks full of information on hotels, restaurants, and shopping, along with sights and detailed maps of the islands. The site also includes links to travel agents and cruise lines that are up on the Web.

Other helpful websites include **Municipality of Ponce** (www.ponce web.org), **Municipality of Rincón** (www.Rincon.org), and **Puerto Rico Travel Maps** (www.travelmaps.com).

You might also want to contact the U.S. State Department for background bulletins, which supply up-to-date information on crime, health concerns, import restrictions, and other travel matters. Write the **Superintendent of Documents, U.S. Government Printing Office,** Washington, DC 20402 (© **202/512-1800**).

A good travel agent can be a source of information. Make sure your agent is a member of the American Society of Travel Agents (ASTA). If you get poor service from an ASTA agent, you can write to the **ASTA Consumer Affairs Department,** 1101 King St., Alexandria, VA 22314 (© **703/ 739-8739;** www.astanet.com).

3 Entry Requirements & Customs

ENTRY REQUIREMENTS

DOCUMENTS Because Puerto Rico is a Commonwealth, **U.S. citizens** coming from mainland destinations do not need any documents to enter Puerto Rico. It is the same as crossing from Georgia into Florida. They do not need to carry proof of citizenship or to produce documents. However, because of new airport security measures, it is necessary to produce a government-issued photo ID (federal, state, or local) to board a plane; this is most often a driver's license.

Be sure to carry plenty of documentation. You might need to show a government-issued photo ID (federal, state, or local) at various airport checkpoints. Be sure that your ID is *up-to-date:* an expired driver's license or passport, for example, might keep you from boarding a plane.

For **Canadians,** proof of citizenship is required to land in Puerto Rico. This could be in the form of a province-issued birth certificate or a Canadian identification card. A valid passport is preferred but not required. In addition, some form of photo ID, usually a driver's license, is also required.

Visitors from **other countries** need a valid passport to land in Puerto Rico. For those from countries requiring a visa to enter the U.S., the same visa is necessary to enter Puerto Rico, unless these nationals are coming directly from the U.S. mainland and have already cleared U.S. Immigration and Customs there.

VACCINATIONS   Vaccinations are not required for entry to Puerto Rico if you're coming from the United States or Canada.

Infectious hepatitis has been reported on other Caribbean islands but less frequently on Puerto Rico. Consult your doctor about the advisability of getting a gamma-globulin shot before you leave home.

Typhoid, poliomyelitis, and tetanus are not common diseases on the island, and inoculations against them are recommended mainly to visitors who plan to rough it in the wilds. If you're staying in a regular Puerto Rican hotel, such preventive measures are generally not needed, but your doctor can advise you based on your destination and travel plans.

CUSTOMS

U.S. citizens do not need to clear Puerto Rican Customs upon arrival by plane or ship from the U.S. mainland. All non-U.S. citizens must clear Customs and are permitted to bring in items intended for their personal use, including tobacco, cameras, film, and a limited supply of liquor (usually 40 oz.).

WHAT YOU CAN TAKE HOME

U.S. CUSTOMS   On departure, U.S.-bound travelers must have their luggage inspected by the U.S. Agriculture Department because laws prohibit bringing fruits and plants to the U.S. mainland. Fruits and vegetables are not allowed, but otherwise, you can bring back as many purchased goods as you want without paying duty.

For more information, contact the **U.S. Customs Service,** 1300 Pennsylvania Ave. NW, Washington, DC 20229 (© **877/287-8867;** www.customs.gov [click on "Traveler Information" and then "Know Before You Go Brochure") and request the free pamphlet *Know Before You Go.*

CANADIAN CUSTOMS   For a clear summary of Canadian rules, write for the booklet *I Declare,* issued by the **Canada Customs and Revenue Agency** (© **800/461-9999** in Canada

---

Tips **Travel Documents**

Before leaving home, make two copies of your most valuable documents, including your passport, your driver's license, or any other identity document; your airline ticket; and any hotel vouchers. If you're on medication, you should also make copies of prescriptions. Keep copies of your documentation safe and separate from the originals.

or 204/983-3500; www.ccra-adrc. gc.ca). Canada allows its citizens a Can$750 exemption, and you're allowed to bring back duty-free one carton of cigarettes, one can of tobacco, 40 imperial ounces of liquor, and 50 cigars. In addition, you're allowed to mail gifts to Canada valued at less than Can$60 per day, provided they're unsolicited and don't contain alcohol or tobacco (write on the package "Unsolicited gift, under $60 value"). All valuables should be declared on the Y-38 form before departure from Canada, including serial numbers of valuables already owned, such as expensive foreign cameras. *Note:* The $750 exemption can only be used once per year and only after an absence of 7 days.

U.K. CUSTOMS U.K. citizens returning from a non-EC country have a customs allowance of 200 cigarettes; 50 cigars; 250 grams of smoking tobacco; 2 liters of still table wine; 1 liter of spirits or strong liqueurs (over 22% volume); 2 liters of fortified wine, sparkling wine, or other liqueurs; 60cc (ml) perfume; 250 cubic centimeters (ml) of toilet water; and £145 worth of all other goods, including gifts and souvenirs. People under 17 do not get the tobacco or alcohol allowance. For more information, contact **HM Customs & Excise,** Passenger Enquiry Point, 2nd Floor Wayfarer House, Great South West Road, Feltham, Middlesex, TW14 8NP (☎ **0181/ 910-3744;** from outside the U.K. 44/181-910-3744), or consult their website at www.open.gov.uk.

AUSTRALIA CUSTOMS The duty-free allowance in Australia is A$400, or for those under 18, A$200. Personal property mailed back from Puerto Rico should be marked "Australian goods returned" to avoid payment of duty. Upon returning to Australia, citizens can bring in 250 cigarettes or 250 grams of loose tobacco, and 1,125 ml of alcohol. If you're returning with valuable goods, you already owned, such as foreign-made cameras, you should file form B263. A helpful brochure, available from Australian consulates or Customs offices, is *Know Before You Go.* For more information, contact **Australian Customs Service,** GPO Box 8, Sydney NSW 2001 (☎ **02/6275-6666**), or see www.customs.gov.au.

NEW ZEALAND CUSTOMS The duty-free allowance for New Zealand is NZ$700. Citizens over 17 can bring in 200 cigarettes or 50 cigars or 250 grams of tobacco (or a mixture of all three if their combined weight doesn't exceed 250g); plus 4.5 liters of wine and beer or 1.125 liters of liquor. New Zealand currency does not carry import or export restrictions. Fill out a certificate of export, listing the valuables you are taking out of the country; that way, you can bring them back without paying duty. Most questions are answered in a free pamphlet available at New Zealand consulates and Customs offices: *New Zealand Customs Guide for Travellers, Notice no. 4.* For more information, contact **New Zealand Customs,** 50 Anzac Ave., P.O. Box 29, Auckland (☎ **09/359-6655**).

4 Money

CURRENCY The U.S. dollar is the coin of the realm. Keep in mind that once you leave Ponce or San Juan, you might have difficulty finding a place to exchange foreign money (unless you're staying at a large resort), so it's wise to handle your exchange needs

before you head off into rural parts of Puerto Rico.

ATMS ATMs are linked to a network that most likely includes your bank at home. **Cirrus** (☎ 800/424-7787; www. mastercard.com) and **Plus** (☎ 800/ 843-7587; www.visa.com) are the two

---

Tips **Small Change**

When you change money, ask for some small bills or loose change. Small cash will come in handy for tipping and public transportation. Consider keeping the change separate from your larger bills, so it's readily accessible and you'll be less of a target for theft.

---

most popular networks in the U.S.; call or check online for ATM locations at your destination. Be sure you know your four-digit PIN before you leave home and be sure to find out your daily withdrawal limit before you depart. You can also get cash advances on your credit card at an ATM. Keep in mind that credit-card companies try to protect themselves from theft by limiting the funds someone can withdraw away from home; it's therefore best to call your credit-card company before you leave and let them know where you're going and how much you plan to spend. You'll get the best exchange rate if you withdraw money from an ATM, but keep in mind that many banks impose a fee every time a card is used at an ATM in a different city or bank. On top of this, the bank from which you withdraw cash may charge its own fee.

CURRENCY EXCHANGE The currency exchange facilities at any large international bank within Puerto Rico's larger cities can exchange non-U.S. currencies for dollars. You can also exchange money at the Luis Muñoz Marín International Airport. Also, you'll find foreign-exchange facilities in large hotels and at the many banks in Old San Juan or Avenida Ashford in Condado. In Ponce, look for foreign-exchange facilities at large resorts and at banks such as **Banco Popular,** Plaza Las Delicias (© 787/843-8000).

TRAVELER'S CHECKS Traveler's checks are something of an anachronism from the days before the ATM made cash accessible at any time.

Traveler's checks used to be the only sound alternative to traveling with large amounts of cash. They were as reliable as currency, but, unlike cash, could be replaced if lost or stolen.

These days, traveler's checks seem less necessary because most cities have 24-hour ATMs that allow you to withdraw small amounts of cash as needed. However, you're likely to be charged an ATM withdrawal fee if the bank is not your own, so if you're withdrawing money every day, you might be better off with traveler's checks—provided that you don't mind showing identification every time you want to cash one.

You can get traveler's checks at almost any bank. **American Express** offers denominations of $20, $50, $100, $500, and (for cardholders only) $1,000. You'll pay a service charge ranging from 1% to 4%. You can also get American Express traveler's checks over the phone by calling © **800/221-7782;** Amex Gold and Platinum cardholders who use this number are exempt from the service charge. AAA members can obtain checks without a fee at most AAA offices.

Visa offers traveler's checks at Citibank locations nationwide, as well as at several other banks. The service charge ranges between 1.5% and 2%; checks come in denominations of $20, $50, $100, $500, and $1,000. Call © **800/732-1322** for information. **MasterCard** also offers traveler's checks. Call © **800/223-9920** for a location near you.

Tips What to Do if Your Wallet Is Stolen

Be sure to block charges against your account the minute you discover that a card has been lost or stolen. Then be sure to file a police report.

Almost every credit-card company has an emergency toll-free number to call if your card is stolen. Yours might be able to wire you a cash advance off your credit card immediately, and in many places, credit-card companies can deliver emergency credit cards in a day or two. The issuing bank's toll-free number is usually on the back of your credit card—though of course, if your card has been stolen, that won't help you unless you recorded the number elsewhere.

Citicorp Visa's U.S. emergency number is ✆ 800/336-8742. American Express cardholders and traveler's check holders should call ✆ 800/221-7282. MasterCard holders should call ✆ 800/307-7309. Otherwise, call the toll-free number directory at ✆ 800/555-1212 to get the number of your card issuer.

Odds are that if your wallet is gone, the police won't be able to recover it for you. However, it's still worth informing the authorities. Your credit-card company or insurer might require a police report number or record of the theft.

If you choose to carry traveler's checks, be sure to keep a record of your serial numbers separate from your checks. You'll get a refund faster if you know the numbers.

If you need emergency cash over the weekend when all banks and American Express offices are closed, you can have money wired to you from Western Union (✆ 800/325-6000; www.westernunion.com). You must generally present valid ID to pick up the cash at the Western Union office. However, in most countries, you can pick up a money transfer without valid identification as long as you can answer a test question provided by the sender. Be sure to let the sender know in advance that you don't have ID. If you need to use a test question instead of ID, the sender must take cash to his or her local Western Union office, rather than transfer the money over the phone or online.

CREDIT CARDS   Credit cards are invaluable when you're traveling. They are a safe way to carry money and provide a convenient record of all your expenses. You can also withdraw cash advances from your credit cards at any bank (though you'll start paying hefty interest on the advance the moment you receive the cash). At most banks, you don't even need to go to a teller; you can get a cash advance at the ATM if you know your PIN. If you've forgotten yours, or didn't even know you had one, call the number on the back of your credit card and ask the card issuer to send it to you. It usually takes 5 to 7 business days, though some banks will provide the number over the phone if you tell them your mother's maiden name or pass some other security clearance.

In San Juan and at all the big resorts on the island, even some of the smaller inns, credit cards are commonly accepted. However, as you tour through rural areas and if you intend to patronize small, out-of-the-way establishments, it's wise to carry

What Things Cost in Puerto Rico	US $	British £
Taxi from airport to Condado	12.00	8.00
Average taxi fare within San Juan	6.00	4.00
Typical bus fare within San Juan	.25–.50	.16–.33
Local telephone call	.10	.07
Double room at the Caribe Hilton (very expensive)	250.00	166.50
Double room at El Canario by the Lagoon (moderate)	145.00	96.50
Double room at At Wind Chimes Inn (inexpensive)	80.00	53.25
Lunch for one at Amadeus (moderate)	16.00	10.50
Lunch for one at La Bombonera (inexpensive)	8.00	5.25
Dinner for one at Ramiro's (expensive)	46.00	30.50
Dinner for one at El Patio de Sam (moderate)	26.00	17.25
Dinner for one at Tony Roma's (inexpensive)	16.00	10.50
Bottle of beer in a bar	3.00	2.00
Glass of wine in a restaurant	3.75	2.50
Roll of ASA 100 color film, 36 exposures	8.50	5.50
Movie ticket	5.00–6.50	3.25–4.25
Theater ticket	15.00–65.00	10.00–43.25

sufficient amounts of the Yankee dollar. Visa and MasterCard are accepted most widely throughout Puerto Rico.

MONEYGRAMS Sponsored by American Express, **MoneyGram** (© **800/MONEYGRAM;** www.money gram.com) is the fastest-growing money-wiring service in the world. Funds can be transferred from one individual to another in less than 10 minutes between thousands of locations throughout the world. You can call MoneyGram to have a phone representative give you the names of four or five offices near you. (Some locations are pharmacies or convenience stores in small communities.) Acceptable forms of payment include cash, Visa, MasterCard, or Discover, and occasionally, a personal check. Service charges collected by MoneyGram are $40 for the first $500 sent, with a sliding scale of commissions for larger sums. Included in the transfer is a 10-word telex-style message. The deal also includes a free 3-minute phone call to the recipient. Funds are transferred within 10 minutes, and they can then be retrieved by the beneficiary at the most convenient location when proper photo ID, and in some cases, a security code established by whomever provides the funds, is presented.

CLIMATE

Puerto Rico has one of the most unvarying climates in the world. Temperatures year-round range from 75°F to 85°F (24°C – 29°C). The island is wettest and hottest in August, averaging 81°F (27°C) and 7 inches of rain. San Juan and the northern coast seem to be cooler and wetter than Ponce and the southern coast. The coldest weather is in the high altitudes of the Cordillera, the site of Puerto Rico's lowest recorded temperature—39°F (4°C).

THE HURRICANE SEASON

The hurricane season, the curse of Puerto Rican weather, lasts—officially, at least—from June 1 to November 30. But there's no cause for panic. In general, satellite forecasts give adequate warnings so that precautions can be taken.

If you're heading to Puerto Rico during the hurricane season, you can call your local branch of the **National Weather Service** (listed in your phone directory under the U.S. Department of Commerce) for a weather forecast.

It'll cost 95¢ per query, but you can get information about the climate conditions in any city you plan to visit by calling ℂ **800/WEATHER.** When you're prompted, enter your Visa or MasterCard account number and then punch in the name of any of 1,000 cities worldwide whose weather is monitored by the **Weather Channel** (www.weather.com).

Average Temperatures on Puerto Rico

	Jan	Feb	Mar	Apr	May	June	July	Aug	Sept	Oct	Nov	Dec
Temp. (°F)	75	75	76	78	79	81	81	81	81	81	79	77
Temp. (°C)	25	24	24	24.4	25.6	26	27	27	27	27	27	26

THE "SEASON"

In Puerto Rico, hotels charge their highest prices during the peak winter period from mid-December to mid-April, when visitors fleeing from cold northern climates flock to the islands. Winter is the driest season along the coasts but can be wet in mountainous areas.

If you plan to travel in the winter, make reservations 2 to 3 months in advance. At certain hotels it's almost impossible to book accommodations for Christmas and the month of February.

SAVING MONEY IN THE OFF-SEASON

Puerto Rico is a year-round destination. The island's "off-season" runs from late spring to late fall, when temperatures in the mid-80s (about 29°C) prevail throughout most of the region. Trade winds ensure comfortable days and nights, even in accommodations without air-conditioning. Although the noonday sun may raise the temperature to around 90°F (32°C), cool breezes usually make the morning, late afternoon, and evening more comfortable here than in many parts of the U.S. mainland.

Dollar for dollar, you'll spend less money by renting a summer house or fully equipped unit in Puerto Rico than you would on Cape Cod, Fire Island, Laguna Beach, or the coast of Maine.

The off-season in Puerto Rico—roughly from mid-April to mid-December (rate schedules vary from hotel to hotel)—amounts to a summer sale. In most cases, hotel rates are slashed from 20% to a startling 60%. It's a bonanza for cost-conscious travelers, especially families who like to go on vacations together. In the chapters ahead, we'll spell out in dollars the specific amounts hotels charge during the off-season.

OTHER OFF-SEASON ADVANTAGES

Although Puerto Rico may appear inviting in the winter to those who live in northern climates, there are many reasons your trip may be much more enjoyable if you go in the off-season:

- After the winter hordes have left, a less-hurried way of life prevails. You'll have a better chance to appreciate the food, culture, and local customs.
- Swimming pools and beaches are less crowded—perhaps not crowded at all.
- Year-round resort facilities are offered, often at reduced rates, which may include snorkeling, boating, and scuba diving.
- To survive, resort boutiques often feature summer sales, hoping to clear the merchandise they didn't sell in February to accommodate stock they've ordered for the coming winter.
- You can often appear without a reservation at a top restaurant and get a table for dinner, a table that in winter would have required a reservation far in advance. Also, when waiters are less hurried, you get better service.
- The endless waiting game is over: no waiting for a rented car (only to be told none is available), no long wait for a golf course tee time, and quicker access to tennis courts and watersports.
- Some package-tour fares are as much as 20% lower, and individual excursion fares are also reduced between 5% and 10%.
- All accommodations and flights are much easier to book.
- Summer is an excellent time for family travel, not usually possible during the winter season.
- The very best of Puerto Rican attractions remain undiminished in the off-season—sea, sand, and surf, with lots of sunshine.

OFF-SEASON DISADVANTAGES

Let's not paint too rosy a picture. Although the advantages of off-season travel far outweigh the disadvantages, there are nevertheless drawbacks to traveling in summer:

- You might be staying at a construction site. Hoteliers save their serious repairs and their major renovations until the off-season, when they have fewer clients. That means you might wake up early in the morning to the sound of a hammer.
- Single tourists find the cruising better in winter, when there are more clients, especially the unattached. Families predominate in summer and there are fewer chances to meet fellow singles than in the winter months.
- Services are often reduced. In the peak of winter, everything is fully operational. But in summer, many of the programs such as watersports might be curtailed. Also, not all restaurants and bars are fully operational at all resorts. For example, for lack of business, certain gourmet or specialty dining rooms might be shut down until house count merits reopening them. In all, the general atmosphere is more laid-back when a hotel or resort might also be operating with a reduced staff. The summer staff will still be adequate to provide service for what's up and running.

HOLIDAYS

Puerto Rico has many public holidays when stores, offices, and schools are closed: New Year's Day, January 6 (Three Kings Day), Washington's Birthday, Good Friday, Memorial Day, July 4, Labor Day, Thanksgiving, Veterans Day, and Christmas, plus such local holidays as Constitution Day (July 25) and Discovery Day (Nov 19). Remember, U.S. federal holidays are holidays in Puerto Rico, too.

PUERTO RICO CALENDAR OF EVENTS

January

Three Kings Day, islandwide. On this traditional gift-giving day in Puerto Rico, there are festivals with lively music, dancing, parades, puppet shows, caroling troubadours, and traditional feasts. January 6.

San Sebastián Street Festival, Calle San Sebastián in Old San Juan. Nightly celebrations with music, processions, crafts, and typical foods, as well as graphic arts and handicraft exhibitions. For more information, call © **787/721-1476.** January 18–21, 2003.

February

San Blas de Illescas Half Marathon, Coamo. International and local runners compete in a challenging 13.1-mile (21km) half-marathon in the hilly south-central town of Coamo. Call **Delta Phi Delta Fraternity** (© **787/825-4077**). February 6, 2003.

Coffee Harvest Festival, Maricao. Folk music, a parade of floats, typical foods, crafts, and demonstrations of coffee preparation in Maricao, a 1-hour drive east of Mayagüez in the center of one of the island's coffee-growing districts. For more information, call © **787/838-2290** or 787/856-1345. February 15–20, 2003.

Carnival Ponceño, Ponce. The island's Carnival celebrations feature float parades, dancing, and street parties. One of the most vibrant festivities is held in Ponce, known for its masqueraders wearing brightly painted horned masks. Live music includes the folk rhythms of the plena, which originated in Africa. Festivities include the crowning of a carnival queen and the closing "burial of the sardine." For more information, call © **787/284-4141.** February 6 through 12, 2003.

March

Emancipation Day, islandwide. Commemoration of the emancipation of Puerto Rico's slaves in 1873, held at various venues. March 22.

April

José de Diego Day, islandwide. Commemoration of the birthday of José de Diego, patriot, lawyer, writer, orator, and political leader who was the first president of the Puerto Rico House of Representatives under U.S. rule. April 17.

Good Friday and Easter, islandwide. Celebrated with colorful ceremonies and processions. April 18 through 20, 2003.

Sugar Harvest Festival, San Germán. This festival marks the end of the island's sugar harvest, with live music, crafts, and typical foods, as well as exhibitions of sugarcane plants and past and present harvesting techniques. Late April.

May

Heineken JazzFest, San Juan. The annual jazz celebration is staged at Parque Sixto Escobar. Each year a different jazz theme is featured. The open-air pavilion is in a scenic oceanfront location in the Puerta de Tierra section of San Juan, near the Hilton. For more information, call © **787/277-9200.** End of May through the beginning of June.

Puerto Rican Danza Week (*Semana de la "Danza" Puertorriqueña*), Convento de los Dominicos, Old San Juan. This week commemorates what is, perhaps, the most expressive art form in the Puerto Rican culture: danza music and dance. Throughout Danza Week, live performances and conferences are held at Convento de los Dominicos's indoor patio. The building is located on Old San

Juan's Cristo Street. For information, call ℭ **787/724-1844.** May 16 through 20, 2003.

June

Casals Festival, Performing Arts Center in San Juan. *Sanjuaneros* and visitors alike eagerly look forward to the annual Casals Festival, the Caribbean's most celebrated cultural event. The bill at San Juan's Performing Arts Center includes a glittering array of international guest conductors, orchestras, and soloists. They come to honor the memory of Pablo Casals, the renowned cellist who was born in Spain to a Puerto Rican mother. When Casals died in Puerto Rico in 1973 at the age of 97, the Casals Festival was 16 years old and attracting the same class of performers who appeared at the Pablo Casals Festival in France, founded by Casals after World War II. When he moved to Puerto Rico in 1957 with his wife, Marta Casals Istomin (former artistic director of the John F. Kennedy Center for the Performing Arts), he founded not only this festival but also the Puerto Rico Symphony Orchestra to foster musical development on the island.

Ticket prices for the Casals Festival range from $20 to $40. A 50% discount is offered to students, people over 60, and persons with disabilities. Tickets are available through the **Performing Arts Center** in San Juan (ℭ **787/721-7727**). Information is also available from the **Puerto Rico Tourism Company,** 666 Fifth Ave., New York, NY 10103 (ℭ **800/223-6530** or 212/586-6262). The festivities take place June 2 through 17, 2003.

San Juan Bautista Day, islandwide. Puerto Rico's capital and other cities celebrate the island's patron saint with weeklong festivities. At midnight, Sanjuaneros and others walk backward into the sea (or nearest body of water) three times to renew good luck for the coming year. June 24.

Aibonito Flower Festival, at Road 722 next to the City Hall Coliseum, in the central mountain town of Aibonito. This annual flower-competition festival features acres of lilies, anthuriums, carnations, roses, gardenias, and begonias. For more information, call ℭ **787/735-3871.** Last week in June and first week in July.

July

Luis Muñoz Rivera's Birthday, islandwide. A birthday celebration commemorating Luis Muñoz Rivera (1829–1916), statesman, journalist, poet, and resident commissioner in Washington, DC. July 15.

Loíza Carnival. An annual folk and religious ceremony honoring Loíza's patron saint, James (Santiago) the Apostle. Colorful processions take place, with costumes, masks, and bomba dancers (the bomba has a lively Afro-Caribbean dance rhythm). This jubilant celebration reflects the African and Spanish heritage of the region. For more information, call ℭ **787/876-3570.** July 24 through August 3, 2003.

August

El Gigante Marathon, Adjuntas. This 15-km (9½-mile) race starts at Puerta Bernasal and finishes at Plaza Pública. For more information call ℭ **787/829-3114.** Early August.

Cuadragésimo Cuarto Torneo de Pesca Interclub del Caribe, Cangrejos Yacht Club. This international blue-marlin fishing tournament features crafts, music, local delicacies, and other activities. For more information, call ℭ **787/791-1015.** August 10 through 13, 2003.

September

International Billfish Tournament, at Club Náutico, San Juan. This is one of the premier game-fishing tournaments and the longest consecutively held billfish tournament in the world. Fishers from many countries angle for blue marlin that can weigh up to 900 pounds. For further information, call © **787/722-6624.** September 3 through 10, 2003.

October

La Raza Day (Columbus Day), islandwide. Commemoration of Columbus's landing in the New World. October 12.

National Plantain Festival, Corozal. This annual festivity involves crafts, paintings, agricultural products, exhibition, and sale of plantain dishes; *neuva trova* music and folk ballet are performed. For more information, call © **787/859-1259.** End of October through the beginning of November.

November

Puerto Rican Day of Bomba and Plena, Ponce. Festivities celebrate two local rhythms and dances, the bomba and the plena, which are still popular today. Groups from all over the island present their repertoires. A colorful parade, handicraft exhibits, and typical food—a selection that ranges from grilled island specialties to hot dogs. For more information, call © **787/844-2540.** Mid-November.

Start of Baseball Season, in Hiram Bithorn Park in San Juan and throughout the island. Six Puerto Rican professional clubs compete. Professionals from North America also play here from December to January. For more information, contact **Professional Baseball of Puerto Rico** (© **787/765-6285**). Early November.

Puerto Rico Discovery Day, islandwide. This day commemorates the "discovery" by Columbus in 1493 of the already inhabited island of Puerto Rico. Columbus is thought to have come ashore at the northwestern municipality of Aguadilla, although the exact location is unknown. November 19.

Festival of Puerto Rican Music, San Juan. Annual classical and folk music festival. One of its highlights is a *cuatro*-playing contest. (A *cuatro* is a guitar-like instrument with 10 strings.) For more information, call © **787/721-5274.** Mid-November.

Jayuya Indian Festival, Jayuya. This fiesta features the culture and tradition of the island's original inhabitants, the Taíno Indians, and their music, food, and games. More than 100 artisans exhibit and sell their works. There is also a Miss Taíno Indian Pageant, in which contestants are judged by their features and garments that are designed to evoke—both in style and materials—the typical dress of a Taíno woman. For more information, call © **787/828-0900.** November 16 through 19, 2003.

December

Old San Juan's White Christmas Festival, Old San Juan. Special musical and artistic presentations take place in stores, with window displays. December 1 through January 12.

Bacardi Artisans' Fair, San Juan. The best and largest artisans' fair on the island features more than 100 artisans who turn out to exhibit and sell their wares. The fair includes shows for adults and children, a Puerto Rican troubadour contest, rides, and typical food and drink—all sold by nonprofit organizations. Held on the grounds of the world's largest rum-manufacturing plant in Cataño, an industrial suburb set on a peninsula jutting into San Juan Bay. For more information, call ℂ 787/788-1500. First two Sundays in December.

Las Mañanitas, Ponce. A religious procession that starts out from Lolita Tizol Street and moves toward the city's Catholic church, led by mariachis singing songs to honor Our Lady of Guadalupe, the city's patron saint. The lead song is the traditional Mexican birthday song, *Las Mañanitas.* There's a 6am mass. For more information, contact **Ponce City Hall** (ℂ 787/284-4141). December 12.

Puerto Rico International Offshore Cup, in San Juan Bay. The first of its kind on the island, this competition matches local speedboat-racing teams with some of the best offshore teams from the United States and the Caribbean. For more information, call Hector Cardona at the **Puerto Rico Offshore Association** (ℂ 787/787-0521). December 14, 2003.

Hatillo Masks Festival, Hatillo. This tradition, celebrated since 1823, represents the biblical story of King Herod's ordering the death of all infant boys in an attempt to kill the baby Jesus. Men with colorful masks and costumes represent the soldiers, who run or ride through the town from early morning, looking for the children. Food, music, and craft exhibits in the town

square. For more information, call ℂ 787/898-3835. December 28.

Lighting of the Town of Bethlehem, between San Cristóbal Fort and Plaza San Juan Bautista in Old San Juan. This is the time that the most dazzling Christmas lights go on, and many islanders themselves drive into San Juan to see this dramatic lighting, the finest display of lights in the Caribbean at Christmas. During the Christmas season.

YEAR-ROUND FESTIVALS

In addition to the individual events described above, Puerto Rico has two year-long series of special events.

Many of Puerto Rico's most popular events are during the **Patron Saint Festivals** (*fiestas patronales*) in honor of the patron saint of each municipality. The festivities, held in each town's central plaza, include religious and costumed processions, games, local food, music, and dance.

At **Festival La Casita,** prominent Puerto Rican musicians, dance troupes, and orchestras perform; puppet shows are staged; and painters and sculptors display their works. It happens every Saturday at Puerto Rico Tourism's "La Casita" Tourism Information Center, Plaza Darsenas, across from Pier 1, Old San Juan.

For more information about all these events, contact the **Puerto Rico Tourism Company,** 666 Fifth Ave., New York, NY 10103 (ℂ 800/223-6530 or 212/586-6262).

6 Insurance, Health & Safety

INSURANCE

Check your existing insurance policies before you buy travel insurance to cover trip cancellation, lost luggage, medical expenses, or car-rental insurance. You're likely to already have partial or complete coverage. But if you need some, ask your travel agent about a comprehensive package. The cost of

travel insurance varies widely, depending on the cost and length of your trip, your age and overall health, and the type of trip you're taking. Insurance for extreme sports or adventure travel, for example, will cost more than coverage for a cruise.

Some credit cards (American Express and certain gold and platinum

Visas and MasterCards, for example) offer automatic flight insurance against death or dismemberment in case of an airplane crash if you charged the cost of your ticket.

For information on travel insurance, contact one of the following popular insurers:

Access America (© **800/284-8300;** www.accessamerica.com)

Travel Guard International (© **800/826-1300;** www.travel guard.com)

Travel Insured International (© **800/243-3174;** www.travel insured.com)

Travelex Insurance Services (© **800/228-9792;** www.travelex insurance.com)

TRIP-CANCELLATION INSURANCE

There are three major types of trip-cancellation insurance—one that covers you in the event that you prepay a cruise or tour that gets cancelled, and you can't get your money back; a second that covers when you or someone in your family gets sick or dies, and you can't travel (but beware that you may not be covered for a preexisting condition); and a third that covers you when bad weather such as a hurricane makes travel impossible. Some insurers provide coverage for events like jury duty, natural disasters close to home, such as floods or fire, and even the loss of a job. A few have added provisions for cancellations because of terrorist activities. Always check the fine print before signing on, and don't buy trip-cancellation insurance from the tour operator that may be responsible for the cancellation; buy it only from a reputable travel insurance agency. Don't overbuy, because you won't be reimbursed for more than the cost of your trip.

MEDICAL INSURANCE

Most health insurance policies cover you if you get sick away from home,

but they are not likely to provide for medical evacuation in case of life-threatening injury or illness. It's a good idea to buy a travel insurance policy that provides for **emergency medical evacuation.** If you have to buy a one-way same-day ticket home and forfeit your nonrefundable round-trip ticket, you might be out big bucks. And the cost of a flying ambulance could wipe out your life's savings.

Check with your insurer, particularly if you're insured by an HMO, about the extent of its coverage while you're overseas. With the exception of certain HMOs and Medicare/Medicaid, your medical insurance should cover medical treatment—even hospital care—overseas. However, most out-of-country hospitals make you pay your bills up front, and they send you a refund after you've returned home and filed the necessary paperwork.

If you require additional insurance, try one of the following companies:

- **MEDEX International** (© **888/ MEDEX-00** or 410/453-6300; fax 410/453-6301; www.medex assist.com)
- **Travel Assistance International** (© **800/821-2828;** www.travel assistance.com)
- **The Divers Alert Network** (DAN) (© **800/446-2671** or 919/684-8181; www.diversalertnetwork. org; for divers only)

LOST-LUGGAGE INSURANCE

On U.S. domestic flights, including those to Puerto Rico, checked baggage is covered up to $2,500 per ticketed passenger. If you plan to check items more valuable than the standard liability, you can purchase "excess valuation" coverage from the airline, up to $5,000. Be sure to take any valuables or irreplaceable items with you in your carry-on luggage. If you file a lost luggage claim, be prepared to

Tips **Quick ID**

Tie a colorful ribbon or piece of yarn around your luggage handle, or slap a distinctive sticker on the side of your bag. This makes it less likely that someone will mistakenly appropriate it. And if your luggage gets lost, it will be easier to find.

answer detailed questions about the contents of your baggage, and be sure to file a claim immediately, as most airlines enforce a 21-day deadline. Before you leave home, compile an inventory of all packed items and a rough estimate of the total value to ensure that you're properly compensated if your luggage is lost. You will only be reimbursed for what you lost, no more. Once you've filed a complaint, persist in securing your reimbursement; there are no laws governing the length of time a carrier can take to reimburse you. If you arrive at a destination without your bags, ask the airline to forward them to your hotel or to your next destination; they will usually comply. If your bag is delayed or lost, the airline might reimburse you for reasonable expenses, such as a toothbrush or a set of clothes, but the airline is under no legal obligation to do so.

Lost luggage may also be covered by your homeowner's or renter's policy. Many platinum and gold credit cards cover you for lost luggage as well, provided your air ticket was purchased using one of the platinum or gold credit cards. If you choose to purchase additional lost-luggage insurance, be sure not to buy more than you need. Buy in advance from an insurer or a trusted agent (prices will be much higher at the airport).

CAR RENTAL INSURANCE (LOSS/DAMAGE WAIVER OR COLLISION DAMAGE WAIVER)

If you hold a private auto insurance policy in the United States, you are probably covered in Puerto Rico for loss or damage to the car, and liability in case a passenger is injured. The credit card you used to rent the car might also provide some coverage.

Car-rental insurance probably does not cover liability if you caused the accident. Check your own auto insurance policy, the rental company policy, and your credit-card coverage for the extent of coverage: Is your destination covered? Are other drivers covered? How much liability is covered if a passenger is injured? (If you rely on your credit card for coverage, you might want to bring a second credit card with you, as damages may be charged to your card and you might find yourself stranded with no money or remaining credit.)

Car-rental insurance in Puerto Rico costs about $14 to $20 a day.

STAYING HEALTHY

Puerto Rico poses no major health problem for most travelers. If you have a chronic condition, however, you should check with your doctor before visiting the islands. For conditions such as epilepsy, diabetes, or heart problems, wear a **MedicAlert Identification Tag** (© 800/825-3785; www.medicalert.org), which will immediately alert doctors to your condition and give them access to your records through MedicAlert's 24-hour hot line.

Finding a good doctor in Puerto Rico is easy, and most speak English. See "Fast Facts: Puerto Rico" later in this chapter, for the locations of hospitals.

If you worry about getting sick away from home, consider purchasing **medical travel insurance** and carry your ID card in your purse or wallet. In most cases, your existing health plan will provide the coverage you need. See the section on insurance earlier in this chapter for more information.

Pack **prescription medications** in your carry-on luggage, and carry prescription medications in their original containers. Also bring along copies of your prescriptions in case you lose your medication or run out. Carry the generic name of prescription medicines, in case a local pharmacist is unfamiliar with the brand name.

And don't forget **sunglasses** and an extra pair of **contact lenses** or **prescription glasses.**

Contact the **International Association for Medical Assistance to Travellers** (IAMAT; © **716/754-4883** or 416/652-0137; www.sentex.net/~iamat) for tips on travel and health concerns in Puerto Rico and lists of local, English-speaking doctors. If you get sick, consider asking your hotel concierge to recommend a local doctor—even his or her own. You can also try the emergency room at a local hospital; many have walk-in clinics for emergency cases that are not life threatening. You might not get immediate attention, but you won't pay the high price of an emergency-room visit (usually a minimum of $300 just for signing your name).

It's best to stick to **bottled mineral water** here. Although tap water is said to be safe to drink, many visitors experience diarrhea, even if they follow the usual precautions. The illness usually passes quickly without medication if you eat simply prepared food and drink only mineral water until you recover. If symptoms persist, consult a doctor.

The **sun** can be brutal, especially if you haven't been exposed to it in some time. Experts advise that you limit your time on the beach the first day. If you do overexpose yourself, stay out of the sun until you recover. If your exposure is followed by fever or chills, a headache, or a feeling of nausea or dizziness, see a doctor.

Sandflies (or "no-see-ums") are one of the biggest insect menaces in Puerto Rico. They appear mainly in the early evening, and even if you can't see these tiny bugs, you sure can "feel-um," as any native Puerto Rican will attest. Screens can't keep them out, so you'll need to use your favorite insect repellent.

Although **mosquitoes** are a nuisance, they do not carry malaria in Puerto Rico.

Hookworm and other **intestinal parasites** are relatively common in the Caribbean, though you are less likely to be affected in Puerto Rico than on other islands. Hookworm can be contracted by just walking barefoot on an infected beach. *Schistosomiasis* (also called *bilharzia*), caused by a parasitic fluke, can be contracted by submerging your feet in rivers and lakes infested with a certain species of snail.

Puerto Rico has been especially hard hit by **AIDS.** Exercise *at least* the same caution in choosing your sexual partners, and in practicing safe sex, as you would at home.

THE SAFE TRAVELER

The U.S. State Department issues no special travel advisories for the Commonwealth of Puerto Rico, the way it might for, say, the more troubled island of Jamaica. However, there are problems in Puerto Rico, especially muggings along San Juan's Condado and Isla Verde beaches. Auto theft and cars getting broken into are other major problems. Do not leave valuables in cars, even when the doors are locked.

Take precautions about leaving valuables on the beach, and exercise extreme care if you're searching for a remote beach where there's no one in sight. The only person lurking nearby might be someone not interested in surf and sand but a robber waiting to make off with your possessions.

Avoid wandering around the darkened and relatively deserted alleys and small streets of San Juan's Old Town at night, especially a section called El Callejón, near the intersection of calles San Sebastián and Tanca. Be especially careful along the narrow alley that connects this intersection with Calle Norzagaray. The district attracts more drug dealers than any other spot in Puerto Rico. A number of muggings also occur in Old Town's Cementerio de San Juan.

7 Tips for Travelers with Special Needs

TRAVELERS WITH DISABILITIES

Most disabilities shouldn't stop anyone from traveling. There are more options and resources out there today than ever before.

The Americans with Disabilities Act is enforced as strictly in Puerto Rico as it is on the U.S. mainland—in fact, a telling example of the act's enforcement can be found in Ponce, where the sightseeing trolleys are equipped with ramps and extra balustrades to accommodate travelers with disabilities. Unfortunately, hotels rarely give much publicity to the facilities they offer persons with disabilities, so it's always wise to contact the hotel directly, in advance, if you need special facilities. Tourist offices usually have little data about such matters.

You can obtain a free copy of *Air Transportation of Handicapped Persons,* published by the U.S. Department of Transportation. Write for *Free Advisory Circular No. AC12032,* Distribution Unit, U.S. Department of Transportation, Publications Division, 3341Q 75 Ave., Landover, MD 20785 (© **301/322-4961;** fax 301/386-5394). No phone requests are accepted, but you can write for a copy of the publication or download it for free at http://isddc.dot.gov.

The U.S. National Park Service offers a Golden Access Passport that gives free lifetime entrance to U.S. national parks, including those in Puerto Rico, for persons who are blind or permanently disabled, regardless of age. You can pick up a Golden Access Passport at any NPS entrance fee area by showing proof of medically determined disability and eligibility for receiving benefits under federal law. Besides free entry, the Golden Access Passport also offers a 50% discount on federal-use fees charged for such facilities as camping, swimming, parking, boat launching, and tours. For more information, go to www.nps.gov/fees_passes.htm or call © **888-GO-PARKS.**

AGENCIES/OPERATORS

Flying Wheels Travel (© **800/535-6790;** www.flyingwheelstravel.com) offers escorted tours and cruises that emphasize sports and private tours in minivans with lifts.

Access Adventures (© **716/889-9096**), a Rochester, N.Y.–based agency, offers customized itineraries for a variety of travelers with disabilities.

Accessible Journeys (© **800/TINGLES** or 610/521-0339; www.disabilitytravel.com) caters specifically to slow walkers and wheelchair travelers and their families and friends.

ORGANIZATIONS

MossRehab ResourceNet (© **215/456-5995;** www.mossresourcenet.org) provides helpful phone assistance through its **Travel Information Service.**

The Society for Accessible Travel and Hospitality (© **212/447-7285;**

fax 212/725-8253; www.sath.org) offers a wealth of travel resources for all types of disabilities and informed recommendations on destinations, access guides, travel agents, tour operators, vehicle rentals, and companion services. Annual membership costs $45 for adults, $30 for seniors and students.

The American Foundation for the Blind (© 800/232-5463; www.afb.org) provides information on traveling with Seeing Eye dogs.

PUBLICATIONS

Mobility International USA (© 541/343-1284; www.miusa.org) publishes *A World of Options,* a 658-page book of resources, covering everything from biking trips to scuba outfitters, and a biannual newsletter, *Over the Rainbow.* Annual membership is $35.

Twin Peaks Press (© 360/694-2462) publishes travel-related books for travelers with special needs.

Open World for Disability and Mature Travel magazine, published by SATH (see above), is full of good resources and information. A year's subscription is $13 ($21 outside the U.S.).

TIPS FOR BRITISH TRAVELERS WITH DISABILITIES

The **Royal Association for Disability and Rehabilitation** (RADAR), Unit 12, City Forum, 250 City Rd., London, EC1V 8AF (© 020/7250-3222; fax 020/7250-0212; www.radar.org.uk), publishes holiday "fact packs," three in all, which sell for £2 each or all three for £5. The first one provides general information, including planning and booking a holiday, insurance, finances, and useful organization and holiday providers. The second outlines transportation available abroad and equipment for rent. The third deals with specialized accommodations.

GAY & LESBIAN TRAVELERS

Puerto Rico is the most gay-friendly destination in the Caribbean, with lots of accommodations, restaurants, clubs, and bars that actively cater to a gay clientele. A free monthly newsletter, *Puerto Rico Breeze,* lists items of interest to the island's gay community. It's distributed at the Atlantic Beach Hotel (p. 94) and many of the gay-friendly clubs mentioned in this book.

The **International Gay & Lesbian Travel Association** (IGLTA; © 800/448-8550 or 954/776-2626; fax 954/776-3303; www.iglta.org) links travelers up with gay-friendly hoteliers, tour operators, and airline and cruise-line representatives. It offers monthly newsletters, marketing mailings, and a membership directory that's updated once a year. Membership is $150 yearly, plus a $100 administration fee for new members.

AGENCIES/OPERATORS

Above and Beyond Tours (© 800/397-2681; www.abovebeyondtours.com) offers gay and lesbian tours worldwide and is the exclusive gay and lesbian tour operator for United Airlines.

Now, Voyager (© 800/255-6951; www.nowvoyager.com) is a San Francisco–based gay-owned and -operated travel service.

Olivia Cruises & Resorts (© 800/631-6277 or 510/655-0364; www.oliviatravel.com) charters entire resorts and ships for exclusively lesbian vacations all over the world.

PUBLICATIONS

Out and About (© 800/929-2268 or 415/644-8044; www.outandabout.com) offers guidebooks, and a newsletter 10 times a year, packed with solid information on the global gay and lesbian scene.

Spartacus International Gay Guide and *Odysseus* are good, annual

English-language guidebooks focused on gay men, with some information for lesbians. You can get them from most gay and lesbian bookstores, or order them from **Giovanni's Room** bookstore, 1145 Pine St., Philadelphia, PA 19107 (© **215/923-2960;** www.giovannisroom.com).

Gay Travel A to Z: The World of Gay & Lesbian Travel Options at Your Fingertips, by Marianne Ferrari (Ferrari Publications), is a very good gay and lesbian guidebook series.

SENIOR TRAVEL

Mention the fact that you're a senior citizen when you first make your travel reservations. All major airlines and many Puerto Rican hotels offer discounts for seniors.

Though much of the island's sporting and nightlife activity is geared toward youthful travelers, Puerto Rico also has much to offer the senior citizen. The best source of information for seniors is the Puerto Rico Tourism Company (see "Visitor Information," above), or, if you're staying in a large resort hotel, the activities director or the concierge.

Members of **AARP** (formerly known as the American Association of Retired Persons), 601 E St. NW, Washington, DC 10049 (© **800/ 424-3410** or 202/434-2277; www. aarp.org), get discounts on hotels, airfares, and car rentals. AARP offers members a wide range of benefits, including *Modern Maturity of My Generation* magazine and a monthly newsletter. Anyone over 50 can join.

The **Alliance for Retired Americans,** 8403 Colesville Rd., Suite 1200, Silver Spring, MD 20910 (© **301/ 578-8422;** www.retiredamericans. org), offers a newsletter six times a year and discounts on hotel and auto rentals; annual dues are $13 per person or couple. *Note:* Members of the former National Council of Senior Citizens receive automatic membership in the Alliance.

The **U.S. National Park Service** offers a **Golden Age Passport** that gives seniors 62 years or older lifetime entrance to U.S. national parks for a one-time processing fee of $10. The pass must be purchased in person at any NPS facility that charges an entrance fee. Besides free entry, a Golden Age Passport also offers a 50% discount on federal-use fees charged for such facilities as camping, swimming, parking, boat launching, and tours. For more information, click onto www.nps.gov/fees_passes.htm or call © **888-GO-PARKS.**

AGENCIES/OPERATORS

Grand Circle Travel (© **800/ 221-2610** or 617/350-7500; fax 617/ 346-6700; www.gct.com) offers package deals for the 50-plus market, mostly of the tour-bus variety, with free trips thrown in for those who organize groups of 10 or more.

SAGA Holidays (© **800/343- 0273;** www.sagaholidays.com) offers tours and cruises for those 50 and older. SAGA also offers a number of single-traveler tours, and sponsors "Road Scholar Tours" (© **800/ 621-2151;** salesinfo@sagaholidays. com), vacations with an educational bent. You can order a free brochure from the website.

Interhostel (© **800/733-9753;** www.learn.unh.edu/interhostel), organized by the University of New Hampshire, also offers educational travel for senior citizens. On these escorted tours, the days are packed with seminars, lectures, and field trips, with sightseeing led by academic experts. **Interhostel** takes travelers 50 and over (with companions over 40), and offers 1- and 2-week trips, mostly international.

PUBLICATIONS

The Book of Deals is a collection of more than 1,000 senior discounts on airlines, lodging, tours, and attractions around the country. It's available for $9.95 by calling ☎ **800/460-6676.**

101 Tips for the Mature Traveler is available from Grand Circle Travel (☎ **800/221-2610** or 617/350-7500; fax 617/346-6700; www.gct.com).

The 50+ Traveler's Guidebook (St. Martin's Press).

Unbelievably Good Deals and Great Adventures That You Absolutely Can't Get Unless You're Over 50 (Contemporary Publishing Co.).

FAMILY TRAVEL

The family vacation is a rite of passage for many households, one that in a split second can devolve into a *National Lampoon* farce. But as any veteran family vacationer will assure you, a family trip can be among the most pleasurable and rewarding times of your life.

Puerto Rico is a terrific family destination. The smallest toddlers can spend blissful hours on sandy beaches and in the shallow seawater or pools specifically constructed for them. There's no end to the fascinating pursuits available for older children, ranging from boat rides to shell collecting to horseback riding and hiking. Perhaps your children are old enough to learn to snorkel and explore the wonderland of underwater Puerto

Rico. Skills such as swimming and windsurfing are taught here, and there are a variety of activities unique to the islands. Most resort hotels will advise you on what there is in the way of fun for the young, and many have play directors and supervised activities for various age groups.

Refer to chapter 4 for some recommendations of family-friendly accommodations, and to chapter 5 for our pick of family-friend restaurants. In chapter 6, look for the section "Especially for Kids" for special activities.

Families will be especially interested in some of the activities outlined in chapter 7, including Arecibo Observatory and Río Camuy cave park. A trip to the El Yunque rain forest and an afternoon at Luquillo Beach are other family favorite highlights. Chapter 7 also contains recommendations of two Hyatt properties at Dorado that are among the most family-friendly accommodations in Puerto Rico.

Family Travel Times, which is published 10 times a year by Travel With Your Children (TWYCH), includes a weekly call-in service for subscribers. Subscriptions cost $40 a year and can be ordered by contacting TWYCH, 40 Fifth Ave., New York, NY 10011 (☎ **212/477-5524;** www.familytraveltimes.com).

AGENCIES/OPERATORS

Familyhostel (☎ **800/733-9753;** www.learn.unh.edu/familyhostel) can help you take the whole family on

---

⟨*Value*⟩ Zero-Cost Lodging

Elder Travelers, 1615 Smelter Ave., Black Eagle, MT 59414 (editor@ eldertravelers.com), is for those who are more than 50 years old and like to travel and meet people. The organization's stated purpose is to provide members with "zero-cost lodging" anywhere in the world. It hooks up senior citizens with their counterpart hosts in the lands in which they travel. For $40 annually, you get a subscription to an informative newsletter, which provides links to the best travel data sites worldwide. For more information on this unique group, seek them out at www.eldertravelers.com.

moderately priced domestic and international learning vacations. All trip details are handled by the program staff, and lectures, field trips, and sightseeing are guided by a team of academics. For kids ages 8 to 15 accompanied by their parents and/or grandparents.

PUBLICATIONS
How to Take Great Trips with Your Kids (The Harvard Common Press) is full of good general advice that can apply to travel anywhere.

WEBSITES
Family Travel Network (www.familytravelnetwork.com) offers travel tips and reviews of family-friendly destinations, vacation deals, and thoughtful features such as "What to Do When Your Kids Are Afraid to Travel" and "Kid-Style Camping."

Travel with Your Children (www.travelwithyourkids.com) is a comprehensive site that offers sound advice for traveling with children.

The Busy Person's Guide to Travel with Children (http://wz.com/travel/TravelingWithChildren.html) offers a "45-second newsletter" where experts weigh in on the best websites and resources for tips for traveling with children.

SINGLE TRAVEL
Puerto Rico's thriving nightlife makes it a stellar destination for singles looking for romance. Two of the best clubs for meeting people are Babylon (if you're straight) and Eros (if you're gay). See the write-up of each club in "San Juan After Dark" in chapter 6.

Many people prefer traveling alone. Unfortunately, the solo traveler is often forced to pay a punishing "single supplement" charged by many resorts, cruise lines, and tours for the privilege of sleeping alone.

OPERATORS/ROOMMATE FINDERS
Travel Companion Exchange (TCE; ℂ 631/454-0880; www.travelcompanions.com) is one of the nation's oldest roommate finders for single travelers. Register with them and find a travel mate who will split the cost of the room with you and be around as little, or as often, as you like during the day.

Travel Buddies Singles Travel Club (ℂ 800/998-9099; www.travelbuddiesworldwide.com) runs small, intimate, single-friendly group trips and will match you with a roommate free and save you the cost of single supplements.

TravelChums (ℂ 212/799-6464; www.travelchums.com) is an Internet-only travel-companion matching service hosted by respected New York–based Shaw Guides travel service.

PUBLICATIONS
Traveling Solo: Advice and Ideas for More than 250 Great Vacations, by Eleanor Berman (Globe Pequot), gives advice on traveling alone, whether on your own or on a group tour.

Outdoor Singles Network, P.O. Box 781, Haines, AK 99827 (http://kcd.com/ci/osn), is a quarterly newsletter for outdoor-loving singles ages 19 to 90. The network will help you find a travel companion, pen pal, or soulmate. Subscriptions are $55, and your own personal ad is printed free in the next issue. Current issues are $15.

8 Getting There: Flying to Puerto Rico

Puerto Rico is by far the most accessible of the Caribbean islands, with frequent airline service. It's also the major airline hub of the Caribbean Basin.

THE AIRLINES
With San Juan as its hub for the entire Caribbean, **American Airlines** (ℂ 800/433-7300; www.aa.com) offers nonstop daily flights to San Juan

from Baltimore, Boston, Chicago, Dallas–Fort Worth, Hartford, Miami, Newark, New York (JFK), Orlando, Philadelphia, Tampa, Fort Lauderdale, and Washington (Dulles), plus flights to San Juan from both Montréal and Toronto with changes in Chicago or Miami. There are also at least two daily flights from Los Angeles to San Juan that touch down in Dallas or Miami.

American, because of its wholly owned subsidiary, **American Eagle,** is also the undisputed leader among the short-haul local commuter flights of the Caribbean. It usually flies in propeller planes carrying between 34 and 64 passengers. Collectively, American Eagle, along with its larger associate, American Airlines, offers service to 37 destinations on 31 islands of the Caribbean and The Bahamas, more than any other carrier.

Delta (© 800/221-1212; www. delta.com) has four daily nonstop flights from Atlanta Monday to Friday, six nonstop on Saturday, and four nonstop on Sunday. Flights into Atlanta from around the world are frequent, with excellent connections from points throughout Delta's network in the South and Southwest. There is also one daily nonstop flight from Cincinnati.

United Airlines (© 800/241-6522; www.ual.com) offers daily nonstop flights from Chicago to San Juan. **Northwest** (© 800/225-2525; www. nwa.com) has one daily nonstop flight to San Juan from Detroit, as well as at least one (and sometimes more) connecting flights to San Juan from Detroit. United also offers flights to San Juan, some of them nonstop, from both Memphis and Minneapolis, with a schedule that varies according to the season and the day of the week.

US Airways (© 800/428-4322; www.usairways.com) has daily direct flights between Charlotte, N.C., and San Juan. The airline also offers three daily nonstop flights to San Juan from Philadelphia, and one daily nonstop flight to San Juan from Pittsburgh.

British travelers can take a **British Airways** (© 0845/773-3377 in the U.K., 800/247-9297 in the U.S.) weekly flight direct from London to San Juan on Sunday. **Lufthansa** (© 01/803-803-803 in Germany, 800/645-3880 in the U.S.) passengers can fly on Saturday (one weekly flight) from Frankfurt to San Juan via Condor (a subsidiary operating the flight). And **Iberia** (© 1/902-400-500 in Spain, 800/772-4642 in the U.S.; www.iberia.com) has two weekly flights from Madrid to San Juan, leaving on Thursday and Saturday.

NEW AIR TRAVEL SECURITY MEASURES

In the wake of the terrorist attacks of September 11, 2001, the airline industry began implementing sweeping security measures in airports. Expect a lengthy check-in process and extensive delays. Although regulations vary from airline to airline, you can expedite the process by taking the following steps:

- **Arrive early.** Arrive at the airport at least 2 hours before your scheduled flight.
- **Avoid driving your car to the airport.** Parking and curbside access to the terminal may be limited. Call ahead to check.
- **Don't count on curbside check-in.** Some airlines and airports have stopped curbside check-in altogether, whereas others offer it on a limited basis. For up-to-date information on specific regulations and

Tips   What You Can Carry On—and What You Can't

In the United States, the Federal Aviation Administration (FAA) has devised new restrictions on carry-on baggage, not only to expedite the screening process but to prevent potential weapons from passing through airport security. Passengers are now limited to bringing just one carry-on bag and one personal item onto the aircraft (previous regulations allowed two carry-on bags and one personal item, like a briefcase or a purse). For more information, go to the FAA's website, **www.faa.gov**. The FAA has released a new list of items passengers are not allowed to carry on to an aircraft:

Not permitted: knives and box cutters, corkscrews, straight razors, metal scissors, metal nail files, golf clubs, baseball bats, pool cues, hockey sticks, ski poles, ice picks.

Permitted: nail clippers, tweezers, eyelash curlers, safety razors (including disposable razors), syringes (with documented proof of medical need), walking canes, and umbrellas (must be inspected first).

The airline you fly may have additional restrictions on items you can and cannot carry onboard. Call ahead to avoid problems.

implementations, check with the individual airline. There is no curbside check-in at the island airports.

- **Be sure to carry plenty of documentation.** A government-issued photo ID (federal, state, or local) is now required (don't forget your passport!). You might need to show this at various checkpoints. And be sure that your ID is *up-to-date:* an expired driver's license, for example, may keep you from boarding the plane altogether, and an expired passport won't get you into any of the island countries.

- **Know what you can carry on and what you can't.** Travelers in the United States are now limited to one carry-on bag, plus one personal bag (such as a purse or a briefcase). The FAA has also issued a list of newly restricted carry-on items; see the box "What You Can Carry On—and What You Can't," above, for more information.

- **Prepare to be searched.** Expect spot-checks. Electronic items, such as laptops and cellphones, should be readied for additional screening. Limit the metal items you wear on your person.

- **Don't make jokes.** When a check-in agent asks if someone other than you packed your bag, don't decide that this is the time to be funny. The agents will not hesitate to call an alarm.

- **No ticket, no gate access.** Only ticketed passengers will be allowed beyond the screener checkpoints, except for people with specific medical or parental needs.

FLYING FOR LESS: TIPS FOR GETTING THE BEST AIRFARE

Passengers within the same airplane cabin are rarely paying the same fare. Business travelers who need to purchase tickets at the last minute, change their itinerary at a moment's notice, or get home for the weekend pay the premium rate. Passengers who can book their ticket long in advance, who can stay over Saturday night, or who are willing to travel on a Tuesday, Wednesday, or Thursday after 7pm, will pay a fraction of the full fare. On many flights, even the shortest hops, the full fare is close to $1,000 or more, while a 7- or 14-day advance purchase ticket may cost less than half that amount. Here are a few other easy ways to save.

Airlines periodically lower prices on their most popular routes. Check the travel section of your Sunday newspaper for advertised discounts or call the airlines directly and ask if any **promotional rates** or special fares are available. You'll almost never see a sale during the peak winter season in Puerto Rico, or during the Thanksgiving or Christmas seasons. If your schedule is flexible, say so, and ask if you can secure a cheaper fare by staying an extra day, by flying midweek, or by flying at less-trafficked hours. If you already hold a ticket when a sale breaks, it may even pay to exchange your ticket, which usually incurs a $100 to $150 charge. *Note:* The lowest-priced fares are often nonrefundable, require advance purchase of 1 to 3 weeks and a certain length of stay,

and carry penalties for changing dates of travel.

Search the **Internet** for cheap fares. Great last-minute deals are available through free weekly e-mail services provided directly by the airlines. See "Planning Your Trip Online," later in this chapter, for more information.

Join a travel club such as **Moment's Notice** (© 718/234-6295; www.moments-notice.com) or **Sears Discount Travel Club** (© 800/433-9383 or 800/255-1487 to join; www.travelersadvantage.com), which supply unsold tickets at discounted prices. You pay an annual membership fee to get the club's hot-line number. Of course, you're limited to what's available, so you have to be flexible.

Join **frequent-flier clubs.** It's best to accrue miles on one program so you can rack up free flights and achieve elite status faster. But it makes sense to open as many accounts as possible, no matter how seldom you fly a particular airline. It's free, and you'll get the best choice of seats, faster response to phone inquiries, and prompter service if your luggage is stolen, your flight is canceled or delayed, or if you want to change your seat.

9 Escorted Tours, Package Deals & Special-Interest Vacations

Before you start your search for the lowest airfare, you might want to consider booking your flight as part of a travel package such as an escorted tour or a package tour. What you lose in adventure, you'll gain in time and money saved when you book accommodations, and maybe even food and entertainment, along with your flight.

PACKAGE TOURS FOR INDEPENDENT TRAVELERS

Package tours are not the same thing as escorted tours. With a package tour, you travel independently but pay a group rate. Packages usually include airfare, a choice of hotels, and car

rentals, and packagers often offer several options at different prices. In many cases, a package that includes airfare, hotel, and transportation to and from the airport will cost you less than just the hotel alone would have, had you booked it yourself. That's because packages are sold in bulk to tour operators—who resell them to the public at a cost that drastically undercuts standard rates.

RECOMMENDED U.S. PACKAGE TOUR OPERATORS

One good source of package deals is the airlines themselves. Most major airlines offer air/land packages, including **American Airlines Vacations** (© 800/321-2121; http://aav1.aavacations.com), **Delta Vacations** (© 800/221-6666; www.deltavacations.com), **US Airways Vacations** (© 800/455-0123 or 800/422-3861; www.usairwaysvacations.com), **Continental Airlines Vacations** (© 800/301-3800; www.coolvacations.com), and **United Vacations** (© 888/854-3899; www.unitedvacations.com).

Online Vacation Mall (© 800/839-9851; www.onlinevacationmall.com) allows you to search for and book packages offered by a number of tour operators and airlines. The **United States Tour Operators Association's** website (www.ustoa.com) has a search engine that allows you to look for operators that offer packages to a specific destination. Travel packages are also listed in the travel section of your local Sunday newspaper. **Liberty Travel** (© 888/271-1584; www.libertytravel.com), one of the biggest packagers in the Northeast, often runs full-page ads in Sunday papers. Or check ads in the national travel magazines such as *Arthur Frommer's Budget Travel Magazine, Travel & Leisure, National Geographic Traveler,* and *Condé Nast Traveler.*

To save time comparing the price and value of all the package tours out there, consider calling **TourScan Inc.,** P.O. Box 2367, Darien, CT 06820 (© 800/962-2080 or 203/655-8091; fax 203/655-6689; www.tourscan.com). Every season the company gathers and computerizes the contents of about 200 brochures containing 10,000 different vacations in the Caribbean, The Bahamas, and Bermuda. TourScan selects the best value at each hotel and condo. Two catalogs are printed each year. Each lists a broad-based choice of hotels on most of the islands of the Caribbean, in all price ranges. Write to TourScan for their catalogs, costing $4 each, the price of which is credited to any TourScan vacation.

Other options for general independent packages include:

Horizon Tours, 1634 Eye St. NW, Suite 301, Washington, DC 20006 (© 877/TRIPSAI or 202/393-8390; fax 202/393-1547; www.horizontours.com), specializes in all-inclusive upscale resorts in Puerto Rico.

AAA Tours, 1759 Pinero Ave., Summit Hills, San Juan (© 787/793-3678), offers some good packages ranging from 2 days to 2 weeks.

PACKAGES FOR BRITISH TRAVELERS

British travelers can contact **Caribbean Connection,** Concorde House, Forest Street, Chester, CH1 1QR (© 01244/355300; www.Caribbean-connections.co.uk), which offers airfare-and-hotel packages to the Caribbean and customizes tours for independent travel. It publishes two catalogs of Caribbean offerings, one featuring more than 160 properties on all the major islands, and a 50-page catalog of luxury all-inclusive properties.

Other Caribbean specialists operating out of England include **Kuoni Travel,** Kuoni House, Dorking, Surrey, RH5 4AZ (© 01306/742-222; www.kuoni.co.uk). **Caribtours,** Kiln House, 210 New Kings Rd., London, SW6 4NZ (© 020/7751-0660; www.caribtours.co.uk), a small, very knowledgeable organization, also specializes in Caribbean travel and will tailor itineraries.

Although Australians are welcome to visit Puerto Rico, as are New Zealanders and other nationals, there are no special packages or deals for them.

THE PROS & CONS OF PACKAGE TOURS

Packages can save you money because they are sold in bulk to tour operators, who sell them to the public. They offer group prices but allow for independent travel. The disadvantages are that you're usually required to make a large payment up front; you may end up on a charter flight; and you have to deal with your own luggage and with transfers between your hotel and the airport, if transfers are not included in the package price. Packages often don't allow for complete flexibility or a wide range of choices. For instance, you might prefer a quiet inn but have to settle for a popular chain hotel instead. Your choice of travel days might be limited as well.

ESCORTED TOURS

An escorted tour is a structured group tour with a group leader. The price usually includes everything from airfare to hotel, meals, tours, admission costs, and local transportation.

RECOMMENDED ESCORTED TOUR OPERATORS

Puerto Rico Tours, Condo Inter-Suite, Suite 5M on Isla Verde in San Juan (© **787/306-1540;** fax 787/791-5479), offers specially conducted private sightseeing tours of Puerto Rico, including trips to the rain forest, Luquillo Beach, the caves of Camuy, and other attractions, such as a restored Taíno Indian village.

Backstage Partners (© **787/791-0099;** fax 787/791-2760) offers customized tours that take in a wide range of island attractions, including ecotours, deep-sea fishing, scuba diving and snorkeling, safaris, and golf packages.

Other leading escorted tour operators include **Crown Imperial Travel,** Loiza Street Station in San Juan (© **787/791-7075**), known for such major destinations as Ponce, El Yunque, and the Camuy Caverns; **Northwestern Land Tour** (© **787/447-7804**), which helps you take in all the major sights of the island from Ponce to El Yunque; and **Sunshine Tours** (© **787/791-4500;** www.puerto-rico-sunshinetours.com), which covers much the same ground as the others.

SPECIAL-INTEREST TOURS

If you'd like to explore Puerto Rico as part of a horseback riding tour package, consult **PRwest Vacation Services** (© **888/779-3788**). A dozen well-trained Paso Fino horses are available to accommodate both the advanced and novice rider. In northwest Puerto Rico, you can explore cavernous cliffs and tropical forests—all on horseback. Tours last 7 days and 6 nights.

Several other tour operators cater to special tastes, including **Castillo Tours & Travel Service,** 2413C Laurel St., Punta Las Marias, San Juan (© **787/791-6995;** www.castillotours.com), which is known for some of the best deep-sea fishing tours. **Encantada Tours,** 654 Muñoz Rivera Ave., Suite 908, IBM Plaza, San Juan (© **888/711-2901;** www.encantadatours.com), offers gastronomical tours of the island.

Tips Questions to Ask if You Book a Package Tour

- What are the **accommodation choices** available, and are there price differences? Once you find out, look them up in a Frommer's guide.
- What **type of room** will you be staying in? Don't take whatever is thrown your way. Request a nonsmoking room, a quiet room, a room with a view, or whatever you fancy.
- What type of **hidden expenses** might I face? Ask whether airport departure fees and taxes are included in the total cost.

Hillbilly Tours, Route 181, km 13.4, San Juan (© **787/760-5618**), specializes in nature-based and countryside tours in the rain forest.

AdvenTours, Luquillo (© **787/530-8311;** aventura@coqui.net), features customized private tours that include such activities as bird-watching, hiking, camping, visits to coffee plantations, and kayaking. **Aventuras Tierra Adentro,** 268 Piñero Avenue, San Juan (© **787/766-0470;** www.aventurastierraadentro.com), specializes in rock climbing, body rafting, caving, and canyoning.

Eco Xcursion Aquatica, Route 191, km 1.7, Rio Grande, Fajardo (© **787/888-2887**), offers some of the best rain-forest hikes and mountain bike tours for both individuals and groups.

10 For the Cruise-Ship Traveler

If you'd like to sail the Caribbean in a hotel with an ocean view, a cruise ship might be for you. Cruises are slow and easy and are no longer enjoyed only by the idle rich who have months to spend away from home. In fact, most cruises today appeal to the middle-income traveler who often has no more than 3 to 5 days to vacation.

Miami is the cruise capital of the world, but San Juan is second. Unless you have never visited Miami and would like to include it as part of your extended Caribbean itinerary, there is justification in flying directly to San Juan by plane and beginning your cruise here. It puts you immediately in the Caribbean, which means you save a 2-day ocean voyage just to get here. Instead of sailing from Florida, you can spend the time getting to know Puerto Rico.

Most cruise-ship operators emphasize the concept of a total vacation. Some are mostly activity centered; others offer the chance to do nothing but relax. Cruise ships are self-contained resorts, offering a large variety of services and activities onboard and sightseeing once you arrive in a port of call.

For those who don't want to spend all their time at sea, some lines offer a fly-and-cruise vacation. You spend a week cruising the Caribbean and another week staying at a first-class hotel at reduced prices. These total packages generally cost less than the cruise and air portions would cost if purchased separately.

Another version of fly-and-cruise is to fly to and from the cruise. Most plans offer a package deal from the principal airport closest to your residence to the major airport nearest to the cruise departure point. It's possible to purchase your air ticket on your own and book your cruise ticket separately, but you'll save money by combining the fares in a package deal.

Most cruise ships travel at night, arriving the next morning at the day's port of call. In port, passengers can go ashore for sightseeing, shopping, and a local meal. Cruise prices vary widely. Sometimes the same route with the same ports of call can carry different fares, depending on the ship's luxury (as well as your accommodations onboard). Consult a good travel agent for the latest offerings.

Some of the most likely contenders include the following: **Ambassador Tours,** 120 Montgomery St., Suite 400, San Francisco, CA 94104 (© **800/989-9000** or 415/357-9876); **Cruises, Inc.,** 1415 NW 62 St., Suite 205, Fort Lauderdale, FL 33309 (© **800/854-0500** or 954/958-3700); **Cruises of Distinction,** 2750 S. Woodward Ave., Bloomfield Hills, MI 48304 (© **800/634-3445**); **Cruise Masters,** Century Plaza Towers, 2029 Century Park E., Suite 950,

---

> **Tips** While Waiting for Your Ship to Sail
>
> While waiting for the departure of your cruise vessel, you might spend the day enjoying the historic district of Old San Juan with its endless sightseeing possibilities and merchandise-crammed shops. Another day can be devoted to the beaches, gambling casinos, and sporting possibilities in the greater San Juan area, including almost unlimited golf, tennis, and watersports. Even if you have only hours to spend before your ship's departure, you can explore the historic old city, either by taking an organized tour or going on your own.

Los Angeles, CA 90067 (© **800/242-9000** or 310/556-2925); **Kelly Cruises,** 1315 W. 22nd St., Suite 105, Oak Brook, IL 60521 (© **800/837-7447** or 630/990-1111); and **Hartford Holidays Travel,** 129 Hillside Ave., Williston Park, NY 11596 (© **800/828-4813**). Any of these stay tuned to last-minute price wars brewing among such megacarriers as Carnival, Princess, Royal Caribbean, and Holland America, as well as such low-budget contenders as Premier.

Vacations to Go, 1502 Augusta Dr., Suite 415, Houston, TX 77057 (© **800/338-4962** or 713/974-2121; www.vacationstogo.com), provides catalogs and information on discount cruises through the Caribbean, as well as the Atlantic and Mediterranean.

WHEN YOUR SHIP COMES IN

The Port of San Juan is the busiest ocean terminal in the West Indies, with an estimated half of the Caribbean's trade passing through here. There are about 710 cruise-ship arrivals every year, bringing nearly 850,000 passengers.

A spacious walkway connects the piers to the cobblestone streets of Old San Juan, so you can walk there to shop. You can also take a waiting taxi to the beaches of Condado. For advice and maps, contact the **Tourist Information Center** at La Casita, near Pier 1 in Old San Juan (© **787/721-2400**). The dock area, now restored, is an attractive place for strolling, with its plazas, fountains, promenades, and beaches.

THE CRUISE LINES

Here's a brief rundown of some of the cruise lines that serve San Juan and the Caribbean. For detailed information, pick up a copy of one of our companion guides in this series, *Frommer's Caribbean Cruises & Ports of Call, Frommer's Caribbean Ports of Call,* or *Unofficial Guide to Cruises.*

- **Carnival Cruise Lines** (© **800/327-9501** or 305/599-2200; fax 305/406-4740; www.carnival.com), a specialist in the maintenance of some of the biggest and most brightly decorated ships afloat, is the richest, boldest, brashest, and most successful mass-market cruise line in the world. Nine of its vessels depart from Florida or Caribbean ports that include, among others, San Juan, Miami, Tampa, and New Orleans. Two of the ships (*Carnival Holiday* and *Carnival Destiny*) define San Juan as their home port, from which 7-day excursions are made to such southern Caribbean ports as St. Thomas, St. Maarten, Dominica, Barbados, Guadalupe, Martinique, Grenada, St. Lucia, and Santo Domingo. If you prefer to depart from one of the ports of Florida (especially Miami), know in advance that many of the company's cruises make San Juan a focal point of their stopovers. Most of the company's Caribbean cruises offer good value, last between 4 and 11 days (in most cases, 7 days), and feature nonstop activities, lots of glitter, and the hustle and bustle of armies of clients and crew members embarking and disembarking at every port. Cuisine and party-colored drinks are plentiful, although with vessels of this size, they are, by necessity, mass-produced. The overall atmosphere is comparable to that of a floating theme park with hordes of visitors, loaded with whimsy, and with lots of emphasis on partying in a style you might have expected in Atlantic City. Lots of single passengers, some of them with gleams in their eye, opt for this line, and some actually get lucky. Despite the presence of lots of unattached or loosely attached adults, the line makes special efforts to amuse and entertain children between 2 and 17. The average onboard age ranges from 38 to 42, although individual passengers range from 3 to 95.

- **Celebrity Cruises** (© **800/722-5941** or 800/280-3423; www.celebrity-cruises.com) maintains nine medium-to-large ships offering cruises of between 7 and 10 nights to such ports as Key West, Grand Cayman, St. Thomas, Aruba, Antigua, and Cozumel, Mexico, among others. Passengers interested in maximum exposure to Puerto Rico usually opt to cruise aboard *Galaxy,* a 77,713-ton megaship that's based (late Oct–late Apr only) in San Juan, and which embarks every week throughout the year for tours to such southern Caribbean islands as Barbados, St. Kitts, and Aruba. Despite a merger of Celebrity with the larger and better-financed Royal Caribbean International, Celebrity maintains its own identity and corporate structure within the larger framework. The niche this line has created is unpretentious but classy, several notches above mass market, but with pricing that's nonetheless relatively competitive. Accommodations are roomy and well equipped, and the cuisine is among the most intensely cultivated of any of its competitors afloat.

- **Costa Cruise Lines** (© **800/462-6782** or 954/266-5600; fax 305/358-7325; www.costacruises.com), the U.S.-based branch of an Italian cruise line that has thrived for about a century, maintains hefty to megasize vessels that are newer than those of many other lines afloat. Two of these offer virtually identical jaunts through the western and eastern Caribbean on alternate weeks, each of them departing from Fort Lauderdale, Florida. Ports of call during the eastern Caribbean itineraries of both vessels include a stopover in San Juan, followed by visits to St. Thomas, Catalina Island (a private island off the coast of the Dominican Republic known for its beaches), and Cozumel. There is an Italian flavor and lots of Italian design onboard here, and an atmosphere of relaxed indulgence. The ships—*CostaAtlantica* and *CostaVictoria*—feature tame versions of ancient Roman Bacchanalia, as well as such celebrations as *Festa Italiana,* and focaccia and pizza parties by the pool.

- **Princess Cruises** (© **800/421-0522** or 310/553-1770; fax 310/284-2845; www.princesscruises.com) has a large and far-flung fleet that totals seven megavessels. The ships cruise at various times of the year through Caribbean and

Bahamian waters, sometimes with stops at San Juan as part of the itinerary. The *Dawn Princess,* a state-of-the-art megaship, defines San Juan as its home port. Departing every Saturday, it pays calls at ports that include St. Thomas, Trinidad, Barbados, Martinique, and Antigua. The *Dawn Princess's* sibling ship, *Sun Princess,* pinpoints San Juan and Costa Rica as the beginning or end point of transcanal cruises that last 10 days. Princess is one of the very few lines in the world to offer luxury accommodations and upscale service as a standard feature aboard its megaships. These usually carry a smaller number of passengers than similarly sized vessels on less elegant lines. The company's clientele is upscale, with an average passenger age of 55 or over. A respectable percentage of the staff is British.

- **Radisson Seven Seas Cruises** (© **800/285-1835** or 954/776-6123; fax 954/772-3763; www.rssc.com) is noted for the level of glamour and prestige that permeates its cruises. It sends all three of its ships—the *Radisson Diamond, Seven Seas Mariner,* and *Seven Seas Navigator*—into the Caribbean on a regular basis. Designed along lines distinctly different from those of every other cruise line afloat, the *Radisson Diamond* is a relatively slow but stable ship that floats atop submerged pontoons similar to those used by catamarans or oil-drilling platforms in the North Sea. Despite the fact that its design is not likely to be duplicated anytime soon within the cruise industry, passengers appreciate it for its fine cuisine, upscale service, and suitability for corporate conventions at sea. The *Mariner,* carrying 700 passengers, is an all-suite vessel, and the *Navigator* carries 490 passengers on luxe cruises. Cruises are relatively expensive compared to those offered by less prestigious lines, and roam freely, with less allegiance to a fixed home port than many other vessels. The *Diamond* defines San Juan as its home port between March and April, when it embarks on short-term cruises of no more than 4 or 5 days in duration. Stopovers include Virgin Gorda, St. Barts, and St. Maarten. The rest of the time, the ship's Caribbean ports include cities along the coast of Costa Rica, as well as Curaçao, Aruba, Grand Cayman, Cayman Brac, Cartagena, St. Barts, St. Maarten, St. Thomas, and Cozumel.

- **Royal Caribbean International** (© **800/327-6700** or 305/539-6000; fax 800/722-5329; www.royalcaribbean.com) leads the industry in the development of megaships. Most of this company's dozen or so vessels weigh in at around 73,000 tons, are among the largest of any line afloat, and represent a roster of floating hardware that's more impressive than that of many national navies. Marketed as a mainstream mass-market cruise line whose components have been fine-tuned through endless repetition, the line encourages a restrained house-party theme that's somehow a bit less frenetic than that found aboard the more raucous megaships of other cruise lines, including Carnival. The company is well run, and there are enough onboard activities to suit virtually any taste and age level. Though accommodations and accoutrements are more than adequate, they are not upscale, and cabins aboard some of the line's older vessels tend to be a bit more cramped than the industry norm.

Using either Florida ports or San Juan as their home port, RCI ships call regularly at such oft-visited ports as St. Thomas, Ocho Rios, St. Maarten, Grand Cayman, St. Croix, and Curaçao. Most of the company's cruises last for 4 to 7 days. If Puerto Rico is the focal point of your cruise, your best bet is the midsize ship, the 48,563-ton *Nordic Empress,* based in San Juan from October to April and specializing in 4-day cruises with stopovers in St. Thomas, St. Maarten, and St. Croix. These cruises alternate with 5-night cruises of St. Kitts, St. Lucia, and Barbados, or Tortola, St. Martin, and Antigua. Royal Caribbean is the only cruise line in the business that owns, outright, two tropical beaches (one in The Bahamas, the other along an isolated peninsula in northern Haiti) whose sands and watersports facilities are the focus of many of the company's Caribbean cruises.

11 Planning Your Trip Online

Researching and booking your trip online can save time and money. Then again, it might not. It is simply not true that you always get the best deal online. Most booking engines do not include schedules and prices for budget airlines, and from time to time you'll get a better last-minute price by calling the airline directly, so it's best to call the airline to see if you can do better before booking online.

On the plus side, Internet users today can tap into the same travel-planning databases that were once accessible only to travel agents—and do it at the same speed. Sites such as **Frommers.com, Travelocity.com, Expedia.com,** and **Orbitz.com** allow consumers to comparison shop for airfares, access special bargains, book flights, and reserve hotel rooms and rental cars.

But don't fire your travel agent just yet. Although online-booking sites offer tips and hard data to help you bargain-shop, they cannot endow you with the hard-earned experience that makes a seasoned, reliable travel agent an invaluable resource, even in the Internet age. And for consumers with a complex itinerary, a trusty travel agent is still the best way to arrange the most direct flights to and from the best airports.

Still, there's no denying the Internet's emergence as a powerful tool in researching and plotting travel time. The benefits of researching your trip online can be well worth the effort.

Last-minute specials, such as weekend deals or Internet-only fares, are offered by airlines to fill empty seats. Most of these are announced on Tuesday or Wednesday and must be purchased online. They are only valid for travel that weekend, but some can be booked weeks or months in advance. Sign up for weekly e-mail alerts at airline websites or check mega-sites that compile comprehensive lists of last-minute specials, such as **Smarter Living** (www.smarter living.com) and **WebFlyer** (www. webflyer.com).

Some sites, such as Expedia.com, will send you **e-mail notification** when a cheap fare becomes available to your favorite destination. Some will also tell you when fares to a particular destination are lowest.

TRAVEL-PLANNING & -BOOKING SITES

Because several airlines are no longer willing to pay commissions on tickets sold by online travel agencies, these agencies may either add a $10 surcharge to your bill if you book on that carrier or neglect to offer those carriers' schedules.

The list of sites below is selective, not comprehensive. Some sites will have evolved or disappeared by the time you read this:

- **Travelocity** (www.travelocity.com or www.frommers.travelocity.com) and **Expedia** (www.expedia.com) are among the most popular sites, each offering an excellent range of options. Travelers search by destination, dates, and cost.
- **Orbitz** (www.orbitz.com) is a popular site launched by United, Delta, Northwest, American, and Continental airlines. (Stay tuned: At press time, travel-agency associations were waging an antitrust battle against this site.)
- **Qixo** (www.qixo.com) is a powerful search engine that allows you to search for flights and accommodations from some 20 airline and travel-planning sites (such as Travelocity) at once. Qixo sorts results by price.
- **Priceline** (www.priceline.com) lets you "name your price" for airline tickets, hotel rooms, and rental cars. For airline tickets, you

can't say what time you want to fly or on what airline—you have to accept any flight between 6am and 10pm on the dates you've selected, and you may have to make one or more stopovers. Tickets are nonrefundable, and no frequent-flyer miles are awarded.

SMART E-SHOPPING

The savvy traveler is armed with insider information. Here are a few tips to help you navigate the Internet successfully and safely:

- **Know when sales start.** Last-minute deals may vanish in minutes. If you have a favorite booking site or airline, find out when last-minute deals are released to the public.
- **Shop around.** If you're looking for bargains, compare prices on different sites and airlines—and against a travel agent's best fare. Try a range of times and alternative airports before you make a purchase.
- **Stay secure.** Book only through secure sites (some airline sites are not secure). Look for a key icon (Netscape) or a padlock (Internet

 Frommers.com: The Complete Travel Resource

For an excellent travel-planning resource, we highly recommend Frommers.com (www.frommers.com). We're a little biased, of course, but we guarantee that you'll find the travel tips, reviews, monthly vacation giveaways, and online-booking capabilities thoroughly indispensable. Among the special features are our popular Message Boards, where Frommer's readers post queries and share advice (sometimes even our authors show up to answer questions); Frommers.com Newsletter, for the latest travel bargains and inside travel secrets; and Frommer's Destinations Section, where you'll get expert travel tips, hotel and dining recommendations, and advice on the sights to see for more than 2,500 destinations around the globe. When your research is done, the Online Reservation System (www.frommers.com/booktravelnow) takes you to Frommer's favorite sites for booking your vacation at affordable prices.

Tips All About E-Ticketing

Electronic tickets (E-tickets) are the fast and easy ticket-free alternative to paper tickets. E-tickets allow passengers to avoid long lines at airport check-in, all the while saving the airlines money on postage and labor. With the increased security measures in airports, however, an E-ticket no longer guarantees an accelerated check-in. You often can't go straight to the boarding gate, even if you have no bags to check. You'll probably need to show your printed E-ticket receipt or confirmation of purchase, as well as a photo ID, and sometimes even the credit card with which you purchased your E-ticket. That said, buying an E-ticket is still a fast, convenient way to book a flight; instead of having to wait for a paper ticket to come through the mail, you can book your fare by phone or on the computer, and the airline will immediately confirm by fax or e-mail. In addition, airlines often offer frequent-flier miles as incentive for electronic bookings.

Explorer) at the bottom of your Web browser before you enter credit-card information or other personal data.

- **Avoid online auctions.** Sites that auction airline tickets and frequent-flier miles are the No. 1 perpetrators of Internet fraud,

according to the National Consumers League.

- **Maintain a paper trail.** If you book an e-ticket, print out a confirmation, or write down your confirmation number, and keep it safe and accessible—or your trip could be a virtual one!

12 Getting Around

BY PLANE

American Eagle (*©* **800/433-7300** or 787/749-1747; www.aa.com) flies from Luis Muñoz Marín International Airport to Mayagüez, which can be your gateway to western Puerto Rico. Round-trip fares are $99 to $242. For information about air connections to the offshore islands of Vieques and Culebra, see chapter 11.

BY RENTAL CAR

There is good news and bad news about driving in Puerto Rico. First, the good news. Puerto Rico offers some of the most scenic drives in all the Caribbean. Driving around and discovering its little hidden beaches, coastal towns, mountain villages, vast forests, and national parks is reason enough to visit the island. In fact, if you want to explore the island in any

depth, driving a private car is about the only way, as public transportation is woefully inadequate.

Of course, if you want to stay only in San Juan, having a car is not necessary. You can get around San Juan on foot or by bus, taxi, and in some cases, hotel minivan.

Now the bad news. Renting a car and driving in Puerto Rico, depending on the routes you take, can lead to a number of frustrating experiences, as our readers relate to us year after year. These readers point out that local drivers are often dangerous, as evidenced by the number of fenders with bashed-in sides. The older coastal highways provide the most scenic routes but are often congested. Some of the roads, especially in the mountainous interior, are just too narrow for automobiles. If you do rent a car, proceed with caution along these poorly paved and maintained roads, which most often follow circuitous routes. Cliffslides or landslides are not uncommon.

Some local agencies may tempt you with special reduced prices. But if you're planning to tour the island by car, you won't find any local branches that will help you if you experience trouble. And some of the agencies widely advertising low-cost deals won't take credit cards and want cash in advance. Also, watch out for "hidden" extra costs, which sometimes proliferate among the smaller and not very well known firms, and difficulties connected with resolving insurance claims.

If you do rent a vehicle, it's best to stick with the old reliables: **Avis** (© **800/331-1212** or 787/253-5926; www.avis.com), **Budget** (© **800/527-0700** or 787/791-3685; https://rent.drivebudget.com), or **Hertz** (© **800/654-3131** or 787/791-0840; www.hertz.com). Each of these companies offers minivan transport to its office and car depot. Be alert to the minimum-age requirements for car rentals in Puerto Rico. Both Avis and Hertz require that renters be 25 or older; at Budget, renters must be 21 or older, but those between the ages of 21 and 24 pay a $5 daily surcharge to the agreed-upon rental fee. None of these companies rents Jeeps, SUVs, or convertibles.

Added security comes from an antitheft double-locking mechanism that has been installed in most of the rental cars available in Puerto Rico. Car theft is common in Puerto Rico, so extra precautions are always needed.

Distances are often posted in kilometers rather than miles (1km = 0.62 mile), but speed limits are displayed in miles per hour.

INSURANCE Each company offers an optional collision damage waiver priced at around $14 to $20 a day. Purchasing the waiver eliminates most or all of the financial responsibility you would face in case of an accident. With it, you can simply go home, leaving the rental company to sort it all out. Without it, you would be liable for up to the full value of the car in case it was damaged. Paying for the rental with certain credit or charge cards sometimes eliminates the need to buy this extra insurance. Also, your own automobile insurance policy might cover some or all of the damages. You should check with both your own insurer and your credit-card issuers before leaving home. (See "Insurance, Health & Safety," earlier in this chapter.)

GASOLINE There is usually an abundant supply of gasoline in Puerto Rico, especially on the outskirts of San Juan, where you'll see all the familiar signs, such as Mobil. Gasoline stations are also plentiful along the main arteries traversing the island. However, if you're going to remote areas of the island, especially on Sunday, it's advisable to start out with a full tank. *Note:* In Puerto Rico, gasoline is sold by the liter, not by the gallon. The cost of gasoline is often somewhat cheaper than in the United States. A liter usually sells for 26¢, which comes to about $1.25 per gallon.

DRIVING RULES Driving rules can be a source of some confusion. Speed limits are often not posted on the island, but when they are, they're given in miles per hour. For example, the limit on the San Juan–Ponce *autopista* (superhighway) is 70 mph. Speed limits elsewhere, notably in heavily populated residential areas, are much lower. Because you're not likely to know what the actual speed limit is in some of these areas, it's best to confine your speed to no more than 30 mph. The highway department places *lomas* (speed bumps) at strategic

Highway Signs

Road signs using international symbols are commonplace in the San Juan metropolitan area and other urban centers, but they are written in Spanish. The following translations will help you figure out what they mean:

Spanish	English
Autopista	Expressway
Balneario	Public beach
Calle sin salida	Dead end
Carretera cerrada	Road closed to traffic
Carretera dividida	Divided highway
Carretera estrecha	Narrow road
Cruce	Crossroad
Cruce de peatones	Pedestrian crossing
Cuesta	Hill
Desprendimiento	Landslide
Desvío	Detour
Estación de peaje	Toll station
Manténgase a la derecha	Keep right
No entre	Do not enter
No estacione	Do not park
Parada de guaguas	Bus stop
Peligro	Danger
Puente estrecho	Narrow bridge
Velocidad máxima	Speed limit
Zona escolar	School zone

points to deter speeders. Sometimes these are called "sleeping policemen."

Like U.S. and Canadian motorists, *Puerto Ricans drive on the right-hand side of the road.*

ROAD MAPS One of the best and most detailed road maps of Puerto Rico is published by **International Travel Maps** and distributed in the United States by Rand McNally. It's available in some bookstores and is a good investment at $8.95. The **Gousha Puerto Rico Road Map,** which sells for $8.95 in the United States and Canada, has a good street map of San Juan but lacks detailed information about minor highways on the island and is very similar to the map of Puerto Rico distributed free at tourist offices.

BREAKDOWNS & ASSISTANCE
All the major towns and cities have garages that will come to your assistance and tow your vehicle for repairs if necessary. There's no national emergency number to call in the event of a mechanical breakdown. If you have a rental car, call the rental company first. Usually, someone there will bring motor assistance to you. If your car requires extensive repairs because of a mechanical failure, a new one will be sent to replace it.

BY PUBLIC TRANSPORTATION
Cars and minibuses known as *públicos* provide low-cost transportation around the island. Their license plates have the letters "P" or "PD" following the numbers. They serve all the main

towns of Puerto Rico; passengers are let off and picked up along the way, both at designated stops and when someone flags them down. Rates are set by the Public Service Commission. *Públicos* usually operate during daylight hours, departing from the main plaza (central square) of a town.

Information about público routes between San Juan and Mayagüez is available at **Lineas Sultana,** Calle Esteban González 898, Urbanización Santa Rita, Río Piedras (© **787/765-9377**). Information about público routes between San Juan and Ponce is available from **Choferes Unidos de Ponce,** Terminal de Carros Públicos, Calle Vive in Ponce (© **787/764-0540**).

Fares vary according to whether the público will make a detour to pick up or drop off a passenger at a specific locale. (If you want to deviate from the predetermined routes, you'll pay more than if you wait for a público beside the main highway.) Fares from San Juan to Mayagüez range from $16 to $30; from San Juan to Ponce, from $15 to $25. Be warned that although prices of públicos are low, the routes are slow, with frequent stops, often erratic routing, and lots of inconvenience.

13 The Active Vacation Planner

Puerto Rico offers a wide variety of sports, including golf, tennis, horseback riding, and all kinds of watersports—from scuba diving to deep-sea fishing.

Many resorts offer a large choice of sports activities, and various all-inclusive sports-vacation packages are available from hotels and airlines serving Puerto Rico.

Dorado Beach, Cerromar Beach, and Palmas del Mar are the chief centers for golf, tennis, and beach life. San Juan's hotels on the Condado–Isla Verde coast also generally offer a complete array of watersports.

BEACHES

With 272 miles (438km) of Atlantic and Caribbean coastline, Puerto Rico obviously has plenty of beaches—more than 250 of them. No two beaches are alike. Some are long, straight, and very popular, with active and lively waves. Others have calmer waters, are more intimate, and are off the beaten path.

Puerto Rico's public beaches are called *balnearios;* they charge for parking and for use of facilities such as lockers and showers. Some of Puerto Rico's balnearios are practically deserted. They are closed on Monday, except if Monday is a holiday; in that case, they are open then but closed on Tuesday. In winter, public beach hours are 9am to 5pm; in summer, 9am to 6pm. For more information about the island's many beaches, call the **Department of Sports and Recreation** at © **787/728-5668.**

The most frequented beaches in San Juan are **Condado Beach, Isla Verde Beach,** and **Ocean Park Beach** (see "Diving, Fishing, Tennis & Other Outdoor Pursuits" in chapter 6 for more details). The largest concentration of hotels in Puerto Rico—it's like Miami Beach—opens onto these golden sands, which have public facilities. The big resorts have been built, naturally, on the most idyllic sands. Even so, the beaches, including those fronting resorts, are open to the public in general. If, however, you use any of the facilities of the hotel or its services, you have to pay a fee, of course. Condado and Isla Verde beaches, in particular, are often overcrowded, especially during the winter season.

In the northeast of the island are 6 miles (9.5km) of relatively unspoiled beaches, with waters ranging from calm to raging. Visits to El Yunque, the rain forest, are often combined with a stopover at the most popular (and the best) beach in the northeast, **Luquillo Beach,** a balneario. There's a huge stand of majestic coconut palms that shade more than a mile (1.5km) of sand. Dressing facilities, parking, and lockers are available here. It is the major beach used by residents of San Juan, and it tends to be overcrowded on weekends, especially at places where the most facilities are located. One of the unique aspects of Luquillo Beach is its wheelchair-accessible pathway, *Mar Sin Barreras,* which allows the physically challenged to easily enter and cool off in the refreshing waters of the Atlantic Ocean. After a relaxing day in the sun, travelers can take romantic rides on horseback or continue to sit back, relax, and enjoy the sunset.

For more information on the El Yunque rain forest and Luquillo Beach, refer to chapter 7.

Some of the best beaches of Puerto Rico are in the east—but offshore— on the two small islands of **Culebra** and **Vieques.** In Culebra, the white-sand beaches, particularly **Flamenco Beach,** have clear waters and scenic coral reefs, including a mile-long (1.5km) formation off Culebrita, where there is also a lighthouse. Vieques contains numerous scalloped beaches along the north and northwest coasts, all of which lie on U.S. Navy land and are open to the public when no military maneuvers are going on. For more details on these beaches, refer to chapter 11.

On the west coast the best beach is along the bay at **Boquerón**, part of the municipality of Cabo Rojo. The area opens onto a mile (1.5km) of white sand bordered by clear water. Long a balneario, it is frequented mainly by locals. The beach is popular for swimming and picnicking under coconut palms. Nearby is the Boquerón Lagoon, a refuge for ducks and other birds.

Some of the best deserted beaches stretch between Cabo Rojo, on the southwesterly tip of Puerto Rico, eastward all the way to Ponce. Beginning in the west, directly east of Cabo Rojo, you'll discover **Bahia Sucia Beach, Rosado Beach, Santa Beach, Caña Gorda Beach, Tamarindo Beach,** and **Ballena Beach.** Access to many of these beaches is limited because of poor roads, but the effort to reach them is worth it. Bring along any supplies you'll need.

The best surfing beaches in the Caribbean are on the west coast, north of Mayagüez, including the beach at **Punta Higüero,** on Route 413 near the town of Rincón, which is said to be one of the finest surfing spots in the world.

For more details on the beaches of western Puerto Rico, refer to chapter 9.

For a quick overview of where the most popular of the dozens upon dozens of beaches in Puerto Rico are located, refer to the "Puerto Rico" map earlier in this chapter, on p. 20.

BOATING & SAILING
The waters off Puerto Rico provide excellent boating in all seasons. Winds

---

Beach Warning
Don't go walking along the beaches at night, even as tempting as it may be to do with your lover. Even if you find the secluded, hidden beach of your dreams, proceed with caution. On unguarded beaches, you will have no way to protect yourself or your valuables should you be approached by a robber or mugger, which happens frequently.

average 10 to 15 knots virtually year-round. Marinas provide facilities and services on par with any others in the Caribbean, and many have power-boats or sailboats for rent, crewed or bareboat charter.

Major marinas include the **San Juan Bay Marina,** Fernandez Juncos Avenue (© 787/721-8062); **Marina Puerto Chico,** at Puerto Chico (© 787/863-0834); **Marina de Palmas Shipyard** at Palmas del Mar in Humacao (© 787/850-2065); and **Marina de Salinas** (© 787/752-8484) in Salinas. The Caribbean's largest and most modern marina, **Puerto del Rey,** RD 3, km 51.4 (© 787/860-1000), is located on the island's east coast, in Fajardo.

One of the sailing regattas in Puerto Rico is the Copa Velasco Regatta for ocean racing, at Palmas del Mar in Humacao.

For the typical visitor interested in watersports—not the serious yachter—our favorite place for fun in the surf is the aptly named **San Juan Water Fun,** Isla Verde Beach in back of the Wyndham El San Juan Hotel and Casino, Avenida Isla Verde in Isla Verde, San Juan (© 787/644-2585). Here you can rent everything from a two-seater kayak for $30 per hour or a "banana boat" that holds eight passengers and costs $12 for a 20-minute ride.

If you're staying in eastern Puerto Rico, the best place for watersports rentals is **Iguana Water Sports,** Westin Rio Mar Beach Resort, 6000 Rio Mar Blvd., Rio Grande (© 787/888-6000), which has the island's best selection of small boats. Waverunners cost $60 per hour, and two-seat kayaks go for $35 per hour.

For more serious boating needs, we head for **Karolette Charter,** Palmas del Mar, AB-12 St., RD 3, km 86.4, Humacao (© 787/850-7442). You can be taken out on a combined fishing and snorkeling cruise for $95 per person for 4½ hours. More serious

fishers can book an entire boat, which holds six comfortably and costs $600 for 4 hours or $750 for 6 hours.

CAMPING

Puerto Rico abounds in sandy beaches and forested hillsides that are suitable for erecting a tent. It is best and safest to camp only in the sites maintained by the government-sponsored **Campanias de Parques Nacionales.** (See the map "Camping in Puerto Rico," p. 62.) Some of these are simple places where you erect your own tent, although they are outfitted with electricity and running water; some are simple cabins, sometimes with fireplaces. Showers are communal. To stay at a campsite costs between $15 and $22 per night per tent. For more information and an application to rent one of the units or reserve a site, call © 787/622-5200.

Many sites offer very basic cabins for rent. Each cabin is equipped with a full bathroom, a stove, a refrigerator, two beds, and a table and chairs. However, most of your cooking will probably be tastier if you do it outside at one of the on-site barbecues. In nearly all cases, you must provide your own sheets and towels.

You might want to camp along or near a lovely beach. On the western coast of Puerto Rico, the best camping site is **Tres Hermanos Beach,** which opens onto Anasco Bay, lying between Rincón to the north and Mayagüez to the south.

Heading west from San Juan en route to Isabella, there are two excellent beach camps: **Cerro Gordo,** east of the city of Arecibo, and **Punta Maracayo,** to the west of Arecibo, both reached along Route 22. The Atlantic waters here can be turbulent, even in summer.

If you'd like to camp in the east of Puerto Rico, the finest site is the beach at **Seven Seas** to the south of Fajardo.

Arroyo on the southern coast to the east of the town of Guayama is yet

Take Me Out to the *Beisbol* Game

Baseball has a long, illustrious history in Puerto Rico. Imported around the turn of the 20th century by plantation owners as a leisure activity for workers, *beisbol* quickly caught fire, and local leagues have produced such major-league stars as Roberto Alomar, Bernie Williams, and the late great Roberto Clemente.

A top-notch league of six teams—featuring many rising professionals honing their skills during the winter months—begins its season in October and plays in ballparks throughout Puerto Rico. Many baseball fans from the U.S. mainland come down specifically to see these teams play. For a chance to see good baseball in a more intimate setting than is afforded in the U.S. major leagues, call **Professional Baseball of Puerto Rico (© 787/765-6285)** for information about professional games and, if available, a schedule.

another site on mainland Puerto Rico that has both cabins and regular campsites, although this location is a bit bare-boned.

Both Culebra and Vieques offer camping by the beach. The best for camping on Culebra is **Flamenco Beach,** on the north shore. On Vieques, the best beach camping is at **Sun Bay,** on the island's south coast.

For information about camping on or near a beach, call © 787/721-2800.

Puerto Rico also allows camping in various state forests, provided that permits are obtained. Except for cabins at Monte Guilarte State Forest, which cost $20 per night, camping sites are available at $4 per person. For further information about permits, call the **forest service office** at San Juan Bay Marina (© 787/724-3724).

There are seven major on-island camping sites in various state forests: **Cambalache State Forest,** near Barceloneta; **Carite State Forest,** near Patillas; **Guajataca State Forest,** near Quebradillas; **Monte Guilarte State Forest,** near Adjuntas; **Susua State Forest,** near Yauco; **Río Abajo State Forest,** near Arecibo; and our favorite, **Toro Negro Forest**

Reserve, near Villaba, where you can camp in the shadow of Puerto Rico's highest peaks, in the Toro Negro Forest.

In addition, the **Caribbean National Forest/El Yunque (© 787/888-1800)** allows primitive camping within the rain forest. For more information, call © 787/888-1880.

It's also possible to camp at either of two wildlife refuges, **Isla de Mona Wildlife Refuge (© 787/724-3724),** lying some 50 miles (81km) off the rough seas of Mona Passage, and at **Lago Lucchetti Wildlife Refuge (© 787/844-4660),** between Yauco and Ponce.

The **Parks and Recreation Association of Puerto Rico (© 787/721-2800)** can provide you with a map and detailed instructions about how to reach all these sites.

DEEP-SEA FISHING

The offshore fishing here is top-notch! Allison tuna, white and blue marlin, sailfish, wahoo, dolphin, mackerel, and tarpon are some of the fish that can be caught in Puerto Rican waters, where some 30 world records have been broken.

Charter arrangements can be made through most major hotels and

Camping in Puerto Rico

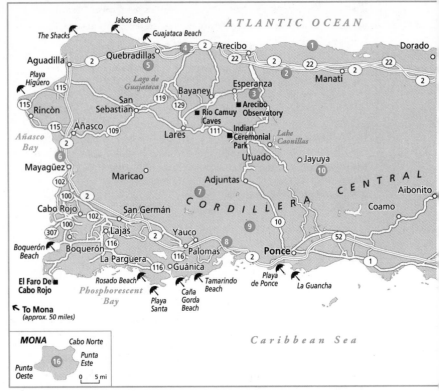

resorts. In San Juan, **Benitez Fishing Charters** sets the standard by which to judge other captains (see "Diving, Fishing, Tennis & Other Outdoor Pursuits" in chapter 6). In Palmas del Mar, which has some of the best year-round fishing in the Caribbean, you'll find **Capt. Bill Burleson** (see "Palmas del Mar" in chapter 10).

GOLF

Home to 13 golf courses, including 8 championship links, Puerto Rico is justifiably known as the "Scotland of the Caribbean." In fact, the 72 holes at the Hyatt resorts at Dorado offer the greatest concentration of golf in the Caribbean.

The courses at the **Hyatt Dorado Beach Resort & Country Club** and

the **Hyatt Regency Cerromar Beach Resort** are among the 25 best courses created by Robert Trent Jones, Sr. Jack Nicklaus rates the challenging 13th hole at the Hyatt Dorado as one of the top 10 in the world. See chapter 7 for more details.

On the southeast coast, crack golfers consider holes 11 through 15 at the **Golf Club at Palmas del Mar** to be the toughest five successive holes in the Caribbean. At **Wyndham El Conquistador Resort & Country Club,** the spectacular $250 million resort at Las Croabas east of San Juan, the course's 200-foot changes in elevation provide panoramic vistas. With the exception of the El Conquistador Resort and Country Club, these

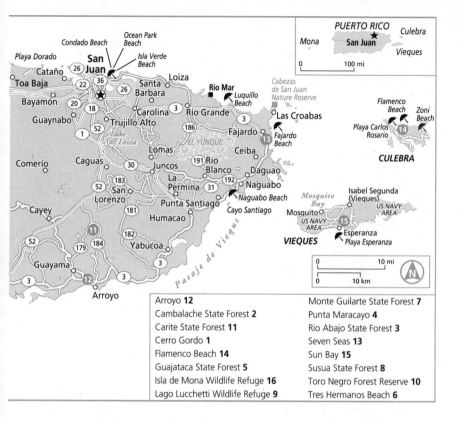

Arroyo **12**	Monte Guilarte State Forest **7**
Cambalache State Forest **2**	Punta Maracayo **4**
Carite State Forest **11**	Rio Abajo State Forest **3**
Cerro Gordo **1**	Seven Seas **13**
Flamenco Beach **14**	Sun Bay **15**
Guajataca State Forest **5**	Susua State Forest **8**
Isla de Mona Wildlife Refuge **16**	Toro Negro Forest Reserve **10**
Lago Lucchetti Wildlife Refuge **9**	Tres Hermanos Beach **6**

courses are open to the public. See chapter 10 for more details on the major golf clubs east of San Juan.

HIKING

The mountainous interior of Puerto Rico provides ample opportunities for hill climbing and nature treks. These are especially appealing because panoramas open at the least-expected moments, often revealing spectacular views of the distant sea.

The most popular, most beautiful, and most spectacular trekking spot is **El Yunque,** the sprawling "jungle" maintained by the U.S. Forest Service and the only rain forest on U.S. soil. El Yunque is part of the **Caribbean National Forest,** which lies a 45-minute drive east of San Juan. More

than 250 species of trees and some 200 types of ferns have been identified here. Some 60 species of birds inhabit El Yunque, including the increasingly rare Puerto Rican parrot. Such rare birds as the elfin woods warbler, the green mango hummingbird, and the Puerto Rican lizard-cuckoo live here.

Park rangers have clearly marked the trails that are ideal for walking. See "El Yunque" in chapter 7 for more details.

A lesser forest, but one that is still intriguing to visit, is the **Maricao State Forest,** near the coffee town of Maricao. This forest is in western Puerto Rico, east of the town of Mayagüez. For more details, see "Mayagüez" in chapter 8.

Ponce is the best center for exploring some of the greatest forest reserves in the Caribbean Basin, notably **Toro Negro Forest Reserve** with its **Lake Guineo** (the lake at the highest elevation on the island), the **Guánica State Forest,** ideal for hiking and bird-watching, and the **Carite Forest Reserve,** a 6,000-acre park known for its dwarf forest. For more details, see "Ponce" in chapter 8.

Equally suitable for hiking are the protected lands (especially the **Río Camuy Cave Park**) whose topography is characterized as "karst"—that is, limestone riddled with caves, underground rivers, and natural crevasses and fissures. Although these regions pose additional risks and technical problems for trekkers, some people prefer the opportunities they provide for exploring the territory both above and below its surface. See "Arecibo & Camuy" in chapter 7 for details about the Río Camuy Caves.

For more information about any of the national forest reserves of Puerto Rico, call the **Department of Sports & Recreation** at ✆ 787/728-5668.

SCUBA DIVING & SNORKELING

SCUBA DIVING The continental shelf, which surrounds Puerto Rico on three sides, is responsible for an abundance of coral reefs, caves, sea walls, and trenches for scuba diving and snorkeling.

Open-water reefs off the southeastern coast near **Humacao** are visited by migrating whales and manatees. Many caves are located near Isabela on the west coast. The **Great Trench,** off the island's south coast, is ideal for experienced open-water divers. Caves and the sea wall at **La Parguera** are also favorites. **Vieques** and **Culebra islands** have coral formations. **Mona Island** offers unspoiled reefs at depths averaging 80 feet; seals are one of the attractions. Uninhabited islands, such as **Icacos,** off the northeastern coast near Fajardo, are also popular with both snorkelers and divers.

These sites are now within reach because many of Puerto Rico's dive operators and resorts offer packages that include daily or twice-daily dives, scuba equipment, instruction, and excursions to Puerto Rico's popular attractions.

In San Juan, **Caribe Aquatic Adventures** offers an array of sailing, scuba, and snorkeling trips, as well as boat charters and fishing (see chapter 6). At the Palmas del Mar Resort, **Palmas Dive Center** features daily two-tank open-water dives for certified divers, plus snorkeling trips to Monkey Island (see chapter 10). Elsewhere on the island, several other companies offer scuba and snorkeling instruction. We provide details in each chapter.

SNORKELING Because of its overpopulation, the waters around San Juan aren't the most ideal for snorkeling. In fact, the entire north shore of Puerto Rico fronts the Atlantic, where the waters are often turbulent. Windsurfers—not snorkelers—gravitate to the waves and surf in the northwest.

Safety for Tropical Hikers

When you hike in the tropics, you can quickly become dehydrated and also sustain more serious insect bites and sunburn than you would while hiking in more temperate climes. Take plenty of water and drink it frequently, wear a sun hat, and consider the advisability of long-sleeved shirts and sunscreen to protect yourself from heat exhaustion and sunstroke.

The most ideal conditions for snorkeling in Puerto Rico are along the shores of the remote islands of **Vieques** and **Culebra** (see chapter 11).

The best snorkeling on the main island is found near the town of **Fajardo,** to the east of San Juan and along the tranquil eastern coast (see chapter 10).

The calm, glasslike quality of the clear Caribbean along the south shore is also ideal for snorkeling. The most developed tourist mecca here is the city of Ponce. Few rivers empty their muddy waters into the sea along the south coast, resulting in gin-clear waters offshore. You can snorkel off the coast without having to go on a boat trip. One good place is at **Playa La Parguera,** where you can rent snorkeling equipment from kiosks along the beach. This beach lies east of the town of Guánica, to the east of Ponce. Here tropical fish add to the brightness of the water, which is generally turquoise. The addition of mangrove cays in the area also makes La Parguera more alluring for snorkelers. Another good spot for snorkelers is **Caja de Muertos** off the coast of Ponce. Here a lagoon coral reef boasts a large number of fish species (see chapter 8).

SURFING

Puerto Rico's northwest beaches attract surfers from around the world. Called the "Hawaii of the East," Puerto Rico has hosted a number of international competitions. October through February are the best surfing months, but the sport is enjoyed in Puerto Rico from August through April. The most popular areas are from Isabela around Punta Borinquén to Rincón—at beaches such as Wilderness, Surfers, Crashboat, Los Turbos in Vega Baja, Pine Grove in Isla Verde, and La Pared in Luquillo. Surfboards are available at many watersports shops.

International competitions held in Puerto Rico have included the 1968 and 1988 World Amateur Surfing Championships, the annual Caribbean Cup Surfing Championship, and the 1989 and 1990 Budweiser Puerto Rico Surfing Challenge events.

TENNIS

Puerto Rico has approximately 100 major tennis courts. Many are at hotels and resorts; others are in public parks throughout the island. Several paradores also have courts. A number of courts are lighted for nighttime play.

In San Juan, the **Caribe Hilton** and the **Condado Plaza Hotel & Casino** have tennis courts. Also in the area are the **public courts** at the San Juan Central Municipal Park. See chapter 6.

The **Hyatt Regency Cerromar Beach Hotel** and the **Hyatt Dorado Beach Resort & Country Club** maintain a total of 21 courts between them (see chapter 7). The **Tennis Center** at **Palmas del Mar** in Humacao, the largest in Puerto Rico, features 20 courts (see chapter 10).

WINDSURFING

Windsurfing is a popular watersport in Puerto Rico; the sheltered waters of the **Condado Lagoon** in San Juan are a favorite spot. Other sites include **Ocean Park, Enseñada, Boquerón, Honda Beach,** and **Culebra.** Puerto Rico hosted its first major windsurfing tournament, the Ray-Ban Windsurfing World Cup, in 1989.

Many companies that offer snorkeling and scuba diving also provide windsurfing equipment and instruction, and dozens of hotels have facilities on their own premises.

One of the best places to arrange for windsurfing in San Juan is **Caribe Aquatic Adventures** (see chapter 6). Windsurfing is excellent at the beachfront of the Hyatt Dorado Beach Resort & Country Club, where **Penfield Island Adventures** offers lessons and rentals (see chapter 7).

14 Tips on Choosing Your Accommodations

HOTELS & RESORTS

There is no rigid classification of Puerto Rican hotels. The word "deluxe" is often used—or misused—when "first class" might be a more appropriate term. Self-described first-class hotels often aren't that nice. We've presented fairly detailed descriptions of the hotels in this book, so you'll get an idea of what to expect once you're there.

Even in the real deluxe and first-class properties, however, don't expect top-rate service and efficiency. The slow tropical pace is what folks mean when they talk about "island time." Also, things often don't work as well in the tropics as they do in some of the fancy resorts of California or Europe. You might even experience power failures.

Ask detailed questions when booking a room. Don't just ask to be booked into a certain hotel, but specify your likes and dislikes. There are several logistics of getting the right room in a hotel. Entertainment in Puerto Rico is often alfresco, so light sleepers obviously won't want a room directly over a steel band. In general, back rooms cost less than oceanfront rooms, and lower rooms cost less than upper-floor units. Therefore, if budget is a major consideration for you, opt for the cheaper rooms. You won't have a great view, but you'll pay less. Just make sure that it isn't next to the all-night drummers.

Transfers from the airport or the cruise dock are included in some hotel bookings, most often in a package plan but usually not in ordinary bookings. This is true of first-class and deluxe resorts but rarely of medium-priced or budget accommodations. Always ascertain whether transfers (which can be expensive) are included.

When using the facilities at a resort, make sure that you know exactly what is free and what costs money. For example, swimming in the pool is nearly always free, but you might be charged for use of a tennis court. Nearly all watersports cost extra, unless you're booked on some special plan such as a scuba package. Some resorts seem to charge every time you breathe and might end up costing more than a deluxe hotel that includes most everything in the price.

Some hotels are right on the beach. Others involve transfers to the beach by taxi or bus, so factor in transportation costs, which can mount quickly if you stay 5 days to a week. If you want to go to the beach every day, it might be wise to book a hotel on the Condado and not stay in romantic Old San Juan, from which you'll spend a lot of time and money transferring back and forth between your hotel and the beach.

Most hotels in Puerto Rico are on the windward side of the island, with lots of waves, undertow, and surf. If a glasslike smooth sea is imperative for your stay, you can book on the leeward (eastern shore) or Caribbean (southeast coast) sides, which are better for snorkeling. The major centers in these areas are the resort complex of Palmas del Mar and the "second city" of Ponce.

MAP VS. AP, OR DO YOU WANT TO GO CP OR EP?

All resorts offer a **European Plan** (EP) rate, which means you pay for the price of a room. That leaves you free to dine around at night at various other resorts or restaurants without restriction. Another plan preferred by many is the **Continental Plan** (CP), which means you get your room and a continental breakfast of juice, coffee, bread, jam, etc., included in a set price. This plan is preferred by many because most guests don't like to "dine around" at breakfast time.

Another major option is the **Modi-fied American Plan** (MAP), which includes breakfast and one main meal of the day, either lunch or dinner. The final choice is the **American Plan** (AP), which includes breakfast, lunch, and dinner.

At certain resorts you will save money by booking either the MAP or AP because discounts are granted. If you dine a la carte for lunch and dinner at various restaurants, your final dining bill will no doubt be much higher than if you stayed on the MAP or AP.

These plans might save you money, but if as part of your holiday you like to eat in various places, you might be disappointed. You face the same dining room every night, unless the resort you're staying at has many different restaurants on the dining plan. Often they don't. Many resorts have a lot of specialty restaurants, serving, say, Japanese cuisine, but these more expensive restaurants are not included in MAP or AP; rather, they charge a la carte prices.

One option is to ask if your hotel has a dine-around plan. You might still keep costs in check, but you can avoid a culinary rut by taking your meals in some other restaurants if your hotel has such a plan. Such plans are rare in Puerto Rico, which does not specialize in all-inclusive resorts the way that Jamaica and some other islands do.

Before booking a room, check with a good travel agent or investigate on your own what you are likely to save by booking in on a dining plan. Under certain circumstances in winter, you might not have a choice if MAP is dictated as a requirement for staying there. It pays to investigate, of course.

SPAS

The best spas in San Juan are previewed in chapter 6, "Exploring San Juan." For an idyllic spa outside San Juan, refer to the box "Portal of Luxury" in chapter 10.

PUERTO RICAN GUESTHOUSES

A unique type of accommodation is the guesthouse, where Puerto Ricans themselves usually stay when they travel. Ranging in size from 7 to 25 rooms, they offer a familial atmosphere. Many are on or near the beach, some have pools or sun decks, and a number serve meals.

In Puerto Rico, however, the term "guesthouse" has many meanings. Some guesthouses are like simple motels built around pools. Others have small individual cottages with their own kitchenettes, constructed around a main building in which you'll often find a bar and a restaurant serving local food. Some are surprisingly comfortable, often with private baths and swimming pools. You may or may not have air-conditioning. The rooms are sometimes cooled by ceiling fans or by the trade winds blowing through open windows at night.

For value, the guesthouse can't be topped. If you stay at a guesthouse, you can journey over to a big beach resort and use its seaside facilities for only a small fee. Although bereft of frills, the guesthouses we've recommended are clean and safe for families or single women. However, the cheapest ones are not places where you'd want to spend a lot of time because of their modest furnishings.

For further information on guesthouses, contact the **Puerto Rico Tourism Company,** 666 Fifth Ave., New York, NY 10103 (© **800/223-6530** or 212/586-6262).

PARADORES

In an effort to lure travelers beyond the hotels and casinos of San Juan's historic district to the tranquil natural beauty of the island's countryside, the Puerto Rico Tourism Company offers *paradores puertorriqueños* (charming country inns) which are comfortable bases for exploring the island's varied attractions. Vacationers seeking a peaceful idyll can also choose from several privately owned and operated guesthouses.

Using Spain's *parador* system as a model, the Puerto Rico Tourism Company established the paradores in 1973 to encourage tourism across the island. Each of the paradores is situated in a historic place or site of unusual scenic beauty and must meet high standards of service and cleanliness. (See the map "Paradores of Puerto Rico" p. 69.)

Some of the paradores are located in the mountains and others by the sea. Most have pools, and all offer excellent Puerto Rican cuisine. Many are within easy driving distance of San Juan.

Our favorite paradores are all in western Puerto Rico (see chapter 9). **Parador Posada Porlamar** in La Parguera gives you a taste of the good life in a simple fishing village. For a plantation ambience and an evocation of the Puerto Rico of colonial times, there is the **Parador Hacienda Gripiñas** at Jayuya, some 30 miles (48km) southwest of San Juan; it was a former coffee plantation. **Parador Vistamar,** at Quebradillas, one of the largest paradores in Puerto Rico, enjoys a mountain location with beautiful gardens of tropical flowers.

VILLAS & VACATION HOMES

You can often secure good deals in Puerto Rico by renting privately owned villas and vacation homes.

Almost every villa has a staff, or at least a maid who comes in a few days a week. Villas also provide the essentials of home life, including bed linen and cooking paraphernalia. Condos usually come with a reception desk and are often comparable to life in a suite at a big resort hotel. Nearly every condo complex has a swimming pool, and some have more than one.

Private apartments are rented either with or without maid service. This is more of a no-frills option than the villas and condos. An apartment might not be in a building with a swimming pool, and it might not have a front desk to help you. Among the major categories of vacation homes, cottages offer the most freewheeling way to live. Most cottages are fairly simple, many opening in an ideal fashion onto a beach, whereas others may be clustered around a communal pool. Many contain no more than a simple bedroom together with a small kitchen and bath. For the peak winter season, reservations should be made at least 5 or 6 months in advance.

Dozens of agents throughout the United States and Canada offer these types of rentals (see "Rental Agencies," below, for some recommendations). You can also write to local tourist-information offices, which can advise you on vacation-home rentals.

Travel experts agree that savings, especially for a family of three to six people, or two or three couples, can range from 50% to 60% over what a hotel would cost. If there are only two in your party, these savings probably don't apply.

RENTAL AGENCIES

Agencies specializing in renting properties in Puerto Rico include:

- **Villas of Distinction,** P.O. Box 55, Armonk, NY 10504 (© **800/ 289-0900** or 914/273-3331; fax 914/273-3387; www.villasof distinction.com), is one of the best rental agencies offering "complete vacations," including airfare, rental car, and domestic help. Some private villas have two to five bedrooms, and almost every villa has a swimming pool.
- **Caribbean Connection Plus Ltd.,** P.O. Box 261, Trumbull, CT 06611 (© **800/634-4907** or

Paradores & Country Inns of Puerto Rico

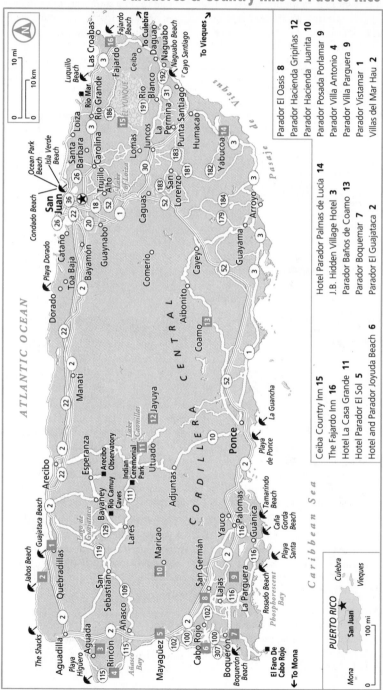

Parador El Oasis **8**
Parador Hacienda Gripiñas **12**
Parador Hacienda Juanita **10**
Parador Posada Porlamar **9**
Parador Villa Antonio **4**
Parador Villa Parguera **9**
Parador Vistamar **1**
Villas del Mar Hau **2**

Ceiba Country Inn **15**
The Fajardo Inn **16**
Hotel La Casa Grande **11**
Hotel Parador El Sol **5**
Hotel and Parador Joyuda Beach **6**

Hotel Parador Palmas de Lucía **14**
J.B. Hidden Village Hotel **3**
Parador Baños de Coamo **13**
Parador Boquemar **7**
Parador El Guajataca **2**

203/261-8603; fax 203/261-8295; www.islandhoppingexperts.com), offers many apartments, cottages, and villas in the Caribbean. Caribbean Connection specializes in island hopping with JetAir, and it offers especially attractive deals for U.S. West Coast travelers. This is one of the few reservations services whose staff has actually been on the islands, so members can talk to people who know from experience and not from a computer screen.

- **VHR, Worldwide,** 235 Kensington Ave., Norwood, NJ 07648 (© **800/633-3284** or 201/767-9393; fax 201/767-5510; www.vhrww.com), offers the most comprehensive portfolio of luxury villas, condominiums, resort suites, and apartments for rent in the Caribbean, including complete

packages for airfare and car rentals. The company's more than 4,000 homes and suite resorts are handpicked by the staff, and accommodations are generally less expensive than comparable hotel rooms.

- **Hideaways International,** 767 Islington St., Portsmouth, NH 03801 (© **800/843-4433** or 603/430-4433; fax 603/430-4444; www.hideaways.com), provides a 144-page guide with illustrations of its accommodations in the Caribbean so that you can get an idea of what you're renting. Most of its villas, which can accommodate up to three couples or a large family of about 10, come with maid service. You can also ask this travel club about discounts on plane fares and car rentals.

15 Recommended Reading

GENERAL

Babin, Theresa Maria. *The Puerto Ricans' Spirit: Their History, Life, and Culture.* Provides good background information on the island's history and its people, along with a survey of its fine arts and literature.

Garver, Susan, and Paula McGuire. *Coming to North America.* Explores the subject of the massive migration from Puerto Rico to America, where immigrants settled mainly in New York.

Gonzáles, José Luís. *Puerto Rico: The Four Storeyed Country.* A collection of essays examining Puerto Rican society, culture, and national identity; it assumes that you already know a lot about the island.

Gordon Raoul. *Puerto Rican Culture: An Introduction.* Provides an in-depth study of this subject for those interested in understanding the art and traditions of the island.

Hanberg, Clifford A. *Puerto Rico and the Puerto Ricans.* Offers a broad-based look at the history and background of Puerto Rico.

Santiago, Esmeralda. *When I Was Puerto Rican.* The president of a film company describes her childhood as 1 of 11 Puerto Rican siblings, born into poverty. From the island countryside to the crime-ridden streets of Brooklyn, Santiago's memoir is rich in the ambience of Puerto Rican life.

Steiner, Stan. *The Islands.* A journalistic portrayal of the island people, both within Puerto Rico itself and in North American barrios, such as those of the South Bronx.

HISTORY

Carrion, Artura Morales. *Puerto Rico: A Political and Cultural History.* One of the best major overviews of Puerto Rican history and culture. Most of the book focuses on the political history of the island, with extensive chapters devoted to 18th-century society, the plantation society, and the challenge to Spanish colonialism. Part II traces the conflicts, hopes, and trauma that followed the U.S. takeover of the island in 1898. The final section provides a good cultural survey of Puerto Rico, covering folklore, literature, music, and art.

Dor-Ner, Zvi, and William G. Scheller. *Columbus and the Age of Discovery.* The companion book to the PBS series about the explorer. This is a good general survey of what is known about the voyages of Columbus.

Golding, Morton. *A Short History of Puerto Rico.* For those who want their history readable and condensed.

Honychurch, Reginald. *The Caribbean People.* In three volumes, this is a well-balanced account written by one of the so-called new historians of the Caribbean.

Scarano, Francisco A. *Sugar and Slavery in Puerto Rico: The Plantation Economy of Ponce, 1800–1850.* A scholarly study of an agrarian region of Puerto Rico far removed from the Spanish-controlled capital of San Juan.

Wagenheim, Kal, and Olga Jimenez, eds. *The Puerto Ricans: A Documentary History.* A sourcebook that provides a better understanding of Puerto Ricans. Its fast-paced rhythm makes it engrossing, if prejudicial, reading.

Williams, Eric. *From Columbus to Castro: The History of the Caribbean.* The former prime minister of Trinidad and Tobago takes you on a grand tour of a region dominated by slavery, sugar, and often sheer greed.

POLITICS

Carr, Ramon. *Puerto Rico: A Colonial Experiment.* One of the most insightful views of island politics, which has been called the national religion of Puerto Rico. This book, funded by the Twentieth Century Fund (established in 1919 by philanthropist Edward A. Filene), discusses ways to loosen the economic bonds between a superpower and what is today a quasi-colonial possession.

Johnson, Roberta. *Puerto Rico: Commonwealth or Colony?* This book attempts to answer the title's provocative question.

Melendez, Edgardo. *Puerto Rico's Statehood Movement.* Melendez reviews the statehood movement, presenting the pros and cons of a complicated issue.

Perl, Lila. *Puerto Rico, Island Between Two Worlds.* Describes the dilemma of an island caught between its Spanish heritage and its contemporary American ties.

Perusse, Roland I. *The United States and Puerto Rico: Breaking the Bonds of Economic Colonialism.* This book traces the history of trade relations in Puerto Rico, the second-largest western trading partner of the United States, after Canada. A cultural and economic survey with a strongly politicized point of view.

Williams, Byron. *Puerto Rico: Commonwealth, State, or Nation?* A pointed discussion of the major Puerto Rican self-determination movements.

FICTION, LANGUAGE & LITERATURE
FICTION

Baldwin, James. *If Beale Street Could Talk.* An acclaimed work by the famed novelist. The setting of this story ranges from the streets of New York to Puerto Rico.

Coll y Toste, Cayetano. *Puerto Rican Tales, Legends of Spanish Colonial Times.* Translated and adapted by José Ramírez Rivera. A highly readable collection of 12 Caribbean vignettes that provide an insight into the life of the Spanish conquistadors, the Taíno peoples, and the African slaves, in rich juxtaposition one to another. Dr. Ramírez Rivera, a medical academic, translated into English these original stories collected by Coll y Toste; originally published in the 1920s, they are tales of adventure, romance, religion and superstition, and history.

Michener, James A. *Caribbean*. A good epic from the master. His sweep of the Caribbean, including Puerto Rico, begins with the 1310 conquest of the peaceful Arawaks by the cannibalistic Caribs and proceeds through 7 centuries to Castro's Cuba. Perhaps it's a lot to cover in one book, but Michener has a way of recapturing the past that his many imitators don't.

LANGUAGE

Del Rosario, Ruben. *Vocabulario Puertorriqueño*. The first major compilation of the Puerto Rican vocabulary.

LITERATURE

Babin, Theresa Maria. *Borinquén: An Anthology of Puerto Rican Literature*. A pioneering work and the best survey of several generations of island writing.

 FAST FACTS: Puerto Rico

American Express See "Fast Facts: San Juan" in chapter 3.

Area Code The telephone area code for Puerto Rico is **787**. For calls on the island, the area code is not used.

ATM Networks See "Money," earlier in this chapter.

Banks All major U.S. banks have branches on Puerto Rico; their hours are 8am to 2:30pm Monday through Friday and 9:45am to noon on Saturday.

Business Hours Regular business hours are Monday through Friday from 8am to 5pm. Shopping hours vary considerably. Regular shopping hours are Monday through Thursday and Saturday from 9am to 6pm. On Friday, stores have a long day: 9am to 9pm. Many stores also open on Sunday from 11am to 5pm.

Camera & Film It's important to protect your camera not only from theft but also from saltwater and sand; furthermore, your camera can become overheated and any film it contains can be ruined if left in the sun or locked in the trunk of a car. See "Fast Facts: San Juan" in chapter 3.

Car Rentals See "Getting Around," earlier in this chapter.

Climate See "When to Go," earlier in this chapter.

Currency See "Money," earlier in this chapter.

Customs See "Entry Requirements & Customs," earlier in this chapter.

Driving Rules See "Getting Around," earlier in this chapter.

Drugs A branch of the Federal Narcotics Strike Force is permanently stationed on Puerto Rico, where illegal drugs and narcotics are a problem. Convictions for possession of marijuana can bring severe penalties, ranging from 2 to 10 years in prison for a first offense. Possession of hard drugs, such as cocaine or heroin, can lead to 15 years or more in prison.

Drugstores It's a good idea to carry enough prescription medications with you to last the duration of your stay. If you're going into the hinterlands, take along the medicines you'll need. If you need any additional medications, you'll find many drugstores in San Juan and other leading cities. One of the most centrally located pharmacies in Old San Juan is the **Puerto Rican Drug Co.,** Calle San Francisco 157 (© **787/725-2202**); it's open daily from 7:30am to 9:30pm.

Electricity   The electricity is 110 volts AC, as it is in the continental United States and Canada.

Embassies & Consulates   Because Puerto Rico is part of the United States, there is no U.S. embassy or consulate. Instead, there are branches of all the principal U.S. federal agencies. Canada has no embassy or consulate either. There are no special provisions or agencies catering to British travel needs in Puerto Rico, nor are there agencies serving citizens of Australia or New Zealand.

Emergencies   In an emergency, dial © **911.** Or call the local police (© **787/343-2020**), fire department (© **787/343-2330**), ambulance (© **787/343-2550**), or medical assistance (© **787/754-3535**).

Gambling   In addition to **casino gambling** at major Puerto Rico resorts, the country also has a **lottery,** for which tickets can be purchased at hundreds of kiosks, stores, and shops around the island. The major casino gambling on the island is Caribbean stud poker, blackjack, roulette, and craps, along with thousands of slot machines. Under Puerto Rican law, alcoholic beverages cannot be served in a casino.

Health Care   Medical-care facilities, including excellent hospitals and clinics, in Puerto Rico are on par with those in the United States. Hotels can arrange for a doctor in case of an emergency. Most major U.S. health insurance plans are recognized here, but it's advisable to check with your carrier or insurance agent before your trip, because medical attention is very expensive. See "Insurance, Health & Safety," earlier in this chapter.

Holidays   See "When to Go," earlier in this chapter.

Hospitals   In a medical emergency, call © **911. Ashford Presbyterian Community Hospital,** Av. Ashford 1451, San Juan (© **787/721-2160**), maintains 24-hour emergency service. Service is also provided at **Clinica Las Americas,** 400 Franklin Delano Roosevelt Ave., Hato Rey (© **787/ 765-1919**), and at **Río Piedras Medical Center,** Av. Americo Miranda, Río Piedras (© **787/777-3535**).

Information   See "Visitor Information," earlier in this chapter.

Internet Access   Public access to the Internet is available at some large-scale resorts; the staff often provides access from their own computers. Another place to try is **Cybemet Café,** Av. Ashford Condado 1126 (© **787/724-4033**), which is open Monday to Thursday from 9am to 10pm, Friday and Saturday from 9am to midnight, and Sunday from 10am to 9pm. It charges $3 for 15 minutes, $5 for 30 minutes, $7 for 45 minutes, and $9 for 1 hour.

Language   English is understood at the big resorts and in most of San Juan. Out in the island, Spanish is still *numero uno.*

Liquor Laws   You must be 21 years of age to purchase liquor in stores or buy drinks in hotels, bars, and restaurants.

Maps   See "Getting Around," earlier in this chapter.

Marriage Requirements There are no residency requirements for getting married in Puerto Rico. You need parental consent if either of you is under 18. Blood tests are required, although a test conducted in your home country within 10 days of the ceremony will suffice. A doctor must sign the license after an examination of the bride and groom. For complete details, contact the **Commonwealth of Puerto Rico Health Department,** Demographic Register, Franklin Delano Roosevelt Ave., Hato Rey (P.O. Box 11854), San Juan, PR 00910 (✆ **787/281-8868).**

Newspapers & Magazines **The San Juan Star,** a daily English-language newspaper, has been called the "*International Herald Tribune* of the Caribbean." It concentrates extensively on news from the United States. You can also pick up copies of *USA Today* at most news kiosks. If you read Spanish, you might enjoy *El Nuevo Día,* the most popular local tabloid. Few significant magazines are published on Puerto Rico, but *Time* and *Newsweek* are available at most newsstands.

Passports See "Visitor Information," earlier in this chapter.

Pets To bring your pet in, you must produce a health certificate from a U.S. mainland veterinarian and show proof of vaccination against rabies. Very few hotels allow animals, so check in advance.

Postal Services Because the U.S. Postal Service is responsible for handling mail on Puerto Rico, the regulations and tariffs are the same as on the mainland United States. Stamps can be purchased at any post office, all of which are open Monday through Friday from 8am to 5pm. Saturday hours are from 8am to noon (closed Sun). As on the mainland, you can purchase stamps at vending machines in airports, stores, and hotels. First-class letters to addresses within Puerto Rico, the United States, and its territories cost 34¢; postcards, 20¢. Letters and postcards to Canada both cost 48¢ for the first half-ounce. Letters and postcards to other countries cost 60¢ for the first half-ounce. *Note:* These rates will rise during the life of this edition.

Safety Crime exists here as it does everywhere. Use common sense and take precautions. Muggings are commonplace on the Condado and Isla Verde beaches, so you might want to confine your moonlit beach nights to the fenced-in and guarded areas around some of the major hotels. The countryside of Puerto Rico is safer than San Juan, but caution is always in order. Avoid narrow country roads and isolated beaches, night or day.

Smoking Antismoking regulation is less stringent here than it is on the U.S. mainland. Anyone over 18 can smoke in any bar here. Smoking is permitted in restaurants, within designated sections, but not necessarily everywhere. Most hotels have smoking and nonsmoking rooms.

Taxes All hotel rooms in Puerto Rico are subject to a tax, which is not included in the rates given in this book. At casino hotels, the tax is 11%; at noncasino hotels, it's 9%. At country inns you pay a 7% tax. Most hotels also add a 10% service charge. If they don't, you're expected to tip for services rendered. When you're booking a room, it's always best to inquire about these added charges. There is no airport departure tax.

Telephone & Fax Coin-operated phones can be found throughout the island, with a particularly dense concentration in San Juan. After depositing your coins, you can dial a seven-digit number at the sound of the dial tone. If you're calling long distance within Puerto Rico, add a **1** before the numbers. When you're placing a call to the U.S. mainland or to anywhere else overseas, preface the number with **011**. An operator (or a recorded voice) will tell you how much money to deposit, although you'll probably find it more practical to use a calling card issued by such long-distance carriers as Sprint, AT&T, or MCI. Public phones that allow credit cards such as American Express, Visa, or MasterCard to be inserted or "swiped" through a magnetic slot are rare on the island. Most of these are located at the San Juan airport. Most phone booths contain printed instructions for dialing. Local calls are 10¢. Most Puerto Ricans buy phone cards valid for between 15 and 100 units. The 30-unit card costs $13.50; the 60-unit card, $27.50. The card provides an even less expensive and usually more convenient way of calling within Puerto Rico or to the U.S. mainland. They are for sale in most drugstores and gift shops on the island.

Most hotels can send a telex or fax for you and bill the costs to your room, and in some cases, they'll even send a fax for a nonguest if you agree to pay a charge. Barring that, several agencies in San Juan will send a fax anywhere you want for a fee. Many are associated with print shops/photocopy stands. **Eagle Print,** 1229 Franklin Delano Roosevelt Blvd., Puerto Nuevo, San Juan, PR 00920 (© **787/782-7830**), charges $2 per page for faxes sent to the U.S. mainland.

Time Puerto Rico is on Atlantic standard time, which is 1 hour later than eastern standard time. Puerto Rico does not go on daylight saving time, however, so the time here is the same year-round.

Tipping Tipping is expected here, so hand over the money as you would on the U.S. mainland. That usually means 15% in restaurants, 10% in bars, and 10% to 15% for taxi drivers, hairdressers, and other services, depending on the quality of the service rendered. Tip a porter, either at the airport or at your hotel, $1 per bag. The U.S. government imposes income tax on wait staff and other service-industry workers whose income is tip-based according to the gross receipts of their employers; therefore, if you don't tip them, those workers could end up paying tax anyway.

Visitor Information See "Visitor Information," earlier in this chapter.

Water See "Insurance, Health & Safety," earlier in this chapter.

Weights & Measures There's a mixed bag of measurements in Puerto Rico. Because of its Spanish tradition, most weights (meat and poultry) and measures (gasoline and road distances) are metric. But because of the U.S. presence, speed limits appear in miles per hour and liquids such as beer are sold by the ounce.

3

Getting to Know San Juan

All but a handful of visitors arrive in San Juan, the capital city. It is the political base, economic powerhouse, and cultural center of the island, and it's home to about one-third of all Puerto Ricans.

The second-oldest city in the Americas (behind Santo Domingo in the Dominican Republic), this metropolis presents two different faces. On one hand, the charming historic district, Old San Juan, is strongly reminiscent of the Spanish Empire. On the other hand, modern expressways outside the historic district cut through urban sprawl to link towering concrete buildings and beachfront hotels resembling those of Miami Beach.

Old San Juan is a 7-square-block area that was once completely enclosed by a wall erected by the Spanish with slave labor. The most powerful fortress in the Caribbean, this fortified city repeatedly held off would-be attackers. By the 19th century, however, it had become one of the Caribbean's most charming residential and commercial districts. Today it's a setting for restaurants and shops. Most of the major resort hotels are located nearby, along the Condado beachfront and at Isla Verde (see chapter 4).

1 Orientation

ARRIVING BY PLANE & GETTING FROM THE AIRPORT INTO THE CITY

Visitors from overseas arrive at **Luis Muñoz Marín International Airport** (© 787/791-1014), the major transportation center of the Caribbean. The airport is on the easternmost side of the city, rather inconvenient to nearly all hotels except the resorts and small inns at Isla Verde.

The airport offers services such as a tourist-information center, restaurants, hair stylists, coin lockers for storing luggage, bookstores, banks, currency-exchange kiosks, and a bar (open daily from noon–4pm) that offers Puerto Rican rums.

BY TAXI　Some of the larger hotels send vans to pick up airport passengers and transport them to various properties along the beachfront. It's wise to find out if your hotel offers this service when making a reservation. If your hotel doesn't have shuttle service between the airport and its precincts, you'll have to get there on your own steam—most likely by taxi. Dozens of taxis line up outside the airport to meet arriving flights, so you rarely have to wait. Fares can vary widely, depending on traffic conditions. Again depending on traffic, figure on about a 30-minute drive from the airport to your hotel along the Condado.

Although technically cab drivers should turn on their meters, more often than not they'll quote a flat rate before starting out. The rate system seems effective and fair, and if you're caught in impenetrable traffic, it might actually work to your advantage. The island's **Public Service Commission,** or PSC (© 787/756-1401), establishes flat rates between the Luis Muñoz Marín International

Airport and major tourist zones as listed here: From the airport to any hotel in Isla Verde, the fee is $8; to any hotel in the Condado district, the charge is $12; and to any hotel in Old San Juan, the cost is $16. Normal tipping supplements of between 10% and 15% of that fare are appreciated.

BY MINIVAN OR LIMOUSINE   A wide variety of vehicles at the San Juan airport call themselves *limosinas* (their Spanish name). One outfit whose sign-up desk is in the arrivals hall of the international airport, near American Airlines, is the **Airport Limousine Service** (© 787/791-4745). It offers minivan service from the airport to various San Juan neighborhoods for prices that are lower than what a taxi would charge. When 8 to 10 passengers can be accumulated, the fare for transport, with luggage, is $35 to $55 per van to any hotel in Isla Verde, $55 to $75 per van to the Condado or Old San Juan.

For conventional limousine service, **Bracero Limousine** (© 787/253-1133) offers cars with drivers that will meet you and your entourage at the arrivals terminal for luxurious, private transportation to your hotel. Transport to virtually anywhere in San Juan ranges from $85 to $105; transport to points throughout the island varies from $150 to $275. Ideally, transport should be arranged in advance, so that a car and driver can be waiting for you near the arrivals terminal.

BY CAR   All the major car-rental companies have kiosks at the airport. Although it's possible to rent a car once you arrive, your best bet is to reserve one before you leave home. See the "Getting Around" section of chapter 2 for details.

To drive into the city, head west along Route 26, which becomes Route 25 as it enters Old San Juan. If you stay on Route 25 (also called Avenida Muñoz Rivera), you'll have the best view of the ocean and the monumental city walls.

Just before you reach the capital building, turn left between the Natural Resources Department and the modern House of Representatives office building. Go 2 blocks, until you reach the intersection of Paseo de Covadonga, and then take a right past the Treasury Building, and park your car in the **Covadonga Parking Garage** (© 787/7222-337) on the left. The garage is open 24 hours; the first hour costs $1, the second hour 65¢, and 24 hours costs $15.95. A free shuttle-bus service loops the Old Town from here on two different routes.

BY BUS   Those with little luggage can take the T1 bus, which runs to the center of the city.

VISITOR INFORMATION

Tourist information is available at the **Luís Muñoz Marín Airport** (© 787/791-1014). Another office is at **La Casita,** Pier 1, Old San Juan (© 787/722-1709). These offices are open Sunday to Wednesday from 9am to 8pm, Thursday and Friday from 9am to 5:30pm.

The Way to Go: Tren Urbano in 2003

San Juan will be linked to its major suburbs such as Santurce, Bayamón, and Guaynabo in summer 2003 by a $1.25 billion urban train called *Tren Urbano.* This will be the first mass-transit project in the history of Puerto Rico. The new train system is designed to bring a fast and easy mode of transportation to the most congested areas of metropolitan San Juan. Trains will run every 4 minutes during peak hours in the morning and afternoon. For more information, call © 787/765-0927.

San Juan Orientation

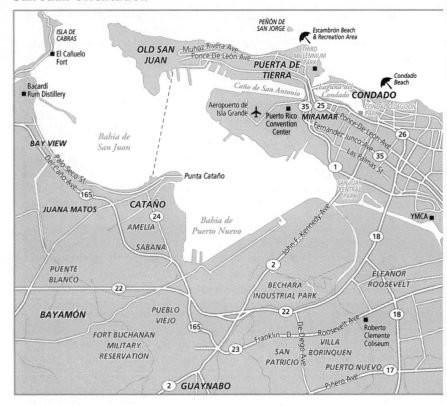

CITY LAYOUT

Metropolitan San Juan includes the old walled city on San Juan Island; the city center on San Juan Island (called Puerta de Tierra), containing the capitol building; Santurce, on a larger peninsula, which is reached by causeway bridges from San Juan Island (the lagoon-front section here is called Miramar); Condado, the narrow peninsula that stretches from San Juan Island to Santurce; Hato Rey, the business center; Río Piedras, site of the University of Puerto Rico; and Bayamón, an industrial and residential quarter.

The Condado strip of beachfront hotels, restaurants, casinos, and nightclubs is separated from Miramar by a lagoon. Isla Verde, another resort area, is near the airport, which is separated from the rest of San Juan by an isthmus.

FINDING AN ADDRESS   Finding an address in San Juan isn't always easy. You'll have to contend not only with missing street signs and numbers but also with street addresses that appear sometimes in English and at other times in Spanish. The most common Spanish terms for thoroughfares are *calle* (street) and *avenida* (avenue). When it is used, the street number follows the street name; for example, the El Convento hotel is located at Calle del Cristo 100, in Old San Juan. Locating a building in Old San Juan is relatively easy. The area is only 7 square blocks, so by walking around, it's possible to locate most addresses.

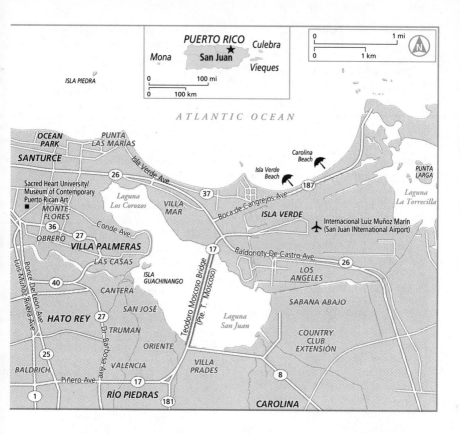

STREET MAPS *Qué Pasa?,* the monthly tourist magazine distributed free by the tourist office, contains accurate, easy-to-read maps of San Juan and the Condado that pinpoint the major attractions.

NEIGHBORHOODS IN BRIEF

OLD SAN JUAN This is the most historic area in the West Indies. Filled with Spanish colonial architecture and under constant restoration, it lies on the western end of an islet. It's encircled by water; on the north is the Atlantic Ocean and on the south and west is the tranquil San Juan Bay. Ponte San Antonio bridge connects the Old Town with "mainland" Puerto Rico. Ramparts and old Spanish fortresses form its outer walls.

PUERTA DE TIERRA Translated as "gateway to the land" or "gateway to the island," Puerta de Tierra lies just east of the old city walls of San Juan. It is split by Avenida Ponce de León and interconnects Old San Juan with the Puerto Rican "mainland." Founded by freed black slaves, the settlement today functions as the island's administrative center and is the site of military and government buildings, including the capital and various U.S. naval reserves.

MIRAMAR Miramar is an upscale residential neighborhood across the bridge from Puerta de Tierra.

Yachts anchor in its waters on the bay side of Ponte Isla Grande, and some of the finest homes in Puerto Rico are found here. It's also the site of Isla Grande Airport, where you can board flights to the islands of Vieques and Culebra.

CONDADO Linked to Puerta de Tierra and Old San Juan by a bridge built in 1910, the Condado was once known as the Riviera of the Caribbean, enjoying a voguish reputation in the 1920s. This beach-bordering district is wedged between the Atlantic Ocean and several large inland bodies of water, including the lakelike Los Corozos and Lagunas Condado. Over the years the area has declined. It is now a cliché to compare it to Miami Beach. But like Miami Beach, the Condado is making major improvements, although many parts of it remain seedy and in need of restoration. The *putas* (prostitutes), pimps, and drug dealers are still here, but there are many fine deluxe hotels as well. Much of the Condado architecture today is viewed as "kitsch," the way Art Deco on Miami Beach is prized. The area is especially popular with gays, but straights also flock here, especially those attracted to the beaches during cruise-ship stopovers. Much of the Condado has been turned into time-share condos.

OCEAN PARK Dividing the competitive beach resort areas of the Condado and Isla Verde, Ocean Park is a beachfront residential neighborhood that's sometimes plagued by flooding, especially during hurricanes. It's completely built up today with houses that are smaller and more spread out than those in the Condado district. Beaches here are slightly less crowded than those at Condado or Isla Verde. Because several gay guesthouses are located here, some

of the beaches of Ocean Park are popular with gay men.

VILLA PALMERAS Villa Palmeras is a residential sector and business area of San Juan, an eastern extension of the Santurce district. Its far eastern frontier opens onto Laguna Los Corozos. On the eastern side of the water is the international airport. From the Old Town, Route 26 east takes you to this district.

ISLA VERDE East of the Condado, en route to the airport, Isla Verde—technically known as the "Carolina" section of San Juan—is the chief rival of the Condado. Because much of the Condado is in need of massive rejuvenation, many of the great resorts have fled east to Isla Verde, which has better, cleaner beaches. Don't come here for history or romance. Two features put Isla Verde on the tourist map: some of San Juan's best beaches and its most deluxe hotels. This district appeals to travelers who like a hotel to be a virtual theme park, with everything under one roof—entertainment, vast selections of dining, convenient shopping, pools, and an array of planned activities. Isla Verde is the Las Vegas of San Juan. The area roughly lies between Ocean Park and the San Juan airport. When visitors get tired of all this glamour and glitz, they can taxi into Old San Juan for museum hopping and shopping.

HATO REY Situated to the south of the Martín Peña canal, this area was a marsh until landfill and concrete changed it forever. Today it is the Wall Street of the West Indies, filled with many high-rises, a large federal complex, and many business and banking offices.

RIO PIEDRAS South of Hato Rey and Santurce, this is the site of the University of Puerto Rico. It's dominated by the landmark Roosevelt Bell Tower, named for Theodore Roosevelt, who donated the money for its construction. The main thoroughfare is Paseo de Diego, site of a popular local produce market. The Agricultural Experimental Station of Puerto Rico maintains a botanical garden that includes many tropical plants, including 125 species of palms.

BAYAMON The San Juan sprawl has reached this once-distant southwestern suburb, which was once farmland. Some 200,000 people and nearly 200 factories are now located in this large district. Bus no. 46 from the center of San Juan runs out here.

2 Getting Around

BY TAXI Except for a handful of important, high-profile tourist routes, public taxis are metered within San Juan (or should be). Normal tipping supplements of between 10% and 15% are appreciated. Passengers traveling between most other destinations within greater San Juan are charged by meter readings. The initial charge is $1, plus 10¢ for each quarter mile (.5km) and 50¢ for every suitcase, with a minimum fare of $3. These rates apply to conventional *taxis turisticos,* which are usually white-painted vehicles with official logos on their doors. Owned by a medley of individual outfitters within San Juan, they maintain standards that are higher than those of the cheaper but more erratic and inconvenient *públicos,* which are described in chapter 2. Call the **PSC** (© 787/756-1401) to request information or to report any irregularities.

Taxis are invariably lined up outside the entrance to most of the island's hotels, and if they're not, a staff member can almost always call one for you. But if you want to arrange a taxi on your own, call the **Rochdale Cab Company** (© 787/721-1900) or the **Mejor Cab Company** (© 787/723-2460).

You'll have to negotiate a fare with the driver, usually at a flat rate, for trips to far-flung destinations within Puerto Rico.

BY BUS The **Metropolitan Bus Authority** (© 787/767-7979 for route information) operates buses in the greater San Juan area. Bus stops are marked by upright metal signs or yellow posts that say PARADA. There's one bus terminal in the dock area and another at the Plaza de Colón. A typical fare is 25¢ to 50¢.

Most of the large hotels of the Condado and Isla Verde maintain air-conditioned buses that make free shuttle runs into Old San Juan. Clients are usually deposited at the Plaza de Colón. Public buses also make the run along the Condado, stopping at clearly designated bus stops placed near the major hotels. Public buses usually deposit their clients at the Plaza Colón and the main bus terminal across the street from the Cataño ferryboat pier. This section of Old San Juan is the starting point for many of the city's metropolitan bus routes.

Here are some useful public bus routes: bus no. 2 goes from the Plaza de Colón along the Condado, eventually reaching the commercial section of San Juan, Hato Rey; bus no. A7 passes from Old San Juan to the Condado and goes on to Avenida Isla Verde; and no. T1 heads for Avenida de Diego in the Condado district, then makes a long run to Isla Verde and the airport.

ON FOOT This is the only way to explore Old San Juan. All the major attractions can easily be covered in a day. If you're going from Old San Juan to Isla Verde, however, you'll need to rely on public transportation.

⌒Value   **Great Discounts Through the LeLoLai VIP Program**

For the $10 it will cost you to join San Juan's **LeLoLai VIP** (Value in Puerto Rico) program, you can enjoy the equivalent of up to $250 in travel benefits. You'll get discounts on admission to folklore shows, guided tours of historic sites and natural attractions, lodgings, meals, shopping, activities, and more. Of course, most of the experiences linked to LeLoLai are of the rather touristy type, but it can still be a good investment.

With membership, the *paradores puertorriqueños,* the island's modestly priced network of country inns, give cardholders 10% to 20% lower room rates Monday through Thursday. Discounts of 10% to 20% are offered at many restaurants, from San Juan's toniest hotels to several *mesones gastronómicos,* government-sanctioned restaurants that serve Puerto Rican fare. Shopping discounts are offered at many stores and boutiques, and, best yet, cardholders get 10% to 20% discounts at many island attractions.

The card also entitles you to free admission to some of the island's folklore shows. At press time, the pass included *Jolgorio,* presented every Wednesday at 8:30pm at the Caribe Terrace of the Caribe Hilton, although the specifics might change by the time you arrive in Puerto Rico.

For more information about this card, call ⓒ **787/722-1709** or go to the El Centro Convention Center at Avenida Ashford on the Condado. Although you can call for details before you leave home, you can only sign up for this program once you reach Puerto Rico. Many hotel packages include participation in this program as part of their offerings.

BY TROLLEY   When you tire of walking around Old San Juan, you can board one of the free trolleys that run through the historic area. Departure points are the Marina and La Puntilla, but you can board along the route by flagging the trolley down (wave at it and signal for it to stop) or by waiting at any of the clearly designated stopping points. Relax and enjoy the sights as the trolleys rumble through the old and narrow streets.

BY RENTAL CAR   See "Getting Around" in chapter 2 for details—including some reasons you shouldn't plan to drive in Puerto Rico.

BY FERRY   The **Agua Expreso** (ⓒ **787/788-1155**) connects Old San Juan with the industrial and residential communities of Hato Rey and Cataño, across the bay. Ferries depart daily every 30 minutes from 6am to 9pm. The one-way fare to Hato Rey is 75¢, and the one-way fare to Cataño is 50¢. Departures are from the San Juan Terminal at the pier in Old San Juan. However, it's best to avoid rush hours because hundreds of locals who work in town use this ferry. Each ride lasts about 20 minutes.

FAST FACTS: **San Juan**

Airport See "Arriving by Plane & Getting from the Airport into the City," earlier in this chapter.

American Express The agency is represented in San Juan by **Travel Network,** Av. Ashford 1135, Condado (✆ **787/725-0960**). The office is open Monday to Friday from 9am to 5pm, Saturday from 9 to 11:30am.

Bus Information For information about bus routes in San Juan, call ✆ **787/729-1512.**

Camera & Film Both **Cinefoto** (✆ **787/753-7238**) and **Foto World** (✆ **787/753-8778**), located in the Plaza Las Americas Shopping Mall in Hato Rey, offer a wide variety of photographic supplies. Cinefoto is open Monday through Saturday from 9am to 9pm. Foto World is open Monday to Saturday from 9am to 9pm, Sunday from 11am to 5pm.

Car Rentals See "Getting Around" in chapter 2. If you want to reserve after you've arrived in Puerto Rico, call **Avis** (✆ **787/791-2500**), **Budget** (✆ **787/791-3685**), or **Hertz** (✆ **787/791-0840**).

Currency Exchange The unit of currency is the U.S. dollar. Most banks provide currency exchange, and you can also exchange money at the **Luis Muñoz Marín International Airport.** See "Money" in chapter 2.

Drugstores One of the most centrally located pharmacies is **Puerto Rican Drug Co.,** Calle San Francisco 157 (✆ **787/725-2202**), in Old San Juan. It's open daily from 7:30am to 9:30pm. **Walgreen's,** Av. Ashford 1130, Condado (✆ **787/725-1510**), is open 24 hours.

Emergencies In an emergency, dial ✆ **911.** Or call the local police (✆ **787/343-2020**), fire department (✆ **787/343-2330**), ambulance (✆ **787/343-2550**), or medical assistance (✆ **787/754-3535**).

Eyeglasses Services are available at **Pearle Vision Express,** Plaza Las Americas Shopping Mall (✆ **787/753-1033**). Hours are Monday to Saturday from 9am to 9pm and Sunday from 11am to 5pm.

Hospitals **Ashford Presbyterian Community Hospital,** Av. Ashford 1451 (✆ **787/721-2160**), maintains a 24-hour emergency room.

Information See "Visitor Information" earlier in this chapter.

Internet Access Public access to the Internet is available at **Soapy's Station,** 111 Gilberto Concepción de Gracia, Old San Juan (✆ **787/289-0344**), in an annex of the Wyndham Old San Juan Hotel & Casino.

Maps See "City Layout" earlier in this chapter.

Police Call ✆ **787/343-2020** for the local police.

Post Office In San Juan, the **General Post Office** is at Av. Roosevelt 585 (✆ **787/767-3604**). If you don't know your address in San Juan, you can ask that your mail be sent here "c/o General Delivery." This main branch is open Monday to Friday from 6am to 9pm, Saturday from 8am to 2pm. A letter from Puerto Rico to the U.S. mainland will arrive in about 4 days. See "Fast Facts: Puerto Rico" in chapter 2, for more information.

Restrooms Restrooms are not public facilities accessible from the street. It's necessary to enter a hotel lobby, cafe, or restaurant to gain access to a toilet. Fortunately, large-scale hotels are familiar with this situation, and someone looking for a restroom usually isn't challenged during his or her pursuit.

Safety At night, exercise extreme caution when walking along the back streets of San Juan, and don't venture onto the unguarded public stretches of the Condado and Isla Verde beaches at night. All these areas are favorite targets for muggings.

Salons Most of San Juan's large resort hotels, including the Condado Plaza, the Marriott, and the Wyndham Old San Juan, maintain hair salons.

Taxis See "Getting Around" earlier in this chapter.

Telephone/Fax Many public telephones are available at **World Service Telephone (AT&T),** Pier 1, Old San Juan (© **787/721-2520**). To send a fax, go to **Eagle Print,** 1229 F. D. Roosevelt Blvd., Puerto Nuevo (© **787/782-7830**). For more information, see "Fast Facts: Puerto Rico" in chapter 2.

Tourist Offices See "Visitor Information" earlier in this chapter.

4

Where to Stay in San Juan

Whatever your preferences in accommodations—a beachfront resort or a place in historic Old San Juan, sumptuous luxury or an inexpensive base from which to see the sights—you can find a perfect fit in San Juan.

In addition to checking the recommendations listed here, you might want to contact a travel agent; there are package deals galore that can save you money and match you with an establishment that meets your requirements. See "Package Tours for Independent Travelers" in chapter 2.

Before talking to a travel agent, you should refer to our comments about how to select a room in Puerto Rico. See "Hotels & Resorts" under "Tips on Choosing Your Accommodations" in chapter 2. You should also refer to "Package Tours for Independent

Travelers" in the same chapter, particularly if you're planning to book a deal with all your meals included.

Not all hotels here have air-conditioned rooms. We've pointed them out in the recommendations below. If air-conditioning is important to you, make sure "A/C" appears after "*In room.*" at the end of the listing.

If you prefer shopping and historic sights to the beach, then Old San Juan might be your preferred nest. The high-rise resort hotels lie primarily along the Condado beach strip and the equally good sands of Isla Verde. The hotels along Condado and Isla Verde attract the cruise-ship and casino crowds. The hotels away from the beach in San Juan, in such sections as Santurce, are primarily for business clients.

TAXES & SERVICE CHARGES

All hotel rooms in Puerto Rico are subject to a tax that is not included in the rates given in this book. At casino hotels, the tax is 11%; at noncasino hotels, it's 9%. At country inns you pay a 7% tax. Most hotels also add a 10% service charge. If they don't, you're expected to tip for services rendered. When you're booking a room, it's a good idea to ask about these charges.

MAKING RESERVATIONS

You can make accommodations reservations via telephone, mail, fax, and, in some cases, the Internet. If you're booking into a chain hotel, such as a Hilton, you can easily make your reservations by calling the chain's toll-free numbers in many countries. We provide the North American toll-free numbers in this book.

You can usually cancel a room reservation 1 week ahead of time and get a full refund. A few places will return your money on cancellations up to 3 days before the reservation date; others won't return any of your deposit, even if you cancel far in advance. It's best to clarify this issue when you make your reservation. If booking by mail, include a stamped, self-addressed envelope with your payment so that the hotel can easily send you a receipt and confirmation.

If you arrive without a reservation, you need to begin your search for a room as early in the day as possible. If you arrive late at night and without a reservation, you might have to take what you can get, often in a price range much higher than you'd like.

San Juan has become a year-round destination, and summers are no longer as tranquil as they used to be. Nonetheless, hotels still have lower occupancy from mid-April to mid-December. Off-season discounts, which can be substantial, are often granted at the resort hotels during this slower period.

1 Old San Juan

Old San Juan is 1½ miles (2.5km) from the beach. You should choose a hotel here if you're more interested in shopping and attractions than you are in water-sports. For the locations of hotels in Old San Juan, see the map "Old San Juan Accommodations & Dining" on p. 87.

EXPENSIVE

El Convento ★★ Puerto Rico's most famous hotel had deteriorated into a shabby version of its former self, but it came majestically back to life when it was restored and reopened in 1997, at cost of $275,000 per room. El Convento offers some of the most charming and historic hotel experiences anywhere in the Caribbean. As one observer put it, El Convento "is an exquisitely wrought David on an island of otherwise glitzy Goliaths." Built in 1651 in the heart of the old city, it was the New World's first Carmelite convent, but over the years it played many roles, from a dance hall to a flophouse to a parking lot for garbage trucks. It first opened as a hotel in 1962.

The roomy accommodations include Spanish-style furnishings, throw rugs, elaborate paneling, and handmade Andalusian terra-cotta floor tiles. Each unit contains two double or twin beds, fitted with fine linen. The small bathrooms, with tub-and-shower combinations, contain scales and second phones. For the ultimate in luxury, ask for Gloria Vanderbilt's restored suite or ask for no. 508, a corner room with dramatic views. Although the facilities here aren't as diverse as those of some resorts on the Condado or in Isla Verde, this hotel's sweeping charm and Old Town location usually compensate. The reason we like to stay here is that the swimming pool on the fourth floor overlooks the historic port. A possible drawback for some is that El Convento is a 15-minute walk to the nearest beach. The lower two floors feature a collection of shops, bars, and restaurants.

Calle de Cristo 100, San Juan, PR 00901. © **800/468-2779** or 787/723-9020. Fax 787/721-2877. www.elconvento.com. 58 units. Winter $265–$375 double; off-season $150–$285 double. Year-round from $400 suite. AE, DC, DISC, MC, V. Parking $10. Bus: Old Town trolley. **Amenities:** 4 restaurants, 2 bars; indoor pool; fitness center; Jacuzzi; massage. *In room:* A/C, TV, VCR, coffeemaker, hair dryer, iron, safe, stereo.

Wyndham Old San Juan Hotel & Casino ★ Opened in 1997, this digni-fied, nine-story waterfront hotel is part of a $100 million renovation of San Juan's cruise-port facilities. The hotel has an unusual and desirable position between buildings erected by the Spanish monarchs in the 19th century and the city's busiest and most modern cruise-ship terminals. Most of the major cruise ships dock nearby, making this a worthwhile choice if you want to spend time in San Juan before boarding a ship. On days when cruise ships pull into port, the hotel's lobby and bars are likely to be jammed with passengers stretching their legs after a few days at sea.

Although the pastel building is modern, iron railings and exterior detailing convey a sense of colonial San Juan. The triangular shape of the building encircles an inner courtyard that floods light into the tasteful and comfortable bedrooms, each of which has two phone lines and a modem connection for

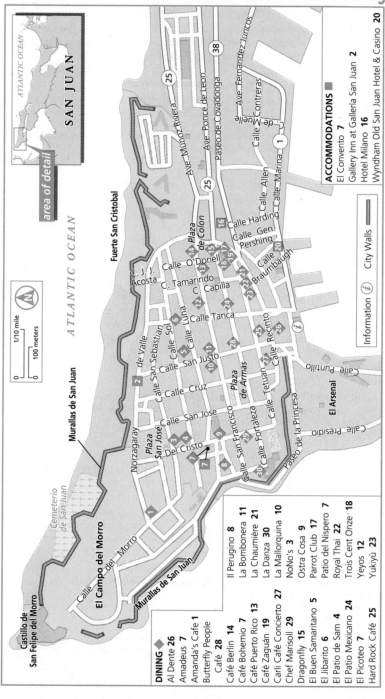

Old San Juan Accommodations & Dining

ATLANTIC OCEAN

ACCOMMODATIONS ■
El Convento **7**
Gallery Inn at Galleria San Juan **2**
Hotel Milano **16**
Wyndham Old San Juan Hotel & Casino **20**

Information ⓘ   City Walls

Castillo de
San Felipe del Morro

Cemeterio
de San Juan

El Campo del Morro

Muallas de San Juan

Calle del Morro

Muallas de San Juan

Fuerte San Cristobal

Muallas de San Juan

ATLANTIC OCEAN

SAN JUAN

area of detail

N
0   1/10 mile
0   100 meters

Norzagaray

Plaza
San José

Del Cristo

de Valle

Calle San Sebastián

Calle Sol

Calle Luna

Calle Tanca

Calle Cruz

Calle San Justo

Plaza
de Armas

Calle San Jose

Calle San Francisco

Calle Tetuan

Calle Fortaleza

Paseo de la Princesa

Calle Presidio

El Arsenal

Calle Puntillo

Calle Recinto

C. J. J.
Acosta

C. Tamarindo

C. Capilla

Calle O'Donell

Plaza
de Colon

Calle Harding

Calle Gen.
Pershing

Calle
Braumbaugh

Calle Allen

Calle Marina

Ave. Muñoz Rivera

Ave. Ponce de León

Paseo de Covadonga

Ave. Fernandez Juncos

Calle Contreras

de Muelle

25

38

25

1

DINING ◆
Al Dente **26**
Amadeus **7**
Amanda's Cafe **1**
Butterfly People
Café **28**
Café Berlin **14**
Café Bohemio **7**
Café Puerto Rico **13**
Café Zaguán **19**
Carli Café Concierto **27**
Chef Marisoll **29**
Dragonfly **15**
El Buen Samaritano **5**
El Jibarito **6**
El Patio de Sam **4**
El Patio Mexicano **24**
El Picoteo **7**
Hard Rock Café **25**

Il Perugino **8**
La Bombonera **11**
La Chaumière **21**
La Danza **30**
La Mallorquina **10**
NoNo's **3**
Ostra Cosa **9**
Parrot Club **17**
Patio del Nispero **7**
Royal Thai **22**
Trois Cent Onze **18**
Yeyos **12**
Yukiyú **23**

laptop computers. Other than that, the smallish rooms lack character. Each room has a compact bathroom with a shower stall. Think of a Holiday Inn geared for business travelers. If you want Old Town character and atmosphere, head for El Convento (see above) instead. Most of the lobby level here is devoted to a 10,000-square-foot casino. The upscale dining room serves perfectly fine, if unremarkable, international cuisine, with some regional specialties.

Calle Brumbaugh 100, San Juan, PR 00902. (©) 800/WYNDHAM or 787/721-5100. Fax 787/721-1111. www. wyndham.com. 240 units. Winter $230–$340 double; $290–$390 suite. Off-season $135–$200 double; $185–$290 suite. AE, DC, DISC, MC, V. Free self-parking; valet parking $15. Bus: A7. **Amenities:** 8 restaurants, 14 bars, nightclub, casino; 2 pools; 3 tennis courts; fitness center; 5 Jacuzzis; room service (6:30–11:30pm). *In room:* A/C, TV, dataport, minibar, coffeemaker, hair dryer, iron.

MODERATE

Gallery Inn at Galería San Juan *(★) (Finds)*   This hotel's location and ambience are unbeatable, though the nearest beach is a 15-minute ride away. Set on a hilltop in Old Town, with a sweeping sea view, this unusual hotel contains a maze of verdant courtyards. In the 1700s it was the home of an aristocratic Spanish family. Today it's the most whimsically bohemian hotel in the Caribbean. Jan D'Esopo and Manuco Gandia created this inn out of their art studio. They cast bronze in their studio when not attending to their collection of birds, including macaws and cockatoos. The entire inn is covered with clay and bronze figures as well as other original art. We suggest booking one of the least expensive doubles; even the cheapest units are fairly roomy and attractively furnished, with good beds and small but adequate shower-only bathrooms. *Note to lovers:* The honeymoon suite has a Jacuzzi on a private balcony with a panoramic view of El Morro. From the rooftop terrace there is a 360-degree view of the historic Old Town and the port. This is the highest point in San Juan and the most idyllic place to enjoy a breeze at twilight and a glass of wine.

Calle Norzagaray 204-206, San Juan, PR 00901. (©) 787/722-1808. Fax 787/977-3929. www.thegalleryinn. com. 22 units (some with shower only). Year-round $145–$270 double; $350 suite. Rates include continental breakfast. AE, DC, MC, V. There are 6 free parking spaces, plus parking on the street. Bus: Old Town trolley. **Amenities:** Breakfast room. *In room:* A/C, hair dryer, safe.

Hotel Milano   Old Town's newest hotel was created in April 1999 in a 1920s warehouse. You enter a wood-sheathed lobby at the lower, less desirable end of Calle Fortaleza before ascending to one of the clean, well-lit bedrooms. Despite its location in historic Old Town, there's not much charm about this place. The simple, modern rooms have cruise-ship–style decor and unremarkable views. The more expensive accommodations contain small refrigerators and dataports.

The building's fifth floor (the elevator goes only to the fourth floor) contains an alfresco Italian and Puerto Rican restaurant called the Panoramic, which has views of San Juan's harbor.

Calle Fortaleza 307, San Juan, PR 00901. (©) 877/729-9050 or 787/729-9050. Fax 787/722-3379. 30 units. Winter $85–$150 double; off-season $75–$125 double. Rates include continental breakfast. AE, MC, V. Bus: Old Town trolley. **Amenities:** Restaurant, bar; babysitting. *In room:* A/C, TV, dataport (in some), fridge (in some), hair dryer.

2 Puerta de Tierra

Stay in Puerta de Tierra only if you have a desire to be at either the Caribe Hilton or the Normandie Hotel, because when you stay there, you're sandwiched halfway between Old San Juan and the Condado, but you're not getting the advantages of staying right in the heart of either. For the location of hotels

Puerta de Tierra, Miramar, Condado & Ocean Park Accommodations & Dining

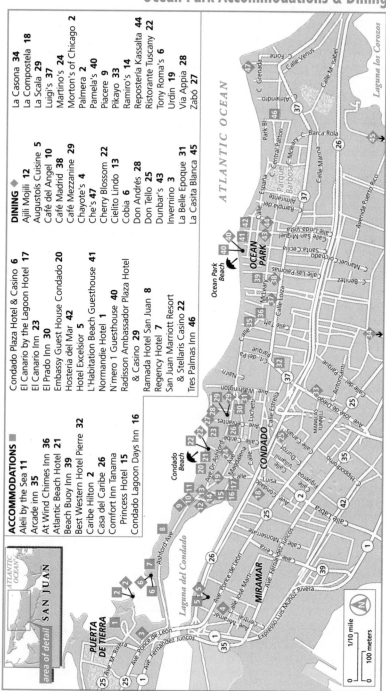

ACCOMMODATIONS

Aleli by the Sea 11
Arcade inn 35
At Wind Chimes Inn 36
Atlantic Beach Hotel 21
Beach Buoy Inn 39
Best Western Hotel Pierre 32
Caribe Hilton 2
Casa del Caribe 26
Comfort Inn Tanama Princess Hotel 15
Condado Lagoon Days Inn 16
Condado Plaza Hotel & Casino 6
El Canario by the Lagoon Hotel 17
El Canario Inn 23
El Prado Inn 30
Embassy Guest House Condado 20
Hostería del Mar 42
Hotel Excelsior 5
L'Habitation Beach Guesthouse 41
Normandie Hotel 1
N'mero 1 Guesthouse 40
Radisson Ambassador Plaza Hotel & Casino 29
Ramada Hotel San Juan 8
Regency Hotel 7
San Juan Marriott Resort & Stellaris Casino 22
Tres Palmas Inn 46

DINING ◆

Ajili Mojili 12
Augustois Cuisine 5
Café del Angel 10
Café Madrid 38
Café Mezzanine 29
Chayote's 4
Che's 47
Cherry Blossom 22
Cielito Lindo 13
Cobia 6
Don Andrés 28
Don Tello 25
Dunbar's 43
Invernino 3
La Belle Epoque 31
La Casita Blanca 45
La Casona 34
La Compostela 18
La Scala 29
Luigi's 37
Martino's 24
Morton's of Chicago 2
Palmera 2
Pamela's 40
Piacere 9
Pikayo 33
Ramiro's 14
Repostería Kassalta 44
Ristorante Tuscany 22
Tony Roma's 6
Urdin 19
Via Appia 28
Zabó 27

in Puerta de Tierra, see the map "Puerta de Tierra, Miramar, Condado & Ocean Park Accommodations & Dining" on p. 89.

Caribe Hilton ★★ Thanks to rivers of money being poured into its radical renovation, this deluxe hotel is one of the most up-to-date spa and convention hotels in San Juan. Thanks to an unusual configuration of natural barriers and legal maneuverings, the hotel has the only private beach on the island (and the only garden incorporating an antique naval installation: the semi-ruined colonial Fort San Gerónimo). Because this beachfront hotel was the first Hilton ever built outside the U.S. mainland (in 1949), the chain considers it its most historic property. The Caribe's size (17 acres of parks and gardens) and sprawling facilities often attract conventions and tour groups. Only the Condado Plaza and the Wyndham El San Juan rival it for nonstop activity.

Rooms were radically upgraded in the late 1990s; variations in price are related to the views outside and the amenities within. Each room has a larger-than-expected bathroom with a tub-and-shower combo, as well as comfortable tropical-inspired furniture. In the Caribe Terrace Bar, you can order the bartender's celebrated piña colada, which was once enjoyed by movie legends Joan Crawford and Errol Flynn. A newly restored oceanfront spa and fitness center is the only beachside spa in Puerto Rico. It features such tantalizing delights as couples massages, body wraps, hydrotherapy tub treatments, and soothing cucumber sun therapies. A 12,400-square-foot casino is adjacent to the lobby atrium area.

Calle Los Rosales, San Juan, PR 00902. © **800/HILTONS** or 787/721-0303. Fax 787/725-8849. www. caribehilton.com. 644 units. Winter $310–$365 double; off-season $205–$290 double. Year-round $255–$1,000 suite. Children 16 and under stay free in parents' room (maximum 4 people per room). AE, DC, DISC, MC, V. Self-parking $10; valet parking $20. Bus: B21. **Amenities:** 6 restaurants, 3 bars, casino; pool; 6 tennis courts; health club and spa; playground, business center (6am–1am), babysitting, laundry/dry cleaning. *In room:* A/C, TV, minibar, hair dryer, safe.

Normandie Hotel It isn't as well accessorized as its nearby competitor the Hilton, but for a clientele of mostly business travelers, it doesn't really matter. One guest, however, found the Hilton bright and festive, the Normandie "dark and haunting." The hotel first opened in 1939 and remains one of the purest examples of Art Deco architecture in Puerto Rico. Originally built for a Parisian cancan dancer by her tycoon husband, the building has a curve-sided design that was inspired by the famous French ocean liner, *Le Normandie*. The gardens are not particularly extensive, and the beach is unexceptional. But several multimillion-dollar renovations, most recently in 2000 after devastation by a 1998 hurricane, have given the place a conservative, vaguely historic charm. Bedrooms are tastefully outfitted, each with a neatly tiled tub-and-shower bathroom. The lobby retains its original Art Deco zest, soaring upward into an atrium whose centerpiece is a bubbling aquarium.

Av. Muñoz-Rivera, San Juan, PR 00902. © **877/987-2929** or 787/729-2929. Fax 787/729-3083. www. normandiepr.com. 176 units. Winter $250–$350 double; $550 suite. Off-season $185–$205 double; $450 suite. AE, DC, MC, V. Parking $10. Bus: B5 or B21. **Amenities:** Restaurant, bar; pool; gym; room service; babysitting; laundry/dry cleaning. *In room:* A/C, TV, coffeemaker, hair dryer, iron, safe.

3 Condado

This is where you'll find the city's best beaches. Once the Condado area was filled with the residences of the very wealthy, but all that changed with the construction of the Puerto Rico Convention Center. Private villas gave way to high-rise hotel blocks, restaurants, and nightclubs. The Condado shopping area, along Ashford and Magdalena avenues, has an extraordinary number of boutiques. There are good bus connections into Old San Juan, and taxis are plentiful. For the locations of hotels in Condado, see the map "Puerta de Tierra, Miramar, Condado & Ocean Park Accommodations & Dining" on p. 89.

VERY EXPENSIVE

Condado Plaza Hotel & Casino ★★ *Kids* This is one of the busiest hotels in Puerto Rico, with enough facilities, restaurants, and distractions to keep visitors occupied for weeks. It is the most prominent of San Juan's hotels, set on a popular strip of beachfront on the Condado. It's a favorite of business travelers, tour groups, and conventions, but it also attracts independent travelers, especially families (see "Especially for Kids" under "Seeing the Sights" in chapter 6), because of its wide array of amenities. The Hilton is its major rival, but we prefer this hotel's style and flair, especially after its recent $40 million overhaul.

Each unit has a private terrace and is spacious, bright, and airy, fitted with deluxe beds, either one king-size, two doubles, or two twins. The good-size bathrooms contain tub-and-shower combos. The complex's most deluxe section, the Plaza Club, has 80 units (including 5 duplex suites), a VIP lounge reserved exclusively for the use of its guests, and private check-in/checkout service.

The hotel is owned by the same consortium that owns the somewhat more upscale Wyndham El San Juan Hotel & Casino (see below). Use of the facilities at one hotel can be charged to a room at the other. Only the Wyndham El San Juan Hotel has a more dazzling array of dining options. This place is known for its charming restaurants with culinary diversity that attract many local residents. The hotel's premier restaurant—a hot ticket on San Juan's dining scene—is Cobia, winner of several culinary awards (see p. 120).

Av. Ashford 999, San Juan, PR 00907. © **800/468-8588** or 787/721-1000. Fax 787/721-4613. www. condadoplaza.com. 570 units. Winter $325–$475 double; $460–$1,350 suite. Off-season $225–$390 double; $350–$945 suite. AE, DC, DISC, MC, V. Valet parking $10. Bus: A7. **Amenities:** 6 restaurants, 3 bars, casino; 3 pools; 2 tennis courts; health club & spa; 3 Jacuzzis; watersports; children's programs, car rental; salon; 24-hour room service; laundry/dry cleaning. *In room:* A/C, TV, minibar, coffeemaker, hair dryer, iron, safe.

San Juan Marriott Resort & Stellaris Casino ★ It's the tallest building on the Condado, a 21-story landmark that Marriott spent staggering sums to renovate in a radically different format after a tragic fire gutted the premises in 1989. The current building packs in lots of postmodern style, and one of the best beaches on the Condado is right outside. Furnishings in the soaring lobby were inspired by Chippendale. If there's a flaw, it's the decor of the comfortable but bland bedrooms, with pastel colors that look washed out when compared to the rich mahoganies and jewel tones of the rooms in the rival Condado Plaza Hotel. Nonetheless, the units here boast one of the most advanced telephone networks on the island, and good security and fire-prevention systems. They're generally spacious, with good views of the water, and each has a tiled bathroom with tub-and-shower combination. We suggest having only one dinner in-house—at Ristorante Tuscany (see p. 122).

Av. Ashford 1309, San Juan, PR 00907. © **800/464-5005** or 787/722-7000. Fax 787/722-6800. www. marriottpr.com. 538 units. Winter $205–$340 double. Off-season $180–$225 double. Year-round $610 suite. Suite rate includes breakfast. AE, DC, DISC, MC, V. Parking $10. Bus: B21. **Amenities:** 3 restaurants, 2 bars, casino; 2 pools; 2 tennis courts; health club; Jacuzzi; sauna; concierge; tour desk; car rental; salon; 24-hour room service; babysitting, laundry/dry cleaning. *In room:* A/C, TV, dataport, minibar, coffeemaker, hair dryer, iron, safe.

EXPENSIVE

Radisson Ambassador Plaza Hotel & Casino ⭐   At the eastern edge of the Condado, a short walk from the beach, the Ambassador is now competitive with its more glamorous neighbors, after a local entrepreneur poured $40 million into its restoration in 1990. Since then, it has evolved into a competent but not particularly exciting hotel. What's missing (especially at these prices) are the resort amenities associated with the Hilton, the Condado Plaza, the Ritz-Carlton, and the Wyndham El San Juan. Nor does this hotel have the sense of whimsy and fun that's so much a part of those glitzy competitors.

Accommodations are in a pair of towers, one of which is devoted to suites. The decor is inspired variously by 18th-century Versailles, 19th-century London, imperial China, and Art Deco California. However, despite the gaudy, glitzy overlay, the hotel used to be a Howard Johnson's, a fact that's evident in the relatively small size of the standard rooms. Each unit has a balcony with outdoor furniture. The beds (twins or doubles) are fitted with fine linen, and each bathroom has generous shelf space and a tub-and-shower combination.

Av. Ashford 1369, San Juan, PR 00907. ℂ 800/333-3333 or 787/721-7300. Fax 787/723-6151. www. radisson.com. 233 units. Winter $260–$290 double; $290–$320 suite. Off-season $185–$215 double; $215–$225 suite. Self-parking $8. Bus: B21 or C10. **Amenities:** 3 restaurants, 3 bars, casino; rooftop pool; gym; sauna; babysitting; laundry/dry cleaning. *In room:* A/C, TV, coffeemaker, hair dryer, iron, safe (in suites).

MODERATE

Best Western Hotel Pierre ⭐ *Value*   The seven-floor "Lucky Pierre" is one of San Juan's major bargains. It's 4 blocks from the beach and an easy drive to most major San Juan attractions if you rent a car. It's a small resort, with a large pool and deck in a setting of palm trees. The bedrooms, although hardly grand, have recently been remodeled. Each has a tiled bathroom with tub and shower. Its two restaurants are moderately priced and serve respectable cuisine.

Av. José de Diego 105, Condado, San Juan, PR 00914. ℂ 800/528-1234 or 787/721-1200. Fax 787/ 721-3118. www.hotelpierresanjuan.com. 184 units. Winter $155–$175 double; off-season $125–$135 double. AE, DC, DISC, MC, V. Children 11 and under stay free in parents' room. Bus: 5, 9, 21, or 22. **Amenities:** 2 restaurants, bar; pool; gym; room service; babysitting; laundry/dry cleaning. *In room:* A/C, TV, coffeemaker, hair dryer, iron, safe.

Condado Lagoon Days Inn *Kids*   This family-oriented hotel, remodeled in 1996, rises seven stories above a residential neighborhood across the street from Condado Beach. The accommodations are small and not particularly imaginative in their decor. Each room has either one or two queen beds, and each has a tub-and-shower bathroom. Some rooms have sofas that convert into beds for children. There's a small swimming pool on the premises. The bars, restaurants, and facilities of the Condado neighborhood are within walking distance.

Calle Clemenceau 6, Condado, San Juan, PR 00907. ℂ 800/858-7407 or 787/721-0170. www.daysinn.com. 50 units. Winter $119 double; $200–$210 suite. Off-season $89 double; $149–$189 suite. AE, DC, DISC, MC, V. Parking $7. Bus: 5, 9, 21, or 22. **Amenities:** Pool; babysitting; laundry/dry cleaning. *In room:* A/C, TV, hair dryer, iron, safe.

El Canario by the Lagoon Hotel   A relaxing, informal European-style hotel, El Canario is in a quiet residential neighborhood just a short block from Condado Beach. The place is a bit run-down and the staff is not too helpful, but it charges affordable rates. The hotel is very much in the Condado styling, which evokes Miami Beach in the 1960s. The bedrooms are generous in size and have balconies. Most of them have twin beds and a sleek and contemporary bathroom, with a shower stall and enough space to spread out your stuff. If the hotel doesn't have room for you, it can book you into El Canario Inn.

Calle Clemenceau 4, Condado, San Juan, PR 00907. ℂ **800/533-2649** or 787/722-5058. Fax 787/723-8590. www.canariohotels.com. 40 units. Winter $145 double; off-season $95–$105 double. Rates include continental breakfast and morning newspaper. AE, DISC, MC, V. Bus: B21 or C10. **Amenities:** Access to health club; tour desk; laundry. *In room:* A/C, TV, safe.

El Prado Inn ★ *Finds*   An undiscovered oasis, this Mediterranean-style inn lies only a 3-minute walk from the beach. Some guests don't bother, preferring to linger around the inviting Spanish-style patio and pool for most of the day. El Prado is also within an easy walk of major hotels, with their dining and entertainment possibilities, casinos, and dozens of restaurants. Each of the midsize bedrooms is well furnished and has a neatly tiled tub-and-shower bathroom. Some of the accommodations are large enough to house four comfortably.

Calle Luchetti 1350, San Juan, PR 00907. ℂ **800/468-4521** or 787/728-5925. Fax 787/725-6978. 22 units. Winter $89–$139 double; $99–$149 suite. Off-season $69–$105 double; $79–$119 suite. Rates include continental breakfast. AE, DC, MC, V. Free parking. Bus: B21 or C10. **Amenities:** Coffee shop; pool; gym; coin-op laundry. *In room:* A/C, TV, kitchenette (in some).

Embassy Guest House Condado   Sandwiched between a vacant lot and a hamburger joint, this acceptable choice lies in a district heavily frequented by gay vacationers. The staff here is helpful and friendly, and restaurants, casinos, and nightlife are within easy walking distance; the famous Condado Beach lies just across the street. Guests usually stay here for economy. This is far from the luxury of Ritz-Carlton, but it offers a relaxed atmosphere—you could live in a swimsuit or shorts for your entire stay. The small bedrooms are simply furnished, many with rattan, and the small shower-only bathrooms are tiled. Each unit has a kitchenette or access to one. The most winning features are the rooftop sun deck, which has a view directly over the beach, and the pool and whirlpool.

Calle Seaview 1126, Condado, San Juan, PR 00907. ℂ **787/725-8284** or 787/724-7440. Fax 787/725-2400. EmbassyGuestHouse@worldnet.att.net. 22 units (shower only). Winter $75–$125 double; off-season $55–$95 double. AE, MC, V. Bus: B21. **Amenities:** Pool; whirlpool. *In room:* A/C, TV, kitchenette, coffeemaker, safe.

Ramada San Juan   This standard hotel is right on the oceanfront in the heart of the Condado. It lacks the style and facilities of some of its very expensive neighbors, but you can bask in the sun by the pool, have lunch or drinks on the sun deck, and dance the night away to live music in the Polo Lounge. The onsite Restaurant Papaya specializes in many Puerto Rican dishes, including *asopao* (the local gumbo), often made with shrimp and lobster. A selection of seafood is featured nightly. Shopping, sights, and island nightlife are within walking distance or just a short ride away. The rooms are classified as standard, superior, and deluxe. The deluxe rooms are larger than the others and open onto the beach; the superior rooms are slightly smaller than the deluxe rooms, and they are on the upper floors, overlooking the water. The standard rooms face the busy street and are a bit cramped. All the bathrooms are well maintained and medium in size, with adequate shelf space; each contains a shower and tub. The price seems rather high for what you get, but you must pay dearly for a beachfront Condado location, even though the shoreline adjacent to the hotel is rocky (head instead for the sandy beach at the Condado Plaza, a 5-min. walk away).

Av. Ashford 1045, San Juan, PR 00907. ℂ **800/468-2040** or 787/723-8000. Fax 787/723-8230. www.ramadasanjuan.com. 95 units. Winter $195 double; off-season $155 double. AE, DC, DISC, MC, V. Parking $12. Bus: 21 or 27. **Amenities:** Restaurant; bar; pool; room service; babysitting; laundry/dry cleaning. *In room:* A/C, TV, hair dryer, iron.

Regency Hotel   This modest choice occupies prime Condado real estate, although the beach here is approached through an underground parking garage. The generally spacious rooms aren't style-setters by any means, but most are comfortable and clean, and they are a good value for the tab-happy Condado district. Many are equipped with kitchenettes, and each of the suites contains a fully equipped kitchen. Whether you like this hotel or not may depend on your room assignment. All rooms have balconies but not all face the ocean. Although the units are constantly being renovated, some are shabbier than others and of unequal quality, and many have a musty smell. Discuss the rooms in detail with management before making reservations, and if possible, see the room before accepting it. Each unit has a small tub-and-shower bathroom. On the premises are a bar and a restaurant that serves conservatively classic food. Although the hotel has its own small-scale pool, some guests prefer to do their swimming, gambling, dining, and drinking at the Condado Plaza, next door.

Av. Ashford 1005, San Juan, PR 00907. ✆ **800/468-2823** or 787/721-0505. Fax 787/722-2909. 125 units. Winter $160–$170 double; $285 suite. Off-season $99–$119 double; $165 suite. Children 11 and under stay free in parents' room. Rates include continental breakfast. AE, DC, DISC, MC, V. Parking $5. Bus: A7. **Amenities:** Restaurant, bar; pool; room service; babysitting; laundry/dry cleaning. *In room:* A/C, TV, kitchen or kitchenette (in some), hair dryer, iron.

INEXPENSIVE

Aleli by the Sea *Value*   This is a lone budget holdout in a sea of expensive hotel options. Right on the Condado, it's a charming little guesthouse that opens onto the beach 1 block off Ashford Avenue. Most of the bedrooms, which are small to midsize, overlook the ocean, and all of them have rattan furnishings and compact, tiled, shower-only bathrooms. A pleasant touch is the second-floor terrace overlooking the Atlantic, where guests gather to watch the sunsets.

Calle Seaview 1125, Condado, San Juan, PR 00907. ✆ **787/725-5313**. Fax 787/721-4744. 9 units (shower only). Winter $70–$100 double; off-season $60–$90 double. AE, MC, V. Bus: B21 or C10. **Amenities:** Communal kitchen; laundry. *In room:* A/C, TV, no phone.

Arcade Inn *Value*   This inn, originally built as a private home in 1943 and transformed into a simple hotel in 1948, didn't become well known until the late 1960s, when its reasonable rates began to attract families with children and college students traveling in groups. It's a stucco-covered building with vaguely Spanish colonial detailing on a residential street lined with similar structures. Each unit has simple, slightly battered furniture and a small shower-only bathroom. There's no pool and few amenities on-site, but the beach is only a 5-minute walk away.

Calle Taft 8, Condado, San Juan, PR 00911. ✆ **787/725-0668.** Fax 787/728-7524. 19 units (shower only). Winter $70–$80 double; $130 suite. Off-season $60–$70 double; $110 suite. MC, V. Free parking. Bus: A5 or B21. **Amenities:** Bar; babysitting. *In room:* A/C, TV, fridge.

Atlantic Beach Hotel   This is the most famous gay hotel in Puerto Rico. Housed in a five-story building with vaguely Art Deco styling, the hotel is best known for its ground-floor indoor/outdoor bar—the most visibly gay bar in Puerto Rico. It extends from the hotel lobby onto a wooden deck about 15 feet above the sands of Condado Beach. The units are simple cubicles with stripped-down but serviceable and clean decor. Some of the rooms are smaller than others, but few of the short-term guests seem to mind—maybe because the place can have the spirit of a house party. Each unit has a small, shower-only bath-room with plumbing that might not always be in prime condition. There's a whirlpool on the rooftop; an on-again, off-again in-house restaurant; and the above-mentioned bar. The top floor is devoted to a duplex penthouse with a soaring pyramid-shaped ceiling. The space was originally conceived as a disco that thrived in the 1970s and early 1980s.

Several readers have written in to complain about the restrictive policy of not allowing a guest to take a visitor back to the bedrooms. One disgruntled patron wrote, "Lighten up, folks! We're big boys and can decide for ourselves who we want to bring up to our room. If you're going with a lover, fine. If you want to play with the locals, stay in another hotel."

Calle Vendig 1, Condado, San Juan, PR 00907. © 787/721-6900. Fax 787/721-6917. www.atlantic beachhotel.net. 35 units (shower only). Winter $100–$135 double; off-season $70–$100 double. AE, DC, MC, V. Bus: A7. **Amenities:** Restaurant, bar; whirlpool, laundry/dry cleaning. *In room:* A/C, TV, safe.

At Wind Chimes Inn *Kids* This restored and renovated Spanish manor, 1 short block from the beach and 3½ miles (5.5km) from the airport, is one of the best guesthouses on the Condado. Upon entering a tropical patio, you'll find tile tables surrounded by palm trees and bougainvillea. There's plenty of space on the deck and a covered lounge for relaxing, socializing, and eating breakfast. Dozens of decorative wind chimes add melody to the daily breezes. The good-size rooms offer a choice of size, beds, and kitchens; all contain ceiling fans and air-conditioning. Beds are comfortable and come in four sizes, ranging from twin to king. The shower-only bathrooms, though small, are efficiently laid out. Families like this place not only because of the accommodations and the affordable prices but because they can also prepare light meals here, cutting down on food costs.

Av. McLeary 1750, Condado, San Juan, PR 00911. © 800/946-3244 or 787/727-4153. Fax 787/728-0671. www.atwindchimesinn.com. 17 units (shower only). Winter $80–$129 double; $125–$140 suite. Off-season $65–$110 double; $120 suite. Rates include continental breakfast. AE, DISC, MC, V. Parking $5. Bus: B21 or A5. **Amenities:** Pool. *In room:* A/C, TV, kitchen.

Casa del Caribe *Value* Don't expect the Ritz, but if you're looking for a bargain on the Condado, this is it. This renovated guesthouse was built in the 1940s, later expanded, and then totally refurbished with tropical decor in 1995. A very Puerto Rican ambience has been created, with emphasis on Latin hospitality and comfort. On a shady side street just off Ashford Avenue, behind a wall and garden, you'll discover Casa del Caribe's wraparound veranda. The small but cozy guest rooms have ceiling fans and air conditioners, and most feature original Puerto Rican art. The bedrooms are inviting, with comfortable furnishings and efficiently organized shower-only bathrooms. The front porch is a social center for guests, and you can also cook out at a barbecue area. The beach is a 2-minute walk away, and the hotel is also within walking distance of some mega-resorts, with their glittering casinos.

Calle Caribe 57, San Juan, PR 00907. © 877/722-7139 or 787/722-7139. Fax 787/723-2575. 13 units (shower only). Winter $75–$130 double; off-season $55–$99 double. Rates include continental breakfast. AE, DISC, MC, V. Parking $5. Bus: B21. **Amenities:** Babysitting; laundry/dry cleaning. *In room:* A/C, TV.

Comfort Inn Tanama Princess Hotel A seven-story white-painted structure, this recently expanded hotel offers a desirable Condado location but without the towering prices of the grand resorts along the beach. Tanama is about a 2-minute walk from Condado Beach and is convenient to Old San Juan (a 15-min. drive) and the airport (a 20-min. drive). Most accommodations have two double beds (ideal for families) and ceiling fans, and each has a small bathroom with tub and shower. Many open onto balconies with water views. It's about a 5-minute walk to major casinos at the Condado Plaza and San Juan Marriott hotels (see above).

Calle Marinao Ramirez Bages 1, Condado, San Juan, PR 00907. © **888/826-2621** or 787/724-4160. Fax 787/723-2282. www.choicecaribbean.com. 117 units. Winter $99–$109 double; off-season $79–$89 double. Children 18 and under stay free in parents' room. Rates include continental breakfast. AE, DC, DISC, MC, V. Parking $7. Bus: T1. **Amenities:** Pool; gym; laundry/dry cleaning. *In room:* A/C, TV, hair dryer, iron.

El Canario Inn *(Value)* Affiliated with El Canario by the Lagoon Hotel (see above), this little bed-and-breakfast, originally built as a private home, is one of the best values along the high-priced Condado strip. The location is just 1 block from the beach (you can walk there in your bathing suit). This well-established hotel lies directly on the landmark Ashford Avenue, center of Condado action, and is close to casinos, nightclubs, and many restaurants in all price ranges. Although surrounded by mega-resorts, it is a simple inn, with rather small but comfortable rooms and good maintenance by a helpful staff. Each unit has a small, tiled, shower-only bathroom. You can relax on the hotel's patios or in the whirlpool area, which is surrounded by tropical foliage. There is no elevator.

Av. Ashford 1317, Condado, San Juan, PR 00907. © **787/722-3861.** Fax 787/722-0391. www.canariohotels. com. 25 units (shower only). Winter $128 double; off-season $96 double. AE, DC, MC, V. Bus: B21 or C10. **Amenities:** Whirlpool. *In room:* A/C, TV, safe.

4 Miramar

Miramar, a residential neighborhood, is very much a part of metropolitan San Juan, and a brisk 30-minute walk will take you where the action is. Regrettably, the beach is at least half a mile (1km) away. For the location of hotels in Miramar, see the map "Puerta de Tierra, Miramar, Condado & Ocean Park Accommodations & Dining" on p. 89.

Hotel Excelsior Handsome accommodations and good service are offered at this family-owned and -operated hotel. Some of the bedrooms have been refurbished; many have fully equipped kitchenettes, and each has two phones (one in the bathroom), marble vanities, and a tub-and-shower combo. Included in the rates are shoeshines and transportation to the nearby beach, as well as parking in the underground garage or the adjacent parking lot. A lot of your reaction to this hotel will depend on your room assignment. Some units on the same floor can vary in quality. If possible, ask to see the room before checking in. One disgruntled reader called the Excelsior "an overexaggerated dump."

Av. Ponce de León 801, San Juan, PR 00907. © **800/298-4274** or 787/721-7400. Fax 787/723-0068. 140 units. Winter $195–$215 double; $259 suite. Off-season $165–$199 double; $229 suite. Children 9 and under stay free in parents' room; cribs free. AE, DC, MC, V. Free parking. Bus: B1 or A5. **Amenities:** 2 restaurants; pool; gym; room service; babysitting; laundry/dry cleaning. *In room:* A/C, TV, hair dryer.

5 Santurce & Ocean Park

Less fashionable (and a bit less expensive) than their nearest neighbors Condado (to the west) and Isla Verde (to the east), Santurce and Ocean Park are wedged into a modern, not particularly beautiful neighborhood that's bisected with lots of roaring traffic arteries and commercial enterprises. Lots of *Sanjuaneros* come here to work in the district's many offices and to eat in its many restaurants. The coastal subdivision of Ocean Park is a bit more fashionable than landlocked Santurce, but with the beach never more than a 20-minute walk away, few of Santurce's residents seem to mind. For the location of hotels in Santurce and

Ocean Park, see the map "Puerta de Tierra, Miramar, Condado & Ocean Park Accommodations & Dining" on p. 89.

MODERATE

Hosteria del Mar ⭐ Lying a few blocks from the Condado casinos and right on the beach are the white walls of this distinctive landmark. It's in a residential seaside community that's popular with locals looking for beach action on weekends. The hotel boasts medium-size ocean-view rooms. Those on the second floor have balconies; those on the first floor open onto patios. The guest-room decor is invitingly tropical, with wicker furniture, good beds, pastel prints, and ceiling fans, plus small but efficient bathrooms, some with shower, some with tub only. The most popular unit is no. 208, with a king-size bed, private balcony, kitchenette, and a view of the beach; it's idyllic for a honeymoon. There's no pool, but a full-service restaurant here is known for its vegetarian, macrobiotic, and Puerto Rican plates, all freshly made. The place is simple, yet with its own elegance, and the hospitality is warm.

Calle Tapía 1, Ocean Park, San Juan, PR 00911. ℂ 877/727-3302 or 787/727-3302. Fax 787/268-0772. hosteria@caribe.net. 8 units. Winter $75–$125 double without ocean view; $165–$185 double with ocean view; $195–$240 apt. Off-season $75–$90 double without ocean view; $120–$130 double with ocean view; $185–$195 apt. Children 11 and under stay free in parents' room. AE, DC, DISC, MC, V. Bus: A5. **Amenities:** Restaurant; room service; babysitting; laundry/dry cleaning. *In room:* A/C, TV, kitchenette (in 3 units), coffeemaker (in some), safe.

L'Habitation Beach Guesthouse This small hotel sits on a tranquil tree-lined street with a sandy beach right in its backyard. Located only a few blocks from the Condado, this inn has a laid-back atmosphere. The good-size and well-maintained bedrooms have ceiling fans, comfortable beds, and fairly simple furnishings. The most spacious rooms are numbers 8 and 9, which also open onto ocean views. Each unit has a small, tiled, shower-only bathroom. Chairs and beverage service are provided in a private beach area, and guests can enjoy breakfast alfresco. You can also eat or drink on the breezy patio overlooking the sea. Ask for one of the bar's special margaritas.

Calle Italia 1957, Ocean Park, San Juan, PR 00911. ℂ 787/727-2499. Fax 787/727-2599. www.habitation beach.com. 10 units (shower only). Winter $75–$96 double; off-season $60–$83 double. Extra person $15. Rates include continental breakfast. AE, DISC, MC, V. Free parking. Bus: T1. **Amenities:** Laundry. *In room:* A/C, TV, coffeemaker, safe.

INEXPENSIVE

Beach Buoy Inn *(Finds* About a block from the beach, this B&B deserves to be better known. This place is a comfortable, snug nest, and the staff is helpful and friendly. The rooms are not decorated as nicely as those at the At Wind Chimes Inn (see above), but they're clean and decent. Each efficiency has two double beds or two twin beds. Some units have small refrigerators, and each unit has a tiled bathroom with either a tub or a shower. It has no restaurant, bar, or pool, but many of these features are available nearby. You can enjoy the complimentary breakfast outdoors on the patio if you wish.

Av. McLeary 1853, Ocean Park, San Juan, PR 00911. ℂ 800/221-8119 or 787/728-8119. Fax 787/268-0037. 15 units (some with shower only, some with tub only). Winter $65–$77 double; $80 efficiency. Off-season $60–$65 double; $70 efficiency. Children 11 and under stay free in parents' room. Rates include continental breakfast. AE, MC, V. Free parking. Bus: A5 or A7. *In room:* Fridge (in some).

Número 1 Guest House ⭐⭐ *(Finds* As a translation of its name implies, this is the best of the small-scale low-rise guesthouses in Ocean Park. It was originally built in the 1950s, in a prestigious residential neighborhood adjacent to the wide sands of Ocean Park Beach. A massive renovation in 1999 transformed the place into the closest thing in Ocean Park to the kind of stylish boutique hotel you might find in an upscale California neighborhood. Much of this is thanks to the hardworking owner, Esther Feliciano, who cultivates within her walled compound a verdant garden replete with splashing fountains, a small swimming pool, and manicured shrubbery and palms. Stylish-looking bedrooms contain tile floors, wicker or rattan furniture, and comfortable beds, plus tiled, shower-only bathrooms. Some repeat clients, many of whom are gay, refer to it as their fantasy version of a private villa beside a superb and usually convivial beach. The staff can direct you to watersports emporiums nearby for virtually any tropical watersport. Whereas it lacks the staggering diversity of the big hotels of the nearby Condado or Isla Verde, some guests value its sense of intimacy and small-scale charm.

Calle Santa Ana 1, Ocean Park, San Juan, PR 00911. Ⓒ **866/726-5010** or 787/726-5010. Fax 787/727-5482. 13 units (shower only). Winter $135 double; $265 apt. Off-season $80 double; $165 apt. $20 each additional occupant of a double room. Rates include continental breakfast. AE, MC, V. Bus: A5. **Amenities:** Restaurant, bar; pool; babysitting. *In room:* A/C, TV, minibar, hair dryer, iron, safe.

Tres Palmas Inn *(Value)*   Across the street from the ocean, this apartment-style guesthouse overlooks the surf. It's one of the best values for those seeking a beach vacation. Recently renovated, the hotel is a lot like a B&B, lying between two main tourist destinations, the Condado to the west and Isla Verde to the east. If you don't want to swim in the ocean, try the hotel's pool, located in a secluded courtyard. You can also relax on the rooftop sun deck while soaking in the whirlpool. The medium-size bedrooms are simply but comfortably furnished, with rather standard motel items. Each guest room has a private entrance and a ceiling fan, and most have small refrigerators. Larger rooms also have small kitchens, and each unit has a small, tiled bathroom with either a tub or a shower.

2212 Ocean Park Blvd., San Juan, PR 00913. Ⓒ **888/290-2076** or 787/727-4617. Fax 787/727-5434. www. trespalmasinn.com. 17 units (some with shower only, some with tub only). Winter $72–$129 double; off-season $69–$115 double. Extra person $15. Rates include continental breakfast. AE, MC, V. Bus: A5 or A7. **Amenities:** Pool; whirlpool; babysitting. *In room:* A/C, TV, kitchen (in some), fridge (in some), hair dryer.

6 Isla Verde

Beach-bordered Isla Verde is closer to the airport than the Condado and Old San Juan. The hotels here are farther from Old San Juan than those in Miramar, Condado, and Ocean Park. It's a good choice if you don't mind the isolation and want to be near fairly good beaches. For the location of hotels in Isla Verde, see the map "Isla Verde Accommodations & Dining" on p. 99.

VERY EXPENSIVE

Inter-Continental San Juan Resort & Casino ✦   Thanks to an extensive $15.2 million restoration, this resort on the beach now competes with Wyndham El San Juan Hotel next door, but it still doesn't overtake it. You'll get the sense of living in a sophisticated beach resort rather than a hotel where the sun rises and sets around the whims of high-rolling gamblers.

Most of the comfortable, medium-size rooms have balconies and terraces and tasteful furnishings with a lot of pizzazz. Top-floor rooms are the most expensive, even though they lack balconies. Each bathroom has a power showerhead, a deep tub, and a scale. The most desirable units are in the Plaza Club, a mini-hotel within the hotel that sports a private entrance, concierge service,

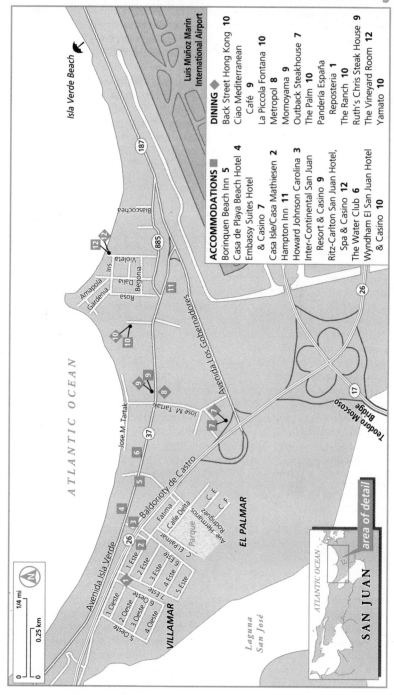

DINING ◆
Back Street Hong Kong **10**
Ciao Mediterranean
    Café **9**
La Piccola Fontana **10**
Metropol **8**
Momoyama **9**
Outback Steakhouse **7**
The Palm **10**
Panadería España
    Repostería **1**
The Ranch **10**
Ruth's Chris Steak House **9**
The Vineyard Room **12**
Yamato **10**

ACCOMMODATIONS ■
Borinquen Beach Inn **5**
Casa de Playa Beach Hotel **4**
Embassy Suites Hotel
    & Casino **7**
Casa Isle/Casa Mathiesen **2**
Hampton Inn **11**
Howard Johnson Carolina **3**
Inter-Continental San Juan
    Resort & Casino **9**
Ritz-Carlton San Juan Hotel,
    Spa & Casino **12**
The Water Club **6**
Wyndham El San Juan Hotel
    & Casino **10**

Luis Muñoz Marín
International Airport

Isla Verde Beach

ATLANTIC OCEAN

Biascochea

Violeta
Iris
Amapola
Gardenia
Dalia
Begonia
Rosa

Avenida Los Gobernadores

Jose M. Tartak
Jose M. Tartak

Baldorioty de Castro

Avenida Isla Verde

Fátima
Calle Delta
Ave. Hermanos
    Rodríguez
C. El Palmar
Parque

C. E
C. F

EL PALMAR

1 Este
2 Este
3 Este
4 Este
5 Este
6 Este
7 Este

1 Oeste
2 Oeste
3 Oeste
4 Oeste
5 Oeste
6 Oeste
7 Este

VILLAMAR

Laguna
San José

Teodoro Moscoso
Bridge

187
885
37
26
17

1/4 mi
0.25 km

ATLANTIC OCEAN
SAN JUAN
area of detail

complimentary food and beverage buffets, and suite/spa and beach facilities. Dining within any of this hotel's six restaurants merits attention, although the choice is vaster at the neighboring Wyndham El San Juan Hotel. Even if you're not a guest, consider a visit to the Inter-Continental, to Ruth's Chris Steak House (see p. 130), which serves the best steaks in San Juan. Momoyama (see p. 131) is also worth a trek across town, and its sushi bar is the finest along the beachfront. However, we find the Market Cafe, with its made-to-order foods and snacks, overrated.

Av. Isla Verde 5961, Isla Verde, PR 00937. © **800/443-2009** or 787/791-6100. Fax 787/253-2510. www. interconti.com. 400 units. Winter $269–$489 double; $409–$1,699 suite. Off-season $199–$339 double; $279–$450 suite. Children 15 and under stay free in parents' room. AE, DC, DISC, MC, V. Self-parking $10; valet parking $15. Bus: M7. **Amenities:** 6 restaurants, 3 bars; the Caribbean's largest free-form pool; gym; scuba diving; business center, room service (6am–2pm and 5pm–2am), massage, babysitting, laundry/dry cleaning, limousine service. *In room:* A/C, TV, coffeemaker, hair dryer, iron, safe.

Ritz-Carlton San Juan Hotel, Spa & Casino ★★★ This is one of the most spectacular deluxe hotels in the Caribbean. Set on 8 acres of prime beachfront, within a 5-minute drive of the airport, it appeals to both business travelers and vacationers. The decor reflects Caribbean flavor and the Hispanic culture of the island, with artwork from prominent local artists. More visible, however, is an emphasis on continental elegance. Some of the most opulent public areas anywhere, these include wrought-iron balustrades and crystal chandeliers.

Beautifully furnished guest rooms open onto ocean views or the gardens of nearby condos. Rooms are very large, with excellent furnishings, and fine linen. The bathrooms are exceptionally plush, with tub-and-shower combos, scales, bathrobes, and deluxe toiletries. Some rooms are accessible for guests with disabilities. Preferred accommodations are in the 9th-floor Ritz-Carlton Club, which has a private lounge and personal concierge staff.

The scope and diversity of dining here is second only to that at the Wyndham El San Juan, and for top-shelf dining venues, the Ritz-Carlton has no equal. The Vineyard Room is one of the finest restaurants in San Juan (see p. 130). The hotel has the Caribbean's largest casino (see p. 172).

Av. de los Gobernadores (State Rd.) 6961, no. 187, Isla Verde, PR 00979. © **800/241-3333** or 787/253-1700. Fax 787/253-0700. www.ritzcarlton.com. 414 units. Winter $279–$399 double; off-season $199–$299 double. Year-round from $975 suite. AE, DC, DISC, MC, V. Valet parking $15. Bus: A7, M7, or T1. **Amenities:** 3 restaurants, 3 bars, nightclub, Caribbean's largest casino; 7,200-sq.-ft. pool; 2 tennis courts; gym; children's program; salon; 24-hour room service; babysitting; laundry/dry cleaning. *In room:* A/C, TV, dataport, minibar, hair dryer, iron, safe.

The Water Club ★★★ A refreshing change from the mega-chain resorts of San Juan, this ultrachic hotel is hip and contemporary. It's the city's only "boutique hotel" on a beach. We find much to praise at this small and exclusive hotel because of its highly personalized and well-trained staff. Although avant-garde, the design is not daringly provocative. Behind glass are "waterfalls," even on the elevators, and inventive theatrical-style lighting is used to bring the outdoors inside. The one-of-a-kind glass art doors are from Murano, the fabled center of glassmaking outside Venice. The hotel overlooks Isla Verde's best beach area, and all the bedrooms are spacious, opening onto views of the water and containing custom-designed beds positioned to face the ocean. Bathrooms are tiled and elegant, with tub-and-shower combinations. Unique features are the open-air 11th-floor exotic bar, with the Caribbean's only rooftop fireplace. The pool is a level above; it's like swimming in an ocean in the sky.

Calle José M. Tartak 2, Isla Verde, Puerto Rico 00979. ℂ **888/265-6699** or 787/253-0100. Fax 787/253-0220. www.waterclubsanjuan.com. Winter $395–$485 double; $995 suite. Off-season $205–$310 double; $825 suite. AE, DC, MC, V. Bus: T1 or A5. **Amenities:** Restaurant, 2 bars; rooftop pool; fitness center; Jacuzzi; room service; babysitting; laundry/dry cleaning. *In room:* A/C, TV, minibar, hair dryer, safe.

Wyndham El San Juan Hotel & Casino ★★★ *(Kids)* One of the best hotels in Puerto Rico, this place evokes Havana in its heyday. Built in the 1950s, it was restored with an infusion of millions—some $80 million in 1997 and 1998 alone. It's also a great choice for (well-to-do) families, with lots of activities for children. The beachfront hotel is surrounded by 350 palms, century-old banyans, and gardens. Its 700-yard-long sandy beach is the finest in the San Juan area. The hotel's river pool, with currents, cascades, and lagoons, evokes a jungle stream, and the lobby is the most opulent and memorable in the Caribbean. Entirely sheathed in red marble and hand-carved mahogany paneling, the public rooms stretch on almost endlessly.

The large, well-decorated rooms have intriguing touches of high-tech; each contains three phones and a VCR. Bedrooms are the ultimate in luxury in San Juan, with honey-hued woods and rattans and king or double beds. Bathrooms have all the amenities and tub-and-shower combos; a few feature Jacuzzis. About 150 of the units, designed as comfortable bungalows, are in the outer reaches of the garden. Known as *casitas,* they include Roman tubs, atrium showers, and access to the fern-lined paths of a tropical jungle a few steps away. A 17-story, $60 million wing with 120 suites, all oceanfront, was completed in 1998. The ultra-luxury tower features 103 one- or two-bedroom units, 8 garden suites, 5 governor's suites, and 4 presidential suites.

No other hotel in the Caribbean offers such a rich diversity of dining options and such high-quality food. Japanese, Italian, Mexican, and 24-hour American/Caribbean restaurants are just a few of the options. (See chapter 5 for

---

Kids Family-Friendly Accommodations

Wyndham El San Juan Hotel & Casino (p. 101) This hotel, although expensive, offers more programs for children than any other hotel in Puerto Rico. Its supervised Kids' Klub provides daily activities—ranging from face painting to swimming lessons—for children 5 to 12 years of age.

Hampton Inn (p. 102) For families seeking the kind of lodging values found on the mainland, this new hotel is highly desirable, as many of its rooms have two double beds. There's also a beautiful swimming pool in a tropical setting. Suites have microwaves and refrigerators.

Condado Plaza Hotel & Casino (p. 91) For the family seeking an upmarket resort with lots of facilities, this is the best choice along the Condado. Its Camp Taíno is guided by experts and occupies children under 12 throughout the day for a fee. See "Especially for Kids" in chapter 6.

At Wind Chimes Inn (p. 95) Families like this hotel not only because of the accommodations and the affordable prices but because they can prepare meals here, cutting down on food costs.

reviews of The Palm, Back Street Hong Kong, La Piccola Fontana, Yamato, and The Ranch.)

Av. Isla Verde 6063, San Juan, PR 00979. © 800/WYNDHAM or 787/791-1000. Fax 787/791-0390. www. wyndham.com. 389 units. Winter $415–$565 double; from $625 suite. Off-season $145–$495 double; from $515 suite. AE, DC, DISC, MC, V. Self-parking $10; valet parking $15. Bus: M7. **Amenities:** 8 restaurants, 3 bars; 2 pools; tennis courts; health club and spa; steam room; sauna; watersports; children's program; 24-hour room service; massage; babysitting; dry cleaning. *In room:* A/C, TV/VCR, minibar, coffeemaker, hair dryer, safe.

EXPENSIVE

Embassy Suites Hotel & Casino ⋆   The location is 2 blocks from the beach, and the hotel has its own water world, with waterfalls and reflecting ponds set against a backdrop of palms. As you enter, you're greeted with an aquarium, giving a tropical-resort aura to the place. The excellent accommodations are all suites, and they're comfortably furnished and roomy, with bedrooms separated from the living rooms. Each has a wet bar, a tub-and-shower combination bathroom, two phones, a safe, and a dining table. The most spacious suites are those with two double beds; each of the smaller suites is furnished with a king-size bed. The best view of the water is from units above the third floor. Two restaurants are on the premises, including the Embassy Grill, a low-key indoor/outdoor affair, and an independently managed Outback Steakhouse branch. There's also a small-scale casino on the property.

Calle José M. Tartak 8000, Isla Verde, San Juan, PR 00979. © **800/362-2779** or 787/791-0505. Fax 787/ 791-0555. www.embassysuites.com. 300 suites. Winter $205–$275 1-bedroom suite; $550 2-bedroom suite; $700 presidential suite. Off-season $170–$205 1-bedroom suite; $350 2-bedroom suite; $500 presidential suite. Rates include breakfast and free drinks 5:30–7:30pm. AE, DC, MC, V. Self-parking $6; valet parking $10. Bus: M7. **Amenities:** 2 restaurants, bar, small casino; pool; gym; business center; room service; babysitting; laundry/dry cleaning. *In room:* A/C, TV, wet bar (in suites), fridge, coffeemaker, hair dryer, iron, safe, microwave.

MODERATE

Hampton Inn *Kids*   Opened in 1997, this chain hotel is set across the busy avenue from Isla Verde's sandy beachfront, far enough away to keep costs down but within a leisurely 10-minute walk of the casinos and nightlife. Two towers, with four and five floors, hold the well-maintained, well-furnished, and comfortable bedrooms. There's no restaurant on the premises, no real garden; other than a whirlpool and a swimming pool with a swim-up bar, there are very few facilities or amenities. Because of its reasonable prices and location, however, this Isla Verde newcomer could be a good choice. Families are especially fond of staying here, despite the fact that there are no special children's programs; many of the rooms have two double beds and suites have microwaves and refrigerators.

Av. Isla Verde 6530, Isla Verde, PR 00979. © **800/HAMPTON** or 787/791-8777. Fax 787/791-8757. 201 units. Winter $179 double; $199 suite. Off-season $129 double; $149 suite. Rates include breakfast bar. AE, DC, MC, V. Free parking. Bus: A5 or C45. **Amenities:** Bar; pool; gym; whirlpool; babysitting; laundry/dry cleaning. *In room:* A/C, TV, minibar (in suites), fridge (in suites), coffeemaker, hair dryer, iron, microwave (in suites).

Howard Johnson Carolina   Rising eight stories above the busy traffic of Isla Verde, this chain hotel offers comfortable but small bedrooms, furnished simply with bland, modern furniture. They're done in typical motel style, with small but serviceable tub-and-shower bathrooms. Many guests carry a tote bag to the beach across the street, and then hit the bars and restaurants of the expensive hotels nearby. There's a restaurant, a pool, and a bar, which features live dance music Wednesday through Saturday nights. Though it's simple and not very personal, this is a good choice for the money.

Av. Isla Verde 4820, Isla Verde, PR 00979. ✆ **800/728-1300.** Fax 787/268-0637. www.hojo.com. 115 units. Winter $130 double; off-season $105 double. Suite from $150 year-round. AE, DC, MC, V. Parking $6.50. Bus: T1. **Amenities:** Restaurant, bar; pool; gym; laundry/dry cleaning. *In room:* A/C, TV, coffeemaker, hair dryer, iron.

INEXPENSIVE

Borinquen Beach Inn *Value*   Lying just 1 block from the beach and a 5-minute drive from the airport, this is a good deal. This modest one-story guesthouse has been popular with islanders and visitors for more than 2 decades. The unassuming white facade is in keeping with the plain interior decor, with its pastel-painted walls, communal lounge and kitchen, and small serving area where guests can order coffee. The rooms are small and plain, but they're clean and comfortable enough, and each has a small bathroom with a shower stall. The overall aura here is very laid-back, but the low prices and convenient location keep the place booked with holidaymakers year-round.

Av. Isla Verde 5451, Isla Verde, San Juan, PR 00979. ✆ **787/728-8400.** Fax 787/268-2411. www.borinquen beachinn.com. 12 units. Year-round $83–$98 double. AE, MC, V. Free parking. Bus: A5. **Amenities:** Communal kitchen. *In room:* A/C, TV, no phone.

Casa de Playa Beach Hotel *Finds*   Jutting out over the sand on the mile-long (1.5km) Isla Verde beach, this bargain oasis is a find. If you're less interested in being in the center of San Juan than you are in spending time on the beach, check out this modest choice. The hotel consists of two two-story buildings, with a porch around the second floor and a small garden in front. Furnishings are modest and functional but comfortable nonetheless. Each room has a tidily maintained, small bathroom with a tiled shower. Standard but inexpensive Italian food is served at a beach bar and restaurant. The hotel doesn't have everything—no pool, no room service—but the price is hard to beat in Isla Verde.

Av. Isla Verde 4851, San Juan, PR 00979. ✆ **800/916-2272** or 787/728-9779. Fax 787/727-1334. 21 units. Winter $90 double; $175 suite. Off-season $80 double; $120 suite. Children 9 and under stay free in parents' room. Rates include continental breakfast. AE, DC, DISC, MC, V. Free parking. Bus: A5. **Amenities:** Restaurant, bar; babysitting. *In room:* A/C, TV, fridge (in some), coffeemaker (in suites), safe.

Green Isle Inn/Casa Mathiesen   Across the busy avenue from the larger and much more expensive San Juan Grand Beach Resort & Casino, this is really two hotels in one. They stand side by side and charge the same prices. Both of them are equally comfortable, though modest. The beach is a 5-minute walk away, and each of the hotels has a pool. There are 25 rooms at the Green Isle. Casa Mathiesen is only slighter larger, with 29 units. The furnishings are summery, simple, and comfortable. Each has a tiled tub-and-shower bathroom.

Calle Uno 36, Villamar, Isla Verde, PR 00979. ✆ **800/677-8860** or 787/726-8662. Fax 787/268-2415. www. greenisleinn.com. 54 units. Winter $79–$84 double; off-season $73–$82 double. AE, MC, V. Free parking. Bus: A5. **Amenities:** Restaurant, bar; 2 small pools; laundry. *In room:* A/C, TV, kitchenette (in some), safe.

5

Where to Dine in San Juan

San Juan has the widest array of restaurants in the Caribbean. You can enjoy fine continental, American, Italian, Chinese, Mexican, and Japanese cuisines, to name a few. In recent years, many restaurants have shown a greater appreciation for traditional Puerto Rican cooking, and local specialties now appear on the menus of numerous restaurants. When possible, many chefs enhance their dishes with native ingredients.

Many of San Juan's best restaurants are in the resort hotels along the Condado and at Isla Verde. There has been a restaurant explosion in San Juan in the past few years, but many of the newer ones are off the beaten tourist path, and some have not yet achieved the quality found at many of the older, more traditional restaurants.

Local seafood is generally in plentiful supply, but no restaurant guarantees that it will have fresh fish every night, especially during winter, when the sea can be too turbulent for fishing. In those cases, the chef relies on fresh or frozen fish flown in from Miami. If you want fresh fish caught in Puerto Rican waters, ask your server about the catch of the day. Make sure he or she can guarantee that the fish was recently caught rather than resting for a while in the icebox.

The restaurants listed in this chapter are classified first by area and then by price, using the following categories: **Very Expensive,** dinner from $40 per person; **Expensive,** dinner from $30 per person; **Moderate,** dinner from $20 per person; and **Inexpensive,** dinner under $20 per person. These categories reflect prices for an appetizer, a main course, a dessert, and a glass of wine.

1 Best Bets

- **Best Caribbean Chef** Reigning supreme as chef of the year, Jeremie Cruz holds forth at **La Belle Epoque,** an elegant Condado setting in the Casabella Building, Av. Magdalena 1400 (© **787/977-1765**), with a superb blend of French and fusion cuisine. The service is peerless, and top-quality ingredients are used to fashion noble dishes.
- **Best Classic Creole Cooking** In its new location in Old Town's Museum of Art of Puerto Rico, Chef Wilo Benet at **Pikayo,** Av. José de Diego 299 (© **787/721-6194**), holds forth. He's a master specialist in the *criolla* cooking of the colonial age, emphasizing the Spanish, Indian, and African elements in his unusual recipes.
- **Best Wine List** The luxurious **Vineyard Room** in the dazzling Ritz-Carlton, 6961 State Road #187, Isla Verde (© **787/253-1700**), serves a refined California/Mediterranean cuisine, but we'd go there just for the wine list. The countries best represented on the wine *carte* are France, Australia, Germany, Italy, Spain, and even South Africa. The California selection will

make you think you're back in the Napa Valley. There is also a good selection of the increasingly fashionable wines from Chile.

- **Best Female Chef**   Acclaimed as one of Puerto Rico's finest chefs, Marisoll Hernández presides over **Chef Marisoll,** Calle del Cristo 202 (© 787/725-7454). *Gourmet* magazine and some of the most savvy foodies in San Juan's Old Town love her imaginative dishes. She even makes soup aficionados out of those who usually aren't. Try her cream of exotic wild mushroom soup with essence of black truffles or her butternut squash soup with crisp ginger.

- **Best Classic French Cuisine**   If you like classic French food, then head to **La Chaumière,** Calle Tetuán 367 (© 787/722-3330), in San Juan's Old Town. In back of the Tapía Theater, this two-story restaurant is intimate and inviting. The cuisine follows time-tested recipes of which Escoffier might have approved: onion soup, oysters Rockefeller, scallops Provençal, and a perfectly prepared rack of baby lamb Provençal.

- **Best Nuevo Latino Cuisine**   **Parrot Club,** Calle Fortaleza 363 (© 787/725-7370), wows tastebuds with its modern interpretation of Puerto Rican specialties. Even San Juan's mayor and the governor have made it their favorite. Husband-and-wife team Emilio Figueroa and Gigi Zafero borrow from a repertoire of Puerto Rican and Spanish recipes, and they also use Taíno and African influences in their cuisine. Their ceviche is the best in town, and their Créole-style flank steak is worth the trek from Condado Beach.

- **Best Japanese & Best Sushi Restaurant**   In San Juan's Old Town, **Yukiyú,** Calle Recinto Sur 311 (© 787/721-0653), pioneered a style of Japanese and Asian cuisine unfamiliar here. Locals learned to sushi, and a few have even become addicted. Other than its sushi bar—acclaimed as the best in the Caribbean—a wide array of Japanese- and Asian-inspired dishes are available, including a delectable yellowfin tuna with teriyaki.

- **Best Burgers**   Patrons freely admit that **El Patio de Sam,** Calle San Sebastián 102 (© 787/723-1149), is not always on target with its main dishes. But they agree on one thing: The hamburgers are the juiciest and most delectable in San Juan. The Old Town atmosphere is also intriguing—you almost expect to encounter Bogey and Bacall.

- **Best Asopao**   Soul food to Puerto Ricans, *asopao* is the regional gumbo, made in as many different ways as there are chefs on the island. Some versions are too thick to be called soup, such as the seafood variety at **La Bombonera,** Calle San Francisco 259 (© 787/722-0658), in San Juan's Old Town, which is more like a stew. One popular version of asopao includes pigeon peas, although the one with chicken is better known.

- **Best Spanish Cuisine**   You'd have to go all the way to Madrid to find Spanish food as well prepared as it is at **Ramiro's,** Av. Magdalena 1106 (© 787/721-9049). The chefs take full advantage of fresh island produce to create an innovative cuisine. In fact, the style is New Creole, although its roots are firmly planted in Spain. Their fresh fish and chargrilled meats are succulent, and any dessert with the strawberry-and-guava sauce is a sure palate pleaser.

- **Best Local Cuisine**   Devoted to *la cocina criolla,* the term for the often starchy local cuisine, **Ajili Mójili,** Av. Ashford 1052 (© 787/725-9195), features food that islanders might have enjoyed in their mama's kitchens. Try such specialties as *mofongos* (green plantains stuffed with veal, chicken, shrimp, or pork) or the most classic *arroz con pollo* (stewed chicken with saffron rice) in town.

- **Best Hotel Restaurant** In 1997 *San Juan City Magazine* bestowed best hotel restaurant status on **Ristorante Tuscany** in the San Juan Marriott Resort, Av. Ashford 1309 (© 787/722-7000). It has continued to maintain high standards that won it the accolade in the first place. We've found it even better in the early 21st century than it was in the 1990s. The chef searches the markets for some of the best and freshest ingredients to whip into succulent northern Italian cuisine that is smooth and refined to the palate.

- **Best Italian Restaurant** In Wyndham El San Juan Hotel & Casino, **La Piccola Fontana,** Av. Isla Verde 6063 (© 787/791-0966), takes you on a culinary tour of sunny Italy. Plate after plate of delectable northern Italian food is presented nightly—everything from grilled filets of fresh fish to succulent pastas. Service is first-rate, the welcome warm.

- **Best Late-Night Dining** If you have hunger pangs late at night, forget the fast-food joints and head to **Amadeus,** Calle San Sebastián 106 in Old San Juan (© 787/722-8635). It offers Caribbean ingredients deftly handled with a nouvelle twist. And it does so Tuesday through Sunday until 2am. An attractive, trendy, generally young crowd arrives late to feast on the refined cuisine, enjoying such delights as Cajun-grilled mahimahi.

- **Best Family Meals** **Ciao Mediterranean Café,** in the Inter-Continental San Juan Grand Resort & Casino, Av. Isla Grande 187 (© 787/791-5000), offers an excellent and reasonably priced menu. Many tables are placed on a private boardwalk adjacent to the beach. Pizza and pasta are favorite dishes, and you can also choose from a large selection of other Mediterranean fare.

- **Best Pizza** At **Via Appia,** Av. Ashford 1350 (© 787/725-8711), you should try the special: a delectable blend of sausages, onions, mushrooms, pepperoni, green pepper, and bubbling cheese. Or sample a pizza with meatballs or one with vegetarian ingredients.

- **Best Sunday Brunch** Both locals and American visitors flock to **Palmera** at the Caribe Hilton, Calle Los Rosales (© 787/721-0303), for its delectable all-you-can-eat Sunday brunch. Good food, glamour, and live music are combined here. The freshly prepared seafood alone is worth the set price, which includes champagne.

- **Best Aphrodisiac Cuisine** Take someone special to **Ostra Cosa,** Calle del Cristo 154 (© 787/722-2672), for a night of romance. Even if you aren't in the mood, the owner promises that you will be after consuming his dishes, which are "chock full of aphrodisiacs." All the food is guaranteed to enhance your performance in the bedroom.

- **Best Ice Cream** On a cobble-covered street in Old San Juan, **Ben & Jerry's,** Calle del Cristo 61 (© 787/977-6882), is a block from the landmark cathedral, Catedral de San Juan, across from the entrance to the El Convento Hotel. This North American chain offers the best ice cream in San Juan. Any of the 32 flavors—10 of them low-fat—taste particularly good on hot, steamy days, when their names, such as Chubby Hubby and Phish Food, seem especially ironic and/or flavorful, depending on your point of view.

- **Best Drinks** Even when we're just in San Juan waiting for plane connections and have time available, we take a taxi to **Maria's,** Calle del Cristo 204 (© 787/721-1678), in Old San Juan, for the coolest and most original drinks in the city. On a hot day, there is no finer place to enjoy a mixed-fruit frappé; a banana, pineapple, or chocolate frost; or an orange, papaya, or lime freeze. See p. 169.

2 Cocina Criolla & Kill-Devil Rum

Although Puerto Rican cooking is somewhat similar to both Spanish and Mexican cuisine, it has a unique style, using such indigenous seasonings and ingredients as coriander, papaya, cacao, nispero (a tropical fruit that's brown, juicy, and related to the kiwi), apio (a small African-derived tuber that's sort of a more pungent type of turnip), plantains, and yampee (a tuber that's similar to an apio, but bigger, growing as big as 5–10 lb.).

Cocina criolla (Creole cooking) can be traced back to the Arawaks and Taínos, the original inhabitants of the island, who thrived on a diet of corn, tropical fruit, and seafood. When Ponce de León arrived with Columbus in 1493, the Spanish added beef, pork, rice, wheat, and olive oil to the island's foodstuffs.

The Spanish soon began planting sugarcane and importing slaves from Africa, who brought with them okra and taro (known in Puerto Rico as *yautia*). The mingling of flavors and ingredients passed from generation to generation among the different ethnic groups that settled on the island, resulting in the exotic blend of today's Puerto Rican cuisine.

APPETIZERS & SOUPS

Lunch and dinner generally begin with hot appetizers such as *bacalaítos,* crunchy cod fritters; *surullitos,* sweet and plump cornmeal fingers; and *empañadillas,* crescent-shaped turnovers filled with lobster, crab, conch, or beef.

Strange Fruit

Reading of Capt. James Cook's explorations of the South Pacific in the late 1700s, West Indian planters were intrigued by his accounts of the breadfruit tree, which grew in abundance on Tahiti. Seeing it as a source of cheap food for their slaves, they beseeched King George III to sponsor an expedition to bring the trees to the Caribbean. In 1787 the king put Capt. William Bligh in command of H.M.S. *Bounty* and sent him to do just that. One of Bligh's lieutenants was a former shipmate named Fletcher Christian. They became the leading actors in one of the great sea yarns when Christian overpowered Bligh, took over the *Bounty,* threw the breadfruit trees into the South Pacific Ocean, and disappeared into oblivion.

Bligh survived by sailing the ship's open longboat 3,000 miles to the East Indies, where he hitched a ride back to England on a Dutch vessel. Later he was given command of another ship and sent to Tahiti to get more breadfruit. Although he succeeded on this second attempt, the whole operation went for naught when the West Indies slaves refused to eat the strange fruit of the new tree, preferring instead their old, familiar rice.

Descendants of those trees still grow in the Caribbean, and the islanders prepare the head-size fruit in a number of ways. A thick green rind covers its starchy, sweet flesh whose flavor is evocative of a sweet potato. *Tostones*—fried green breadfruit slices—accompany most meat, fish, or poultry dishes served today in Puerto Rico.

Soups are also a popular beginning. There is a debate about whether one of the world's best-known soups, *frijoles negros,* is Cuban or Puerto Rican in origin. Wherever it started, black-bean soup makes a savory if filling opening to a meal. Another classic soup is *sopón de pollo con arroz*—chicken soup with rice—which manages to taste somewhat different in every restaurant. One traditional method of preparing this soup calls for large pieces of pumpkin and diced potatoes or *yautias* (the starchy root of a large-leaved tropical plant whose flesh is usually yellow or creamy white).

The third classic soup is *sopón de pescado* (fish soup), prepared with the head and tail intact. Again, this soup varies from restaurant to restaurant, and it may depend on the catch of the day. Traditionally, it is made with garlic and spices plus onions and tomatoes, the flavor enhanced by a tiny dash of vinegar and varying amount of sherry. *Caldo gallego* (Galician broth) is a dish imported from Spain's northwestern province of Galicia. It is prepared with salt pork, white beans, ham, and *berzas* (collard greens) or *grelos* (turnip greens), and the whole kettle is flavored with spicy *chorizos* (Spanish sausages).

Garbanzos (chickpeas) are often added to give flavor, body, and texture to Puerto Rican soups. One of the most authentic versions of this is *sopón de garbanzos con patas de cerdo* (chickpea soup with pig's feet). Into this kettle is added a variety of ingredients, including pumpkin, chorizos, salt pork, chile peppers, cabbage, potatoes, tomatoes, and fresh cilantro leaves.

Not really a soup, the most traditional Puerto Rican dish is **asopao,** a hearty gumbo made with either chicken or shellfish. One well-known version, consumed when the food budget runs low, is *asopao de gandules* (pigeon peas asopao). Every Puerto Rican chef has his or her own recipe for asopao. *Asopao de pollo* (chicken asopao) takes a whole chicken, which is then flavored with spices such as oregano, garlic, and paprika, along with salt pork, cured ham, green peppers, chile peppers, onions, cilantro, olives, tomatoes, chorizos, and pimientos. For a final touch, green peas or asparagus might be added.

MAIN COURSES

The aroma that wafts from kitchens throughout Puerto Rico comes from adobo and sofrito—blends of herbs and spices that give many of the native foods their distinctive taste and color. Adobo, made by crushing together peppercorns, oregano, garlic, salt, olive oil, and lime juice or vinegar, is rubbed into meats before they are roasted. Sofrito, a potpourri of onions, garlic, and peppers browned in either olive oil or lard and colored with achiote (annatto seeds), imparts the bright yellow color to the island's rice, soups, and stews.

Stews loom large in the Puerto Rican diet. They are usually cooked in a *caldera* (heavy kettle). A popular one is *carne guisada puertorriqueña* (Puerto Rican beef stew). The ingredients that flavor the chunks of beef vary according to the cook's whims or whatever happens to be in the larder. These might include green peppers, sweet chile peppers, onions, garlic, cilantro, potatoes, olives stuffed with pimientos, or capers. Seeded raisins may be added on occasion.

Pastelon de carne, or **meat pies,** are the staple of many Puerto Rican dinners. Salt pork and ham are often used for the filling and are cooked in a *caldero* (small cauldron). This medley of meats and spices is covered with a pastry top and baked.

Other typical main dishes include fried beefsteak with onions (*carne frita con cebolla*), veal (*ternera*) a la parmesana, and roast leg of pork, fresh ham, lamb, or veal a la criolla. These roasted meats are cooked in the Creole style, flavored with adobo. *Chicharrónes*—fried pork with the crunchy skin left on top for added flavor—is very popular, especially around Christmastime.

Puerto Ricans also like such dishes as *sesos empanados* (breaded calf's brains), *riñones guisados* (calf's kidney stew), and *lengua rellena* (stuffed beef tongue).

A festive island dish is *lechón asado,* or **barbecued pig,** which is usually cooked for a party of 12 to 15. It is traditional for picnics and alfresco parties; one can sometimes catch the aroma of this dish wafting through the palm trees, a smell that must have been familiar to the Taíno peoples. The pig is basted with *jugo de naranja agria* (sour orange juice) and achiote coloring. Green plantains are peeled and roasted over hot stones, then served with the barbecued pig as a side dish. The traditional dressing served with the pig is *aji-li-mojili,* a sour garlic sauce. The sauce combines garlic, whole black peppercorns, and sweet seeded chile peppers, flavored further with vinegar, lime juice, salt, and olive oil.

Puerto Ricans adore **chicken,** which they flavor with various spices and seasonings. *Arroz con pollo* (chicken with rice) is the most popular chicken dish on the island, and it was brought long ago to the U.S. mainland. Other favorite preparations include *pollo al Jerez* (chicken in sherry), *pollo en agridulce* (sweet-and-sour chicken), and *pollitos asados à la parrilla* (broiled chickens).

Most visitors to the island prefer the fresh **fish and shellfish.** A popular dish is *mojo isleno* (fried fish with Puerto Rican sauce). The sauce is made with olives and olive oil, onions, pimientos, capers, tomato sauce, vinegar, and a flavoring of garlic and bay leaves. Fresh fish is often grilled and perhaps flavored with garlic and an overlay of freshly squeezed lime juice—a very tasty dinner indeed. Caribbean lobster is usually the most expensive item on any menu, followed by shrimp. Puerto Ricans often cook *camarones en cerveza* (shrimp in beer). Another delectable shellfish dish is *jueyes hervidos* (boiled crab).

Many tasty **egg dishes** are served, especially *tortilla española* (Spanish omelet), cooked with finely chopped onions, cubed potatoes, and olive oil.

The rich and fertile fields of Puerto Rico produce a wide variety of **vegetables.** A favorite is the **chayote,** a pear-shaped vegetable called *christophine* throughout most of the English-speaking Caribbean. Its delicately flavored flesh is often compared to that of summer squash.

Fried tostones are made with both **breadfruit** (see "Strange Fruit" above) and **plantains.** In fact, the plantain is the single most popular side dish served on the island. Plantains are a variety of banana that cannot be eaten raw. They are much coarser in texture than ordinary bananas and are harvested while green, then baked, fried, or boiled. When made into tostones, they are usually served as an appetizer with before-dinner drinks. Fried to a deep golden yellow, plantains may accompany fish, meat, or poultry dishes.

THE AROMA OF COFFEE

It is customary for most Puerto Ricans to end a meal with the strong, black aromatic coffee grown here. Originally imported from the nearby Dominican Republic, coffee beans have been produced in the island's high-altitude interior for more than 300 years and still rank among the island's leading exports.

Puerto Rican coffee, in the view of many connoisseurs, rivals that of the more highly touted product from Colombia. Coffee has several degrees of quality, of course, the lowest-ranking one being *café de primera,* which is typically served at the ordinary family table. The top category is called *café super premium.* Only three coffees in the world belong to super-premium class: Blue Mountain coffee of Jamaica, Kona coffee from Hawaii, and Puerto Rico's homegrown Alto Grande, coffee beans sought by coffee connoisseurs around the world. The best brand names for Puerto Rican coffee are Café Crema, Café Rico, Rioja, and Yaucono.

You can ask for your brew *puya* (unsweetened), *negrito con azúcar* (black and sweetened), *cortao* (black with a drop of milk), or *con leche* (with milk).

RUM: KILL-DEVIL OR WHISKEY-BELLY VENGEANCE

Rum is the national drink of Puerto Rico, and you can buy it in almost any shade. Because the island is the world's leading rum producer, it's little wonder that every Puerto Rican bartender worthy of the profession likes to concoct his or her own favorite rum libation. You can call for Puerto Rican rum in many mixed drinks such as rum Collins, rum sour, and rum screwdriver. The classic sangria, which is prepared in Spain with dry red wine, sugar, orange juice, and other ingredients, is often given a Puerto Rican twist with a hefty dose of rum.

Today's version of rum bears little resemblance to the raw, grainy beverage consumed by the renegades and pirates of Spain. Christopher Columbus brought sugarcane, from which rum is distilled, to the Caribbean on his second voyage to the New World, and in almost no time rum became the regional drink.

It is believed that Ponce de León introduced rum to Puerto Rico during his governorship, which began in 1508. In time, there emerged large sugarcane plantations. From Puerto Rico and other West Indian islands, rum was shipped to colonial America, where it lent itself to such popular and hair-raising 18th-century drinks as Kill-Devil and Whiskey-Belly Vengeance. After the United States became a nation, rum was largely displaced as the drink of choice by whiskey, distilled from grain grown on the American plains.

It took almost a century before Puerto Rico's rum industry regained its former vigor. This occurred during a severe whiskey shortage in the United States at the end of World War II. By the 1950s, sales of rum had fallen off again, as more and different kinds of liquor had become available on the American market.

The local brew had been a questionable drink because of inferior distillation methods and quality. Recognizing this problem, the Puerto Rican government drew up rigid standards for producing, blending, and aging rum. Rum factories were outfitted with the most modern and sanitary equipment, and sales figures (encouraged by aggressive marketing campaigns) began to climb.

No one will ever agree on what "the best" rum is in the Caribbean. There are just too many of them to sample. Some are so esoteric as to be unavailable in your local liquor store. But if popular tastes mean anything, then Puerto Rican rums, especially Bacardi, head the list. There are 24 different rums from Puerto Rico sold in the United States under 11 brand names—not only Bacardi, but Ron Bocoy, Ronrico, Don Q, and many others.

Puerto Rican rums are generally light, gold, or dark. Usually white or silver in color, the biggest seller is light in body and dry in taste. Its subtle flavor and delicate aroma make it ideal for many mixed drinks, including the daiquiri, rum Collins, rum Mary, and rum and tonic or soda. It also goes with almost any fruit juice, or on the rocks with a slice of lemon or lime. Gold or amber rum is aromatic and full-bodied in taste. Aging in charred oak casks adds color to the rum.

Gold rums are usually aged longer for a deeper and more mellow flavor than light rums. They are increasingly popular on the rocks, straight up, or in certain mixed drinks in which extra flavor is desired—certainly in the famous piña colada, rum and Coke, or eggnog.

Dark rum is full-bodied with a deep, velvety, smooth taste and a complex flavor. It can be aged for as long as 15 years. You can enjoy it on the rocks, with tonic or soda, or in mixed drinks when you want the taste of rum to stand out.

The best introduction to Puerto Rican rum making is to visit the Bacardi distillery in Cataño, a short ferry ride across the San Juan harbor (see chapter 6).

3 Old San Juan

For the locations of Old San Juan restaurants, see the map "Old San Juan Accommodations & Dining" on p. 87.

VERY EXPENSIVE

Chef Marisoll ★★ INTERNATIONAL   Marisoll Hernández is one of the top chefs of Puerto Rico. Trained in Hilton properties, including one in London, she broke away to become an independent restaurateur in Old San Juan. In a Spanish colonial building, with a courtyard patio for dining, her eight-table restaurant is warm and intimate. Service is low key and slightly formal. Her list of appetizers is Old Town's finest selection, including peppers stuffed with codfish and a creamy Italian polenta with wild-mushroom fricassee. Two of our favorite dishes here are the Cajun-spiced blackened shrimp and andouille sausages with linguine and the loin of veal medallions with shiitake mushrooms and oven-dried tomatoes. Another delight is the curried chicken breast with basmati rice and homemade mango chutney.

Calle del Cristo 202. ✆ **787/725-7454.** Reservations required. Main courses $25–$40. AE, MC, V. Thurs–Sat noon–2:30pm; Tues–Sun 7–10pm. Bus: Old Town trolley.

Yukiyú ★★ JAPANESE   Traditional Japanese and other Asian cooking techniques are combined in this Old Town restaurant. Tabs can mount quickly at the sushi bar, acclaimed as the best in the Caribbean. Sushi is available at both lunch and dinner, but the teppanyaki grill at the front, where your own personal chef cooks your meal, is open only at dinner. The dining room itself is postmodern and monochromatic. The various chefs tempt you with hibachi chicken or chicken with scallops and sesame seeds. You might begin with miso soup or steamed pork dumplings, then go on to shrimp and vegetable tempura, or perhaps filet of sole with capers. Fresh yellowfin tuna with teriyaki is a favorite, as is New York sirloin in teriyaki sauce.

Calle Recinto Sur 311. ✆ **787/721-0653.** Reservations recommended. Main courses $20–$35; fixed-price teppanyaki dinners $30–$40; sushi $3–$4 per piece. AE, DISC, MC, V. Mon–Fri noon–2:20pm and 5–11pm, Sat noon–2:20pm and 7–11pm; Sun 5–9pm. Bus: Old Town trolley.

EXPENSIVE

Il Perugino ★ TUSCAN/UMBRIAN   This is one of the most elegant Italian restaurants in San Juan, with a courtyard containing covered tables. It's located in a 270-year-old town house, a short walk uphill from Catedral de San Juan. The entrance is filled with dozens of photographs of owner/chef Franco Seccarelli with friends and well-known patrons, the most notable being Luciano Pavarotti. Dishes and flavors are perfectly balanced. Examples include shrimp salad (usually a mundane dish, but quite special here), scallop salad, perfectly marinated fresh salmon, veal entrecôte with mushrooms, and medallions of beef flavored with balsamic vinegar. In season, there's an emphasis on black and white truffles, although these ingredients can raise the dish price substantially. Want something adventurous? Try the black pasta with crayfish and baby eels.

Calle del Cristo 105. ℰ **787/722-5481**. Reservations required. Main courses $18–$39. AE, MC, V. Daily
6:30–11pm. Bus: Old Town trolley.

La Chaumière ⭐⭐ CLASSIC FRENCH   The classic cuisine here has a loyal
following of foodies. Just steps from the famous Tapía Theater, this restaurant
has cafe-style decor in a greenhouse setting. You might begin with a Marseilles-
style fish soup or a hearty country paté, then follow with a perfectly prepared
rack of baby lamb Provençal, filet mignon with béarnaise sauce, magret of duckling, or Dover sole meunière. Or you might choose the tender chateaubriand for
two. Old standbys include chitterling sausage with red wine sauce, veal Oscar,
and oysters Rockefeller.

Calle Tetuán 367. ℰ **787/722-3330**. Reservations required. Main courses $25–$32. AE, DC, MC, V. Mon–Sat
6pm–midnight. Closed July–Aug. Bus: Old Town trolley.

Parrot Club ⭐⭐⭐ NUEVO LATINO   Parrot Club is the hottest restaurant
in Old San Juan. This bistro and bar serves Nuevo Latino cuisine that blends traditional Puerto Rican cookery with Spanish, Taíno, and African influences. It's
set in a stately looking 1902 building that was originally a hair-tonic factory.
Today you'll find a cheerful-looking dining room where San Juan's mayor and
the governor of Puerto Rico can sometimes be spotted, and a verdantly landscaped courtyard where tables for at least 200 diners are scattered amid potted
ferns, palms, and orchids. Live music, either Brazilian, salsa, or Latino jazz, is
offered nightly, as well as during the popular Sunday brunches.

   Menu items are updated interpretations of old Puerto Rican specialties. They
include ceviche of halibut, salmon, tuna, and mahimahi; delicious crab cakes;
criolla-style flank steak; and pan-seared tuna served with a sauce made from dark
rum and essence of oranges. Everybody's favorite drink is a "Parrot Passion,"
made from lemon-flavored rum, triple sec, oranges, and passion fruit.

Calle Fortaleza 363. ℰ **787/725-7370**. Reservations not accepted. Main courses $17–$29 at dinner,
$12–$20 at lunch. AE, DC, MC, V. Mon–Fri 11:30am–3pm; Sat noon–3pm; Sun noon–4pm and 6–11pm;
Fri–Sat 6pm–midnight. Closed 2 weeks in July. Bus: Old Town trolley.

Trois Cent Onze ⭐ FRENCH/INTERNATIONAL   This former film studio
lures some of the most demanding foodies. The bill of fare offers a variety of
dishes half influenced by the light, provincial cuisine of southern France. Other
dishes evoke the provinces of Normandy and Burgundy. The repertoire reflects
a commitment to creative flavors. We like such appetizers as tuna tartare marinated in olive oil and lemon juice and avocado stuffed with tomato, basil, and
balsamic vinaigrette. From the extensive list of main courses, you can select such
delicacies as roasted baby chicken with herbs and olive oil, roast rack of lamb
with potato crust, and Maine lobster stew with mushroom gratin.

Calle Fortaleza 311. ℰ **787/725-7959**. Reservations required. Sun brunch $19.50; main courses
$14.50–$29.50. AE, DISC, MC, V. July–Dec 15 Tues–Thurs 6–10:30pm; Fri–Sat 6–11:30pm; Sun noon–4pm
(brunch) and 4–10pm (dinner). Dec 16–June Mon–Thurs 6–10:30pm; Fri–Sat 6–11:30pm; Sun noon–4pm
(brunch) and 4–10pm (dinner). Bus: Old Town trolley.

MODERATE

Al Dente ITALIAN/SICILIAN   Located in the heart of Old San Juan, this
unpretentious and well-established restaurant has a decor that evokes a trattoria
in Palermo. Both the dress code and the ambience are relaxed and casual. You
might sample the scallops on a bed of spinach sautéed in cream, or gnocchi with
pesto, fettuccine maestro, ravioli (cheese or shrimp versions), or well-seasoned
calamari. The chef also makes his own desserts, including cheesecake, tiramisu,

---

Tips **Take a Strong Coffee Break**

A coffee break in Old San Juan might last an afternoon. *Taza* (cup) after *taza* of Puerto Rico's rich brew might make you desert Jamaican Blue Mountain coffee or Hawaiian Kona forever. By law, Puerto Rican coffeehouses must serve coffee made from homegrown beans, most often from the mountains in the center of the island. For years we've taken our espresso—from early morning until our final "nightcap"—at **Cuatro Estaciones** (no phone), a rather ugly kiosk at the end of the bustling Plaza de Armas. You'll get a quick jolt from this tasty brew, which attracts local java heads day and night.

---

and chocolate tortes. Nearly all dishes are genuinely satisfying, and the restaurant delivers quality food at reasonable prices. Brochettes of fresh tuna laced with pepper and Mediterranean herbs is an excellent choice.

Calle Recinto Sur 309. ✆ 787/723-7303. Reservations recommended. Main courses $13–$20. AE, MC, V. Mon–Fri noon–2:30pm and 5–11pm; Sat noon–11pm. Bus: Old Town trolley.

Amadeus ★★ CARIBBEAN   Housed in a brick-and-stone building that was constructed in the 18th century by a wealthy merchant, Amadeus offers Caribbean ingredients with a nouvelle twist. The appetizers alone are worth the trip here, especially the Amadeus dumplings with guava sauce and arrowroot fritters. And try the smoked-salmon-and-caviar pizza. One zesty specialty is pork scaloppine with sweet-and-sour sauce.

Calle San Sebastián 106 (across from the Iglesia de San José). ✆ 787/722-8635. Reservations recommended. Main courses $8.75–$12.75 lunch, $12–$26 dinner. AE, MC, V. Mon 6pm–2am; Tues–Sun noon–2am (kitchen closes at midnight). Bus: Old Town trolley.

Amanda's Café MEXICAN   The color scheme of turquoise and hot pink is appealingly garish. But if you're feeling a bit reckless after too many hours of shopping in Old San Juan, this might be just what you need. Come here for a sidewalk table and colorful daiquiris, which might make a continued exploration of Old Town seem beside the point. Food is presented as something of an afterthought to the drinks. The menu includes belly-busting platters of Mexican staples, as well as shrimp with garlic, stuffed chiles with tacos, a daily fish platter, and enchiladas (the Swiss version with peanuts and raisins is intriguing).

Calle Norzagaray 424. ✆ 787/722-0187. Reservations not necessary. Main courses $12.75–$25. AE, MC, V. Daily 11am–1:30pm. Bus: Old Town trolley.

Café Berlin INTERNATIONAL   Other than the hardworking staff, there's very little about this place that's particularly Hispanic. What you'll get is a corner of Central Europe, identified by a Jugendstil-inspired sign, serving coffee, pastries, and a limited array of light platters, such as pasta, on tiny marble-top tables like what you'd expect in Vienna. Paintings, all of them for sale, are displayed on scarlet-colored walls, and lavishly caloric pastries are arranged behind glass display cases. More substantial, rib-sticking fare includes salmon in orange- and garlic-flavored herb broth, scallops in pesto sauce, and turkey breast Stroganoff.

407 Plaza de Colón. ✆ 787/722-5205. Main courses $14–$21. AE, MC, V. Mon–Fri 11am–10pm; Sat–Sun 9am–10pm. Bus: Old Town trolley.

Café Zaguán INTERNATIONAL New Jersey–born owners Billy and Diana Karmazyn have created a catch-all eatery that combines aspects of an indoor/outdoor cafe, a take-away sandwich shop, and a venue that becomes more formal after 6pm. Lunch features simple dishes such as club sandwiches, stir-fried tofu, and salads. Dinners show off Billy's culinary training at other creative restaurants. His entrees include sesame-crusted tuna served with vegetable sushi rolls and spicy Szechuan sauce, and pulled pork quesadillas with papaya salsa. He also serves *mangu-longo,* a Dominican–Puerto Rican dish that consists of plantains topped with sautéed shrimp and wine-flavored cream sauce.

Calle Tetuán 359 at the Plaza Arturo Somohano. ℂ **787/724-3359.** Reservations recommended for dinner Fri–Sat, otherwise not necessary. Lunch sandwiches and salads $5–$10; dinner main courses $14–$30. AE, MC, V. Mon–Sat 9:30am–4pm and 6–11pm; Sun 10am–6pm. Bus: Old Town trolley.

Carli Café Concierto ⭐ INTERNATIONAL This stylish restaurant is owned by Carli Muñoz. The gold discs hanging on the walls attest to Carli's success in his previous role as a pianist for The Beach Boys. Nowadays, Carli entertains his dinner guests nightly with a combination of standards, romantic jazz, and original material on his grand piano. Diners can sit outside on the Plazoleta, where they can enjoy a panoramic view of the bay, or they can eat inside against a backdrop of a tasteful decor of terra-cotta walls and black marble tables. The chef tempts visitors with an imaginative international menu, including such delights as quail rockettes stuffed with dried fruits and sage. The filet of salmon and a mouthwatering rack of lamb are among the finest main dishes. The bar, with its mahogany and brass fittings, is an ideal spot to chill out.

Edificio Banco Popular, Calle Tetuán 206, off Plazoleta Rafael Carrión. ℂ **787/725-4927.** Reservations recommended. Main courses $17–$29. AE, MC, V. Mon–Thurs 4–11:30pm; Fri–Sat 4pm–1:30am. Bus: M2 or M3.

Dragonfly ⭐⭐⭐ LATIN/ASIAN This is San Juan's hottest new restaurant. The decor has been compared to that of a bordello in Old San Francisco. You pass through the beaded curtains into a world of red ceilings, fringed lamps, and

---

 A Toothpick on Your Table

When you've had too many hotel meals or patronized too many first-class restaurants and want something authentic, head for **El Jibarito,** Calle Sol 280 (ℂ **787/725-8375**), where locals flock for food like their mamas used to make.

Don't be put off by the setting. We're not talking luxe here. Established in the mid-1970s by Pedro and his wife, Aïda, two self-professed *jibaros* (peasants), the restaurant is a dive, complete with the mandatory fluorescent lighting, vinyl tablecloths, and blinking Christmas bulbs (at any time of the year). The waiter, as one diner observed, is likely to take out his toothpick and lay it on your table as he scribbles down your menu selections for the evening.

Stick to the simple dishes and you'll rarely go wrong here. The lamb stew is perfectly seasoned and tender. Other specialties that have endured over time are yellow rice with green beans and shredded pork, shrimp with garlic sauce, and several kinds of mofongo. Main courses range from $7 to $12.50, and American Express, Diners Club, MasterCard, and Visa are accepted. El Jibarito is open daily from 11am to 10pm.

gilded mirrors. The restaurant lies right across the street from the Parrot Club, and these two dining enclaves have put the newly named SoFo district (south of Calle Fortaleza in Old Town) on the culinary map. In the bar the drink of choice is a Cosmopolitan, the preferred cigarette Marlboro, and the most popular drink, a lethal "Dragon Punch." Night after night Dragonfly is the fun party place in town, unlike the more staid Parrot Club. Along with the latest gossip, you can enjoy live Latin jazz as background music.

This new-generation San Juan restaurant offers sexy cookery, such as seafood ceviche scooped up with yucca, and plantain chips, *chicharrónes* (pork rinds), spicy crab cakes, and a host of other dishes, such as marinated grilled meats. We applaud the chefs for their use of root vegetables such as yucca. The red snapper and grouper are excellent, and we love the pumpkin and beans of every type. The barbecued lamb shanks are very hearty and filling. Ravioli, timbales, confits, cassoulets—it's a dizzy array of taste temptations.

Calle Fortaleza 364. (C) **787/977-3886.** Reservations required. Main courses $8–$21. AE, MC, V. Mon–Wed 6:30–10:30pm; Thurs–Sat 6:30pm–midnight. Bus: A5 or T1.

El Patio de Sam AMERICAN/PUERTO RICAN   Established in 1953, this joint has survived several generations of clients, who came here for booze, fantastic juicy burgers, Puerto Rican food, and dialogue. The setting includes an exterior space with tables that overlook a historic statue of Ponce de León and a well-known church, and a labyrinth of dark, smoked-stained inner rooms with high-beamed ceilings and lots of potted plants. The menu includes paella, grilled chicken and steak, black-bean soup, calamari, and codfish croquettes.

Calle San Sebastián 102 (across from the Iglesia de San José). (C) **787/723-1149.** Sandwiches, burgers, and salads $9–$9.50; platters $13–$33. AE, DC, DISC, MC, V. Daily 11am–midnight. Bus: Old Town trolley.

El Picoteo SPANISH   In the courtyard of the historic El Convento hotel, this is the best place in Old Town to go for tapas. You get real Spanish flavor here, in such dishes as garbanzo salad, sausages, and ceviche. Fresh octopus is also a delight, as are the Spanish-style pizzas. *Sanjuaneros* along with visitors enjoy this informal place for lunch or a drink at the bar. Many spend the afternoon playing backgammon and sipping a pitcher of sangria. Dinner is festive, accompanied by salsa and lights in the courtyard. The menu has some 80 tapas from which to choose, and the selection of imported Spanish cheeses is Old Town's finest.

In El Convento hotel, Calle del Cristo 100. (C) **787/723-9020.** Reservations recommended. Main courses $8–$20. AE, MC, V. Tues–Sun noon–midnight. Bus: Old Town trolley.

La Mallorquina ✮ PUERTO RICAN   This is San Juan's oldest restaurant, founded in 1848, and it has been run by the Rojos family since 1900. If you look carefully at the floor adjacent to the old-fashioned mahogany bar, you'll see the building's original gray-and-white marble flooring, which the owners are laboriously restoring, square foot by square foot, to its original condition. Lunches here tend to attract local office workers; dinners are more cosmopolitan and more leisurely, with many residents of the Condado and other modern neighborhoods selecting this place specifically because of its old-fashioned, old-world charm.

The food has changed little here over the decades, with special emphasis on asopao made with rice and either chicken, shrimp, or lobster and shrimp. Arroz con pollo is almost as popular. Begin with either garlic soup or gazpacho, end with flan, and you'll have eaten a meal that's authentically Puerto Rican.

Calle San Justo 207. (C) **787/722-3261.** Reservations not accepted at lunch, recommended at dinner. Dinner main courses $15–$36 (highest price is for lobster). AE, MC, V. Mon–Sat noon–10pm. Closed Sept. Bus: Old Town Trolley.

Ostra Cosa ★★ (Finds) ECLECTIC   This is the most artfully promoted restaurant in San Juan, with a growing clientele who swear that the ambience here is one of the most sensual and romantic in Old San Juan. It was created by a former advertising executive, Alberto Nazario, a lifestyle guru who mingles New Age thinking with good culinary techniques to promote love, devotion, and a heightened sexuality. Couples dine beneath a massive quenepe tree—waiters will tell you to hug the tree and make a wish—in a colonial courtyard surrounded by a 16th-century building that was once the home of the colony's governor. The atmosphere, enhanced by domesticated quail and chirping tree frogs, will make you feel far removed from the cares of the city. Featured foods are high in phosphorus, zinc, and flavor, designed to promote an "eat-up, dress-down experience." The ceviche is superb, as are the grilled prawns. But it is the conch, known as Caribbean Viagra, that rates "Wow!!" or "Ay Ay Ay!!!"

Calle del Cristo 154. ℂ 787/722-2672. Reservations recommended. Main courses $12–$25. AE, MC, V. Aug–Sept Mon–Fri 6–10pm; Sat–Sun noon–10pm. Oct–July daily noon–10pm. Bus: Old Town trolley.

Royal Thai ★ THAI   Thai cuisine arrived in Puerto Rico long after it was a familiar sight in urban areas of the U.S. mainland. If you're an aficionado of the cuisine, this is as good as it gets anywhere on the island. The setting is a long and narrow room filled with Thai embroideries and sculpture, outfitted in tones of pink and blue. Menu items include some of the best duck in town, served in either curry or tamarind sauce; sea bass steamed with prawns and ginger or deep-fried with curry sauce; and a medley of sautéed seafood with brown sauce and cooking sherry. An excellent beginning is chicken with coconut milk.

Calle Recinto Sur 315. ℂ 787/725-8401. Reservations recommended. Main courses $16–$36. AE, MC, V. Mon–Sat noon–3pm and 6–11pm; Sun 6–11. Bus: Old Town trolley.

INEXPENSIVE

Butterfly People Café (Kids) CONTINENTAL/AMERICAN   This rather cramped restaurant is on the second floor of a restored mansion, next to the world's largest gallery devoted to butterflies. Wherever you look, thousands of framed butterflies will delight or horrify you. You can dine at one of the tables inside the cafe, which overlooks a courtyard. This is among the most kid-welcoming place in town, and most children take delight in eating in a setting surrounded by the framed butterflies, viewing it as a sort of fantasy world. The cuisine is tropical and light European fare, made with fresh ingredients appealing to children, as opposed to the more heavy-handed Puerto Rican cuisine offered at nearby dining spots. You might begin with gazpacho or vichyssoise, follow with quiche or one of the daily specials, and finish with chocolate mousse or the tantalizing raspberry chiffon pie with fresh raspberry sauce. A full bar offers tropical specialties such as piña coladas, fresh-squeezed Puerto Rican orange juice, and Fantasia, a frappé of seven fresh fruits.

Calle Fortaleza 152. ℂ 787/723-2432. Salads, sandwiches, and quiches $4–$8. AE, MC, V. Mon–Wed and Fri–Sat 10am–5pm. Bus: Old Town trolley.

Café Bohemio INTERNATIONAL   Accessible via a side entrance of the Old Town's most historic hotel, within a high-ceilinged room that evokes the 18th century, this popular singles bar attracts a congenial group of fans. Lots of people come just for a drink or to enjoy the live music presented every Tuesday through Friday beginning at 9:30pm. If you're in the mood for a meal, you can order well-prepared versions of ceviche in tequila sauce, blackened calamari,

Cajun-crusted red snapper, or spinach and ricotta crepes. Pizzas and burgers are also available.

In El Convento hotel, Calle del Cristo 100. ✆ **787/723-9200.** Reservations not necessary. Main courses $9.50–$14.50. AE, MC, V. Daily 11am–11pm. Closed Aug–Sept. Bus: Old Town trolley.

Café Puerto Rico CREOLE/PUERTO RICAN   On the Plaza de Colón, this restaurant offers balconies overlooking one of the most charming of Old Town squares. The setting is colonial, with beamed ceilings and tile floors, and with ceiling fans whirling overhead. The menu features hearty regional fare. Tasty options include fried fish filet, paella, and lobster cooked as you like it. Eggplant parmagiana is an excellent vegetarian option, and you might also order eye round stuffed with ham in Creole sauce. On weekends live bands play here, and the sound of romantic boleros or salsa fill the air. The cafe is an especially good value then because you get your food and entertainment for just the price of dinner.

Calle O'Donnell 208. ✆ **787/724-2281.** Main courses $9–$20. AE, MC, V. Daily 11:30am–11pm (bar open till 2am Thurs–Sat). Bus: Old Town trolley.

El Buen Samaritano PUERTO RICAN   Only the most experimental foreign tourists would venture in here, despite the fact that it provides lots of insights into the subculture of this thriving inner-city neighborhood. In fact, we have included this authentic little eatery to answer the often-posed question "Where do the locals dine?" It stands adjacent to the back door of city hall, near the corner of Calle San Justo, on one of our favorite "backwater" streets of the historic Old Town. Almost no English is spoken; it's as Creole and ethnic as anything on the island, and it contains no more than four well-scrubbed tables in a setting Hemingway would have praised. All the food is predictably filling and starchy, including roast pork with yellow rice and beans and filet of red snapper in pungent tomato sauce. The menu, which depends largely on what was available in the market that morning, is recited lethargically by a member of the family who owns the joint. Except during the midday crush, no one will mind if you opt for just a cup of thick Puerto Rican coffee, a beer, or a soda.

Calle Luna 255 (near Calle San Justo). ✆ **787/721-6184.** Reservations not accepted. Platters and main courses $6–$15. No credit cards. Daily 7am–7pm. Bus: Old Town trolley.

El Patio Mexicano MEXICAN   A tour of this restaurant reveals all the charm of a 19th-century country store in an isolated Mexican puebla. There's memorabilia commemorating folk heroes such as Francisco Villa, photographs of Mexican movie stars of the 1930s and 1950s, elaborately carved beams and columns, and handicrafts, which probably required months of labor by entire villages. The best way to begin is with a mango margarita in an absolutely enormous glass. The menu retains an allegiance to "pure" Mexican (not Tex-Mex) cuisine, as shown in such dishes as chicken breast with tamarind sauce and *enchiladas divorciadas* (divorced enchiladas), consisting of red and green enchiladas divided by a "fence" of refried beans. *Sopa trasca* is a rich broth laced with three kinds of meat, two kinds of cheeses, avocados, and sour cream.

Calle Fortaleza 260. ✆ **787/723-5449.** Reservations not necessary. Main courses $7.50–$23. AE, DISC, MC, V. Wed–Mon noon–3pm and 6pm–midnight. Closed Aug 15–Sept 15. Bus: Old Town trolley.

Hard Rock Cafe *Kids* AMERICAN   This is San Juan's most blatant example of gringo-derived cultural imperialism. Set near the cruise-ship terminals on a historic avenue in the Old Town, it's loaded with rock-and-roll memorabilia and permeated with an engaging friendliness. One dining room is devoted to the Beatles, complete with symbol-rich murals that only the most fervent fans can interpret. Standard menu items include barbecued ribs and pork sandwiches, chicken and rib combos, smoked pork chops, pastas, steaks, fiery chili, and a selection of well-stuffed sandwiches. On days when cruise ships pull into port (usually Tues and Sun), the place is likely to be mobbed.

Calle Recinto Sur 253. © 787/724-7625. Burgers, sandwiches, and platters $7–$22. AE, DC, DISC, MC, V. Daily 11am–11pm. Bus: Old Town trolley.

La Bombonera ★★ (Value PUERTO RICAN   This place offers exceptional value in its homemade pastries, well-stuffed sandwiches, and endless cups of coffee—and it has done so since 1902. Its atmosphere evokes turn-of-the-20th-century Castille transplanted to the New World. The food is authentically Puerto Rican, homemade, and inexpensive, with regional dishes such as rice with squid, roast leg of pork, and seafood asopao. For dessert, you might select an apple, pineapple, or prune pie, or one of many types of flan. Service is polite, if a bit rushed, and the place fills up quickly at lunchtime.

Calle San Francisco 259. © 787/722-0658. Reservations recommended. American breakfast $4–$8; main courses $7–$15. AE, DISC, MC, V. Daily 7:30am–8pm. Bus: Old Town trolley.

La Danza (Value PUERTO RICAN   The friendly, jovial Señora Burgos welcomes guests to this choice dining room and has done so for some 4 decades. Opposite the Chapel of Christ, La Danza is known in Old Town for its all-day special, paella for two with fried plantains, garlic bread, two glasses of wine, and coffee—all for $23. Smoking is permitted at the outside tables, and weekend diners are often treated to live street entertainment. There is also an intimate bar, where locals sometimes pop in for a fast pick-me-up. Begin with one of the choice appetizers, especially the salt cod cakes or the small boiled sweet corn cakes. Main dishes include breaded fish and fish in a traditional Creole sauce. Some diners prefer to fill up on asopao, the thick stew of Puerto Rico. Other regional fare includes chicken-and-rice stew accompanied by fried plantains.

Calle Fortaleza 56. © 787/723-1642. Main courses $10–$20. MC, V. Fri–Wed 11:30am–8pm. Bus: Old Town trolley.

NoNo's AMERICAN/FAST FOOD   In the heart of Old San Juan in a 2-century-old building overlooking Plaza San José, NoNo's brings stateside food to those eager for salads, mozzarella sticks, triple-decker sandwiches, chicken-fried steaks, hamburgers (here called NoNo burgers), and onion rings. You'll sit beneath a beamed ceiling, near a large and accommodating bar where folks seem only peripherally interested in the food.

Calle San Sebastián 100 (at Calle del Cristo). © 787/725-7819. Hamburgers and main courses $5–$10. AE, MC, V. Daily 11am–6pm; bar 11am–4am. Bus: Old Town trolley.

Patio del Nispero INTERNATIONAL   Surrounded by the soaring atrium of Old San Juan's most historic hotel, this restaurant provides a charming oasis of calm and quiet. Pots of verdant plants thrive under the direct sunlight of the open sky, and big canvas umbrellas shield diners from the rain. No one will mind if you order just a drink (the daiquiris are excellent) or a cup of coffee while resting after a tour of the Old Town or the cathedral next door. But if you want food, consider filet of red snapper with Creole sauce, chicken breast with chestnuts and mushrooms in cognac sauce, broiled veal chop with Marsala sauce, and one of a wide selection of desserts. Live music is featured two evenings a week.

In the El Convento hotel, Calle del Cristo 100. ℂ **787/723-9260**. Reservations not necessary. Sandwiches $9.50–$12; platters $14–$24. AE, DC, MC, V. Daily 11am–10pm. Bus: Old Town trolley.

Yeyos *Value* PUERTO RICAN/CREOLE   You decide to bypass the store next door, Condom World. This tiny little joint that has only eight tables is a real insider's place, and it serves decent food that's full of flavor under bare fluorescent bulbs. The spartan decor is more than compensated for by the really bargain food served in this working-class neighborhood. The breakfast served here is Old San Juan's most reasonable in price, complete with eggs, potatoes, and ham. For your main course, you could enjoy a generous helping of roast chicken, or something light—such as codfish salad. Pork is smothered in onions and served with yellow rice, and you can also order *sancocho*, a robust meat-and-vegetable stew. Many dishes come with *mangú*, a plantain mash. The fixed-price menu is the town's greatest food buy. The place doesn't have a liquor license.

Calle San Francisco 353. ℂ **787/725-9362**. Breakfast $2–$4; main courses $5–$10; fixed-price menu $5. No credit cards. Mon–Sat 6am–6pm. Bus: Old Town trolley.

4 Puerta de Tierra

For the locations of restaurants in Puerta de Tierra, see the map "Puerta de Tierra, Miramar, Condado & Ocean Park Accommodations & Dining" on p. 89.

Invernino ★★ ITALIAN   Presenting a tempting array of foodstuff from all the major culinary zones of Italy, this restaurant has already become a hit since its opening in late 2001. It received worldwide fame as the setting of the wedding of Oscar de la Hoya to Millie Corretijer. The restaurant is named for a sculpture in its foyer that was created in 1790 by the Italian artist Sau Frilli. The ambience is one of the most sophisticated and inviting in San Juan; the restaurant is filled with paintings and stainless-steel sculptures. A former warehouse, Invernino has been transformed into an up-market restaurant that serves some of the Caribbean's finest Italian cuisine, made with top-quality ingredients handpicked by the chefs. Chef Gerard Cribbin, known in the past for his pasta and steak restaurants, likes diners to "taste every ingredient in a particular dish." Nothing he serves is overpowered with sauces, including succulent steaks such as filet mignon and pastas such as striped lobster ravioli. The fettuccine with fresh clams merits a prize, and the tiramisu is the best in San Juan. A much-frequented watering hole is the cigarette bar on the second floor, where live piano music is played.

Atlantic View Building, Av. Ponce de León 162. ℂ **787/724-2166**. Reservations required. Main courses $18–$34. AE, MC, V. Mon–Fri 11:30am–3pm; Mon–Sat 5–11pm. Bus: B21.

Morton's of Chicago ★★   When it comes to steaks, Ruth's Chris Steak House in Isla Verde enjoys a slight edge, but otherwise Morton's is king of the steaks and other choice meats. The chain of gourmet steakhouses was founded in 1978 by Arnie Morton, former executive vice president of the *Playboy* empire. Beef lovers, from Al Gore to Liza Minnelli, know they'll get quality meats perfectly cooked at Morton's. Carts laden with your selection, ranging from prime Midwestern beefsteaks to succulent lamb or veal chops, are wheeled around for your selection. And Morton's has the island's best prime rib. This is a place where the bartenders make stiff drinks, and the waiters tempt you with their fresh fish, lobster, and chicken dishes. The vegetables here are among the freshest in the area. The house specialty is a 24-ounce porterhouse. Appetizers include perfectly cooked jumbo shrimp with cocktail sauce and smoked Pacific salmon. For dessert, we always gravitate to one of the soufflés, such as raspberry or Grand Marnier.

In the Caribe Hilton, Calle Los Rosales. (© 787/977-6262. Reservations required. Main courses $20–$40. AE, DC, MC, V. Mon–Sat 5:30–11pm; Sun 5–10pm. Bus: B21.

Palmera (★ (Kids INTERNATIONAL   Every Sunday the Hilton's brunch captivates the imagination of island residents and U.S. visitors with its combination of excellently prepared food, glamour, and entertainment. There's a clown to keep the children amused, as well as live music on the bandstand for anyone who cares to dance. Champagne is included in the price. Food is arranged at several different stations: Puerto Rican dishes, seafood, paella, ribs, cold cuts, steaks, pastas, and salads. Afterward, you might like to stroll amid the boutiques and seafront facilities of this famous hotel. In the evening you can order from a standard international menu. However, we recommend this restaurant mainly for its buffet. If you're visiting the Hilton for the evening for dining and entertainment, we'd recommend the cuisine at Morton's (see above) over Palmera.

In the Caribe Hilton, Calle Los Rosales. (© 787/721-0303. Reservations recommended. All-you-can-eat buffet brunch $39 for adults, half price for children under 7; main courses $14–$20. AE, DC, MC, V. Sun buffet 12:30–4pm; daily 6am–midnight. Bus: B21.

5 Condado

For the locations of Condado restaurants, see the map "Puerta de Tierra, Miramar, Condado & Ocean Park Accommodations & Dining" on p. 89.

EXPENSIVE

Ajili Mójili (★★ PUERTO RICAN/CREOLE   This restaurant is devoted exclusively to *la cucina criolla,* the starchy, down-home cuisine that developed on the island a century ago. Though the building housing it is quite modern, you can see artful replicas of the kind of crumbling brick walls you'd expect in Old San Juan and a bar that evokes Old Spain. The staff will willingly describe menu items in colloquial English. Locals come here for a taste of the food they enjoyed at their mother's knee, like *mofongos* (green plantains stuffed with veal, chicken, shrimp, or pork), arroz con pollo, *medallones de cerdo encebollado* (pork loin sautéed with onions), *carne mechada* (beef rib eye stuffed with ham), and *lechon asado con maposteado* (roast pork with rice and beans). Wash it all down with an ice-cold bottle of local beer.

Av. Ashford 1052 (at the corner of Calle Joffre). (© 787/725-9195. Reservations recommended. Main courses $16–$35; children's menu $6. AE, MC, V. Mon–Fri 11:30am–3pm; Mon–Sat 6–10pm; Sun 12:30–4pm and 6–10pm. Bus: B21.

Cobia (★ CARIBBEAN/PACIFIC RIM   Set within the Condado Plaza Hotel, this restaurant presents a stylish, much-praised blend of Caribbean and Asian cuisine. The setting is an artfully contemporary room—with bubbling aquariums, maple trim, and comfortable chairs—which overlooks the glittering lights surrounding the nearby lagoon. Enjoy a drink at the bar outside before heading in to dinner. The menu items developed by resident chef Phil Bellshaw include roasted West Indian pumpkin soup; cream of native root vegetable soup; pan-roasted salmon with cilantro-flavored risotto, smoked yellow pepper coulis, and black-bean salsa; and seafood paella with calamari, mojo chicken, pigeon peas, and chorizo sausage. Even the lobster at this place is likely to be served in ways you might not recognize, including a version with yucca mofongo and black-bean sofrito broth. One of the most enduringly popular desserts is

America Online Keyword: Travel
Booked seat 6A, open return.
Rented red 4-wheel drive.
Reserved cabin, no running water.
Discovered space.
With over 700 airlines, 50,000 hotels, 50 rental car companies and 5,000 cruise and vacation packages, you can create the perfect get-away for you. Choose the car, the room, even the ground you walk on.
Travelocity.com
A Sabre Company
Go Virtually Anywhere.
Travelocity,® Travelocity.com® and the Travelocity skyline logo are trademarks and/or servicemarks of Travelocity.com L.P.,

Book your air, hotel, and transportation all in one place.

Hotel or hostel? Cruise or canoe? Car? Plane? Camel? Wherever you're going, visit Yahoo! Travel and get total control over your arrangements. Even choose your seat assignment. So. One hump or two? travel.yahoo.com

powered by **COMPAQ**

YAHOO!
Travel

chocolate-enriched *tres leches*, with chocolate mousse and peanut-butter-brittle ice cream.

In the Condado Plaza Hotel, Av. Ashford 999. ℭ **787/721-1000**. Reservations recommended. Main courses $22–$52. AE, DC, MC, V. Daily 5–11pm. Bus: A5, A7, B10.

La Belle Epoque ★★★ FUSION/FRENCH   Twice in recent years, master chef Jeremie Cruz has been voted "Caribbean Chef of the Year," and he currently reigns supreme as Puerto Rico's greatest talent in the kitchen. Expect spectacular dining at this elegant enclave of exquisitely prepared cuisine. The Condado setting is one of Murano chandeliers, hand-painted custom-made plates, and Italian damask tablecloths. In addition to two exquisite dining rooms, there is a Smoker Terrace with a wide collection of fine cigars, plus a cozy wine cellar with a selection of more than 1,000 vintage bottles. Even a basic onion soup for an appetizer is prepared with flair, although you can order more luxurious concoctions such as lobster bisque. Another starter might be in seafood mousse resting under a brown potato crust or perhaps a watercress and arugula salad studded with walnuts and savory bits of blue cheese. For a main course, opt for the poached salmon with "lobster potatoes," one of the best dishes we've ever sampled here. Other options might include a classic coq au vin, given added dimension by the use of wild mushrooms, or seared bay scallops with spinach and saffron-laced mussel sauce. Between courses a palate cleanser is served, a refreshing fermented cider with frozen white grapes. Desserts are among the most unusual, delicious, and imaginative on the island—try the lemongrass soup with sorbet, pieces of fresh fruit, and candied carrots.

Casabella Building, Av. Magdalena 1400. ℭ **787/977-1765**. Reservations required. Main courses $12–$25 lunch, $17–$28.50 dinner. AE, MC, V. Mon–Sat noon–3pm and 5–11pm. Bus: B21.

La Compostela ★ INTERNATIONAL   This restaurant offers formal service from a battalion of well-dressed waiters. Established by a Galician-born family, the pine-trimmed restaurant has gained a reputation as one of the best in the capital. The chef made his name on the roast peppers stuffed with salmon mousse. Equally delectable are duck with orange and ginger sauce and baby rack of lamb with fresh herbs. The shellfish grilled in brandy sauce is a sure winner. The chef also makes two different versions of paella, both savory. The wine cellar, comprising some 10,000 bottles, is one of the most impressive in San Juan.

Av. Condado 106. ℭ **787/724-6088**. Reservations required. Main courses $24–$39. AE, MC, V. Mon–Fri noon–2:30pm; Mon–Sat 6:30–10:30pm. Bus: M2.

La Scala ★ NORTHERN ITALIAN   One of the most sophisticated Italian restaurants in San Juan, La Scala caters to discerning diners who appreciate the nuances of fine cuisine and service. The decor includes neutral colors, stucco arches, and murals. The menu lists just about the entire repertoire of northern Italian cuisine. You'll find a specialty version of Caesar salad, fresh mushrooms in garlic sauce, and a succulent half-melted version of fresh mozzarella in carozza. The fresh fish and seafood are flown in from New York and Boston. Specialties include halibut cooked in parchment, rigatoni with shiitake mushrooms and ricotta, and rack of lamb in red wine sauce. Most meals here are memorable, and the cookery, for the most part, is creative and delicate. Service is attentive.

In the Radisson Ambassador Plaza Hotel & Casino, Av. Ashford 1369. ℭ **787/721-7300**. Reservations recommended. Main courses $17–$40. AE, MC, V. Tues–Fri noon–3pm; daily 6–11pm. Bus: A7.

Martino's ★ NORTHERN ITALIAN   This restaurant offers some of the finest service on the Condado and a classic Italian cuisine, centered primarily in the north of Italy, especially Lombardy. It's the domain of chef and owner Martin Acosta. His restaurant's picture windows open onto views of the Atlantic and the night lights of the Condado. Appetizers include hot seafood antipasti and Caesar and spinach salads. The Caesar salad is made tableside with real panache. For a main course you can order one of the homemade pasta dishes or choose from such appetizing dishes as seafood suprême, vitello Martino (with shrimp), gnocchi with cream sauce and Parmesan, and filet mignon Monnalisa, which is flambéed at your table. In fact, almost any dish can receive a tableside flambé if you want. Good and reasonably priced wines add to the dining pleasure.

In the Diamond Palace Hotel & Casino, Av. Condado 55. ℂ **787/722-5256.** Reservations recommended. Main courses $14–$26 lunch, $16.50–$45 dinner. AE, DC, MC, V. Daily 6–11:30pm and Wed–Fri noon–3pm. Bus: A7.

Ramiro's ★★ SPANISH/INTERNATIONAL   This restaurant boasts the most imaginative menu on the Condado. Its refined "New Creole" cooking is a style pioneered by owner and chef Jesús Ramiro. You might begin with breadfruit mille-feuille with local crabmeat and avocado. For your main course, any fresh fish or meat can be chargrilled on request. Some recent menu specialties have included paillard of lamb with spiced root vegetables and guava sauce, charcoal-grilled black Angus steak with shiitake mushrooms, and grilled striped sea bass with citrus sauce. Among the many homemade desserts are caramelized mango on puff pastry with strawberry-and-guava sauce, and "four seasons" chocolate.

Av. Magdalena 1106. ℂ **787/721-9049.** Reservations recommended off-season, required in winter. Main courses $23–$40. AE, DC, MC, V. Sun–Fri 6–10pm; Sat 6–11pm. Bus: A7, T1, or M2.

Ristorante Tuscany ★★★ NORTHERN ITALIAN   This is the showcase restaurant of one of the most elaborate hotel reconstructions in the history of Puerto Rico, and the kitchen continues to rack up culinary awards. Notable entrees include grilled veal chops with shallots and glaze of Madeira, and grilled chicken breast in cream sauce with chestnuts, asparagus, and brandy, surrounded with fried artichokes. The seafood selections are excellent, especially the fresh red snapper sautéed in olive oil, garlic, parsley, and lemon juice. The risottos prepared al dente in the traditional northern Italian style are the finest on the island, especially the one made with seafood and herbs. The cold and hot appetizers are virtual meals unto themselves, with such favorites as grilled polenta with sausages or fresh clams and mussels simmered in herb-flavored tomato broth.

In the San Juan Marriott Resort, Av. Ashford 1309. ℂ **787/722-7000.** Reservations recommended. Main courses $19.50–$34. AE, DC, DISC, MC, V. Daily 6–11pm. Bus: B21.

MODERATE

Most main courses in the restaurants below are at the low end of the price scale. These restaurants each have only two or three dishes that are expensive, almost invariably involving shellfish.

Cherry Blossom JAPANESE   Set on the street level of the San Juan Marriott, with direct access to the busy pedestrian traffic of Avenida Ashford, this is one of the genuinely charming Japanese restaurants of the Condado. There are sections devoted to sushi, including a long bar where you can view the fish available that day, and to teppanyaki, where a corps of carefully trained chefs will fast-sear your meal on a sizzling griddle in front of you. The staff is charming, the food excellent.

In the San Juan Marriott Resort, Av. Ashford 1309. ℂ **787/723-7300.** Reservations recommended. Main courses $11.75–$22.50 at lunch, $18.50–$42.50 at dinner. AE, DC, MC, V. Mon–Sat 12:30–3pm and 5:30–11pm; Sun 1–11pm. Bus: B21.

Luigi's ✰✰ ITALIAN/GENOVESE   There's a formal and even romantic atmosphere here at night. When chef-owner Luigi Sanguineti came to Puerto Rico from Genoa in the late 1980s, he liked the place so much he decided to bring "a little bit of Genoa" to the old town. After gaining a reputation as one of the island's foremost European chefs, Luigi finally opened his own place in 2000. Since then he's been delighting the palates of locals and visitors with high-quality Italian cuisine. Try the gnocchi with pesto or the eggplant lasagna, and perhaps start with a savory antipasto prepared by Luigi himself. His lobster ravioli is San Juan's finest, and another dish we like a lot is the shrimp risotto.

104 Diez de Andino. ⓒ **787/977-0134.** Reservations recommended. Main courses $10–$22. AE, MC, V. Mon–Sat noon–10pm; Sun noon–5pm. Bus: B5.

Piacere NORTHERN ITALIAN   Its decor and the brisk efficiency of its staff might remind you of a neighborhood trattoria in New York City, and, in fact, Piacere has become the preferred neighborhood restaurant of many Condado residents who hail from New York. It's one of the most popular places around for pasta because of its low prices and simple but down-to-earth food. Menu items include savory seafood pasta, grilled meat, an especially good veal steak, and a fresh fish of the day. The antipasti is a good bet, as is the carpaccio of salmon.

Av. Ashford 1104. ⓒ **787/723-6876.** Main courses $15–$29. AE, DC, MC, V. Daily 6–11pm. Bus: B21 or C10.

Urdin ✰✰ PUERTO RICAN/INTERNATIONAL   Urdin is proud of its reputation as one of the capital's bright young restaurants. It occupies a low-slung, stucco-covered house set near a slew of competitors. Inside, a fanciful decor of postmodern, Caribbean-inspired accents and metal sculptures brings a touch of Latino New York. Popularity has brought an unexpected development to this highly visible restaurant: The bar is almost more popular than the food. Consequently, you're likely to find the bar area jam-packed every day between 6 and 10pm. Cliquish, heterosexual, and fashionable, some of this crowd eventually gravitates toward the tables. Yes, that was Ricky Martin we spotted here one evening. Filled with authentic Spanish flavor that's not necessarily geared to the palates of timid diners, the food is innovative, flavorful, strong, and earthy. For starters, there are baby eels Bilbaina style and Castilian lentil soup. Main courses include fresh filet of salmon in mustard sauce, filet of fish "Hollywood style" (with onions, raisins, and mango slices, served in white wine sauce), and rack of lamb with orange sauce. One always-pleasing dish is piquillo peppers stuffed with seafood mousse and black-olive sauce. Savvy locals finish their meal with a slice of sweet-potato cheesecake. The staff can put a damper on (if they're sulky) or enhance (if they're welcoming) a meal here.

Av. Magdalena 1105. ⓒ **787/724-0420.** Reservations recommended. Main courses $14–$27. AE, MC, V. Mon–Sat noon–3pm and 6–11pm. Bus: A7.

Zabó ✰ INTERNATIONAL   This restaurant enjoys citywide fame, thanks to its blend of bucolic charm and superb innovative food. It's set in a dignified villa that provides some low-rise dignity in a sea of skyscraping condos. The creative force here is owner and chef/culinary director Paul Carroll, who built the place from its origins as a simple deli into one of the most sought-after restaurants on the Condado. Menu items fuse the cuisines of the Mediterranean, the Pacific Rim, and the Caribbean into a collection that includes dishes such as blinis stuffed with medallions of lobster with ginger, thyme, and beurre blanc; carpaccio of salmon with mesclun salad and balsamic vinegar; and baked chorizo stuffed with mushrooms, sherry, paprika, and cheddar. The black-bean soup is among the very best in Puerto Rico, served with parboiled cloves of garlic marinated in olive oil that melt in your mouth like candy.

Calle Candina 14 (entrance is via an alleyway leading from Av. Ashford between avs. Washington and Cervantes). (C) **787/725-9494.** Reservations recommended. Main courses $8.75–$29 at lunch, $20–$29 at dinner. AE, MC, V. Tues–Wed 6–10pm; Thurs–Sat 6–11pm; Fri noon–3pm. Bus: A7.

INEXPENSIVE

Café del Angel CREOLE/PUERTO RICAN   Don't come here for the decor. The juice bar up front looks like it was transported from Miami's Flagler Street in 1950, and the plastic green furniture won't compel you to get *Architectual Digest* on the phone. If indeed there is an "angel," as the cafe's name suggests, it is in the kitchen. The chef serves remarkably good food at affordable prices. The place has been in operation for more than a decade. Paintings and figures of its namesake angels decorate the dining room. Some 100 hungry diners can be fed here at one time, in a relaxed atmosphere that is welcoming and friendly. The service is also efficient. Prepare for some real island flavor, as in the traditional *mofongo relleno con camarones,* which is sautéed, mashed plantain with shrimp. You can order a generous helping of tender beefsteak sautéed with onions and peppers or a perfectly grilled chicken. *Pastel,* a kind of creamy polenta of cornmeal, is served with many dishes, and the fresh garlic bread is complimentary.

Av. Ashford 1106. (C) **787/643-7594.** Reservations not necessary. Breakfast $4; main courses $7–$20. MC, V. Wed–Mon 10am–10pm. Bus: 21.

Café Mezzanine INTERNATIONAL   This comfortable and cozy eatery for many years was the most famous Howard Johnson's in the Caribbean. It attracts some of the most prestigious politicians and financiers (many luminaries live nearby and consider it their neighborhood diner). Depending on the time of day, you can be served pancakes, omelets, muffins, hash browns, and sausages; or you can order lunch and dinner foods like fish fries, teriyaki steaks, clam platters, and an array of sandwiches and burgers, as well as typical Puerto Rican dishes.

In the Radisson Ambassador Plaza Hotel, Av. Ashford 1369. (C) **787/721-7300.** Reservations not necessary. Breakfast $10–$15; main courses $14–$18. AE, MC, V. Mon–Thurs 6:30am–2pm and 5–11pm; Fri–Sun 6:30am–11pm. Bus: B21 or C10.

Cielito Lindo *Value* MEXICAN   One of the most likable things about this restaurant is the way it retains low prices and an utter lack of pretension, despite the expensive Condado real estate that surrounds it. Something about it might remind you of a low-slung house in Puebla, Mexico, home of owner Jaime Pandal, who maintains a vigilant position from a perch at the cash register. Walls are outfitted with an intriguing mix of Mexican arts and crafts and ads for popular tequilas and beer. None of the selections has changed since the restaurant was founded, a policy that long-term clients find reassuring. The place is mobbed, especially on weekends, with those looking for heaping portions of well-prepared, standardized Mexican food. Examples include fajitas of steak or chicken; strips of filet steak sautéed with green peppers and onions, covered with tomatoes and spicy gravy; enchiladas of chicken or cheese, covered with cheese and served with sour cream; and several kinds of tacos.

Av. Magdalena 1108. (C) **787/723-5597.** Reservations recommended for dinner. Main courses $8–$16.50. AE, MC, V. Mon–Sat 11am–10:30pm. Bus: B21 or C10.

Don Andrés MEXICAN   Set on a prominent street corner in the Condado, this venue includes big tables, paper tablecloths, bright lights, and a connection with the busy street life of the Condado. Some of its panache derives from potent drinks, including seven kinds of margaritas, and live presentations of Mexican music every Thursday and Saturday from 7:30pm to midnight and every Friday from 9:30pm to midnight. Standard menu items include tacos, nachos, enchiladas, chimichangas, and beef or chicken tortillas, all served with traditional garnishes. The owner, your host, is Armando (Andrés) Ramos.

Av. Ashford 1350. ✆ 787/723-0222. Reservations not necessary. Main courses $7.75–$16.75. AE, MC, V. Tues–Sat 11:30am–midnight; Sun–Mon 5pm–midnight. Bus: A7.

Tony Roma's BARBECUE   Efficient and unpretentious, this is Puerto Rico's busiest branch of the international chain and one of the least expensive restaurants in the Condado. It's well appreciated for its spicy barbecued food (the honey barbecue is not too fiery). Menu items include a wide range of barbecued dishes, such as chicken and several varieties of ribs, as well as hamburgers and the famous Tony Roma onion ring loaf. The most expensive item in the house, a combination platter containing several kinds of ribs with all the fixings, is a meal in itself that's a particularly good value in this high-priced neighborhood.

In the Condado Plaza Hotel, Av. Ashford 999. ✆ 787/721-1000, ext. 2623. Reservations not accepted. Main courses $8–$20. AE, MC, V. Daily noon–midnight. Bus: A5, A7, or B10.

Via Appia ✦ PIZZA/ITALIAN   A favorite of *Sanjuaneros* visiting Condado for the day, Via Appia offers food that's sometimes praiseworthy. Its pizzas are the best in the neighborhood. The chef's signature pizza, Via Appia, is a savory pie made with sausages, onions, mushrooms, pepperoni, green peppers, cheese, and spices. Vegetarians also have a pizza to call their own (made with wholewheat dough, eggplant, mushrooms, green peppers, onions, tomatoes, and cheese). There's even a pizza with meatballs. Savory pasta dishes, including baked ziti, lasagna, and spaghetti, are also prepared with several of your favorite sauces. All of this can be washed down with sangria. During the day, freshly made salads and sandwiches are also available.

Av. Ashford 1350. ✆ 787/725-8711. Pizza and main courses $9–$16. AE, MC, V. Mon–Fri 11am–11pm; Sat–Sun 11am–midnight. Bus: A5.

6 Miramar

For the locations of restaurants in Miramar, see the map "Puerta de Tierra, Miramar, Condado & Ocean Park Accommodations & Dining" on p. 89.

Augusto's Cuisine ✦✦✦ FRENCH/INTERNATIONAL   With its European flair, this is one of the most elegant and glamorous restaurants in Puerto Rico. Austrian-born owner/chef Augusto Schreiner, assisted by a partly Frenchborn staff, operates from a gray and green dining room set on the lobby level of a 15-story hotel in Miramar. Menu items are concocted from strictly fresh ingredients, including such dishes as lobster risotto; rack of lamb with aromatic herbs and fresh garlic; an oft-changing cream-based soup of the day (one of the best is corn and fresh oyster soup); and a succulent version of medallions of veal Rossini style, prepared with foie gras and Madeira sauce. The wine list is one of the most extensive on the island.

In the Hotel Excelsior, Av. Ponce de León 801. ✆ 787/725-7700. Reservations recommended. Main courses $24–$36. AE, MC, V. Tues–Fri noon–3pm; Tues–Sat 7–9:30pm. Bus: B1 or A5.

Chayote's ✦ PUERTO RICAN/INTERNATIONAL   The cuisine of this restaurant is among the most innovative in San Juan. It draws local business leaders, government officials, and celebs like Sylvester Stallone and Melanie Griffith.

It's an artsy, modern, basement-level bistro in a surprisingly obscure hotel (the Olimpo). The restaurant changes its menu every three months, but you might find appetizers like a yucca turnover stuffed with crabmeat and served with mango and papaya chutney, or ripe plantain stuffed with chicken and served with fresh tomato sauce. For a main dish, you might try red snapper filet with citrus vinaigrette made of passion fruit, orange, and lemon. An exotic touch appears in the pork filet seasoned with dried fruits and spices in tamarind sauce and served with green banana and taro root timbale. To finish off your meal, there's nothing better than the mango flan served with macerated strawberries.

In the Olimpo Hotel, Av. Miramar 603. © 787/722-9385. Reservations recommended. Main courses $21–$28. AE, MC, V. Tues–Fri noon–2:30pm; Tues–Sat 7–10:30pm. Bus: B5.

7 Santurce & Ocean Park

For the locations of restaurants in Santurce and Ocean Park, see the map "Puerta de Tierra, Miramar, Condado & Ocean Park Accommodations & Dining" on p. 89.

VERY EXPENSIVE

La Casona ⊛ SPANISH/INTERNATIONAL   In a turn-of-the-20th-century mansion surrounded by gardens, La Casona offers the kind of dining usually found in Madrid, complete with a strolling guitarist. The much-renovated but still charming place draws some of the most fashionable diners in Puerto Rico. Paella marinara, prepared for two or more, is a specialty, as is *zarzuela de mariscos* (seafood medley). Or you might select filet of grouper in Basque sauce, octopus vinaigrette, osso buco, or rack of lamb. Grilled red snapper is a specialty, and you can order it with almost any sauce you want, although the chef recommends one made from olive oil, herbs, lemon, and toasted garlic. The cuisine here has both flair and flavor.

Calle San Jorge 609 (at the corner of Av. Fernández Juncos). © 787/727-2717. Reservations required. Main courses $17–$48. AE, DC, MC, V. Mon–Fri noon–3pm; Mon–Sat 6–11pm. Bus: 1.

Pikayo ⊛⊛⊛ PUERTO RICAN/CAJUN   This is an ideal place to go for the new generation of Puerto Rican cookery, with a touch of Cajun thrown in for spice and zest. This place not only keeps up with the latest culinary trends, but it often sets them, thanks to the inspired guidance of owner and celebrity chef Wilo Benet. Formal but not stuffy, and winner of more culinary awards than virtually any other restaurant in Puerto Rico, Pikayo is a specialist in the criolla cuisine of the colonial age, emphasizing the Spanish, Indian, and African elements in its unusual recipes. Appetizers include a dazzling array of taste explosions: Try shrimp spring rolls with peanut sofrito sauce; crab cake with aioli; or perhaps a ripe plantain, goat cheese, and onion tart. Main course delights feature charred rare yellowfin tuna with onion *escabeche* and red snapper filet with sweet potato purée served with foie gras butter. Our favorite remains the grilled shrimp with polenta and barbecue sauce made with guava.

Museum of Art of Puerto Rico, Av. José de Diego 299. © 787/721-6194. Reservations recommended. Main courses $29–$34; fixed-price menus $65. AE, DC, MC, V. Tues–Sun noon–3pm; Tues–Sat 6–11pm. Closed 2 weeks in Dec–Jan. Bus: M2, A7, or T1.

EXPENSIVE

Pamela's ⊛ CARIBBEAN FUSION   A sense of cachet and style is very pronounced at this restaurant, a fact that's somewhat surprising considering its out-of-the-way location. Part of its allure derives from a sophisticated blend of Caribbean cuisines that combines local ingredients with Puerto Rican flair and a sense of New York style. Menu items include a salad that marries vine-ripened and oven-roasted tomatoes, each drizzled with a roasted-garlic–and-cilantro vinaigrette; club sandwiches stuffed with barbecued shrimp and cilantro-flavored mayonnaise; plantain-encrusted crab cakes with a spicy tomato-herb emulsion; and grilled island-spiced pork loin served with guava glaze and fresh local fruits. Beer and any of a wide array of party-colored drinks go well with this food.

In the Número 1 Guest House, Calle Santa Ana 1, Ocean Park. © 787/726-5010. Reservations recommended. Sandwiches and salads at lunch $10–$14; main course platters $20–$29. AE, MC, V. Daily noon–3pm and 7–10:30pm. Bus: A5.

INEXPENSIVE

Café Madrid *Finds* PUERTO RICAN   Come here to escape from the gloss and sheen of big-city, big-money tourism. Local residents promote this simple diner for its sense of workaday conviviality and low, low prices. Located on a narrow but busy street in a congested commercial neighborhood of Ocean Park, this joint has a battered facade with plastic lettering—signs that the inside is going to be very tacky. At first glance, that's partially true. But if you retain a sense of humor, you might begin to appreciate the Formica bar tops, rows of mismatched refrigerators, big-lettered menus over sizzling deep-fat fryers, and the kind of industrial accessories that Andy Warhol might have appreciated or even collected. It's been the domain of the Molina family since the 1930s, and the food has changed very little since then. Examples include roasted pork, sold either as a full-size meal platter or stuffed into a sandwich; several kinds of asopao and *carne frita* (fried meat); lasagna; and lots of empanadas. Roasted chicken, the signature dish, is an ongoing favorite.

Calle Loiza 100 (at the corner of Calle Las Flores). © 787/728-5250. Reservations not accepted. Breakfast platters $3.25–$6; sandwiches $2.50–$5; lunch and dinner main courses $5–$10. MC, V. Daily 6am–10pm. Bus: B5 or T1.

Don Tello ★ *Finds* PUERTO RICAN   Right at the Santurce Market Square (Plaza del Mercado), this is a family-run restaurant serving an authentic criolla cuisine. All the locals call the owners, Jorge and Rosin, by their first names. In a casual atmosphere, diners dress informally, eat well, and don't pay a lot of money for the privilege. The service is excellent, and the ingredients are fresh and well prepared. The fish tastes among the freshest in San Juan. We've enjoyed the filet of sea bass in a plantain sauce, or a well-seasoned whole roasted sea bass. Grilled filet of mahimahi is another one of our favorites, as is the grilled filet of hake. You can also enjoy the traditional asopao of Puerto Rico, made with chicken, shrimp, lobster, or shellfish. A savory chicken stew is also served, as is a tender filet of steak roasted with onions.

18 Dos Hermanos, Santurce. © 787/724-5752. Reservations required. Main courses $6–$13. AE, DISC, MC, V. Mon 11am–5pm; Tues–Sat 11am–10pm. Bus: 1.

Dunbar's INTERNATIONAL   Sprawling over at least five distinctly different dining and drinking areas, this is the busiest, most active, and most legendary bar and pub in Ocean Park. Painted an arresting shade of tangerine, it was established in 1982. The best way to navigate the labyrinth of Dunbar's is to wander through its various spaces: A large-screen TV room on the second floor attracts a macho, mostly North American crowd; a ground-floor pool room appeals to a deceptively affluent crowd of Spanish-speaking lawyers and doctors; and the various bars and cubbyholes ripple with possibilities for making friends or influencing your romantic destiny. Well-prepared menu items, each conceived by California-born veteran chef Trent Eichler, pour out of the busy kitchens. Examples include thick sandwiches (Spanish chorizo sausage with roasted peppers is an ongoing favorite), omelets, pastas, and juicy steaks. French fries are made from vitamin-rich yams and conventional potatoes. Favorite drinks include (what else?) Sex on the Beach and lots of margaritas. Dunbar's was named, incidentally, after a particularly eccentric character in Joseph Heller's *Catch-22.*

Av. McLeary 1954. ℂ 787/728-2920. Reservations required Fri and Sun. Burgers and sandwiches $8.50–$12.50; main courses $11–$24. AE, DC, MC, V. Mon–Thurs 11:30am–midnight; Fri 11:30am–1am; Sat 5pm–1am; Sun 10am–2pm. Bus: A5 or A7.

Repostería Kassalta *Value* SPANISH/PUERTO RICAN This is the most widely known of San Juan's cafeterias/bakeries/delicatessens. You'll enter a cavernous room flanked with sun-flooded windows and endless ranks of display cases filled with meats, sausages, and pastries appropriate to the season. Patrons line up to place their orders at a cash register, then carry their selections to one of the many tables. Knowledge of Spanish is helpful but not essential. Among the selections are steaming bowls of Puerto Rico's best caldo gallego, a hearty soup laden with collard greens, potatoes, and sausage slices, served in thick earthenware bowls with hunks of bread. Also popular are Cuban sandwiches (sliced pork, cheese, and fried bread), steak sandwiches, a savory octopus salad, and an assortment of perfectly cooked omelets. Paella Valenciano is a Sunday favorite.

Av. McLeary 1966. ℂ 787/727-7340. Reservations not accepted. Full American breakfast $3.50–$5; soups $3–$6; sandwiches $4–$5.50; platters $4.75–$11. AE, DC, MC, V. Daily 6am–10pm. Bus: A5.

8 Near Ocean Park

For the locations of these restaurants, see the map "Puerta de Tierra, Miramar, Condado & Ocean Park Accommodations & Dining" on p. 89.

Che's ARGENTINE/ITALIAN/INTERNATIONAL Named after the Latino revolutionary Che Guevara, this place re-creates some of the color and drama of the Argentine pampas. It's about 2 miles (3km) east of Condado's resorts. Many of the specialties are grilled in the style preferred by cowherding gauchos. If you're not in the mood for highly seasoned flank steak or any of the grilled meats, you can choose from a variety of pastas and veal dishes. The meats here are very tender and well flavored.

Calle Caoba 35. ℂ 787/726-7202. Reservations recommended for lunch, required for dinner. Main courses $13–$25. AE, DC, MC, V. Sun–Thurs noon–11pm; Fri–Sat noon–midnight. Bus: M7.

Moments **Picnic Fare & Where to Eat It**

Puerto Rico is usually ideal for picnicking year-round. The best place to fill a picnic basket is the **Repostería Kassalta** (see above), a cafeteria/bakery/deli with lots of goodies. Puerto Rican families often come here to order delicacies for their Sunday outings. The best places for a picnic are **Muñoz Marín Park,** along Las Américas Expressway, west of Avenida Piñro, and the **Botanical Gardens** operated by the University of Puerto Rico in the Río Piedras section.

La Casita Blanca ★ (Finds) CREOLE/PUERTO RICAN   Island politicians are said to have the best noses for good home cooking. We don't know if that is true or not, but one of their favorite places is this eatery. Governors or governor wannabes also come here to order excellent regional fare. This is a converted family home that opened its door to diners in the mid-1980s, and it's been a favorite of locals from all walks of Puerto Rican society ever since. In a popular barrio, it is off the tourist trail and best reached by taxi. You'll need to make a reservation for lunch but should have no trouble finding a table at dinner. The traditional Creole menu includes such delights as *guisado y arroz con gandule* (beef stew with rice and small beans), or *bacalao* (salt codfish with yucca). Guaranteed to put hair on your chest is *patita* (pig's trotters in a Creole sauce). Veal with sautéed onions is popular, as is grilled red snapper or the chicken fricassee. A typical chicken asopao, a soupy rice stew, is also served. Fried plantains, rice, and beans come with most dishes.

Calle Tapía 351. ℂ 787/726-5501. Reservations recommended at lunch. Main courses $7–$17; Sun buffet $10–$12. MC, V. Mon–Thurs 11:30am–7pm; Fri–Sat 11:30am–10pm; Sun noon–5pm. Bus: C11.

9 Isla Verde

For the locations of restaurants in Isla Verde, see the map "Isla Verde Accommodations & Dining" on p. 99.

VERY EXPENSIVE

La Piccola Fontana ★★★ NORTHERN ITALIAN   Right off the luxurious Palm Court in the Wyndham El San Juan Hotel, this restaurant takes classic northern Italian cuisine seriously and delivers plate after plate of delectable food nightly. From its white linen to its classically formal service, it enjoys a fine reputation. The food is straightforward, generous, and extremely well prepared. You'll dine in one of two neo-Palladian rooms whose wall frescoes depict Italy's ruins and landscapes. Menu items range from the appealingly simple—such as grilled filets of fish or grilled veal chops—to more elaborate dishes—such as *tortellini San Daniele*, made with veal, prosciutto, cream, and sage; and *linguine scogliere*, with shrimp, clams, and other seafood. Grilled medallions of filet mignon are served with braised arugula, Parmesan cheese, and balsamic vinegar.

In Wyndham El San Juan Hotel & Casino, Av. Isla Verde 6063. ℂ 787/791-0966. Reservations required. Main courses $29–$40. AE, DC, MC, V. Daily 6–11pm. Bus: M7.

The Palm ★★ STEAK/SEAFOOD   The management of San Juan's most elegant hotel invited the Palm, a legendary New York steakhouse, to open a branch on the premises. The setting includes a stylish, masculine-looking saloon, where drinks are stiff, and a dining room with artfully simple linen-covered tables and caricatures of local personalities. If you've hit it big at the nearby casino, maybe you'll want to celebrate with the Palm's famous and famously pricey lobster. Otherwise, there's a tempting number of options, all served in gargantuan portions: jumbo lump crabmeat cocktail, Caesar salad, lamb chops with mint sauce, grilled halibut steak, prime porterhouse steak, and steak "a la stone," which finishes cooking on a sizzling platter directly atop your table. One thing is certain—you'll never go hungry here.

In Wyndham El San Juan Hotel & Casino, Av. Isla Verde 6063. ℂ 787/791-1000. Reservations recommended. Main courses $18–$37, except lobster, which is priced by the lb. and can easily cost $21 per lb. AE, DC, MC, V. Daily 6–10pm. Bus: M7.

Ruth's Chris Steak House ✿✿ STEAK   This Puerto Rican branch of one of the most famous steakhouse chains in the world presents macho food, especially steaks that are among the best beef dishes in San Juan. It obsessively focuses on big drinks and big steaks, grilled in the simplest possible way—usually just with salt, pepper, and a brush-over of butter. These are served within two dark blue, mahogany-trimmed dining rooms, separated by a saloon-style bar.

You might begin with barbecued shrimp, mushrooms stuffed with crabmeat, or seared ahi tuna. Or you might opt for a salad as an appetizer. Portions are large and very filling. Steaks are the finest from the U.S. cattle country. Examples include rib-eyes, veal chops, porterhouse, New York strips, and filet mignons. There's also roasted chicken, lobster, and a fresh catch of the day.

In the Inter-Continental San Juan Resort & Casino, Av. Isla Grande 187. ✆ 787/253-1717. Reservations recommended. Main courses $26–$50. AE, DC, MC, V. Daily 6pm–midnight. Bus: M7.

The Vineyard Room ✿✿✿ CALIFORNIA/MEDITERRANEAN   Within the realm of haute cuisine served with impeccable European credentials, this is the finest restaurant in San Juan. The Vineyard Room duplicates the gourmet citadels of Italy and France more accurately than any other restaurant in Puerto Rico, thanks to a staff of culinary luminaries spearheaded by Philippe Trosch, a prize catch that Ritz-Carlton worked hard to get. The wait staff is the best trained in Puerto Rico. The wine-tasting menus, either four or five courses, are the best on the island. The wine list is superb, with both whites and reds from the Continent, as well as a strong emphasis on California wines. For the exotic, there are bottles from Chile, South Africa, and Australia. You can select innovative appetizers like potato cannelloni filled with Caribbean lobster risotto, or a summer salad of cavallion melon, serrano ham, mozzarella, and olive pesto with ciabatta toast. The main courses are equally appealing: Try Nantucket sea bass with barley tapenade and black olive sabayon, or apple-smoked rabbit with cannellini bean mash. You might precede (or end) an experience here at the bar, where the dark paneling and deep leather seats emulate an Edwardian-era men's club in London.

In the Ritz-Carlton San Juan Hotel, Spa & Casino, 6961 State Rd. #187, Isla Verde, Carolina. ✆ 787/253-1700. Reservations required. Main courses $34–$37. Fixed-price menus $45, $55, $65, $75. AE, DC, MC, V. Daily 6–10pm. Bus: M7.

EXPENSIVE

Back Street Hong Kong ✿ MANDARIN/SZECHUAN/HUNAN   To reach this restaurant, you head down a re-creation of a backwater street in Hong Kong—disassembled from its original home at the 1964 New York World's Fair, and rebuilt here with its original design intact. A few steps later, you enter one of the best Chinese restaurants in the Caribbean, serving consistently good food, filled with fragrance and flavor. Beneath a soaring redwood ceiling, you can enjoy pineapple fried rice served in a pineapple, scallops with orange sauce, Szechuan beef with chicken, or Dragon and Phoenix (lobster with shrimp).

In Wyndham El San Juan Hotel & Casino, Av. Isla Verde 6063. ✆ 787/791-1000, ext. 1758. Reservations recommended. Main courses $18–$29. AE, MC, V. Mon–Sat 5pm–midnight; Sun 1pm–midnight. Bus: M7.

Yamato ✿ JAPANESE   The artfully simple decor at Yamato shows the kind of modern urban minimalism that you might expect in an upscale California restaurant. Separate sections offer conventional seating at tables; at a countertop within view of a sushi display; or at seats around a hot grill where chefs shake, rattle, and sizzle their way through a fast but elaborate cooking ritual. Many visitors include at least some sushi with an entree such as beef sashimi with tataki

---

Kids Family-Friendly Restaurants

Palmera (p. 120)   The Sunday brunch here—which is half price for children—is an all-you-can-eat buffet. There's even a clown on hand to keep the kids entertained.

Hard Rock Cafe (p. 117)   The local branch of this international chain is a sure-fire hit with kids. The burgers are pretty good.

Butterfly People Café (p. 116)   Children love eating lunch in this fantasy world of mounted butterflies. A favorite drink is the Fantasia—a frappé made from seven fresh fruits.

Ciao Mediterranean Café (p. 132)   Right on the beach, this is a family favorite that offers some of the best pizzas and pastas at Isla Verde. Prices are affordable, too.

---

sauce, shrimp tempura with noodle soup, filet mignon or chicken with shrimp or scallops, or several kinds of rice and noodle dishes.

In Wyndham El San Juan Hotel & Casino, Av. Isla Verde 6063. ✆ 787/791-1000. Reservations recommended. Sushi $2.25–$3 per piece; sushi and teppanyaki dinners $24–$40. AE, MC, V. Daily 6pm–midnight. Bus: M7.

MODERATE

Momoyama ✿ JAPANESE   Few other restaurants in Isla Verde are as indelibly associated with one dish: sushi pizza. The subject of rave reviews, it's made by deep-frying compressed rice into something akin to a pizza shell, which is layered with rows of salmon or tuna and garnished with fish roe, shaved ginger, and make-your-eyes-water wasabi. If you prefer your food cooked, you can head for one of several teppanyaki tables, where food is fast-cooked in front of you as part of a highly theatrical culinary show. Choices include chicken teriyaki with shrimp, soy-and-ginger chicken with filet mignon, and several kinds of tempura.

In the Inter-Continental San Juan Resort & Casino, Av. Isla Grande 187. ✆ 787/791-8883. Reservations recommended. Fixed-price lunches $8–$19; lunch and dinner main courses $19–$35. AE, MC, V. Mon–Fri noon–3pm and 5:30–11:30pm; Sat 5:30–11pm; Sun 1–11:30pm. Bus: M7.

Outback Steakhouse *Value* STEAK   This Puerto Rican branch of the two-fisted, Australian-themed restaurant chain occupies a dark-paneled room with booths positioned around a prominent bar area. Here you can study memorabilia devoted to the Land Down Under while ordering such drinks as a genuinely delicious Wallabee Darn. There's a simple steak-and-potato-with-salad special priced at $14, a cost-conscious meal in itself. But more appealing are some of the chain's signature dishes, such as a Bloomin' Onion (a batter-dipped deep-fried onion that fans out from its platter like a demented lotus and tastes delicious with beer); at least four kinds of steaks, including filet mignon; fish, including mahimahi and salmon; and our favorite of the lot, Alice Springs chicken, a breast of chicken layered with bacon, mushrooms, and cheese, and served with honey-mustard sauce and french fries.

In the Embassy Suites Hotel & Casino, Calle José M. Tartak 8000. ✆ 787/791-4679. Reservations not accepted. Main courses $14–$23. AE, MC, V. Mon–Thurs 5:30–10:30pm; Fri–Sat 5:30pm–midnight; Sun 3–10pm. Bus: M7.

The Ranch AMERICAN/STEAK   When the very posh Wyndham El San Juan Hotel carved out a space for this irreverent, tongue-in-cheek eatery on its top (10th) floor, it was viewed as a radical departure from an otherwise grand collection of in-house restaurants. The result is likely to make you smile, especially if you have roots anywhere west of Ohio. You'll be greeted with a hearty "Howdy, partner" and the jangling of spurs from a crew of denim-clad cowboys as you enter a replica of a corral in the North American West. Banquettes and barstools are upholstered in faux cowhide; the decor is appropriately macho and rough-textured, and even the cowgirls on duty are likely to lasso anyone they find particularly appealing. The cowboys sing as they serve your steaks, barbecued ribs, country-fried steaks, Tex-Mex fajitas, and enchiladas. Food that's a bit less beefy includes seared red snapper with a cilantro-laced pico de gallo sauce. Especially succulent are soft-shell crabs layered in a pyramid with blue and yellow tortillas. And if you want to buy a souvenir pair of cowboy spurs, you'll find an intriguing collection of western accessories and uniforms for sale outside. Consider beginning your meal with any of 20 kinds of tequila cocktails at the Tequila Bar, which lies a few steps away, on the same floor.

In Wyndham El San Juan Hotel & Casino, Av. Isla Verde 6063. © 787/791-1000. Reservations recommended at dinner Fri–Sat, otherwise not necessary. Main courses $16.25–$34.25. AE, DC, DISC, MC, V. Sun–Thurs 5:30–11pm; Fri–Sat 5:30pm–midnight. Bus: M7.

INEXPENSIVE

Ciao Mediterranean Café ★★ *Kids* MEDITERRANEAN   This is the most charming restaurant in Isla Verde, and it is one of our enduring favorites. It's draped with bougainvillea and set directly on the sands, attracting both hotel guests and locals wandering in barefoot from the beach. The visual centerpiece is an open-air kitchen set within an oval-shaped bar. A crew of cheerfully animated chefs mingle good culinary technique with Latino theatricality.

Pizzas and pastas are popular here, and even more appealing are such dishes as seafood salad, wherein shrimp, scallops, calamari, peppers, onions, and lime juice create something you might expect in the south of Italy. *Kalamarakia tiganita*, (Greek-style squid) consisting of battered and deep-fried squid served with ratatouille and spicy marinara sauce; rack of lamb with ratatouille, polenta, and Provençal herbs; and a mixed grill of seafood are evocative of what you'd expect in Marseilles, thanks to the roe-enhanced aioli and couscous. Compared to most of the restaurants around here, this cafe serves lighter fare that kids go for, especially in its selection of pizzas and pastas. The desserts are also some of the most luscious at Isla Verde, especially the ice cream.

Inter-Continental San Juan Grand Resort & Casino, Av. Isla Grande 187. © 787/791-5000. Reservations recommended for dinner. Breakfast $5–$8; pizzas and salads $8–$17; main courses $16–$25. AE, MC, V. Daily 6:30am–10pm. Bus: M7.

Metropol CUBAN/PUERTO RICAN/INTERNATIONAL   This is part of a restaurant chain known for serving the island's best Cuban food, although the chefs prepare a much wider range of dishes. Metropol is the happiest blend of Cuban and Puerto Rican cuisine we've ever had. The black-bean soup is among the island's finest, served in the classic Havana style with a side dish of rice and chopped onions. Endless garlic bread accompanies most dinners, including Cornish game hen stuffed with Cuban rice and beans or perhaps marinated steak topped with a fried egg (reportedly Castro's favorite). Smoked chicken and chicken fried steak are also heartily recommended; portions are huge. Plantains,

---

---

yucca, and all that good stuff accompany most dishes. Finish with a choice of thin or firm custard. Most dishes are at the low end of the price scale.

Av. Isla Verde. (🕐 **787/791-4046.** Main courses $7–$29. AE, MC, V. Daily 11:30am–10:30pm. Bus: C41, B42, or A5.

Panadería España Repostería SANDWICHES   The Panadería España makes San Juan's definitive Cuban sandwich—a cheap meal all on its own. The biggest sandwich weighs 3 pounds. Drinks and coffee are dispensed from behind a much-used bar. You can purchase an assortment of gourmet items from Spain, arranged as punctuation marks on shelves set against an otherwise all-white decor. The place has been serving simple breakfasts, drinks, coffee, and Cuban sandwiches virtually every day since it opened around 1970.

Centro Comercial Villamar, Marginal Baldoriti de Castro. (🕐 **787/727-3860.** Reservations not necessary. Soups and tapas $4–$5; sandwiches $4.50–$8.50. AE, DISC, MC, V. Daily 6am–10pm. Bus: B21 or C10.

6

Exploring San Juan

The Spanish began to settle in the area now known as Old San Juan around 1521. At the outset, the city was called Puerto Rico ("Rich Port"), and the whole island was known as San Juan.

The streets are narrow and teeming with traffic, but a walk through Old San Juan—in Spanish, *El Viejo San Juan*—is like a stroll through 5 centuries of history. You can do it in less than a day (see "Walking Tour: Old San Juan" later in this chapter). In this historic 7-square-block area of the western side of the city, you can see many of Puerto Rico's chief sightseeing attractions and do some shopping along the way.

On the other hand, you might want to plop down on the sand with a drink or get outside and play. "Diving, Fishing, Tennis & Other Outdoor Pursuits" later in this chapter, describes the beaches and sports in the San Juan area.

1 Seeing the Sights

SUGGESTED ITINERARIES

In case you would like to drag yourself away from the beach, here are some suggestions for how to see San Juan.

If You Have 1 Day

To make the most of a short stay, head straight for Old San Juan for an afternoon of sightseeing and shopping. Definitely schedule a visit to El Morro Fortress. Try to spend 2 hours at Condado Beach. Enjoy a Puerto Rican dinner at a local restaurant, listen to some salsa music, and enjoy a rum punch before retiring for the night.

If You Have 2 Days

On your first day, spend the morning shopping and sightseeing in Old San Juan. Schedule visits to El Morro and San Juan Cathedral and then relax on Condado Beach for the rest of the day. Enjoy a Puerto Rican dinner and some local music before retiring.

On your second day, spend the morning exploring El Yunque rain forest, a lush 28,000-acre site east of San Juan. Schedule 2 or 3 hours at nearby Luquillo Beach, the finest beach in Puerto Rico. Buy lunch from an open-air kiosk. Return to San Juan for the evening, and attend either a folk-culture show (if available) or a Las Vegas–style revue. Visit the casinos for some action before retiring.

We have outlined a walking tour of Old San Juan later in this chapter, but here is an introduction to some of the sights mentioned there, as well as others you might want to seek out.

FORTS

Castillo de San Felipe del Morro ★ *Kids*   Called "El Morro," this fort stands on a rocky promontory dominating the entrance to San Juan Bay.

Constructed in 1540, the original fort was a round tower, which can still be seen deep inside the lower levels of the castle. More walls and cannon-firing positions were added, and by 1787, the fortification attained the complex design you see today. This fortress was attacked repeatedly by both the English and the Dutch.

The U.S. National Park Service protects the fortifications of Old San Juan, which have been declared a World Heritage Site by the United Nations. With some of the most dramatic views in the Caribbean, you'll find El Morro an intriguing labyrinth of dungeons, barracks, vaults, lookouts, and ramps. Historical and background information is provided in a video in English and Spanish. The nearest parking is the underground facility beneath the Quincentennial Plaza at the Ballajá barracks (Cuartel de Ballajá) on Calle Norzagaray. Sometimes park rangers lead hour-long tours for free, although you can also visit on your own. With the purchase of a ticket here, you don't have to pay the admission for Fort San Cristóbal (see below) if you visit during the same day.

At the end of Calle Norzagaray. ✆ 787/729-6960. Admission $2 adults, $1 ages 13–17, free for children 12 and under. Daily 9am–5pm. Bus: A5, B21, or B40.

Fort San Cristóbal ✦   This huge fortress, begun in 1634 and reengineered in the 1770s, is one of the largest ever built in the Americas by Spain. Its walls rise more than 150 feet above the sea—a marvel of military engineering. San Cristóbal protected San Juan against attackers coming by land as a partner to El Morro, to which it is linked by a half-mile (1km) of monumental walls and bastions filled with cannon-firing positions. A complex system of tunnels and dry moats connects the center of San Cristóbal to its "outworks," defensive elements arranged layer after layer over a 27-acre site. You'll get the idea if you look at the scale model on display. Like El Morro, the fort is administered and maintained by the National Park Service. Be sure to see the Garita del Diablo (the Devil's Sentry Box), one of the oldest parts of San Cristóbal's defenses, and famous in Puerto Rican legend. The devil himself, it is said, would snatch away sentinels at this lonely post at the edge of the sea. In 1898 the first shots of the Spanish-American War in Puerto Rico were fired by cannons on top of San Cristóbal during an artillery duel with a U.S. Navy fleet. Sometimes park rangers lead hour-long tours for free, and you can also visit on your own.

In the northeast corner of Old San Juan (uphill from Plaza de Colón on Calle Norzagaray). ✆ 787/729-6960. Admission $2 adults, $1 ages 13–17, free for children 12 and under. Daily 9am–5pm. Bus: A5, B21, or B40; then the free trolley from Covadonga station to the top of the hill.

CHURCHES

Capilla de Cristo   Cristo Chapel was built to commemorate what legend says was a miracle. In 1753 a young rider lost control of his horse in a race down this very street during the fiesta of St. John's Day and plunged over the precipice. Moved by the accident, the secretary of the city, Don Mateo Pratts, invoked Christ to save the youth, and he had the chapel built when his prayers were answered. Today it's a landmark in the old city and one of its best-known historical monuments. The chapel's gold and silver altar can be seen through its glass doors. Because the chapel is open only 1 day a week, most visitors have to settle for a view of its exterior.

Calle del Cristo (directly west of Paseo de la Princesa). ✆ 787/722-0861. Free admission. Tues 10am–2pm. Bus: Old Town trolley.

Catedral de San Juan   This, the spiritual and architectural centerpiece of Old San Juan, as you see it in its present form, was begun in 1540 as a replacement for a thatch-roofed chapel that was blown apart by a hurricane in 1529.

Old San Juan Attractions

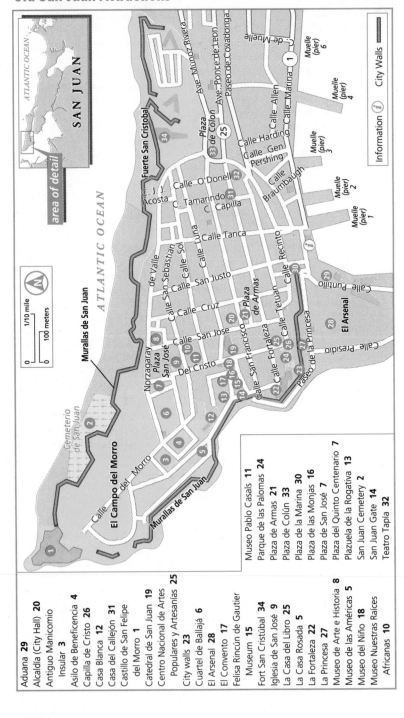

ATLANTIC OCEAN

SAN JUAN

area of detail

ATLANTIC OCEAN

Cemeterio de San Juan

El Campo del Morro

Murallas de San Juan

Calle del Morro

Muelle (pier) 6

Muelle (pier) 4

Muelle (pier) 3

Muelle (pier) 2

Muelle (pier) 1

Information ⓘ

City Walls

1/10 mile

100 meters

Aduana **29**
Alcaldía (City Hall) **20**
Antiguo Manicomio Insular **3**
Asilo de Beneficencia **4**
Capilla de Cristo **12**
Casa Blanca **12**
Casa del Callejón **31**
Castillo de San Felipe del Morro **1**
Catedral de San Juan **19**
Centro Nacional de Artes Populares y Artesanías **25**
City walls **23**
Cuartel de Ballajá **6**
El Arsenal **28**
El Convento **17**
Felisa Rincón de Gautier Museum **15**
Fort San Cristóbal **34**
Iglesia de San José **9**
La Casa del Libro **25**
La Casa Rosada **5**
La Fortaleza **22**
La Princesa **27**
Museo de Arte e Historia **8**
Museo de las Américas **5**
Museo del Niño **18**
Museo Nuestras Raíces Africanas **10**

Museo Pablo Casals **11**
Parque de las Palomas **24**
Plaza de Armas **21**
Plaza de Colún **33**
Plaza de la Marina **30**
Plaza de las Monjas **16**
Plaza de San José **7**
Plaza del Quinto Centenario **7**
Plazuela de la Rogativa **13**
San Juan Cemetery **2**
San Juan Gate **14**
Teatro Tapia **32**

Chronically hampered by a lack of funds and a recurring series of military and weather-derived disasters, it slowly evolved into the gracefully vaulted, Gothic-inspired structure you see today. Among the many disasters to hit this cathedral are the following: In 1598 the Earl of Cumberland led the British Navy in a looting spree, and in 1615 a hurricane blew away its roof. In 1908 the body of Ponce de León was disinterred from the nearby Iglesia de San José and placed in a marble tomb near the transept, where it remains today (see the box "Ponce de León: Man of Myth & Legend" in the appendix for more about Ponce de León). The cathedral also contains the wax-covered mummy of St. Pio, a Roman martyr persecuted and killed for his Christian faith. The mummy has been encased in a glass box ever since it was placed here in 1862. To the right of the mummy is a bizarre wooden replica of Mary with four swords stuck in her bosom. After all the looting and destruction over the centuries, the cathedral's great treasures, including gold and silver, are long gone, although many beautiful stained-glass windows remain. The cathedral faces Plaza de las Monjas (the Nuns' Square), a shady spot where you can rest.

Calle del Cristo 153 (at Caleta San Juan). (✆ 787/722-0861. Free admission. Daily 8:30am–4pm. Bus: Old Town trolley.

Iglesia de San José   Initial plans for this church were drawn in 1523, and Dominican friars supervised its construction in 1532. Both the church and its monastery were closed by decree in 1838, and the property was confiscated by the royal treasury. Later, the Crown turned the convent into a military barracks. The Jesuits restored the badly damaged church. This was the place of worship for Ponce de León's descendants, who are buried here, under the family's coat of arms. The conquistador, killed by a poisoned arrow in Florida, was interred here until his removal to the Catedral de San Juan in 1908.

Although it was badly looted, the church still has some treasures, including *Christ of the Ponces,* a carved crucifix presented to Ponce de León, four oils by José Campeche, and two large works by Francisco Oller. Campeche was the leading Puerto Rican painter of the 18th century, and Oller was Puerto Rico's stellar artist of the late 19th and early 20th centuries. Many miracles have been attributed to a painting in the **Chapel of Belém,** a 15th-century Flemish work called *Virgin of Bethlehem.*

Plaza de San José, Calle del Cristo. (✆ 787/725-7501. Free admission. Church and Chapel of Belém, Mon–Wed and Fri 7am–3pm; Sat 8am–1pm. Bus: Old Town trolley.

Moments Joggers' Trail or Romantic Walk

El Morro Trail, a jogger's paradise, provides Old Town's most scenic views across the harbor. The first part of the trail extends to the San Juan Gate. The walk then goes by El Morro and eventually reaches a scenic area known as Bastion de Santa Barbara. The walk passes El Morro's well-preserved walls, and the trail ends at the entrance to the fortress. The walkway is designed to follow the undulating movement of the ocean, and sea grapes and tropical vegetation surround benches. The trail is romantic at night, when the walls of the fortress are illuminated. Stop at the tourist office for a map, and then set off on the adventure.

San Juan Attractions

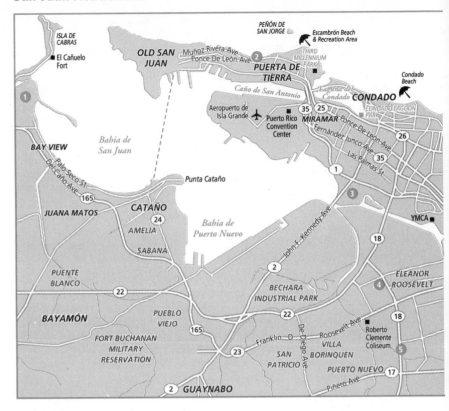

MUSEUMS

Many of the museums in Old San Juan close for lunch between 11:45am and 2pm, so schedule your activities accordingly if you intend to museum-hop.

Felisa Rincón de Gautier Museum   The most heralded woman of modern Puerto Rico served as the mayor of San Juan for 22 consecutive years, between 1946 and 1968. The museum that commemorates her memory is in a 300-year-old building a few blocks downhill from San Juan's cathedral, near one of the medieval gates (La Puerta San Juan) that pierce the walls of the Old City. The interior is devoted to the life and accomplishments of Felisa Rincón de Gautier, and proudly displays some of her personal furniture and artifacts, as well as 212 plaques, 308 certificates of merit, 11 honorary doctorates, and 113 symbolic keys to other cities, such as Gary, I.N., and Perth Amboy, N.J. Her particular areas of influence included child welfare and elementary education. Photographs show her with luminaries from Eleanor Roosevelt to the pope. The oldest of nine children, and the daughter of a local lawyer and a schoolteacher, she shouldered the responsibilities of rearing her younger siblings after the death of her mother when she was 12. Today the museum illuminates Doña Felisa's life as well as the reverence in which Puerto Ricans hold their most celebrated political matriarch. As such, it's a quirky, intensely personalized monument that combines a strong sense of feminism with Puerto Rican national pride.

Caleta de San Juan 51 at Calle Clara Lair. ☎ **787/723-1897.** Free admission. Mon–Fri 9am–4pm. Bus: Old Town trolley.

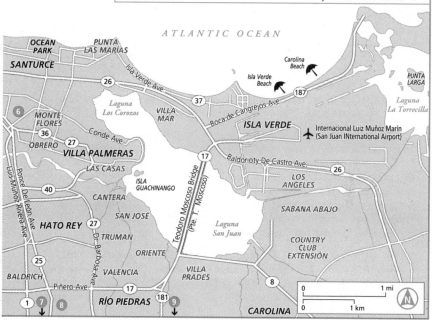

PUERTO RICO ★ San Juan ISLA PIEDRA	Bacardi Distillery **1** Jardín Botánico **7** Luis Muñoz Marin Foundation **9** Luis Muñoz Marin Park **5** Muñoz Rivera Park **2**	Museo de Arte **6** Museum of History, Anthropology & Art **8** Parque Central Municipio de San Juan **3** Time Out Family Amusement Center **4**

Luis Muñoz Marín Foundation

A 30-minute drive south of San Juan, this museum offers a chance to visit the former home of the island's most famous governor, Luis Muñoz Marín. As the first elected governor of Puerto Rico, Marín enjoys somewhat the same position in Puerto Rican history that George Washington does for the mainland United States. A documentary acquaints you with the governor's life and achievements. You can walk through Marín's study and library and view his extensive art collection, and later you can relax in his tropical garden and gazebo. There's also an on-site antique automobile exhibition.

Marginal Rd. 877, km 0.4, Trujillo Alto Expressway. ℂ 787/755-7979. Admission $2 adults, $1 children. Tours Mon–Fri (reservations required) 10am and 2pm; Sun 10am, 11:30am, and 1pm.

Museo de Arte ★★

Puerto Rico's most important gallery, which opened in 2000 and was constructed at a cost of $55 million, is a state-of-the-art showcase for the island nation's rich cultural heritage, as reflected mainly through its painters. Housed in a former city hospital in Santurce, the museum features both a permanent collection and temporary exhibitions. Prominent local artists are the star—for example, Francisco Oller (1833–1917), who brought a touch of Cézanne or Camille Pissarro to Puerto Rico (Oller actually studied in France with both of these Impressionists). Another leading star of the permanent collection is José Campeche, a late 18th-century classical painter. The museum is like a living textbook of Puerto Rico, beginning with its early development and going on to showcase camp aspects, such as the poster art created here in the mid-20th century. All the important modern island artists are also presented, including the best known, the late Angel Botello, and also such contemporaries as Rafael Tufiño and Arnaldo Roche Rabell.

299 Av. José de Diego, Santurce. ✆ **787/977-6277.** Admission $5 adults, $3 children under age 12. Tues and Thurs–Sat 10am–5pm; Wed 10am–8pm; Sun 11am–6pm. Bus: A5.

Museo de Arte e Historia de San Juan Located in a Spanish colonial building at the corner of Calle MacArthur, this cultural center was the city's main marketplace in the mid-19th century. Local art is displayed in the east and west galleries, and audiovisual materials reveal the history of the city. Sometimes major cultural events are staged in the museum's large courtyard. English- and Spanish-language audiovisual shows are presented Monday through Friday every hour on the hour from 9am to 4pm.

Calle Norzagaray 150. ✆ **787/724-1875.** Free admission. Tues–Sun 9am–4pm. Bus: B21 to Old San Juan terminal; then a trolley from the terminal to the museum.

Museo de las Américas ⚘ This museum showcases the artisans of North, South, and Central America, featuring everything from carved figureheads from New England whaling ships to dugout canoes carved by Carib Indians in Dominica. It is unique in Puerto Rico and well worth a visit. Also on display is a changing collection of paintings by artists from throughout the Spanish-speaking world, some of which are for sale, and a permanent collection called "Puerto Rican *Santos,*" donated by Dr. Ricardo Alegría.

Cuartel de Ballajá. ✆ **787/724-5052.** Free admission. Tues–Sun 10am–4pm. Bus: Old Town trolley.

Museo de Pablo Casals This museum is devoted to the memorabilia left to the people of Puerto Rico by the musician Pablo Casals. The maestro's cello is here, along with a library of videotapes (which can be played upon request) of some of his festival concerts. This small 18th-century house also contains manuscripts and photographs of Casals. The annual Casals Festival draws worldwide interest and internationally known performing artists; it's held during the first 2 weeks of June.

Plaza San José, Calle San Sebastián 101. ✆ **787/723-9185.** Admission $1 adults, 50¢ children. Tues–Sat 9:30am–5pm. Bus: Old Town trolley.

Museum of History, Anthropology & Art Here you'll find good collections of paintings by Puerto Rican artists, including Francisco Oller (late 19th and early 20th centuries) and José Campeche, the first important artist of Puerto Rico (18th century). There's also a large collection of pre-Columbian Puerto Rican native artifacts from the Ingeri, sub-Taíno, and Taíno civilizations.

Av. Ponce de León, Río Piedras Campus. ✆ **787/763-3939,** ext. 2452. Free admission. Mon 9am–1pm; Tues and Fri–Sat 9am–4:30pm; Wed–Thurs 9am–8:45pm; Sun 11:30am–4:30pm. Closed holidays. Take the bus marked RÍO PIEDRAS from Plaza de Colón in Old San Juan to stop 36.

HISTORIC SIGHTS

In addition to the forts and churches listed above, you might want to see the sites described below.

San Juan Gate, Calle San Francisco and Calle Recinto Oeste, built around 1635, just north of La Fortaleza, several blocks downhill from the cathedral, was the main point of entry into San Juan if you arrived by ship in the 17th and 18th centuries. The gate is the only one remaining of the several that once pierced the fortifications of the old walled city. For centuries it was closed at sundown to cut off access to the historic old town. Bus: B21.

Plazuela de la Rogativa, Caleta de las Monjas, is a little plaza with a statue of a bishop and three women, commemorating one of Puerto Rico's most famous legends. In 1797, from across San Juan Bay at Santurce, the British held the Old Town under siege. That same year they mysteriously sailed away. Later, the commander claimed he feared that the enemy was well prepared behind those walls; he apparently saw many lights and believed them to be reinforcements. Some people believe that those lights were torches carried by women in a *rogativa,* or religious procession, as they followed their bishop. Bus: T1.

The **city walls** around San Juan were built in 1630 to protect the town against both European invaders and Caribbean pirates. The city walls that remain today were once part of one of the most impregnable fortresses in the New World and even today are an engineering marvel. Their thickness averages 20 feet at the base and 12 feet at the top, with an average height of 40 feet. At their top, notice the balconied buildings that served for centuries as hospitals and also residences of the island's various governors. Between Fort San Cristóbal and El Morro, bastions were erected at frequent intervals. The walls come into view as you approach from San Cristóbal on your way to El Morro. Bus: Old Town trolley.

San Juan Cemetery, on Calle Norzagaray, officially opened in 1814 and has since been the final resting place for many prominent Puerto Rican families. The circular chapel, dedicated to Saint Magdalene of Pazzis, was built in the 1860s. Aficionados of old graveyards can wander among marble monuments, mausoleums, and statues, marvelous examples of Victorian funereal statuary. Because there are no trees, or any other form of shade here, it would be best not to go exploring in the noonday sun. In any case, be careful—the cemetery is often a venue for illegal drug deals and can be dangerous. Bus: Old Town trolley.

Alcaldía (City Hall)   The City Hall, with its double arcade flanked by two towers resembling Madrid's City Hall, was constructed in stages from 1604 to 1789. Still in use, this building today contains a tourist-information center downstairs plus a small art gallery on the first floor.

Calle San Francisco. ✆ 787/724-7171, ext. 2391. Free admission. Mon–Fri 8am–4pm. Closed holidays. Bus: Old Town trolley.

Casa Blanca   Ponce de León never lived here, although construction of the house—built in 1521, 2 years after his death—is sometimes attributed to him. The work was ordered by his son-in-law, Juan García Troche. The parcel of land was given to Ponce de León as a reward for services rendered to the Crown. Descendants of the explorer lived in the house for about 2½ centuries, until the Spanish government took it over in 1779 for use as a residence for military commanders. The U.S. government also used it as a home for army commanders. On the first floor, the **Juan Ponce de León Museum** is furnished with antiques, paintings, and artifacts from the 16th through the 18th centuries. In back is a garden with spraying fountains, offering an intimate and verdant respite.

Calle San Sebastián 1. ✆ 787/724-5477. Admission $2. Tues–Sat 9am–noon and 1–4:30pm. Bus: Old Town trolley.

El Arsenal   The Spaniards used a shallow craft to patrol the lagoons and mangroves in and around San Juan. Needing a base for these vessels, they constructed El Arsenal in the 19th century. It was at this base that they staged their last stand, flying the Spanish colors until the final Spaniard was removed in 1898, at the end of the Spanish-American War. Changing art exhibitions are held in the building's three galleries.

La Puntilla. ✆ 787/723-3068. Free admission. Wed–Sun 8:30am–4:30pm. Bus: Old Town trolley.

La Casa del Libro   This restored 19th-century house shelters a library and museum devoted to the arts of printing and bookmaking, with examples of fine printing, which date back 5 centuries, and some illuminated medieval manuscripts.

Calle del Cristo 255. ✆ 787/723-0354. Free admission. Tues–Sat 11am–4:30pm. Bus: Old Town trolley.

La Fortaleza   The office and residence of the governor of Puerto Rico is the oldest executive mansion in continuous use in the Western Hemisphere, and it has served as the island's seat of government for more than 3 centuries. Its history goes back even further than that, to 1533, when construction began on a fortress to protect San Juan's Spanish settlers during raids by Carib tribesmen and pirates. The original medieval towers remain, but as the edifice was subsequently enlarged into a palace, other modes of architecture and ornamentation were also incorporated, including baroque, Gothic, neoclassical, and Arabian. La Fortaleza has been designated a national historic site by the U.S. government. Informal but proper attire is required.

Calle Fortaleza, overlooking San Juan Harbor. ✆ 787/721-7000, ext. 2211. Free admission. 30-min. tours of the gardens and building (conducted in English and Spanish) given Mon–Fri, every hour 9am–3:30pm. Bus: Old Town trolley

Museo Nuestras Raíces Africanas   Set within the Casa del Contrefueras, this museum documents the African contribution to the sociology of Puerto Rico. You'll find a series of tastefully arranged art objects, including musical instruments, intricately carved African masks, drums, graphics, and maps that show the migratory patterns, usually through the slave trade, from Africa into Puerto Rico. There are graphic depictions of the horrendous disruptions to families and individuals caused by the slave trade during the plantation era.

Plaza San José, Calle San Sebastián. ✆ 787/724-4294. Admission $2 adults and students, free for ages 10 and under. Tues–Sat 9am–4pm. Bus: Old Town Trolley.

Teatro Tapía   Standing across from the Plaza de Colón, this is one of the oldest theaters in the Western Hemisphere, built about 1832. In 1976 a restoration returned the theater to its original appearance. Much of Puerto Rican theater history is connected with the Tapía, named after the island's first prominent playwright, Alejandro Tapía y Rivera (1826–1882). Various productions—some musical—are staged here throughout the year, representing a repertoire of drama, dance, and cultural events.

Av. Ponce de León. ✆ 787/721-0169. Access limited to tickets holders at performances (see "San Juan After Dark" later in this chapter). Bus: B8 or B21.

HISTORIC SQUARES

In Old San Juan, **Plaza del Quinto Centenario** (Quincentennial Plaza) overlooks the Atlantic from atop the highest point in the city. A striking and symbolic feature of the plaza, which was constructed as part of the 1992/1993 celebration of the 500th anniversary of the discovery of the New World, is a sculpture that rises 40 feet from the plaza's top level. The monumental sculpture in black granite and ceramics symbolizes the earthen and clay roots of American history and is the work of Jaime Suarez, one of Puerto Rico's foremost artists. From its southern end, two needle-shaped columns point skyward to the North Star, the guiding light of explorers. Placed around the plaza are fountains, other columns, and sculpted steps that represent various historic periods in Puerto Rico's 500-year heritage.

Sweeping views extend from the plaza to El Morro Fortress at the headland of San Juan Bay and to the Dominican Convent and San José Church, a rare New World example of Gothic architecture. Asilo de Beneficencia, a former indigents' hospital dating from 1832, occupies a corner of El Morro's entrance and is now the home of the Institute of Puerto Rican Culture. Adjacent to the plaza is the Cuartel de Ballajá, built in the mid-19th century as the Spanish army headquarters and still the largest edifice in the Americas constructed by Spanish engineers; it houses the Museum of the Americas.

Centrally located, Quincentennial Plaza is one of modern Puerto Rico's respectful gestures to its colorful and lively history. It is a perfect introduction for visitors seeking to discover the many rich links with the past in Old San Juan.

Once named St. James Square, or Plaza Santiago, **Plaza de Colón** in the heart of San Juan's Old Town is bustling and busy, reached along the pedestrian mall of Calle Fortaleza. The square was renamed Plaza de Colón to honor the 400th anniversary of the explorer's so-called discovery of Puerto Rico. Of course, it is more politically correct today to say that Columbus explored or came upon an already inhabited island. He certainly didn't discover it. But when a statue here, perhaps the most famous on the island, was erected atop a high pedestal, it was clearly to honor Columbus, not to decry his legacy.

PARKS & GARDENS

Jardín Botánico   Administered by the University of Puerto Rico, Jardín Botánico is a lush tropical garden with some 200 species of vegetation. You can pack a picnic lunch and bring it here if you choose. The orchid garden is exceptional, and the palm garden is said to contain some 125 species. Footpaths blaze a trail through heavy forests opening onto a lotus lagoon.

Barrio Venezuela (at the intersection of routes 1 and 847), Río Piedras. ✆ 787/763-4408. Free admission. Daily 6am–6pm. Bus: 19.

Luis Muñoz Marín Park ✪ *Kids*   This park is administered by the Park Trust of Puerto Rico, and it is the best-known, most frequently visited children's playground in Puerto Rico—although it has equal appeal to adults. Conceived as a verdant oasis in an otherwise crowded urban neighborhood, it's a fenced-in repository of swings, jungle gyms, and slides set amid several small lakes. Here you'll also find an incomparable view of San Juan. A small-scale cable car carries passengers aloft at 10-minute intervals for panoramic views of the surrounding landscape ($2 per person).

Av. Piñero, at Alto Rey. ✆ 787/751-3353. Free admission for pedestrians; parking $2 or $3. Wed–Sun 8am–6pm. Bus: A1 to Río Piedras, then switch to bus 52.

Muñoz Rivera Park   This park is affiliated with Luis Muñoz Marín Park (see below), with which it is frequently confused. This green space is administered by the **Park Trust of Puerto Rico** (✆ 787/763-0613). It's a rectangular, seaward-facing park that was built about 50 years ago to honor Luis Muñoz Rivera, the Puerto Rican statesman, journalist, and poet. It's filled with picnic areas, wide walks, shady trees, landscaped grounds, and recreational areas. Its centerpiece, El Pabellon de la Paz, is sometimes used for cultural events and expositions of handicrafts.

Av. Ponce de León. ✆ 787/724-4430. Free admission. Open daily 24 hr. Bus: A1 (or take the Los Américas Expressway to Avenida Piñero, then head west until you reach the entrance).

Parque Central Municipio de San Juan   This mangrove-bordered park was inaugurated in 1979 for the Pan-American Games. It covers 35 acres and lies

The Best Places to See Puerto Rican Art

With its dozen or so museums and even more art galleries, Old San Juan is the greatest repository of Puerto Rican arts and crafts. Galleries sell everything from pre-Columbian artifacts to paintings by relatively contemporary artists such as Angel Botello, who died in 1986. **Galería Botello** (p. 157) was his former home. He restored the colonial mansion himself; now his paintings and sculptures are on display there.

The grandest repository of art in San Juan is at the **Museo de Arte** (p. 139), which is a virtual textbook on all the big names in the art world who rose from Puerto Rico often to international acclaim.

Another good place to see Puerto Rican art is the **Museum of History, Anthropology & Art** (p. 140). Because of space limitations, the museum's galleries can exhibit only a fifth of their vast collection at one time, but the work is always top-notch. The collection ranges from pre-Columbian artifacts to works by today's major painters.

Outside San Juan, the greatest art on the island is at the **Museo de Arte de Ponce,** Avenida de las Américas, #25 (© **787/848-0505**). The collection, donated by former governor Luís A. Ferré, ranges from Jan van Eyck's *Salvatore Mundi* to Rossetti's *Daughters of King Lear.* The museum building was designed by Edward Durell Stone, who also designed New York's Museum of Modern Art. Works are displayed in a honeycomb of skylit hexagonal rooms. In addition to such European masters as Reubens, Van Dyck, and Murillo, the museum features works by Latin American artists, including Diego Rivera. Puerto Rican artists who are represented include José Campeche and Francisco Oller. (See "Ponce" in chapter 8.)

southeast of Miramar. Joggers appreciate its labyrinth of trails, tennis players enjoy the courts, and all city dwellers stroll to relieve the pressures of urban life.

Calle Cerra. © **787/722-1646.** Free admission for pedestrians; parking 75¢. Open Mon–Thurs 6am–10pm; Fri 6am–9pm; Sat and Sun 6am–7pm. Bus: A1.

SIGHTSEEING TOURS

If you want to see more of the island but you don't want to rent a car or manage the inconveniences of public transportation, perhaps an organized tour is for you.

Castillo Sightseeing Tours & Travel Services, 2413 Calle Laurel, Punta La Marias, Santurce (© **787/791-6195**), maintains offices at some of the capital's best-known hotels, including the Caribe Hilton and San Juan Marriott Resort. Using six of their own air-conditioned buses, with access to others if demand warrants it, the company's tours include pickups and drop-offs at hotels as an added convenience.

One of the most popular half-day tours departs most days of the week between 8:30 and 9am, lasts 4 to 5 hours, and costs $35 per person. Leaving from San Juan, it tours along the northeastern part of the island to El Yunque. The company also offers a city tour of San Juan that departs daily around 1pm. The 4-hour trip costs $32 per person and includes a stop at the Bacardi Rum Factory. The company also operates full-day snorkeling tours to the reefs near the coast of a deserted island off Puerto Rico's eastern edge aboard one of two sail- and motor-driven catamarans. With lunch, snorkeling gear, and piña coladas included, the full-day (7:45am–5pm) excursion goes for $69 per person.

Few cities of the Caribbean lend themselves so gracefully to walking tours. You can embark on these on your own, stopping and shopping en route (see "Walking Tour: Old San Juan" below).

ESPECIALLY FOR KIDS

Puerto Rico is one of the most family-friendly islands in the Caribbean, and many hotels offer family discounts. Programs for children are also offered at a number of hotels, including day and night camp activities and babysitting services. Trained counselors at these camps supervise children as young as 3 in activities ranging from nature hikes to tennis lessons, coconut carving, and sand-sculpture contests.

Teenagers can learn to hip-hop dance Latino-style with special salsa and merengue lessons, learn conversational Spanish, indulge in watersports, take jeep excursions, or scuba-dive in some of the best diving locations in the world.

The best kiddies program is offered at **Wyndham El San Juan Hotel & Casino** (p. 172), where camp activities are presented to children between the ages of 5 and 13. Counselors design activities according to the interests of groups of up to 10 children. Kids Klub members receive a T-shirt, membership card, and three Sand Dollars for use in the game room or at a poolside restaurant. The daily fee of $28 includes lunch.

Another worthy choice is the **Condado Plaza Hotel & Casino** (p. 172), where the daily Camp Taíno offers a regular program of activities and special events for children ages 5 to 12. The $25-per-child fee includes lunch. The hotel also has a toddlers' pool, and the kids' water slide in its main pool starts in a Spanish-style castle turret. For teenagers, the hotel has a video game room, a tennis court, several putting greens, and various organized activities.

Children should love **El Morro Fortress** (see "Forts" earlier in this chapter) because it looks just like the castles they have seen on TV and at the movies. On a rocky promontory, El Morro is filled with dungeons and dank places and also has lofty lookout points for viewing San Juan Harbor.

Luis Muñoz Marín Park (see "Parks & Gardens" above) has the most popular children's playground in Puerto Rico. It's filled with landscaped grounds and recreational areas—lots of room for fun in the sun.

Museo del Niño (Children's Museum) *Kids* In the late 1990s, the city of San Juan turned over one of the most desirable buildings in the colonial zone— a 300-year-old villa directly across from the city's cathedral—to a group of sociologists and student volunteers. Jointly, they created the only children's museum in Puerto Rico. Through interactive exhibits, children learn simple lessons, such as the benefits of brushing teeth or recycling aluminum cans, or the value of caring properly for pets. Staff members include lots of student volunteers who play either one-on-one or with small groups of children. Nothing here is terribly cerebral, and nothing will necessarily compel you to return. But it does provide a play experience that some children will remember for several weeks.

Calle del Cristo 150. © 787/722-3791. Admission $3. Tues–Thurs 9am–3:30pm; Fri 9am–5pm; Sat–Sun 12:30–5pm. Bus: Old Town trolley.

Time Out Family Amusement Center *Kids* This is the most popular venue for family outings on Puerto Rico. On weekends, seemingly half the families in the city show up. It has a large variety of electronic games for children and adults alike, but there are no rides.

Plaza de las Américas, Las Américas Expressway at Roosevelt Ave., Hato Rey. ⓒ **787/753-0606.** Free admission (prices of activities vary). Mon–Thurs 9:30am–10pm; Fri–Sun 9:30am–11pm. Bus: B21 from Old San Juan.

WALKING TOUR   OLD SAN JUAN

Start:	Plaza de la Marina
Finish:	Fort San Cristóbal
Time:	2 hours (not counting stops)
Best times:	Any sunny day between 7am and 6pm
Worst times:	When several cruise ships are in port simultaneously

The streets are narrow and teeming with traffic, but a walk through Old San Juan (*El Viejo San Juan*) is like a stroll through 5 centuries of history. Beneficiary of millions of dollars' worth of restoration since the early 1970s, Old San Juan is one of the world's most potent reminders of the power and grandeur of the Spanish Empire. This tour begins at a point just to the west of San Juan's cruise piers and encircles the perimeter of some of the best-preserved fortifications built by the Spaniards during the 16th and 17th centuries. En route, it passes beneath the governor's historic mansion, La Fortaleza, and encircles Casa Blanca, before ending at a point beyond the entrance of one of the most fiercely guarded fortresses of the colonial age, Fort San Cristóbal.

Begin your walking tour near the post office, amid the taxis, buses, and urban congestion of:

❶ Plaza de la Marina

This sloping, many-angled plaza is at the eastern edge of one of San Juan's showcase promenades, Paseo de la Princesa. The 19th-century paseo was an esplanade where the Spanish colonial gentry once strolled while enjoying the balmy Caribbean air.

Towering royal palms shade the broad esplanade, now paved with brick. On the paseo's west side, overlooking the sea, a large bronze fountain, *Raíces* (Roots), sculpted in 1992 by the Spanish artist Luís Sanguino, depicts the Amerindian, African, and Spanish origins of Puerto Rico as human figures, with dolphins cavorting at their feet. Viewed from afar, the entire ensemble looks like a caravel being steered out to sea by dolphins. On the paseo's east side stand five allegorical pieces on the island's heritage sculpted by José Buscaglia in 1992.

This work is said to symbolize the various epochs that Puerto Rico has undergone in the past 5 centuries—from the coming of the Spanish conquistadores to the beginning of Puerto Rico's role as a U.S. protectorate.

A gazebo serves light seafood dishes, salads, and the island's famed rich coffee. Outdoor tables with umbrellas allow parents to keep an eye on their children, who may be enjoying the playground nearby. More than 20 trees were planted to shade the tables. Criollo dishes are also available from food carts with colored awnings.

Walk westward along Paseo de la Princesa, past heroic statues and manicured trees, until you reach:

❷ La Princesa

The gray-and-white building on your right, which served for centuries as one of the most feared prisons in the Caribbean, is called La Princesa. Today it houses the offices of the Puerto Rico Tourism Company and

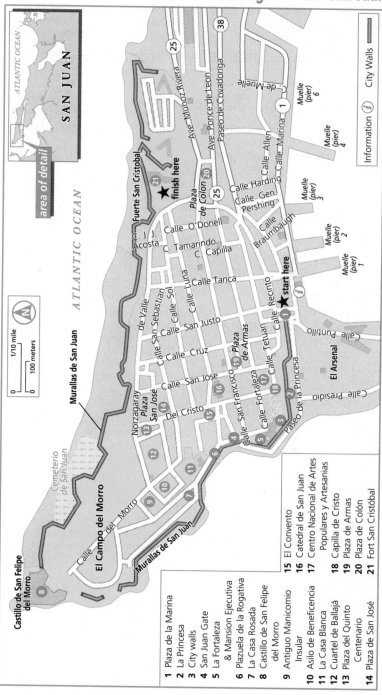

Walking Tour: Old San Juan

1 Plaza de la Marina
2 La Princesa
3 City walls
4 San Juan Gate
5 La Fortaleza
   & Mansion Ejecutiva
6 Plazuela de la Rogativa
7 La Casa Rosada
8 Castillo de San Felipe
   del Morro
9 Antiguo Manicomio
   Insular
10 Asilo de Beneficencia
11 La Casa Blanca
12 Cuartel de Ballajá
13 Plaza del Quinto
   Centenario
14 Plaza de San José

15 El Convento
16 Catedral de San Juan
17 Centro Nacional de Artes
   Populares y Artesanías
18 Capilla de Cristo
19 Plaza de Armas
20 Plaza de Colón
21 Fort San Cristóbal

Information ⓘ   City Walls

an exhibit of work by Puerto Rican artists. Gallery hours are Monday through Friday from 9am to noon and 1 to 4pm, and admission is free. In front of La Princesa stands a sculpture of one of the island's most beloved leaders, Doña Felisa Gautier, mayor of San Juan from 1946 to 1968.

Continue walking westward to the base of the fountain near the edge of the sea. Turn to your right and follow the seaside promenade as it parallels the edge of the:

❸ City Walls

These walls were once part of one of the most impregnable fortresses in the New World. See "Historic Sights" earlier in this chapter.

Continue walking between the sea and the base of the city walls until the walkway goes through the walls at the:

❹ San Juan Gate

This gate was built at Calle San Francisco and Recinto del Oeste, around 1635, as the main point of access from the wharves to the colony's interior. See "Historic Sights" earlier in this chapter.

When you're inside the once-dreaded fortifications, turn immediately right and walk uphill along Calle Recinto del Oeste. The wrought-iron gates at the street's end, which will probably be guarded by a pair of attendants, lead to:

❺ La Fortaleza

The centuries-old residence of the Puerto Rican governor, La Fortaleza is located on Calle Fortaleza. See p. 142.

Now retrace your steps along Calle Recinto del Oeste, walking first downhill and then uphill for about a block, until you reach Caleta de las Monjas. Fork left until you see a panoramic view and a contemporary statue marking the center of:

❻ Plazuela de la Rogativa

The statue on this small square commemorates a time in 1797 when British soldiers mistook a religious procession for the arrival of Spanish reinforcements and fled. See "Historic Sights" earlier in this chapter.

Continue westward, passing between a pair of urn-capped gateposts. You'll be walking parallel to the crenellations of the 17th-century city walls. The cool, tree-shaded boulevard will fork; take the right-hand fork and pass just above the pink walls of:

❼ La Casa Rosada

This graceful villa was built in 1812 for leaders of the Spanish army. It cannot be visited, but you can enjoy the view from outside.

Continue climbing the steeply inclined cobble-covered ramp to its top. Walk westward across the field toward the neoclassical gateway of a fortress believed impregnable for centuries:

❽ Castillo de San Felipe del Morro ("El Morro")

The fortress walls here were designed as part of a network of defenses that made San Juan *La Ciudad Murada* (the Walled City). See p. 134.

After your visit, with El Morro behind you, retrace your steps through the sunlit, tree-less field to the point where you stood when you first sighted the fortress. Walk down Calle del Morro past the:

❾ Antiguo Manicomio Insular

In 1854 the Spanish king decreed that this structure be built as an insane asylum. Converted to a U.S. army barracks after the Spanish-American War, it has functioned since 1965 as the Puerto Rican Academy of Fine Arts. Iron fences of grace and elegance protect a pair of courtyards centered around splashing fountains.

Across the street from Antiguo Manicomio Insular is a stately neoclassical building (painted buff with fern-green trim), the:

❿ Asilo de Beneficencia ("Home for the Poor")

Asilo de Beneficencia, which dates from the 1840s, has two attractive interior patios, an austere dignity, and usually an echoing silence. Today it houses the administrative offices of the Institute of Puerto Rican Culture, with several changing exhibition galleries and an interesting room filled with pre-Columbian artifacts. The galleries are open Tuesday through Saturday from 9am to 4:30pm, charging $1 admission. For more information, call © **787/724-0700.**

Continue walking uphill to the small, formal, and sloping plaza at the street's top. On the right-hand side, within a trio of buildings, is:

⓫ Casa Blanca

Casa Blanca was built by the son-in-law of Juan Ponce de León as the great conquistador's island home (he never actually lived here). See p. 141.

After your visit to Casa Blanca, exit by the compound's front entrance and walk downhill, retracing your steps for a half block, and head toward the massive and monumental tangerine-colored building on your right there:

⓬ Cuartel de Ballajá

This is the 19th-century military barracks of Ballajá, which once housed troops from Spain along with their wives and children, in a setting evocative of the most austere and massive monasteries of old Spain. It is still the largest edifice in the Americas constructed by Spanish engineers. It was declared a National Historic Monument in 1954. On the building's second floor is the Museo de las Américas (see "Museums" earlier in this chapter).

After your visit Cuartel de Ballajá, exit through the extremely narrow eastern door, where you'll immediately spot one of the most dramatic modern plazas in Puerto Rico the:

⓭ Plaza del Quinto Centenario

This plaza is a terraced tribute to the European colonization of the New World and one of the most elaborate and formal piazzas in Puerto Rico.

Walk a short block to the southeast to reach the ancient borders of the:

⓮ Plaza de San José

The center of this plaza is dominated by a statue of Juan Ponce de León that was cast from English cannons captured during a naval battle in 1797. Around the periphery of the square, notice three important sites: the Museo de Pablo Casals (p. 140); the Casa de los Contrafuertes (House of the Buttresses), which is adjacent to the Museo de Pablo Casals; and the Iglesia de San José (p. 137), where the conquistador's coat of arms hangs above the altar. This church is one of the oldest places of Christian worship in the New World.

> ☕ **TAKE A BREAK**
> Plaza de San José is home to several prominent bars and restaurants that serve beer, coffee, and simple meals. They include **El Patio de Sam** and **NoNo's**, where locals occupy virtually every nook and bar stool, especially after sundown (see chapter 5). Also appealing is **El Boquerón**, which is in a narrow storefront midway between the two. Stop at any of these places for some refreshment.

Exit from the plaza's southwestern corner and walk downhill along one of the capital's oldest and best-known streets, Calle del Cristo (also known as Calle Cristo). Two blocks later, at the corner of Calle las Monjas, you'll find the venerable walls of:

⓯ El Convento

El Convento was originally conceived as a convent in the 17th century, but it functioned for many decades as one of the few hotels within the old city (see the recommendation on p. 165).

Diagonally across the street from El Convento lies the island's most famous church and spiritual centerpiece:

⓰ Catedral de San Juan

This distinguished landmark has in recent years been restored to its original Spanish beauty. See p. 135.

Walk 2 more blocks southward along Calle del Cristo, through one of the most attractive shopping districts in the Caribbean. After passing Calle Fortaleza, look on your left for the:

⑰ Centro Nacional de Artes Populares y Artesanías

This building houses the headquarters of the Institute of Puerto Rican Culture. As such, it is assigned to protect the island's precious heritage in arts, crafts, music, and literature. It no longer sells high-quality crafts on these premises, but it uses an outlet on the same street, next to the Iglesia de San José (see "Shopping" below).

Continue to the southernmost tip of Calle del Cristo (just a few steps away), to the wrought-iron gates that surround a chapel no bigger than an oversized newspaper kiosk called:

⑱ Capilla de Cristo

The altar here is dedicated to the "Christ of Miracles." See p. 135.

Retrace your steps north for about a block along Calle del Cristo. Turn right on Calle Fortaleza. One block later, turn left onto Calle de San José, which leads to the site of the capital's most symmetrical and beautiful square:

⑲ Plaza de Armas

This a broad and open Spanish-style plaza was the original main square of Old San Juan and the very hub of the city. It has a lovely fountain with 19th-century statues representing the four seasons. In times gone by, families with unmarried daughters would parade around the square. It was a proper way for chaperoned young women to catch the eye of young, available men. Two important buildings flanking this square are the neoclassic Intendencia (which houses some offices of the U.S. State Department) and San Juan's Alcaldía (see "Historic Sights" earlier in this chapter).

Relax on one of the benches if you like, and then leave the square eastward, along Calle San Francisco.

TAKE A BREAK

 La Bombonera, Calle San Francisco 259 (© **787/ 722- 0658**), offers take-away baked goods, as well as sandwiches, spicy platters of Puerto Rican food, and richly scented coffee. No one will mind if you just order something to drink, but this is a good place for lunch, as the portions are copious and inexpensive. It's rather informal; the place bustles, and no one goes away hungry.

After your pick-me-up, continue your promenade eastward along the length of Calle San Francisco. It will eventually deposit you beside the traffic, parked cars, and open-air conviviality of the very large:

⑳ Plaza de Colón

This plaza features a stone column topped with a statue of Christopher Columbus (see "Historic Squares" earlier in this chapter). To the side of the square is the Teatro Tapía (p. 142), which has been restored to its original 19th-century elegance.

Continue along Calle San Francisco to the intersection with Calle de Valle, turn left, and follow the signs to:

㉑ Fort San Cristóbal

This fort was built as part of the string of fortifications guarding one of Spain's then-most-valuable colonies. Today, like its twin, El Morro, it is maintained by the National Park Service and can be visited throughout the day. See p. 135.

2 Diving, Fishing, Tennis & Other Outdoor Pursuits

Active vacationers have a wide choice of things to do in San Juan, from beaching to windsurfing. The beachside hotels, of course, offer lots of watersports activities (see chapter 4).

THE BEACHES

Some public stretches of shoreline around San Juan are overcrowded, especially on Saturday and Sunday; others are practically deserted. If you find that secluded, hidden beach of your dreams, proceed with caution. On unguarded

The Cathedral of Rum

Called "the Cathedral of Rum," the **Bacardi Distillery** at Route 888, km 2.6 at Cataño (© **787/788-1500**), is the largest of its kind in the world. Reached by taking a 20-minute ferry ride across San Juan Bay (50¢ each way), the distillery produces 100,000 gallons of rum daily. Free 45-minute guided tours take place Monday through Saturday from 8:30am to 4:30pm. Complimentary rum drinks are offered at the beginning of the tour, and a gift shop sells a wide assortment of handsome items, from T-shirts to duffel bags. Naturally, you can purchase Bacardi rums here, at prices that are slightly more reasonable than those at home. Some rums available here are not sold on the U.S. mainland and make unusual gifts.

Upon entering the first floor, you'll get a glimpse of what rum production was like a century ago, including oak barrels used in the aging process and an old sugarcane wagon. On the fifth floor you'll enter the Hall of Rum with a collection of beverages made by the corporation over a period of years. You'll then witness "the birth of rum"—the fermentation processes of molasses (it takes 100 gal. of molasses to produce one barrel of rum).

At the end of the tour, you'll visit the Bacardi Family Museum, documenting the family's history, and you can watch a short video about the bottling process. Afterward, you can stroll through the beautiful grounds overlooking Old San Juan.

beaches you'll have no way to protect yourself or your valuables should you be approached by a robber or mugger, which has been known to happen. For more information about the island's many beaches, call the **Department of Sports and Recreation** at © **787/728-5668.**

All beaches on Puerto Rico, even those fronting the top hotels, are open to the public. Public bathing beaches are called *balnearios* and charge for parking and for use of facilities, such as lockers and showers. Public beaches shut down on Monday; if Monday is a holiday, the beaches are open for the holiday but close the next day. Beach hours are 9am to 5pm in winter, to 6pm off-season. Major public beaches in the San Juan area have changing rooms and showers.

Famous with beach buffs since the 1920s, **Condado Beach** ✯✯ put San Juan on the map as a tourist resort. Backed up by high-rise hotels, it seems more like Miami Beach than any other beach in the Caribbean. From parasailing to sailing, all sorts of watersports can be booked at kiosks along the beach or at the activities desk of the hotels. There are also plenty of outdoor bars and restaurants. People-watching is a favorite sport along these golden strands.

A favorite of *Sanjuaneros* themselves, **Isla Verde Beach** ✯✯ is also ideal for swimming, and it, too, is lined with high-rise resorts a la Miami Beach. Many luxury condos are on this beachfront. Isla Verde has picnic tables, so you can pick up the makings of a lunch and make it a day at the beach. This strip is also good for snorkeling because of its calm, clear waters, and many kiosks will rent you equipment. Isla Verde Beach extends from the end of Ocean Park to the beginning of a section called Boca Cangrejos. The best beach at Isla Verde is at the Wyndham Hotel El San Juan. Most sections of this long strip have separate names, such as El Alambique, which is often the site of beach parties, and Punta El Medio, bordering the new Ritz-Carlton, also a great beach and very popular, even with the locals. If you go past the luxury hotels and expensive condos behind the Luís Muñoz Marín International Airport, you arrive at the major public beach at Isla Verde. Here you'll find parking, showers, fast-food joints, and watersports equipment. The sands here are whiter than those of the Condado, and they are lined with coconut palms, sea-grape trees, and even almond trees, all of which provide shade from the fierce noonday sun.

One of the most attractive beaches in the Greater San Juan area is **Ocean Park Beach** ✹✹, a mile of fine gold sand in a neighborhood east of Condado. This beach attracts both young people and a big gay crowd. Access to the beach at Ocean Park has been limited recently, but the best place to enter is from a section called El Ultimo Trolley. This area is ideal for volleyball, paddleball, and other games. The easternmost portion, known as Punta Las Marias, is best for windsurfing. The waters at Ocean Park are fine for swimming, although they can get rough at times.

Rivaling Condado and Isla Verde beaches, **Luquillo Beach** is the grandest in Puerto Rico and one of the most popular. It's 30 miles (48km) east of San Juan, near the town of Luquillo (see chapter 7).

SPORTS & OTHER OUTDOOR PURSUITS

BIKE RENTALS   Much favored by the dozens of holidaymakers pedaling up and down the Condado, **Condado Bicycles,** Av. Ashford 1024 (© **787/ 722-6288**), rents big-geared mountain bikes for $20 a day. Fortunately for the neighborhood's noise pollution, they don't rent mopeds or motor scooters. The best places to bike are along Avenida Ashford (in Condado), Calle Loiza (between Condado and Ocean Park), and Avenida Baldorioty de Castro (in Santurce). Other streets in this area may be too congested. Similarly, because of the traffic, biking in Old San Juan is not recommended.

CRUISES   For the best cruises of San Juan Bay, go to **Caribe Aquatic Adventures** (see "Scuba Diving" below). Bay cruises start at $25 per person.

DEEP-SEA FISHING ✹   Deep-sea fishing is top-notch here. Allison tuna, white and blue marlin, sailfish, wahoo, dolphin (mahimahi), mackerel, and tarpon are some of the fish that can be caught in Puerto Rican waters, where 30 world records have been broken. Charter arrangements can be made through most major hotels and resorts.

Capt. Mike Benitez, who has chartered out of San Juan for more than 40 years, is one of the most qualified sport-fishing captains in the world. (Past clients include Jimmy Carter.) **Benitez Fishing Charters** can be contacted directly at P.O. Box 9066541, Puerto de Tierra, San Juan, PR 00906 (© **787/ 723-2292** until 6pm). The captain offers a 45-foot air-conditioned deluxe Hatteras called the *Sea Born.* Fishing tours for parties of up to six cost $490 for a half-day excursion and $850 for a full day, with beverages and all equipment included.

GOLF   A 45-minute drive east from San Juan on the northeast coast takes you to Palmer and its 6,145-yard **Westin Rio Mar Golf Course** ✹ (© **787/ 888-6000**). Inexperienced golfers prefer this course to the more challenging and more famous courses at Dorado (see chapter 7), even though trade winds can influence your game along the holes bordering the water, and occasional fairway flooding can present some unwanted obstacles. Greens fees are $160 for hotel guests, $185 for nonguests. A gallery of 100 iguanas also adds spice to your game at Rio Mar.

HORSE RACING   Great thoroughbreds and outstanding jockeys compete year-round at **El Comandante,** Av. 65 de Infantería, Route 3, kilometer 15.3, at Canovanas (© **787/724-6060**), Puerto Rico's only racetrack, a 20-minute drive east of the center of San Juan. Post time varies from 2:15 to 5:30pm on Monday, Wednesday, Friday, Saturday, and Sunday. Entrance to the clubhouse costs $3; no admission is charged for the grandstand.

RUNNING   The cool, quiet, morning hours before 8am are a good time to jog through the streets of Old San Juan. Head for the wide thoroughfares adjacent to El Morro and then San Cristóbal, whose walls jut upward from the flat ground. You might join Puerto Rico's governor, a dedicated runner, in making several laps around the seafront Paseo de la Princesa at the base of his home, La Fortaleza.

If you don't mind heading out into the island a bit from your base in Old San Juan, you might opt for a run through the palm trees of the Parque Central, near Calle Cerra and Route 2 in Santurce. Condado's Avenida Ashford is a busy site for morning runners as well.

SCUBA DIVING   In San Juan, the best outfitter is **Caribe Aquatic Adventures,** P.O. Box 9024278, San Juan Station, San Juan, PR 00902 (© **787/ 281-8858**), which operates a dive shop in the rear lobby of the Normandie Hotel that's open daily from 8am to 4pm. The company offers diving certification from both PADI and NAUI as part of 40-hour courses priced at $465 each. A resort course for first-time divers costs $100. Also offered are local daily dives in the waters close to San Juan, as well as the option of traveling farther afield into waters near the reefs of Puerto Rico's eastern shore. If time permits, we recommend a full-day dive experience; if time is limited, try one of the many worthy dive sites that lie closer to San Juan and can be experienced in a half day.

SNORKELING   Snorkeling is better in the outlying portions of the island than in overcrowded San Juan. But if you don't have time to explore greater Puerto Rico, you'll find that most of the popular beaches, such as Luquillo and Isla Verde, have pretty good visibility and kiosks that rent equipment. Snorkeling equipment generally rents for $15. If you're on your own in the San Juan area, one of the best places is the San Juan Bay marina near the Caribe Hilton.

Watersports desks at the big San Juan hotels at Isla Verde and Condado can generally make arrangements for instruction and equipment rental and can also lead you to the best places for snorkeling, depending on where you are in the sprawling metropolis. If your hotel doesn't offer such services, you can contact **Caribe Aquatic Adventures** (see "Scuba Diving" above), which caters to both snorkelers and scuba divers. You can also rent equipment from **Caribbean School of Aquatics,** Taft No. 1, Suite 10F, San Juan (© **787/728-6606**).

Tips **Swimmers Beware**

You have to pick your spots carefully if you want to swim along Condado Beach. The waters along the Condado Plaza Hotel are calmer than in other areas because of a coral breakwater. The beach near the Marriott is not good for swimming because of rocks and an undertow.

SPAS & FITNESS CENTERS If a spa figures into your holiday plans, the grandest and largest such facility in San Juan is found at **Ritz-Carlton San Juan Hotel, Spa & Casino** ✦, Avenida de los Gobernadores 6961, no. 187, Isla Verde (© 787/253-1700). You get it all here: the luxury life, with state-of-the-art massages, body wraps and scrubs, facials, manicures, pedicures, and a salon guaranteed to make you look like a movie star.

In an elegant marble-and-stone setting, there are 11 rooms for pampering, including hydrotherapy and treatments custom-tailored for individual needs. The spa also features a 7,200-square-foot outdoor swimming pool.

The Ritz-Carlton facility is the only spa in the Caribbean to offer the exotic and ritualistic treatments known to spa lovers around the world as the Balinese Massage and the Javanese Lulur. The fragrant Balinese Massage uses compression, skin-rolling, wringing, and percussion and thumb-walking to "de-stress" the most uptight guests. The Lulur originated centuries ago in the royal palaces of Central Java as part of a ritual for royal brides-to-be. The Lulur was performed daily to beautify, soften, and "sweeten" the bride's skin. Today it is enjoyed by women and men alike.

The only resort spa that challenges the Ritz-Carlton is the runner-up, the newly launched Olas Spa at the **Carib Hilton,** Calle Los Rosales (© 787/721-0303). The spa offers everything from traditional massages to more exotic body and water therapies, using such products as honey, cucumber, sea salts, seaweed, or mud baths. You can choose your delight among the massages, including one called "Rising Sun," a traditional Japanese form of massage called shiatsu that uses pressure applied with hands, elbows, and knees on specific body points. Among body wraps is one known as Firm Away, a super firming, brown and green algae body cocoon therapy for a soft, toned, and smooth skin.

The Hilton Spa has the town's best program for hair treatments, including thinning hair and "tired perm." It also has a state-of-the-art fitness center with Universal and Nautilus weight machines, aerobics and yoga classes, treadmills, aerobicycles, loofah body polishes, and facials.

After the extravaganza of these two spas, it's a bit of a comedown at the other leading resorts. The Plaza Spa at the **Condado Plaza Hotel & Casino,** Av. Ashford 999 (© 787/721-1000), features Universal weight-training machines, video exercycles, a sauna, whirlpools, and a spa program of facials and massage. We'd recommend this mainly for people who want only minor spa or fitness-center facilities during their stay, and not for those who want to make a spa the No. 1 goal of their sojourn in San Juan.

The Penthouse Spa at **Wyndham El San Juan Hotel & Casino,** Av. Isla Verde 6063 (© 787/791-1000), offers a stunning panoramic view of San Juan that almost competes with the facilities. You'll find full amenities, including fitness evaluations, supervised weight-loss programs, aerobics classes, a sauna, a steam room, and luxury massages. A daily fee for individual services is assessed if you want special treatment or care.

If your hotel doesn't have a gym or health club of its own, consider working the kinks out of your muscles at **Muscle Factory** ✦, Av. Ashford 1131, Condado (© 787/721-0717). It's air-conditioned, well equipped, and popular with residents of the surrounding high-rent district. Entrance costs $10 per visit, $35 for 5 days, or $45 for a week. Hours are Monday through Thursday from 6am to 9pm, Friday from 6am to 9pm, and Saturday from 8am to 6pm.

TENNIS In San Juan, courts can be found at the **Caribe Hilton & Casino,** Puerta de Tierra (© 787/721-0303), open daily 24 hours, and the **Condado**

Finds La Vida Loca & La Criolla Chic

Puerto Rico's newly acquired Latino chic is putting it closer into competition with the very hip South Miami Beach scene in Florida.

There is no hipper venue in San Juan today than the new **Museo de Arte** (p. 139). It took $55 million to turn this 1920s city hospital in Santurce, an eyesore for decades, into this new home for art. The new museum has become a way of life for some Puerto Ricans, many of whom go here at least once a week—perhaps to see a production in the 400-seat theater, named for Raúl Juliá, the late Puerto Rican actor, or perhaps to go for a romantic stroll through the museum's 5-acre garden. Many chic trendsetters return at night for a nuevo criolla meal at **Pikayo** (p. 126).

The emerging neighborhood for the chic set is called **SoFo,** a sector that lies south of Calle Fortaleza in Old Town. This place is becoming so trendy that it is the first of the Old San Juan neighborhoods to be awarded its own acronym, no doubt inspired by New York's SoHo. The **Parrot Club** (p. 112) is the hot spot of the neighborhood, quickly rivaled by **Trois Cent Onze** (p. 112).

Even beaches attract trendsetters. Students, surfers, gay people, and those on the see-and-be-seen circuit avoid the beaches of Condado and Isla Verde, heading for **Ocean Park Beach** instead.

Tired of chic? To mix with the locals, head for the **Mercado de Río Piedras** (Paseo José de Diego), with its 4 blocks of shops and cheap restaurants. (You can reach this area by taxi or car. From the Condado or Santurce, take Avenida Ponce de León south until you come to the intersection with Route 47 going east. The route is also called Paseo José de Diego. The market will soon appear on your right.) This vast outdoor mall is scented with everything from recently caught fish to just-picked citrus. When _Sanjuaneros_ want to buy anything, they head here. Open from early morning to late evening (but not on Sun), these stores and markets provide a whiff of local life that's unseen anywhere else in San Juan.

When you're tired of museums and shopping, you can head for the boardwalk at **Parque Lineal Marti Coli,** which stretches for nearly 2 miles (3km) along Caño de Martín Peña, from Hato Rey to Parque Central. Eventually this boardwalk will reach a distance of nearly 12 miles (19km), linking Old Town with Río Piedras. Biking, hiking, and jogging pathways are planned; one day bikers will be able to go along the breadth of San Juan without having to encounter traffic. In the meantime, enough trails have been completed for a memorable stroll.

When the sun goes down, head for a party at the hot spot Ñapa, Av. Ashford 1018, Condado (© **787/724-3686**), which in local slang means "something extra." Owner Luis Moscoso took a rundown cinema and fancied it up with marble and flattering lighting for a minimalist aura. The location is on the waterfront; the cocktails are superb, and the menu of fusion cookery inventive.

Later you can head for **Rumba** (p. 167) to dance the night away to the sounds of salsa and a bomba with an African beat.

Plaza Hotel & Casino, Av. Ashford 999 (© **787/721-1000**), open daily from 6am to 9pm. Nonguests can use these courts if they make reservations. There are also 17 public courts, lit at night, at **San Juan Central Municipal Park,** at Calle Cerra (exit on Route 2; © **787/722-1646**), open daily. Fees are $3 per hour from 8am to 6pm, and $4 per hour from 6 to 10pm.

WINDSURFING   A favorite spot for windsurfing is the sheltered waters of the Condado Lagoon in San Juan. Throughout the island, many of the companies that feature snorkeling and scuba diving also offer windsurfing equipment and instruction, and dozens of hotels offer facilities on their own premises. Another good spot is at the Radisson Normandie Hotel, where **Caribe Aquatic Adventures** has its main branch (see "Scuba Diving" above). Board rentals cost $25 to $30 per hour; lessons cost $45.

3 Shopping

Because Puerto Rico is a U.S. commonwealth, U.S. citizens don't pay duty on items brought back to the mainland. And you can still find great bargains on Puerto Rico, where the competition among shopkeepers is fierce. Even though the U.S. Virgin Islands are duty-free, you can often find far lower prices on many items in San Juan than on St. Thomas.

The streets of Old Town, such as Calle San Francisco and Calle del Cristo, are the major venues for shopping. Malls in San Juan are generally open Monday through Saturday from 9am to 9pm, Sunday from 11am to 5pm. Regular stores in town are usually open Monday through Saturday from 9am to 6pm. In Old San Juan many stores are open on Sunday, too.

Native handicrafts can be good buys, including needlework, straw work, ceramics, hammocks, and papier-mâché fruits and vegetables, as well as paintings and sculptures by Puerto Rican artists. Among these, the carved wooden religious idols known as *santos* (saints) have been called Puerto Rico's greatest contribution to the plastic arts and are sought by collectors. For the best selection of santos, head for Galería Botello (see "Art" below), Olé, or Puerto Rican Arts & Crafts (see "Gifts & Handicrafts" later in this chapter).

Puerto Rico's biggest and most up-to-date shopping mall is **Plaza Las Américas,** in the financial district of Hato Rey, right off the Las Américas Expressway. This complex, with its fountains and modern architecture, has more than 200 mostly upscale shops. The variety of goods and prices is roughly comparable to that of large stateside malls.

Unless otherwise specified, the following stores can be reached via the Old Town trolley.

Tips **Know When the Price Is Right**

The only way to determine if you're paying less for an item in San Juan than you would at home is to find out what the going rate is in your hometown. Obviously, if you can find items in San Juan cheaper than back home, go for it. But know the prices before you go. Otherwise, you could end up lugging merchandise back on an airplane when the same item was available at about the same price, or less, where you live.

ANTIQUES

El Alcazar *Finds*   Established in 1986 by retired career officers with the U.S. Army and the U.S. State Department, this is the largest emporium of antique furniture, silver, and art objects in the Caribbean. The best way to sift through the massive inventory is to begin at the address listed below, on Calle San José between Calle Luna and Calle Sol, and ask the owners, Sharon and Robert Bartos, to guide you to the other three buildings that are literally stuffed with important art and antiques. Each shop lies within a half block of the organization's headquarters, and each is within a historic building of architectural or historic importance (public areas of several large Puerto Rican hotels contain furnishings acquired here). For antique silver, crystal, delicate porcelain, glittering chandeliers, Russian icons, and objects of religious devotion such as santos, look first at the organization's headquarters. Some of the objects, especially the 1930s-era dining-room sets, whose chair backs are composed of wood medallions held in place by woven canes or wicker, derive from Puerto Rico. The majority of the objects, however, are culled from estates and galleries throughout Europe. Calle San José 103. ⓒ 787/723-1229.

ART

Butterfly People   Butterfly People (p. 116) is a gallery and cafe in a handsomely restored building in Old San Juan. Butterflies, sold here in artfully arranged boxes, range from $20 for a single mounting to thousands of dollars for whole-wall murals. The butterflies are preserved and will last forever. The dimensional artwork is sold in limited editions and can be shipped worldwide. Most of these butterflies come from farms around the world, some of the most beautiful hailing from Indonesia, Malaysia, and New Guinea. Tucked away within the same premises is **Malula Antiques.** Specializing in tribal art from the Moroccan sub-Sahara and Syria, it contains a sometimes-startling collection of primitive and timeless crafts and accessories. Calle Fortaleza 152. ⓒ 787/723-2432.

Galería Botello   A contemporary Latin American art gallery, Galería Botello is a living tribute to the late Angel Botello, one of Puerto Rico's most outstanding artists. Born after the Spanish Civil War in a small village in Galicia, Spain, he fled to the Caribbean and spent 12 years in Haiti. His paintings and bronze sculptures, evocative of his colorful background, are done in a style uniquely his own. This galería is his former colonial mansion home, which he restored himself. Today it displays his paintings and sculptures, showcases the works of many outstanding local artists, and offers a large collection of Puerto Rican antique santos. Calle del Cristo 208. ⓒ 787/723-2879.

Galería Fosil Art   This is a specialty gallery, displaying unique art pieces from limestone and coral that may have existed at the time of the dinosaurs. The work is the creation of Radamés Rivera. One of the gallery's most noted artists is Yolanda Velasquez, who paints in an abstract style. The gallery also showcases the work of some 40 other artists, ranging from Mexico to Cuba. Calle Cristo 200B. ⓒ 787/725-4252.

Galería Palomas   This and the also-recommended Galería Botello are the two leading art galleries of Puerto Rico. Here you can find works by some of the leading painters in Latin America. Prices range from $75 to $35,000, and exhibits are rotated every 2 to 3 weeks. The setting is a 17th-century colonial house. Of special note are works by such local artists as Homer, Moya, and Alicea. Calle del Cristo 207. ⓒ 787/725-2660.

Galería San Juan This shop, located at the Gallery Inn, specializes in the sculpture and paintings of Jan D'Esopo, a Connecticut-born artist who has spent a great deal of time in Puerto Rico. Many of her fine pieces are in bronze. In the Gallery Inn, Calle Norzagaray 206. ℂ 787/722-1808.

Magia Artefactos Set across the street from the side entrance to El Convento hotel, about a block uphill from the cathedral, this creatively disorganized art gallery has better and more interesting work than its nearby competitors. Most of the objects were crafted by San Juan native Manolo Díaz, whose art studies in Italy contributed to his zeal for incorporating architectural remnants into his sculptures. Especially poignant are montages that combine battered shutters from colonial buildings with santos carved by Puerto Rican artisans. Calle del Cristo 99. ℂ 787/724-8764.

Sun 'n Sand This is the best store in San Juan for Haitian art and artifacts. Its walls are covered with framed versions of primitive Haitian landscapes, portraits, crowd scenes, and whimsical visions of jungles where lions, tigers, parrots, and herons take on quasi-human personalities and forms. Most paintings range from $35 to $350, although you can usually bargain them down a bit. Look for the brightly painted wall hangings crafted from sheets of metal. Also look for satirical metal wall hangings, brightly painted, representing the *tap-taps* (battered public minivans and buses) of Port-au-Prince. They make amusing and whimsical souvenirs of a trip to the Caribbean. Calle Fortaleza 152. ℂ 787/722-1135.

BOOKS

Bell, Book & Candle For travel guides, maps, and beach-reading material, head here. It is a large, general-interest bookstore that carries fiction and classics in both Spanish and English, plus a huge selection of postcards. Av. José de Diego 102, Santurce. ℂ 787/728-5000. Bus: A5.

Libreria Cronopios This is the leading choice in the Old Town, with the largest selection of titles. It sells a number of books on Puerto Rican culture as well as good maps of the island. Calle San José 255. ℂ 787/724-1815.

CARNIVAL MASKS

La Calle Every Puerto Rican knows that the best, and cheapest, place to buy brightly painted carnival masks (*caretas*) is in Ponce, where the tradition of making them from papier-mâché originated. But if you can't spare the time for a side excursion to Ponce, this store in Old San Juan stocks one of the most varied inventories of vegigantes in the Puerto Rican capital. Depending on their size and composition (some include coconut shells, gourds, and flashy metal trim), they range from $12 to $2,400 each. Side-by-side with the pagan-inspired masks, you'll find a well-chosen selection of paintings by talented local artists, priced from $250 to $2,000 each. Calle Fortaleza 105. ℂ 787/725-1306.

CIGARS

Club Jibarito This is the retail outlet of a Puerto Rican–based manufacturer of genuinely excellent cigars. You can select from the Jibarito cigars that are proudly displayed within one of the best-designed humidors in town. Overall it's our favorite cigar emporium in San Juan, with a polite staff and lots and lots of class. 202 Calle Cristo. ℂ 787/724-7797.

CLOTHING & BEACHWEAR

Casa Marriot *Finds* For more than 50 years, businessmen of San Juan have been coming here for a wide selection of mostly English, tropical-weight fabrics.

Grotesque Masks

The most popular of all Puerto Rican crafts are the frightening **caretas**—papier-mâché masks worn at island carnivals. Tangles of menacing horns, fang-toothed leering expressions, and bulging eyes of these half-demon, half-animal creations send children running and screaming to their parents. At carnival time, they are worn by costumed revelers called *vegigantes*. Vegigantes often wear bat-winged jumpsuits and roam the streets either individually or in groups.

The origins of these masks and carnivals may go back to medieval Spain and/or tribal Africa. A processional tradition in Spain, dating from the early 17th century, was intended to terrify sinners with marching devils in the hope that they would return to church. Cervantes described it briefly in *Don Quijote*. Puerto Rico blended this Spanish procession with the masked tradition brought by slaves from Africa. Some historians believe that the Taínos were also accomplished mask makers, which would make this a very ancient tradition indeed.

The predominant traditional mask colors were black, red, and yellow, all symbols of hellfire and damnation. Today, pastels are more likely to be used. Each vegigante sports at least two or three horns, although some masks have hundreds of horns, in all shapes and sizes. Mask making in Ponce, the major center for this craft, and in Loíza Aldea, a palm-fringed town on the island's northeastern coast, has since led to a renaissance of Puerto Rican folk art.

The premier store selling these masks is **La Calle** (p. 158). Masks can be seen in action at the three big masquerade carnivals on the island: the Ponce Festival in February, the Festival of Loíza Aldea in July, and the Día de las Mascaras at Hatillo in December.

For a suit, most North American men require from 3½ to 4 yards of fabric, priced from $13 to $110 a yard, plus another 2½ yards of lining, priced around $5 a yard. The helpful staff can direct you to any of several local tailors, who will charge from $250 to $350 to whip that fabric into a suit. Calle Tanca 255. ⓒ 787/722-0444.

Lindissima Shop This outlet offers a collection of contemporary sportswear and dresses for women, for both daytime and evening. If you lack an outfit for a formal evening, you are likely to find it here. Calle Fortaleza 300. ⓒ 787/758-6511.

Mrs. and Miss Boutique The most visible article available within this shop is "the magic dress," for $115. Crafted in Morocco of a silky-looking blend of rayon and cotton, it comes in 10 different colors or patterns and can be worn 11 different ways. (A saleswoman will show you how.) The shop also stocks sarongs for $10 and long dresses, sometimes from Indonesia, that begin at only $25. Calle Fortaleza 154. ⓒ 787/724-8571.

Nono Maldonado Named after its owner, a Puerto Rico–born designer who worked for many years as the fashion editor of *Esquire* magazine, this is one of the most fashionable and upscale haberdashers in the Caribbean. Selling both men's and women's clothing, it contains everything from socks to dinner jackets, as well as ready-to-wear versions of Maldonado's twice-a-year collections. Both ready-to-wear and couture are available here. Although this is the designer's main store (midway between the Condado Plaza and the Ramada Hotel), there is also a Maldonado boutique in Wyndham El San Juan Hotel in Isla Verde. Av. Ashford 1051. ℂ **787/721-0456.** Bus: A7.

Polo Ralph Lauren Factory Store *(Value)*   It's as stylish and carefully orchestrated as anything you'd expect from one of North America's leading clothiers. Even better, its prices are often 35% to 40% less than in retail stores on the U.S. mainland. You can find even greater discounts on irregular or slightly damaged garments, but inspect them carefully before buying. The store occupies two floors of a pair of colonial buildings, with one upstairs room devoted to home furnishings. Calle del Cristo 201. ℂ **787/722-2136.**

Speedo Authentic Fitness   This outlet peddles sportswear for women and men, specializing in shorts, jackets, and swimwear. It also has one of the town's best collections of sandals. Calle Fortaleza 65 (at the corner of Calle Cristo). ℂ **787/ 724-3089.**

W. H. Smith   This outlet sells mostly women's clothing, everything from bathing suits and beach attire to jogging suits. For men, there are shorts, bathing suits, and jogging suits. There's also a good selection of books and maps. In the Condado Plaza Hotel, Av. Ashford 999. ℂ **787/721-1000,** ext. 2094.

COFFEE & SPICES

El Alcázar   Here you can find decorative items from almost any part of the world, maybe even remote Tibet. It's like wandering in your grandfather's attic—assuming that he was an ancient mariner with a taste for the exotic. The treasure trove of merchandise is always changing, so drop in for a surprise. Calle San José 103. ℂ **787/723-1229.**

Goa *(Finds)*   Decorators on the lookout for rare and unusual objects consider this shop a dream come true. The inventory is one of the most imaginative in Puerto Rico. Objects hail from Afghanistan, Indonesia, Morocco, India, Brazil, Thailand, and the Philippines, among other places. Exotic birdcages, sub-Saharan tables and chairs, and porcelain vases covered in Arabic writing are just some of the wonderful and sometimes weird objects stocked here. Calle Luna 152 at Calle Cruz. ℂ **787/721-7669.**

Spicy Caribbee   This shop has the best selection of Puerto Rican coffee, which is gaining an increasingly good reputation among aficionados. Alto Grande is the grandest brand. Other favorite brands of Puerto Rican coffee are Café Crema, Café Rico, Rioja, and Yaucono—in that order. The shop also has

---

The Coffee of Kings & Popes

Of all the coffees of Puerto Rico, our favorite is **Alto Grande,** which has been a tradition in Puerto Rican households since 1839. Over the years, this super premium coffee has earned a reputation for being the "Coffee of Popes and Kings," and is hailed as one of the top three coffees in the world. A magnificently balanced coffee, Alto Grande is a rare and exotic coffee with a sweet, pointed aroma and a bright sparkling flavor. The bean is grown in the highest mountains of the Lares range. This coffee is served at leading hotels and restaurants in Puerto Rico. Should you develop a taste for it, it is also available at various specialty stores throughout the United States.

Tips **Shopping for Santos**

The most impressive of the island's crafts are the santos, carved religious figures that have been produced since the 1500s. Craftspeople who make these are called *santeros;* using clay, gold, stone, or cedar wood, they carve figurines representing saints, usually from 8 to 20 inches tall. Before the Spanish colonization, small statues called *zemi* stood in native tribal villages and camps as objects of veneration, and Puerto Rico's santos may derive from that pre-Columbian tradition. Every town has its patron saint, and every home has its santos to protect the family. For some families, worshipping the santos replaces a traditional mass.

Art historians view the carving of santos as Puerto Rico's greatest contribution to the plastic arts. The earliest figures were richly baroque, indicating a strong Spanish influence, but as the islanders began to assert their own identity, the carved figures often became simpler.

In carving santos, craftspeople often used handmade tools. Sometimes such natural materials as vegetable dyes and even human hair were used. The saints represented by most santos can be identified by their accompanying symbols; for example, Saint Anthony is usually depicted with the infant Jesus and a book. The most popular group of santos is the Three Kings. The Trinity and the Nativity are also depicted frequently.

Art experts claim that santos making approached its zenith at the turn of the 20th century, although hundreds of santeros still practice their craft throughout the island. Serious santos collectors view the former craftsmen of old as the true artists in the field. The best collection of santos is found at Puerto Rican Arts & Crafts (p. 162).

Some of the best santos on the island can be seen at the Capilla de Cristo in Old San Juan. Perhaps at some future date, a museum devoted entirely to santos will open in Puerto Rico.

Old Town's best array of hot spicy sauces of the Caribbean. Calle Cristo 154. ✆ 787/725-4690.

Xian Imports   Set within a jumbled, slightly claustrophobic setting, you'll discover porcelain, sculptures, paintings, and Chinese furniture, much of it antique. Island decorators favor this spot as a source for unusual art objects. Calle de la Cruz 153. ✆ 787/723-2214.

DEPARTMENT STORES

Marshalls   This store, part of the U.S. discount chain, is one of our favorite department stores in the whole Caribbean. Thousands of *Sanjuaneros* also consider it their favorite shopping expedition as well. A few dedicated born-to-shop advocates pop in virtually every day to see what new items have gone on sale. At Plaza de Armas, across from the City Hall, expect to see a massive array—at cutrate prices—of designer clothes, housewares, home furnishings, and shoes, plus a variety of other merchandise. Calle Rafael Cordero 154. ✆ 787/722-3020.

GIFTS & HANDICRAFTS

Bared & Sons *Value* Now in its fourth decade, this is the main outlet of a chain of at least 20 upper-bracket jewelry stores on Puerto Rico. It has a worthy inventory of gemstones, gold, diamonds, and wristwatches on the street level, which does a thriving business with cruise-ship passengers. But the real value of this store lies one floor up, where a monumental collection of porcelain and crystal is on display in claustrophobic proximity. It's a great source for hard-to-get and discontinued patterns (priced at around 20% less than at equivalent stateside outlets) from Christofle, Royal Doulton, Wedgwood, Limoges, Royal Copenhagen, Lalique, Lladró, Herend, Baccarat, and Daum. Calle Fortaleza 65 (at the corner of Calle San Justo). ℂ **787/724-4811.**

Bóveda This long, narrow space is crammed with exotic jewelry, clothing, greeting cards with images of life in Puerto Rico, some 100 handmade lamps, antiques, Mexican punched tin and glass, and Art Nouveau reproductions, among other items. Calle del Cristo 209. ℂ **787/725-0263.**

Centro Nacional de Artes Populares y Artesanias This store, a superb repository of native crafts, sells crafts of high-quality work. Centro Nacional scans the islands for artisans who still practice time-treasured crafts and do so with considerable skill. The prices aren't cheap, but the work merits the tab. At Calle del Cristo. ℂ **787/721-6866.**

El Artesano If your budget doesn't allow for an excursion to the Andes, head for this shop. You'll find Mexican and Peruvian icons of the Virgin Mary; charming depictions of fish and Latin American birds in terra-cotta and brass; all kinds of woven goods; painted cupboards, chests, and boxes; and mirrors and Latin dolls. Calle Fortaleza 314. ℂ **787/721-6483.**

El Cundeamor The inventory at this shop includes high-quality trays and serving dishes made from an intricately detailed aluminum-pewter alloy, often from Mexico. There's also a lot of silver jewelry, from Indonesia and Mexico, much of it adaptable to either modern or old-fashioned clothing. Fortaleza 105, Old San Juan. ℂ **787/721-5921.**

Libreria y Tienda de Artesania del Instituto de Cultura Puertorriqueña This store, next to the Convento de los Dominicos, has not only a collection of books on Puerto Rico, but a good display of crafts in the Old Town, including santos, Indian artifacts, carnival masks (many from Ponce), and baskets. All pieces are said to be made in Puerto Rico, rather than in places such as Taiwan, as is so often the case. Calle Norzagaray 98. ℂ **787/721-6866.**

Olé Browsing this store is a learning experience. Even the standard Panama hat takes on new dimensions. Woven from fine-textured *paja* grass and priced from $20 to $1,000, depending on the density of the weave, the hats are all created the same size, then blocked—by an employee on-site—to fit the shape of your head. Dig into this store's diverse inventory to discover a wealth of treasures—hand-beaten Chilean silver, Peruvian Christmas ornaments, Puerto Rican santos—almost all from Puerto Rico or Latin America. Calle Fortaleza 105. ℂ **787/ 724-2445.**

Puerto Rican Arts & Crafts Set in a 200-year-old colonial building, this unique store is one of the premier outlets on the island for authentic artifacts. Of particular interest are papier-mâché carnival masks from Ponce, whose grotesque and colorful features were originally conceived to chase away evil spirits. Taíno designs inspired by ancient petroglyphs are incorporated into most of the sterling silver jewelry sold here. There's an art gallery in back, with silk-screened serigraphs by local artists. The outlet has a gourmet Puerto Rican food section with items like coffee, rum, and hot sauces for sale. A related specialty of this well-respected store involves the exhibition and sale of modern replicas of the Spanish colonial tradition of santos, which are carved and sometimes poly-chromed representations of the Catholic saints and the infant Jesus. Priced from $44 to $225 each, and laboriously carved by artisans in private studios around the island, they're easy to pack in a suitcase because the largest one measures only 12 inches from halo to toe. Calle Fortaleza 204. ℭ 787/725-5596.

JEWELRY

Barrachina's The birthplace, in 1963, of the piña colada (an honor co-claimed by the staff at the Caribe Hilton), Barrachina's is a favorite of cruise-ship passengers. It offers one of the largest selections of jewelry, perfume, cigars, and gifts in San Juan. There's a patio for drinks where you can order (what else?) a piña colada. There is also a Bacardi rum outlet (bottles cost less than stateside but cost the same as at the Bacardi distillery), a costume jewelry department, a gift shop, and a section for authentic silver jewelry, plus a restaurant. Calle Fort-aleza 104 (between Calle del Cristo and Calle San José). ℭ 787/725-7912.

Eduardo Barquet Known as a leading cost-conscious place to buy fine jew-elry in Old San Juan, this shop has 14-karat Italian gold chains and bracelets that are measured, fitted, and sold by weight. You can purchase watches or beau-tiful gems in modern settings in both 14- and 18-karat gold. The store recently expanded its collection to include 18-karat, emerald, ruby, diamond, and pearl jewelry, along with platinum bridal jewelry. Calle Fortaleza 200 (at the corner of Calle La Cruz). ℭ 787/723-1989.

Gaston Bared Jewelry This is an offshoot of the above-recommended Bared & Sons, but with a more contemporary inventory. This shop also has a branch at Calle Fortaleza 208 (same phone) that sells Murano crystal, Hummel and Lladró figurines, watches (including Omega, Seiko, and Tissot), and colored gemstones, such as amethysts, set into gold and silver settings. Calle Fortaleza 154 (at Calle San José). ℭ 787/722-2172.

Joseph Manchini This shop displays the works of its namesake, the shop's owner. He conceives almost anything you'd want in gold, silver, and bronze. Some of Old Town's most imaginative rings, bracelets, and chains are displayed here. If you don't like what's on sale, you can design your own jewelry, includ-ing pieces made from sapphire, emerald, and rubies. Calle Fortaleza 101. ℭ 787/ 722-7698.

Joyería Riviera This emporium of 18-karat gold and diamonds is the island's leading jeweler. Adjacent to Plaza de Armas, the shop has an impeccable reputation. Its owner, Julio Abislaiman, stocks his store from such diamond cen-ters as Antwerp, Tel Aviv, and New York. This is the major distributor of Rolex watches on Puerto Rico. Prices in the store range from $150 into the tens of thousands of dollars—at these prices, it's a good thing you can get "whatever you want," according to the owner. Calle La Cruz 205. ℭ 787/725-4000.

Mount and Gems This shop sells convincing, glittering fake diamonds for those who don't want to wear the real thing. It also stocks real diamond chips, emeralds, sapphires, and rubies. Calle Fortaleza 205. ℭ 787/724-1377.

A Dying Art: Old Lace

Another Puerto Rican craft has undergone a big revival just as it seemed that it would disappear forever: lace. Originating in Spain, *mundillos* (tatted fabrics) are the product of a type of bobbin lace making. This 5-century-old craft exists today only in Puerto Rico and Spain.

The first lace made in Puerto Rico was called *torchon* (beggar's lace). Early examples of beggar's lace were considered of inferior quality, but artisans today have transformed this fabric into a delicate art form, eagerly sought by collectors. Lace bands called *entrados* have two straight borders, whereas the other traditional style, *puntilla,* has both a straight and a scalloped border.

The best outlet in San Juan for lace is **Linen House** (p. 164).

Piercing Pagoda   There's nothing Puerto Rican or glamorous about this branch of a large U.S. chain. But if you're in the market for a gold or silver chain, or perhaps a pendant or set of earrings, the sales here could be worth a detour. Be alert that some displays feature 10-karat gold rather than the more preferable, and expensive, 14- or 18-karat. Calle Fortaleza 203. ✆ **787/725-1765.**

R. Kury   This is the factory outlet for the oldest jewelry factory on Puerto Rico, the Kury Company. Most of the output is shipped stateside. Don't expect a top-notch jeweler here: Many of the pieces are produced in endless repetition. But don't overlook this place for 14-karat-gold ornaments. Some of the designs are charming, and prices are about 20% less than those at retail stores on the U.S. mainland. Plaza los Muchachos, Calle Fortaleza 201. ✆ **787/724-3102.**

LACE & LINENS

Linen House   This unpretentious store specializes in table linens, bed linens, and lace and has the island's best selection. Some of the most delicate pieces are expensive, but most are moderate in price. Inventories include embroidered shower curtains that sell for around $35 each, and lace doilies, bun warmers, place mats, and tablecloths that seamstresses took weeks to complete. Some astonishingly lovely items are available for as little as $30. The aluminum/pewter serving dishes have beautiful Spanish-colonial designs. Prices here are sometimes 40% lower than those on the North American mainland. Calle Fortaleza 250. ✆ **787/721-4219.**

LEATHER & EQUESTRIAN ACCESSORIES

Lalin Leather Shop   Although it lies in an out-of-the-way suburb (Puerto Nuevo), about 2 miles (3km) south of San Juan, this is the best and most comprehensive cowboy and equestrian outfitter in Puerto Rico, probably in the entire Caribbean. Here you'll find all manner of boots, cowboy hats, and accessories. More important, however, is the wide array of saddles and bridles, some from Colombia, some from Puerto Rico, priced from a cost-conscious $159 to as much as $3,100. Even the highest-priced items cost a lot less than their U.S. mainland equivalents, so if you happen to have a horse or pony on the U.S. mainland, a visit here might be worth your while. If you decide to make the rather inconvenient pilgrimage, you won't be alone. Regular clients come from as far away as Iceland, the Bahamas, and New York. Everything can be shipped. Av. Piñero 1617, Puerto Nuevo. ✆ **787/781-5305.** No bus.

MALLS

Belz Factory Outlet World   The largest mall of its kind in Puerto Rico, and the Caribbean as well, opened in 2001 in Canóvanas, east of San Juan en route to El Yunque. Totally enclosed and air-conditioned, it re-creates the experience of strolling through the streets of Old San Juan, sans the traffic and heat. Five interconnected buildings comprise the mall, with dozens of stores from Nike to Gap, from Dockers Levis to Maidenform, from Samsonite to Guess, and from Papaya and Geoffrey Beene. 18400 State Rd. #3, Barrio Pueblo, Canóvanas. ✆ 787/256-7040. No bus.

El Convento Shopping Arcade   Some of the finest merchandise in Old Town is displayed in various shops at the El Convento hotel. Come here for a selection of eclectic jewelry, timepieces, fine china, luxury gift and home-furnishing items, cigars, tobacco, and other items. For example, at the Old City Cigar Emporium, a walk-in humidor contains a collection of the finest tobaccos in the Caribbean. The Oggetti Outlet Store features several bargains in crystal, china, and gift items for the home, and the Oggetti Alessi Boutique carries the renowned Milanese designer line of colorful home accessories. Shop at Oggetti offers an exclusive collection of objets d'art, designer-crafted furnishings, and selected items from Tiffany. Calle Cristo 100. ✆ 787/723-2877.

MARKETS

Plaza del Mercado de Santurce   If you'd like an old-fashioned Puerto Rican market, something likely to be found in a small South American country, visit this offbeat curiosity. In a West Indian structure, the central market is filled with "botanicas" hawking everything from medicinal herbs to Puerto Rican bay rum. Here is your best chance to pick up some patchouli roots. What are they used for? In religious observances and to kill unruly cockroaches. Some little cantinas here offer very typical Puerto Rican dishes, including roast pork, and you can also order the best mango banana shakes on the island. Calle Dos Hermanos at Calle Capitol, Santurce. ✆ 787/723-8022. Bus: B5.

4 San Juan After Dark

San Juan nightlife comes in all varieties. From the vibrant performing-arts scene to street-level salsa and the casinos, discos, and bars, there's plenty of entertainment available almost any evening.

As in a Spanish city, nightlife begins very late, especially on Friday and Saturday nights. Hang out until the late, late afternoon on the beach, have dinner around eight o'clock (nine would be even more fashionable), and then the night is yours. The true party animal will rock until the broad daylight.

Qué Pasa?, the official visitor's guide to Puerto Rico, lists cultural events, including music, dance, theater, film, and art exhibits. It's distributed free by the tourist office.

THE PERFORMING ARTS

Centro de Bellas Artes   In the heart of Santurce, the Performing Arts Center is a 6-minute taxi ride from most of the Condado hotels. It contains the Festival Hall, Drama Hall, and the Experimental Theater. Some of the events here will be of interest only to Spanish speakers; others attract an international audience. Av. Ponce de León 22. ✆ 787/724-4747, or 787/725-7334 for the ticket agent. Tickets $13–$65; 50% discounts for seniors. Bus: 1.

Teatro Tapía   Standing across from Plaza de Colón and built about 1832, this is one of the oldest theaters in the Western Hemisphere (see "Historic Sights" earlier in this chapter). Productions, some musical, are staged throughout the year and include drama, dances, and cultural events. You'll have to call the box office (open Mon through Fri from 9am to 6pm) for specific information. Av. Ponce de León. © 787/721-0169. Tickets $25–$30, depending on the show. Bus: B8 or B21.

THE CLUB & MUSIC SCENE

Babylon   Modeled after an artist's rendition of the once-notorious city in Mesopotamia, this nightclub is designed in the form of a circle, with a central dance floor and a wraparound balcony where onlookers and voyeurs—a 25-to-45-year-old age group—can observe the activities on the floor below. As one patron put it, "Here's where gringos can shake their bon-bons with San Juan's old guard." Equipped with one of the best sound systems in the Caribbean, its location within the most exciting hotel in San Juan allows guests the chance to visit the hotel's bars, its intricately decorated lobby, and its casino en route. In Wyndham El San Juan Hotel & Casino, Av. Isla Verde 6063, Isla Verde. © 787/791-1000. Cover $10, free for residents of El San Juan Hotel. Thurs–Sat 10pm–3am. Bus: M7.

Club Laser   Set in the heart of the old town, this disco is especially crowded when cruise ships pull into town. Once inside, you can wander over the three floors of its historic premises, listening to whatever music happens to be hot in New York at the time, with lots of additional Latino merengue and salsa thrown in as well. Depending on the night, the age of the crowd varies, but in general it's the 20s, 30s, and even 40s set. Calle del Cruz 251 (near the corner of Calle Fortaleza). © 787/725-7581. Cover $8–$10 (free cover for women after midnight on Sat). Usually Thurs–Sun 8pm–4am. Bus: Old Town trolley.

Hacienda Country Club   This glitzy scene unfolds after a 25-minute drive out of San Juan on the signposted road to Caguas. You can't miss the club along the highway. Live musicians entertain here in an alfresco setting surrounded by mountains. A mainly 20- to 30-year-old crowd is attracted to this club, which is evocative of a club where Ricky Ricardo might have appeared in the 1950s. The cover depends on the entertainment being offered. Sometimes some of the hottest Latin groups in the Caribbean appear here. Caguas. © 787/747-9692. Cover: $5–$30. Sat 7:30pm–closing (no set closing); Sun 3pm–closing (no set closing). No bus.

Houlihan's   This two-story casual hangout along the Condado is part of the U.S. chain of restaurants, and it's also one of the best places to hear merengue, Spanish rock music, or salsa. The second floor is used like a pub but only Thursday to Saturday, attracting a relatively young, fun-loving group of both visitors and locals. If you're having dinner or drinks downstairs, you can enter the pub for free; otherwise you pay a $5 cover. In addition to the bar, Houlihan's also serves reasonably good food, such as grilled salmon with vegetables, pasta with chicken, and sirloin steak with cabernet sauce and fresh mushrooms. Main courses cost from $10 to $20. Av. Ashford 1309, Condado. © 787/723-8600. Mon–Thurs 5–10pm; Fri–Sat 5pm–12:30am; Sun 2–10pm. Bus: A7.

Lupi's   You can hear some of the best Spanish rock at this Mexican pub and restaurant. It is a current hot spot, with typical South of the Border decoration and such familiar dishes as fajitas, nachos, and burritos. A wide range of people of all ages are attracted to the place, although after 10pm patrons in their 20s and 30s predominate. Live rock groups perform after 11pm. In addition to the nightly rock bands, Caribbean music is also played on Friday and karaoke on Sunday. Carretera 187, km 1.3, Isla Verde. ℭ 787/253-1664. No cover. Daily 11am–2am. Bus: A5.

Rumba   This bar and pub is one of Old San Juan's hot spots, and it's the best place in Puerto Rico to go for salsa dancing. Hot, hot music is played by live bands. This is where the Puerto Ricans go themselves, leaving the tourists salsa dancing at such hotels as the Wyndham El San Juan or the Marriott on the Condado. The average age is 18 to 28. The club also spins African-tinged bomba favorites for its young patrons. Calle San Sebastián 152. ℭ 787/725-4407. Daily 7pm–closing (no set closing). Bus: Old Town trolley.

St. Mick's   This is a local dive that features food, fun, and rock-n-roll. Near Ocean Park, it's like an Irish pub that draws an under-25 crowd to its simple precincts decorated in wood. It's mainly a bar, but the kitchen on-site serves food, including *churrasco* (braised meat) with potatoes, chicken breast with mozzarella, and a selection of nachos, tapas, and burgers. When live music is featured on Wednesday and Saturday, there's a $2 to $3 cover. Calle Loiza 2473, Punta Las Marias. ℭ 787/727-6620. Tues–Sun 5pm (no set closing). Bus: 21.

San Juan Chateau *(Finds)*   This is the best venue in the city for merengue and salsa. The cover charge depends on what group is appearing. (You no longer get Ricky Martin here, incidentally.) On Friday and Saturday, live Latin groups perform, but Sunday night the club goes gay, with drag shows and the like. The club attracts a wide age range from late teenagers to the middle aged. Av. Chardon 9, Hato Rey. ℭ 787/751-2000. Cover $8–$20. Fri 5pm–closing (no set closing); Sat–Sun 9pm–closing (no set closing). Bus: B21.

Star Gate   This is where the straight young man of San Juan takes his date. Both often dress up to patronize this disco-bar, where they dance and drink until the late hours. Wednesday night is the most casual, Friday and Saturday the most formal nights. Some of the best live music along the Condado/Santurce is played here. Av. Robwert Todd, Santurce. ℭ 787/725-4664. Cover $12. Fri–Sun 9:30pm–4am. Bus: A5.

Unplugged Café *(Finds)*   This trendy hot spot is the place to go to hear live music. Attracting an under-35 crowd, it is also a good choice for island cuisine, so you can dine here and make a whole evening of it. The main lounge is upstairs, with a friendly bar to one side. The repertoire here is called a "musical magazine"—jazz bands on Tuesday, blues and R&B on Wednesday, rock on Thursday and Friday, and local Spanish rock bands or international musicians on the weekends. Sunday afternoons see comedy shows and international music. From 6 to 9pm on Thursday nights you can hear (or participate in) karaoke. Friday night is the best time for dancing to a salsa beat. In between the music, you can order such dishes as breaded shark with mango sauce, which tastes better than your mother's version. Av. José de Diego 365, Santurce. ℭ 787/723-1423. Cover Wed–Sat $3–$5. Tues–Wed 11am–12:30am; Thurs–Fri 11am–2am; Sat 4pm–2am; Sun 3pm–midnight. Bus: 1.

THE BAR SCENE

Unless otherwise stated, there is no cover charge at the following bars.

Café Tabac   If you're in Old Town and would like to sip a good glass of port or smoke a stogie, head for this sector's best-loved cigar bar. The establishment also serves light meals. The place usually closes nightly at midnight, but on

The Birth of the Piña Colada

When actress Joan Crawford tasted the piña colada at what was then the Beachcombers Bar in the **Caribe Hilton,** Calle Los Rosales (✆ **787/ 721-0303**), she claimed it was "better than slapping Bette Davis in the face."

This famous drink is the creation of bartender Ramon "Monchito" Marrero, now long gone, who was hired by the Hilton in 1954. He spent 3 months mixing, tasting, and discarding hundreds of combinations until he felt he had the right blend. Thus, the frothy piña colada was born. It's been estimated that some 100 million of them have been sipped around the world since that fateful time.

Monchito never patented his formula and didn't mind sharing it with the world. Still served at the Hilton, here is his not-so-secret recipe:

2 ounces light rum
1 ounce coconut cream
1 ounce heavy cream
6 ounces fresh pineapple
½ cup crushed ice
Pineapple wedge and maraschino cherry for garnish

Pour rum, coconut cream, cream, and pineapple juice in blender. Add ice. Blend for 15 seconds. Pour into a 12-ounce glass. Add garnishes.

Friday and Saturday nights the drinks and the cigars keep coming until 2am. Calle Fortaleza 262. ✆ **787/725-6785.** Sun–Thurs 5pm–midnight; Fri–Sat 5pm–2am. Bus: Old Town trolley.

Cigar Bar The Palm Court Lobby at the elegant Wyndham El San Juan boasts an impressive cigar bar, with a magnificent repository of the finest stogies in the world. Although the bar is generally filled with visitors, some of San Juan's most fashionable men—and women, too—can be seen puffing away in this chic rendezvous while sipping cognac. Wyndham El San Juan Hotel & Casino, Av. Isla Verde 6063, Isla Verde. ✆ **787/791-1000.** Daily 6pm–3am. Bus: A5.

El Patio de Sam Except for the juicy burgers, we're not so keen on the food served here anymore (and neither are our readers), but we still like to visit Old Town's best-known watering hole, one of the most popular late-night joints with a good selection of beers. Live entertainment is presented here Monday to Saturday. This is a fun joint—that is, if you dine somewhere else before coming here. Calle San Sebastian 102. ✆ **787/723-1149.** Daily 11am–midnight. Bus: Old Town trolley.

Fiesta Bar This bar lures a healthy mixture of local residents and hotel guests, usually the post-35 set. The margaritas are appropriately salty, the rhythms are hot and Latin, and the free admission usually helps you forget any losses you might have suffered in the nearby casinos. From Thursday to Sunday nights you can hear some of the best salsa and merengue music in San Juan here. In the Condado Plaza Hotel & Casino, Av. Ashford 999. ✆ **787/721-1000.** Thurs–Sun 6pm–2am. Bus: C10.

Il Grottino For visitors staying in the Condado area, this is a good address to know about. It's a combined wine bar and cafe, where tables are placed both outdoors and inside. The 36-page wine *carte* features more than 200 different wines, although you can order other drinks as well. If you're hungry, ask about the antipasti, pastas, and other Italian-inspired dishes. Av. Ashford 1372, Condado. ✆ **787/723-0499.** Tues–Sun noon–3pm and 6pm–1am. Bus: A5.

Maria's   Forget the tacky decorations. This is the town's most enduring bar, a favorite local hangout and a prime target for Old Town visitors seeking Mexican food and sangria. The atmosphere is fun, and the tropical drinks include piña coladas and frosts made of banana, orange, and strawberry, as well as the Puerto Rican beer Medalla. Calle del Cristo 204. ✆ **787/721-1678.** Daily 10:30am–3am. Bus: Old Town trolley.

Ñapa   In Puerto Rico the nickname for this place in slang means "something extra." That's what the owner, Luis Moscoso, had in mind when he took over a broken-down film house and restored it into a fancy bar/restaurant with marble and lighting designed to flatter. The club enjoys a waterfront location on the Condado. You can come here to drink and party, but the menu of fusion cuisine is good enough that you might want to dine here as well, as it's far better than the routine club fare. Live music is also a nightly presentation. Av. Ashford 1018. ✆ **787/724-3686.** Mon–Fri 11:30am–2:30pm and 6–11pm; Sat–Sun 11:30am–2:30pm and 6–2am or later. Bus: B21.

Palm Court   This is the most beautiful bar on the island—perhaps in the entire Caribbean. Most of the patrons are hotel guests, but well-heeled locals make up at least a quarter of the business at this fashionable rendezvous. Set in an oval wrapped around a sunken bar area, amid marble and burnished mahogany, it offers a view of one of the world's largest chandeliers. After 7pm on Monday through Saturday, live music, often salsa and merengue, emanates from an adjoining room (El Chico Bar). In Wyndham El San Juan Hotel & Casino, Av. Isla Verde 6063, Isla Verde. ✆ **787/791-1000.** Daily 6pm–3am. Bus: A5.

Shannon's Irish Pub   Ireland and its ales meet the tropics at this pub with a Latin accent. A sports bar with TV monitors and high-energy rock-and-roll, it's the regular watering hole of many university students. There's live music Wednesday through Sunday—everything from rock to jazz to Latin. There are pool tables, and a simple cafe serves inexpensive lunches Monday through Friday. A $3 cover charge is sometimes imposed for a special live performance. Calle Bori 496, Río Piedras. ✆ **787/281-8466.** Daily 11am–1am. No bus.

Violeta's   Stylish and comfortable, Violeta's occupies the ground floor of a 200-year-old beamed house. Because of its location in the Old Town, the bar draws an equal mix of visitors and locals, usually in their 20s and 30s. Sometimes a pianist performs at the oversized grand piano. An open courtyard out back provides additional seating for sipping margaritas or other drinks. Calle Fortaleza 56 (2 blocks from the El Convento). ✆ **787/723-6804.** Daily 5pm–1am. Old Town trolley.

Wet Bar/Liquid   Two chic new drinking spots operate out of San Juan's finest boutique hotel, The Water Club. The main bar, Liquid, is a large area downstairs at the hotel. It's quickly become one of San Juan's most fashionable hangouts for both chic locals and a medley of visitors in all age groups. With its glass walls overlooking the ocean, it features Latino music. The best bar for watching the sun set over San Juan is the Wet Bar on the 11th floor, featuring jazz music and the Caribbean's only rooftop fireplace for those nippy nights in winter when you want to drink outside. The sensuous decor here includes striped zebra-wood stools, futons, pillowy sofas, and hand-carved side tables. The walls feature

---

Moments   Romantic Sunsets

There is no better place on a Sunday night from 5:30 to 7pm to watch the sun set over Old San Juan than at Paseo de la Princesa. In this evocative colonial setting, you can hear local trios serenade you as the sun goes down. After such a romantic interlude, the night is yours. Of course, you should take along a lover.

Indonesian carved teak panels. In the Water Club, Calle José M. Tartak 2. ⒸⒸ **787/728-3666.** Wet Bar Thurs–Sat 7pm–1am; Liquid Bar 6pm–1am. Bus: A5.

Zabó   Among San Juan's young, restless, and unattached, this place is more famous for its bar than its restaurant. The bar is divided into two separate spaces, the more popular being a cottage-like outbuilding on the grounds of a turn-of-the-20th-century villa. There's lots of charm here, from the attractive crowd, stiff drinks such as Cosmopolitans and martinis, and live music every Wednesday and Thursday night from 8 to 11:45pm. Some nights, depending on the operating hours of the restaurant, the bar crowd moves into the restaurant's entrance vestibule, a cozy spot for mingling. 14 Calle Candina. (entrance is via an alleyway on Av. Ashford between Calles Washington and Cervantes.) ⒸⒸ **787/725-9494.** Tues–Sat 5pm–midnight. Bus: B21.

HOT NIGHTS IN GAY SAN JUAN

Straight folks are generally welcome in each of these gay venues, and many local couples show up for the hot music and dancing. Local straight boys who show up to cause trouble are generally ushered out quickly. Unless otherwise stated, there is no cover.

Beach Bar   This is the site of a hugely popular Sunday afternoon gathering, which gets really crowded beginning around 4pm and stretches into the wee hours. There's an open-air bar protected from rain by a sloping rooftop and a space atop the seawall with a panoramic view of the Condado beachfront. Drag shows on Sunday take place on the terrace. On the ground floor of the Atlantic Beach Hotel, Calle Vendig 1. ⒸⒸ **787/721-6900.** Daily 11am–1am or later. Bus: A7.

Cups   Set in a Latino tavern, this place is valued as the only place in San Juan that caters almost exclusively to lesbians. Men of any sexual persuasion aren't particularly welcome. The scene reminds many lesbians of a tropical version of one of the bars they left behind at home. Entertainment such as live music or cabaret is presented Wednesday at 9pm and Friday at 10pm. Calle San Mateo 1708, Santurce. ⒸⒸ **787/268-3570.** Wed–Sat 7pm–4am. Bus: B21.

Eros   This two-level nightclub caters exclusively to the city's growing gay population. Patterned after the dance emporiums of New York, but on a smaller scale, the club has cutting-edge music and bathrooms that are among the most creative in the world. Here, wall murals present fantasy-charged, eroticized versions of ancient Greek and Roman gods. Regrettably, only one night a week (Wed) is devoted to Latino music; on other nights, the music is equivalent to what you'd find in the gay discos of either Los Angeles or New York City. Av. Ponce de León 1257, Santurce. ⒸⒸ **787/722-1131.** Cover $5. Wed–Sun 10pm–3am or 4am. Bus: 1.

Junior's Bar   Lying on a secluded and poorly lit street in Santurce, about a 5-block walk from the more famous gay mecca, Eros (see above), Junior's Bar seems little known to most visitors. It's mainly a place where resident gays go to hang out, talk to each other, and order drinks. Most of the music comes from the jukebox. Drag queens and male strippers are a standard feature Wednesday to Sunday. There is no cover, but you are required to fulfill a two-drink minimum. Av. Condado 602 (off Av. Ponce de León), Santurce. ✆ **787/723-9477.** Daily 8pm–5am. Bus: B21.

Tia Maria's Liquor Store   This is not a liquor store, but a bar that caters to both locals and visitors. As one habitué informed us, "During the day, all the local boys claim they're straight. But stick around until after midnight." The place has a very welcoming and unpretentious attitude, attracting both men and women. Don't come here for entertainment, but to hang out with the locals. Av. José de Diego 326 (near the corner of Av. Ponce de León), Santurce. ✆ **787/724-4011.** Mon–Thurs and Sun 11am–midnight; Fri–Sat 11am–2am. Bus: B1.

CASINOS

Many visitors come to Puerto Rico on package deals and stay at one of the posh hotels at the Condado or Isla Verde just to gamble.

 Barhopping

More than any other place in the Caribbean, San Juan has a nightlife that successfully combines New York hip with Latino zest and the music of the Spanish tropics. For a no-holds-barred insight into what this means, try the recommendations here.

First, head for a pair of holes in the wall across the street from the El Convento hotel. **El Batey,** Calle del Cristo 101 (no phone), and **Don Pablo,** Calle del Cristo 103 (no phone), are battered side-by-side hangouts with a clientele of locals, expatriates, and occasional visitors. (In the 1980s, a Hollywood director selected these spots as the set for a Central American drug den, much to the amusement of the regular clientele.) Whereas El Batey's music remains firmly grounded in the rock-and-roll classics of the 1970s, with a scattering of Elvis Presley hits, Don Pablo prides itself on cutting-edge music that's continually analyzed by the counterculture aficionados who hang out here. El Batey is open daily from 2pm to 6am; Don Pablo, daily from 8pm to 4am.

These bars, along with the dark and smoky **Café Bohemia,** just across the street, in the cellar of the El Convento hotel, Calle del Cristo 100 (✆ **787/723-9020),** are hip hangouts for late-night dialogues. At this hideaway you can often hear live jazz while enjoying fruity cocktails, drinks, and light meals. Older locals mingle with hotel guests, the patronage mainly in the post-35 age group.

You might also stumble into **Carli Café Concierto,** Calle Tetuán 206, off Plazoleta Rafael Carrión (✆ **787/725-4927).** This is one of Old Town's best spots for drinking margaritas and watching the world go by. Owner Carli Muñoz, who earned fame as one of The Beach Boys, plays jazz and piano classics nightly, often with invited guests. On Friday and Saturday nights, there's a $2 cover.

Nearly all the large hotels in San Juan/Condado/Isla Verde offer casinos, and there are other large casinos at some of the bigger resorts outside the metropolitan area. The atmosphere in the casinos is casual, but still you shouldn't show up in bathing suits or shorts. Most of the casinos open around noon and close at 2, 3, or 4am. Guest patrons must be at least 18 years old to enter.

The casino generating all the excitement today is the 18,500-square-foot **Ritz-Carlton Casino,** 6961 State Rd., Isla Verde (© 787/253-1700), the largest casino in Puerto Rico. It combines the elegant decor of the 1940s with tropical fabrics and patterns. This is one of the plushest and most exclusive entertainment complexes in the Caribbean. You almost expect to see Joan Crawford—beautifully frocked, of course—arrive on the arm of Clark Gable. It features traditional games such as blackjack, roulette, baccarat, craps, and slot machines.

One of the splashiest of San Juan's casinos is at the **Wyndham Old San Juan Hotel & Casino,** Calle Brumbaugh 100 (© 787/721-5100), where five-card stud competes with some 240 slot machines and roulette tables. You can also try your luck at the **Caribe Hilton** (one of the better casinos), Calle Los Rosales (© 787/721-0303), **Wyndham El San Juan Hotel & Casino** (one of the most grand), Av. Isla Verde 6063 (© 787/791-1000), or the **Condado Plaza Hotel & Casino,** Av. Ashford 999 (© 787/721-1000). You do not have to flash passports or pay any admission fees.

COCKFIGHTS

A brutal sport not to everyone's taste, cockfights are legal in Puerto Rico. The most authentic are in Salinas, a town on the southern coast with a southwestern ethos, which has *galleras,* or rings, for cockfighting. But you don't have to go all the way there to see a match. About three fights per week take place at the **Coliseo Gallistico,** Av. Isla Verde 6600, Route 37, km 1.5, Isla Verde. Call © 787/791-6005 for the schedule and to order tickets, which cost $10, $15, $20, or $25, depending on the seat. The best time to attend cockfights is from January to May, as more fights are scheduled at that time. The arena is closed during the first 2 weeks of November.

Near San Juan

Within easy reach of San Juan's cosmopolitan bustle are superb attractions and natural wonders. With San Juan as your base, you can explore the island by day and return in time for a final dip in the ocean and an evening on the town. Other places near San Juan, such as the Hyatt resorts at Dorado, are destinations unto themselves.

About 90 minutes west of San Juan is the world's largest radar/radio-telescope, **Arecibo Observatory.** After touring this awesome facility, you can travel west to nearby **Río Camuy,** for a good look at marvels below ground. Here you can plunge deep into the subterranean beauty of a spectacular cave system carved over eons by one of the world's largest underground rivers.

Prefer to stay closer to San Juan? Virtually on the city's doorstep, only 18 miles (29km) to the west, is the **Dorado resort,** home of the famed Hyatt Dorado and Hyatt Regency Cerromar Beach hotels. Both properties open onto beautiful white sandy beaches. If you want to avoid the congestion of the Condado's high-rise hotels, consider a beach holiday here. Both Hyatts are family-friendly.

Just 35 miles (56km) east of San Juan is the Caribbean National Forest, the only tropical rain forest in the U.S. National Park System. Named by the Spanish for its anvil-shaped peak, **El Yunque** receives more than 100 billion gallons of rainfall annually. If you have time for only one side trip, this is the one to take. Waterfalls, wild orchids, giant ferns, towering tabonuco trees, and sierra palms make El Yunque a photographer's and hiker's paradise. Pick up a map and choose from dozens of trails graded by difficulty, including El Yunque's most challenging—the 6-mile (9.5km) El Toro Trail to the peak. At El Yunque is El Portal Tropical Center, with 10,000 square feet of exhibit space, plazas, and patios. This facility greatly expands the recreational and educational programs available to visitors. La Coca Falls and an observation tower are just off Route 191.

Visitors can combine a morning trip to El Yunque with an afternoon of swimming and sunning on tranquil **Luquillo Beach.** Soft white sand, shaded by coconut palms and the blue sea, makes this Puerto Rico's best and best-known beach. Take a picnic or, better yet, sample local specialties from the kiosks.

1 Arecibo & Camuy

68 to 77 miles (190km–124km) W of San Juan

GETTING THERE

Arecibo Observatory lies a 1¼-hour drive west of San Juan, outside the town of Arecibo. From San Juan head west along four-lane Route 22 until you reach the town of Arecibo. At Arecibo, head south on Route 10; the 20-mile (32km) drive south on this four-lane highway is almost as interesting as the observatory itself.

From Route 10, follow the signposts along a roller-coaster journey on narrow two-lane roads. Still following the signposts, you take Routes 626 and 623, crossing the lush Valley of Río Tanamá until you reach Route 625, which will lead you to the entrance to the observatory.

On the same day you visit the Arecibo Observatory, you can also visit the Río Camuy caves. The caves also lie south of the town of Arecibo. Follow Route 129 southwest from Arecibo to the entrance of the caves, which are at km 18.9 along the route, north of the town of Lares. Like the observatory, the caves lie approximately 1½ hours west of San Juan.

EXPLORING THE AREA

Dubbed "an ear to heaven," **Observatorio de Arecibo** ✿ (© 787/878-2612; www.naic.edu) contains the world's largest and most sensitive radar/radio-telescope. The telescope features a 20-acre dish, or radio mirror, set in an ancient sinkhole. It's 1,000 feet in diameter and 167 feet deep, and it allows scientists to monitor natural radio emissions from distant galaxies, pulsars, and quasars, and to examine the ionosphere, the planets, and the moon using powerful radar signals. Used by scientists as part of the Search for Extraterrestrial Intelligence (SETI), this is the same site featured in the movie *Contact* with Jodie Foster. This research effort speculates that advanced civilizations elsewhere in the universe might also communicate via radio waves. The 10-year, $100 million search for life in space was launched on October 12, 1992, the 500-year anniversary of the New World's discovery by Columbus.

Unusually lush vegetation flourishes under the giant dish, including ferns, wild orchids, and begonias. Assorted creatures like mongooses, lizards, and dragonflies have also taken refuge there. Suspended in outlandish fashion above the dish is a 600-ton platform that resembles a space station.

This is not a site where you'll be launched into a *Star Wars* journey through the universe. You are allowed to walk around the platform, taking in views of this gigantic dish. At the Angel Ramos Foundation Visitor Center, you are treated to interactive exhibitions on the various planetary systems and introduced to the mystery of meteors and educated about intriguing weather phenomena.

Tours are available at the observatory Wednesday through Friday from noon to 4pm, Saturday and Sunday from 9am to 4pm. The cost is $4 for adults, $2 for children and seniors. There's a souvenir shop on the grounds. Plan to spend about 1½ hours at the observatory.

Parque de las Cavernas del Río Camuy (Río Camuy Caves) ✿✿✿ (© 787/898-3100) contains the third-largest underground river in the world. It runs through a network of caves, canyons, and sinkholes that have been cut through the island's limestone base over the course of millions of years. Known to the pre-Columbian Taíno peoples, the caves came to the attention of speleologists in the 1950s; they were led to the site by local boys already familiar with some of the entrances to the system. The caves were opened to the public in 1986. Visitors should allow about 1½ hours for the total experience.

Visitors first see a short film about the caves, then descend into the caverns in open-air trolleys. The trip takes you through a 200-foot-deep sinkhole and a chasm where tropical trees, ferns, and flowers flourish, along with birds and butterflies. The trolley then goes to the entrance of Clara Cave of Epalme, one of 16 caves in the Camuy caves network, where visitors begin a 45-minute walk, viewing the majestic series of rooms rich in stalagmites, stalactites, and huge natural "sculptures" formed over the centuries.

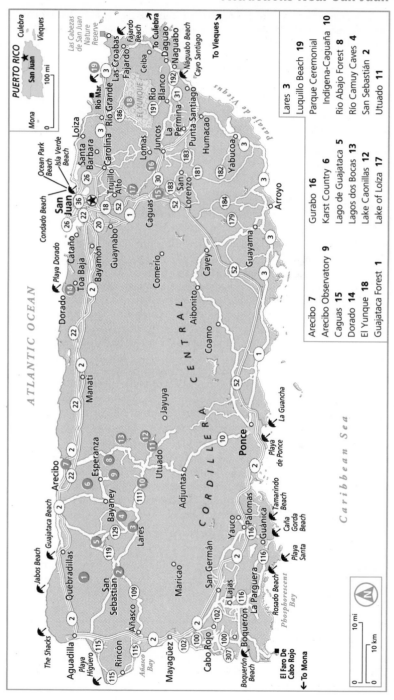

Arecibo **7**
Arecibo Observatory **9**
Caguas **15**
Dorado **14**
El Yunque **18**
Guajataca Forest **1**

Gurabo **16**
Karst Country **6**
Lago de Guajataca **5**
Lagos dos Bocas **13**
Lake Caonillas **12**
Lake of Loíza **17**

Lares **3**
Luquillo Beach **19**
Parque Ceremonial
Indígena-Caguaña **10**
Río Abajo Forest **8**
Río Camuy Caves **4**
San Sebastián **2**
Utuado **11**

Tres Pueblos Sinkhole, located on the boundaries of the Camuy, Hatillo, and Lares municipalities, measures 65 feet in diameter, with a depth of 400 feet—room enough to fit all of El Morro Fortress in San Juan. In Tres Pueblos, visitors can walk along two platforms—one on the Lares side, facing the town of Camuy, and the other on the Hatillo side, overlooking Tres Pueblos Cave and the Río Camuy.

The caves are open Wednesday through Sunday from 8am to 3:45pm. Tickets cost $10 for adults, $7 for children 2 to 12, and $5 for seniors. Parking is $2. For more information, phone the park.

WHERE TO DINE

The closest place for food is the **Hotel La Casa Grande** (p. 225) in Utuado, a little mountain town south of Arecibo.

2 The Karst Country ★★

48 miles (77km) W of San Juan

One of the most interesting areas of Puerto Rico to explore is the large **Karst Country,** south of Arecibo. One of the world's strangest rock formations, karst is formed by the process of water sinking into limestone. As time goes by, larger and larger basins are eroded, forming sinkholes. *Mogotes* (karstic hillocks) are peaks of earth where the land didn't sink into the erosion pits. The Karst Country lies along the island's north coast, directly northeast of Mayagüez in the foothills between Quebradillas and Manatí. The region is filled with an extensive network of caves. One sinkhole contains the 20-acre dish of the world's largest radio/radar telescope at the Arecibo Observatory (see above).

This area was deforested in the late 1940s; alluvial valleys and sinkholes were then used for pastures, shifting cultivation, and coffee plantations. In this region, most of the coffee sites were abandoned in the 1960s, and today most of these sites are covered with secondary forests. The recovery of these forests has been very rapid because of a close seed source—trees left on the steep slopes—and the presence of large populations of dispersers, mainly bats.

GETTING THERE   The only way to explore the Karst Country, which is easy to reach from San Juan, is by car. Leave San Juan on the four-lane highway, Route 22, until you come to the town of Arecibo, a 1½-hour drive, depending on traffic. Once at Arecibo, take Route 10 south, in the direction of Utuado. See "A Driving Tour of the Karst Country" below.

A DRIVING TOUR OF THE KARST COUNTRY

If you'd like a specific goal for exploring in the Karst Country, visit the Arecibo Observatory and the Río Camuy Caves, previewed above. However, you can also spend a day driving at random, exploring lakes and forests at your leisure. If you decide to go this route, make the commercial town of **Arecibo** your base.

Tips Get a Good Map

Arm yourself with the most detailed map you can find at one of the bookstores in San Juan. The free maps dispensed by the tourist office are not sufficiently detailed and do not show the tiny secondary roads you'll need to traverse for a motor tour of the Karst Country.

Although not of tourist interest itself, it is the capital of the Karst Country and the starting point from which you can drive south along many interesting and winding roads. Arecibo is reached after a 1½-hour drive west of San Juan along a four-lane highway, Route 22, one of the best and fastest on the island.

From Arecibo you can take Route 10 south in the direction of Utuado (see chapter 9), which can serve as a refueling stop. Along the way you'll pass **Lagos dos Bocas** ✦, one of the most beautiful lakes of the Karst Country. This is a reservoir adjacent to the Río Abajo Forest (see below). Lagos dos Bocas, which lies 12 miles (19km) south of Arecibo, is in the mountains of Cordillera Central. Along with a nearby lake, **Lake Caonillas,** it forms the major water reservoir for the north-central sector of Puerto Rico.

Take time out at Lagos dos Bocas to ride one of the free government-operated **launches** ✦ that traverse the lake. Established as a taxi service for residents of the area, these launches can be used by sightseers as well. The launches leave from a dock along Route 123 on the west side of the lake, with departures scheduled every hour unless the weather is bad. On weekends many little "restaurants" (really food shacks) are open to serve visitors. If you don't want to get off and patronize one of these ramshackle joints, you can stay on the launch, enjoying one of the most tranquil and scenic 2-hour rides in all of Puerto Rico. The launch will take you back to your car, and then you can continue your journey.

Once at Utuado, you can cut west along Route 111, which leads to the town of Lares. When you come to Route 621 heading north, you can drive into the **Río Abajo Forest** (Bosque Estatal de Río Abajo) ✦, a piece of island beauty riddled with old lumber roads and trail paths. Filled with lush growth, this forest reserve is filled with many tropical trees, such as bamboo, West Indian mahogany, balsa, and teak.

After a look at the region, you can drive south and hook up again with Route 111 going west to Lares. You'll almost immediately come to **Parque Ceremonial Indígena-Caguaña** (Indian Ceremonial Park at Caguaña). The site is signposted and need not take up more than 30 minutes of your time. Built by the Taíno Indians some 1,000 years ago, the site was used for both recreation and worship, and it is encircled by mountains near the Tanama River. You can still see the outlines of the ancient *bateyes* (ball courts), which are bordered by carved stone monoliths decorated with petroglyphs. The best-known petroglyph is the much-photographed *Mujer de Caguaña*, squatting in the position of an earthmother fertility symbol. There is a small and very minor museum of Indian artifacts and skeletons on-site. Charging no admission, the site is open Wednesday to Sunday from 9am to 4:30pm. For more information, call © **787/894-7325.**

Along Route 111, **Lares** comes upon you like a frontier town, lying in the western foothills of the Cordillera Central's principal cluster of peaks. Lares stands at the southernmost spur of the Karst Country. On the island, the residents of Lares live as far from the ocean as you can get in Puerto Rico.

Although there is little of tourist interest in Lares, other than the toylike quality of the town itself, you can use it as a refueling stop, as it has a number of little shops and minor dining joints. In the center of town is a Spanish colonial church dating from the 19th century.

From Lares continue northwest to the town of San Sebastián, and then cut sharply east along Route 119, until you'll reach the shores of **Lago de Guajataca** ✦, one of the most majestic bodies of water on Puerto Rico. In many ways this is our favorite lake for some R&R on the island. It is both a 4-mile-long

(6.5km) body of water and a wildlife refuge. For a scenic look at the lake, drive along its north shore, which is a haven for some of the most skilled anglers of Puerto Rico. You can go fishing here, but you have to bring your own equipment. The most sought-after fish is *tucunare,* with which the lake is stocked. At the dam here, you can gaze upon an evocative "lost valley" of conical peaks.

If you'd like to explore the **Bosque Estatal de Guajataca** (Guajataca Forest) ★★, you can stop in at the **Depto de Recursos Naturales Oficina** (© 787/ 896-7640), at km 22.1 on Route 119 near Lago de Guajataca. The office is open from 6am to 6pm Tuesday to Sunday and usually has a stock of detailed hiking routes through the forest reserve. Set in the thick of the Karst Country, Guajataca Forest sprawls across nearly 2,400 acres of forestland, rising and falling at various elevations, ranging from 500 to 1,000 feet or more.

Reaching the forest from the lake can be difficult. You can return to the town of San Sebastián (see above), following Route 119 until you come to the junction with Route 446 heading north. This road will carry you right into the heart of the forest reserve.

The woodland in the forest is punctuated by mogotes and covered with 25 miles (40km) of hiking trails. It is also home to the endangered Puerto Rico boa (you are unlikely to encounter one) and the habitat of nearly 50 different species of birds. The highlight of the forest is the *Cueva del Viento,* the "Cave of the Wind." The hiking trails have been well marked by park rangers.

At the end of the tour, you can continue north along Route 446, which will hook up with Route 2, continuing to the west coast of Puerto Rico. Otherwise, you can head east via Arecibo to San Juan.

3 Dorado ★

18 miles (29km) W of San Juan

Dorado—the name itself evokes a kind of magic—is a world of luxury resorts and villas that unfolds along the north shore of Puerto Rico. The elegant **Hyatt Dorado Beach Resort & Country Club** and the newer, larger **Hyatt Regency Cerromar Beach Hotel** sit on the choice white-sand beaches here.

The site was originally purchased in 1905 by Dr. Alfred T. Livingston, a Jamestown, N.Y., physician, who developed it as a 1,000-acre grapefruit-and-coconut plantation. Dr. Livingston's daughter, Clara, widely known in aviation circles as a friend of Amelia Earhart, owned and operated the plantation after her father's death. It was she who built the airstrip here.

GETTING THERE

If you're driving from San Juan, take Highway 2 west to Route 693 north to Dorado (trip time: 40 min.). Otherwise, call **Dorado Transport Corp.,** which occupies an office on the site shared by the Hyatt hotels (© **787/796-1234**). Using 18-passenger minibuses, they offer frequent shuttle service between the Hyatt Hotels and the San Juan airport. They operate at frequent intervals, daily between 11am and 10pm. The fare is $20 per person, but a minimum of three passengers must make the trip in order for the bus to operate.

Once you're in Dorado, you can get around via the shuttle bus that travels between the two hotels every 30 minutes during the day.

SPORTS & OTHER OUTDOOR PURSUITS

GOLF The Robert Trent Jones, Sr.–designed courses at the **Hyatt Regency Cerromar** and the **Hyatt Dorado Beach** ★★ match the finest anywhere. The two original courses, known as east and west (© **787/796-8961** for tee times), were carved out of a jungle and offer tight fairways bordered by trees and forests, with lots of ocean holes. The somewhat newer and less noted north and south courses (© **787/796-8915** for tee times) feature wide fairways with well-bunkered greens and an assortment of water traps and tricky wind factors. Each is a par-72 course. The longest is the south course, at 7,047 yards. Guests of the Hyatt hotels get preferred tee times and pay lower fees than nonguests. On the north and south courses, guests pay $70 to $90, and nonguests pay $85 to $115. On the east and west courses guests pay $126 to $145, and nonguests pay from $151 to $181. Golf carts at any of the courses rent for $25, whether you play 9 or 18 holes. There are two pro shops—one for the north and south courses and one for the east and west courses, each with a bar and snack-style restaurant. Both are open daily from 7am until dusk.

WINDSURFING & OTHER WATERSPORTS   The best place for water-sports on the island's north shore is along the well-maintained beachfront of the Hyatt Dorado Beach Resort & Country Club, near the 10th hole of the east golf course. Here, **Penfield Island Adventures** (© **787/382-4631,** ext. 3262, or 787/796-2188) offers 90-minute **windsurfing lessons** for $80 each; board rentals cost $50 per half day. Well-supplied with a wide array of Windsurfers, including some designed specifically for beginners and children, the school benefits from the almost-uninterrupted flow of the north shore's strong, steady winds and an experienced crew of instructors. A **kayaking/snorkeling** trip (© **787/796-4645**), departing daily at 9:15am and 11:45am and lasting 2 hours, costs $69. Two-tank boat **dives** go for $95 per person. **Waverunners** can be rented for $60 per half hour for a single rider or $75 for two riders. A **Sunfish** rents for $50 for 1 hour, $68 for 2 hours.

WHERE TO STAY

Lodgings in Dorado are pretty much limited to the two Hyatts and the Embassy Suites. Either of the Hyatts is a good choice for families. They both offer family getaway packages at Camp Coquí, the Puerto Rican version of Camp Hyatt, featuring professionally supervised day and evening programs for children ages 3 to 12. Certified counselors direct programs of educational, environmental, and cultural activities. In the evening, movies, talent shows, and video games occupy the agenda. All this costs $40 a day per kid. Children also receive a 50% discount on meals. A shuttle bus runs back and forth between the two resorts every half hour, and guests of both can use the facilities at either hotel.

Families interested in massive facilities and the best sports-oriented program in Puerto Rico gravitate to the Cerromar Beach, which is more like a conventional resort hotel. It also attracts more conventions. Those interested in a more peaceful, relaxing ambience cast their vote for the Dorado Beach, whose low-rise buildings sprawl across a former plantation, amid palms, pine trees, and purple bougainvillea, all within a short walk of a beautiful 2-mile (3km) stretch of sandy beach. If forced to choose, we prefer the Dorado, especially because you can take the shuttle to the Cerromar's fabulous pool area even if you don't stay there.

Embassy Suites Dorado del Mar Beach & Golf Resort ⭐   This new beachfront property in Dorado lies less than 2 miles (3km) from the center of Dorado and within easy access from the San Juan airport. It is the only all-suite resort in Puerto Rico, and it has been a success since its opening in 2001. The sparkling new property offers two-room suites with balconies and 55 two-bedroom condos.

The suites are spread over seven floors, each spacious and furnished in a Caribbean tropical motif, with artwork and one king-size bed or two double beds. Most of them have ocean views of the water. Each condo has a living room, kitchen, whirlpool, and balcony.

Although the accommodations are suites or condos, one bedroom in a condo can be rented as a double room (the rest of the condo is shut off). Likewise, it's also possible for two people to rent one bedroom in a condo, with the living room and kitchen facilities available (the other bedroom is closed off). Because condos contain two bedrooms, most of them are rented to parties of four.

The hotel attracts many families because of its very spacious accommodations. It also attracts golfers because of its Chi Chi Rodriguez signature par-72 18-hole golf course set against a panoramic backdrop of mountains and ocean.

210 Dorado del Mar Blvd., Dorado, PR 00646. ⓒ 787/796-6125. Fax 787/796-6145. www.embassysuites dorado.com. 229 units. Year-round $139–$195 double; $165–$259 suite; $205–$299 1-bedroom condo; $315–$440 2-bedroom condo. AE, DC, MC, V. **Amenities:** 2 restaurants, pool and bar grill; pool; golf; 24-hour business center; room service; babysitting; laundry. *In room:* A/C, TV, dataport, kitchenette, hair dryer, iron, safe.

Hyatt Dorado Beach Resort & Country Club ★★ *Kids*

Hyatt has spent millions on improvements here. This is the more elegant and subdued of the two Hyatt properties, the Cerromar attracting more families and rowdy conventions bent on having a good time. The renovated guest rooms have marble bathrooms and terra-cotta floors throughout. Accommodations are available on the beach or in villas tucked in and around the lushly planted grounds. They're fairly spacious, and bathrooms have everything from tubs to bathrobes, deluxe toiletries to power showers. The casitas are a series of private beach or poolside houses.

Dinner is served in a three-tiered main dining room where you can watch the surf. Hyatt Dorado chefs have won many awards, and the food at the hotel restaurants is among the most appealing in Puerto Rico.

Highway 693, Dorado, PR 00646. ⓒ 800/233-1234 or 787/796-1234. Fax 787/796-6560. www.hyatt.com. 298 units, 17 casitas. Winter $395–$595 double; from $705 casita for 2. Off-season $175-$365 double; from $375 casita for 2. MAP (mandatory in winter) $70 extra per day for adults, $35 extra per day for children. AE, DC, DISC, MC, V. **Amenities:** 3 restaurants, 2 bars; 2 pools; 2 18-hole championship golf courses; 7 Laykold tennis courts; spa; windsurfing school; children's camp; 24-hour room service; babysitting; laundry/dry cleaning. *In room:* A/C, minibar, hair dryer, iron, safe.

Hyatt Regency Cerromar Beach Hotel ★★ *Kids*

The name *Cerromar* is a combination of two Spanish words—*cerro* (mountain) and *mar* (sea)—and true to its name, this resort is surrounded by mountains and ocean. Approximately 22 miles (35km) west of San Juan, the high-rise hotel shares the 1,000-acre former Livingston estate with the more elegant Dorado, so guests can enjoy the Robert Trent Jones, Sr., golf courses and other facilities at the hotel next door.

All rooms have first-class appointments and are well maintained; most have private balconies. The floors throughout are tiled and the furnishings are casual tropical, in soft colors and pastels. Many units are wheelchair accessible, and some are reserved for nonsmokers. Bathrooms are equipped with tubs and power showers; the Regency Club units also have robes and hair dryers.

Even if you're trapped at your resort every night because of the isolation of Dorado itself, you'll find a wide variety of cuisine here, ranging from Asian to Italian. The fare is relatively standard but adequate. The water playground contains the world's longest freshwater swimming pool: a 1,776-foot-long fantasy pool with a riverlike current in five connected free-form pools. It takes 15 minutes to float from one end of the pool to the other. There are also 14 waterfalls, tropical landscaping, a subterranean Jacuzzi, water slides, walks, bridges, and a children's pool. A full-service spa and health club provides services for all manner of body and skin care, including massages.

Highway 693, Dorado, PR 00646. © **800/233-1234** or 787/796-1234. Fax 787/796-4647. www.hyatt.com. 506 units. Winter $375–$535 double; from $805 suite. Spring and fall $255–$350 double; from $600 suite. Summer $200–$250 double; from $455 suite. MAP (breakfast and dinner) $70 extra for adults, $35 extra for children. AE, DC, DISC, MC, V. **Amenities:** 4 restaurants, 3 bars, dance club, casino; world's longest freshwater pool, children's pool; 2 golf courses; 14 Laykold tennis courts (2 lit); health club and spa; snorkeling; children's programs; 24-hour room service; babysitting; laundry/dry cleaning. *In room:* A/C, TV, minibar, safe.

WHERE TO DINE

El Malecón PUERTO RICAN   If you'd like to discover an unpretentious local place that serves good Puerto Rican cuisine, then head for El Malecón, a simple concrete structure that's minutes away from a small shopping center. It has a cozy family ambience and is especially popular on weekends. Some members of the staff speak English, and the chef is best with fresh seafood. The chef might also prepare a variety of items not listed on the menu. Most of the dishes are at the lower end of the price scale; only the lobster is expensive. On Wednesday and Friday a live band plays and patrons dance.

Rte. 693, km 8.2 Marginal Costa de Oro. © **787/796-1645.** Main courses $10–$37. AE, MC, V. Daily 11am–11pm.

Steak Co. ★ STEAKS   This restaurant offers the best beef of the fine restaurants at the Hyatts. Frequented by an upscale, usually well-dressed clientele, it occupies a soaring, two-story room with marble and Italian-tile floors. Diners enjoy views of venerable trees draped in Spanish moss, a landscaped pond, and a waterfall while dining on well-conceived cuisine. The best steaks and prime ribs in this part of Puerto Rico are served here. Most dishes are at the lower end of the price scale. The most expensive main course—called "Sea and Earth"—consists of a tender filet mignon and a lobster tail. Most dishes are accompanied by large, perfectly baked potatoes and great sourdough bread. In the highly unlikely event that you have room for dessert, you'll be glad you do.

In the Hyatt Regency Cerromar. © **787/796-1234**, ext. 3240. Reservations required. Main courses $20–$48. AE, DC, DISC, MC, V. Daily 6–10pm.

Su Casa Restaurant ★★★ SPANISH/PUERTO RICAN   This is a restored version of the 19th-century Livingston family plantation home, and it offers the finest dining at all the Dorado Hyatt properties. It's an attractive setting—an old oceanfront hacienda with a red-tile roof, graceful staircases and a courtyard, and verandas in the Spanish style. Strolling musicians and candlelight add to the romantic ambience. The Rockefellers used to entertain their formally dressed guests at this posh Dorado beach hideaway, but today the dress is casual (but no shorts allowed). The chef produces innovative cuisine, using Puerto Rican fruits and vegetables whenever possible. Dining here is such an event that patrons make an evening of it. For a refreshing starter, try the white gazpacho with grapes or a tropical green salad with papaya, avocado, and Caribbean spices. The kitchen whips up a delectable seafood and chicken paella, or you can order mahimahi with a spicy corn sauce served with couscous and a spinach timbale. Meats are also savory, especially the roasted pork chops flavored with tamarind sauce.

In the Hyatt Dorado Beach Resort & Country Club. ⓒ **787/796-1234**. Reservations required. Main courses $27–$48. AE, DC, MC, V. Daily 6:30–10pm.

Zen Garden ⭐ ASIAN   Some of the best Asian food is found not in San Juan but in a Dorado Hyatt hotel. On the lower floor of this resort hotel, the chefs at Zen Garden roam Asia for all your favorite dishes, including both the Chinese and Japanese kitchens, with special attention paid to their very fresh sushi and sashimi collection. The restaurant also has an attractive bar and an elegantly decorated dining room. The larder has a delectable array of such delights as sea urchin, freshwater eel, and smoked salmon. Masters in the kitchen prepare delicious yellowtail, red snapper, octopus, and squid.

In the Hyatt Regency Cerromar Beach Resort & Casino, Dorado. ⓒ **787/796-1234**. Reservations required. Main courses $16–$25; sushi from $2.75 per order. AE, DC, MC, V. Daily 6–9pm.

4 El Yunque ⭐⭐⭐

25 miles (40km) E of San Juan

The El Yunque rain forest, a 45-minute drive east of San Juan, is a major attraction in Puerto Rico. Part of the Caribbean National Forest, this is the only tropical forest in the U.S. National Forest Service system. The 28,000-acre preserve was given its status by President Theodore Roosevelt. Today the virgin forest remains much as it was in 1493, when Columbus first sighted Puerto Rico.

GETTING THERE

From San Juan, road signs direct you to Route 3, which you follow east to the intersection of Route 191, a two-lane highway that heads south into the forest. Take 191 for 3 miles (5km), going through the village of Palmer. As the road rises, you will have entered the Caribbean National Forest. You can stop in at the El Portal Tropical Forest Center to pick up information (see below).

VISITOR INFORMATION

El Portal Tropical Forest Center, Route 191, Rio Grande (ⓒ **787/888-1880**), an $18 million exhibition and information center, has 10,000 square feet of exhibition space. Three pavilions offer exhibits and bilingual displays. The actor Jimmy Smits narrates a documentary called "Understanding the Forest." The center is open daily from 9am to 5pm; it charges an admission of $3 for adults and $1.50 for children under 12.

El Yunque is the most popular spot in Puerto Rico for hiking; for a description of our favorite trails, see "Hiking Trails" below. The **Department of Natural Resources Forest Service** (ⓒ 787/724-8774) administers some aspects of the park, although for the ordinary hiker, more useful information may be available at **El Yunque Catalina Field Office,** near the village of Palmer, beside the main highway at the forest's northern edge (ⓒ **787/888-1880**). The staff can provide material about hiking routes, and, with 10 days' notice, help you plan overnight tours in the forest. If you reserve in advance, the staff will also arrange for you to take part in 2-hour group tours. These tours are conducted Saturday to Monday every hour on the hour from 10:30am to 3:30pm; they cost $5 for adults and $3 for children under 12.

EXPLORING EL YUNQUE

Encompassing four distinct forest types, El Yunque is home to 240 species of tropical trees, flowers, and wildlife. More than 20 kinds of orchids and 50 varieties of ferns share this diverse habitat with millions of tiny tree frogs, whose

A Driving Tour: The Scenic Route to El Yunque

This side trip, the roundabout but most scenic way to reach El Yunque, will take you through some of Puerto Rico's most stunning natural scenery and small towns, such as Trujillo Alto and Gurabo.

From Condado, signs point the way southeast to Route 1. Near Río Piedras on your right, Route 3 is the famous highway and the most direct route that most motorists take to visit Luquillo Beach and El Yunque. Route 1 blends into Route 3, which is sometimes called "Avenida 65 de Infantera" after the Puerto Rican regiment that fought in World War II and the Korean War.

At the intersection of Route 3 and Route 181, head south. South of Trujillo Alto, connect with Route 851, which continues until it comes to an intersection with Route 941. At this point, get on Route 941, which runs in a southwesterly direction. Along 941, and to your right, you'll come to **Lake of Loíza,** which is surrounded by mountains. You might see local farmers (*jíbaros*) riding horses laden with produce, going to or from the marketplace. (Lake of Loíza is not to be confused with the northern coastal town of Loíza, which is known for its music and African heritage.) As you prepare to leave Lake of Loíza, allow an hour of leisurely driving time.

After viewing the lake, continue on Route 941, which now swings in a southeasterly direction through Puerto Rico's tobacco country, to the town of **Gurabo.** You'll know you're nearing the town from the sweet aroma of drying tobacco leaves. Part of Gurabo is set on the side of a mountain, and some of the so-called streets are actually steps carved into the mountain, which you must climb to reach the next level. This means that Gurabo is made for walkers—not drivers.

Leave Gurabo by heading southeast along Route 30. Before you approach the next town, Juncos, signs point the way to Route 185, which will lead you to the small town of Lomas. Continue north along Route 185, following the signs to the major artery of Route 3.

Connect with Route 3 and take it east toward El Yunque and then turn right (south) onto Route 191, which climbs up into the forest surrounding El Yunque's peak and that of its taller sibling, El Toro. You are now in the Caribbean National Forest, the most scenic, panoramic, and dramatic part of the eastern drive through Puerto Rico.

distinctive cry of *coquí* (pronounced "ko-*kee*") has given them their name. Tropical birds include the lively, greenish blue, red-fronted Puerto Rican parrot, once nearly extinct and now making a comeback. Other rare animals include the Puerto Rican boa, which grows to 7 feet. (It is highly unlikely that you will encounter a boa. The few people who have are still shouting about it.)

El Yunque is the best of Puerto Rico's 20 forest preserves. The forest is situated high above sea level, with El Toro its highest peak. You can be fairly sure you'll be showered upon during your visit, since more than 100 billion gallons of rain fall here annually. However, the showers are brief and there are many shelters. On a quickie tour, many visitors reserve only a half-day for El Yunque. But we think it's unique and deserves at least a daylong outing.

HIKING TRAILS The best hiking trails in El Yunque have been carefully marked by the forest rangers. Our favorite, which takes 2 hours for the round-trip jaunt, is called **La Mina & Big Tree Trail,** and it is actually two trails combined. The La Mina Trail is paved and signposted. It begins at the picnic center adjacent to the visitor center and runs parallel to La Mina River. It is named for gold once discovered on the site. After you reach La Mina Falls, the Big Tree Trail begins (also signposted). It winds a route through the towering trees of Tabonuco Forest until it approaches Route 191. Along the trail you might spot such native birds as the Puerto Rican woodpecker, the tanager, the screech owl, and the bullfinch.

Those with more time might opt for the **El Yunque Trail,** which takes 4 hours round-trip to traverse. This trail—signposted from El Caimitillo Picnic Grounds—takes you on a steep, winding path. Along the way you pass natural forests of sierra palm and *palo colorado* before descending into the dwarf forest of Mount Britton, which is often shrouded in clouds. Your major goal, at least for panoramic views, will be the lookout peaks of Roca Marcas, Yunque Rock, and Los Picachos. On a bright, clear day you can see all the way to the eastern shores of the Atlantic.

DRIVING THROUGH EL YUNQUE If you're not a hiker but you appreciate rain forests, you can still enjoy En Yunque. You can drive through the forest on Route 191, which is a tarmac road. This trail goes from the main highway of Route 3, penetrating deep into El Yunque. You can see ferns that grow some 120 feet tall, and at any minute you expect a hungry dinosaur to peek between the fronds, looking for a snack. You're also treated to lookout towers offering panoramic views, waterfalls, picnic areas, and even a restaurant.

WHERE TO STAY

For the location of this *parador,* see the map "Paradores & Country Inns of Puerto Rico" on p. 69.

Ceiba Country Inn *(Finds)* If you're looking for an escape from the hustle and bustle of everyday life, this is the place for you. This small, well-maintained bed-and-breakfast is located on the easternmost part of Puerto Rico, near the Roosevelt Road's U.S. naval base (you must rent a car to reach this little haven in the mountains). El Yunque is only 15 miles (24km) away, and San Juan 40 miles (64km) to the west. The rooms are on the bottom floor of a large, old family home, and each has a private shower-only bathroom. They are decorated in a tropical motif with flowered murals on the walls, painted by a local artist. For a quiet evening cocktail, you might want to visit the small lounge on the second floor.

Road no. 977, km 1.2 (P.O. Box 1067), Ceiba, PR 00735. © **787/885-0471.** Fax 787/885-0471. prinn@juno.com. 9 units (shower only). $75 double. Rate includes breakfast. AE, DISC, MC, V. Free parking. **Amenities:** Patio for outdoor entertainment, bar (guests only). *In room:* A/C, fridge.

WHERE TO DINE

We recommend the dining and drinking facilities at the Westin Rio Mar (see "Luquillo Beach" below), which sits very close to the entrance to El Yunque.

5 Luquillo Beach *(*(*(*

31 miles (50km) E of San Juan

Luquillo Beach is the island's best and most popular public stretch of sand. From here, you can easily explore El Yunque Rain Forest (see above). "Luquillo" is a Spanish adaptation of *Yukiyu*, the god believed by the Taínos to inhabit El Yunque.

GETTING THERE

If you are driving, pass the San Juan airport and follow the signs to Carolina. This leads to Route 3, which travels east toward the fishing town of Fajardo, where you'll turn north to Las Croabas. To reach the Westin, the area's major hotel, follow the signs to El Yunque, and then the signs to the Westin.

A hotel limousine (© 787/608-7666) from the San Juan airport costs $225 per carload to the Westin Rio Mar Beach Resort. A taxi costs approximately $70. Hotel buses make trips to and from the San Juan airport, based on the arrival times of incoming flights; the cost is $27.50 per person, each way, for transport to El Conquistador; $25 per person, each way, to the Westin.

HITTING THE BEACH

Luquillo Beach ★★★, Puerto Rico's finest beach, is palm dotted and crescent-shaped, opening onto a lagoon with calm waters and a wide, sandy bank. It's very crowded on weekends but much better during the week. There are lockers, tent sites, showers, picnic tables, and food stands that sell a sampling of the island's *frituras* (fried fare), especially cod fritters and tacos. The beach is open daily from 9am to 6pm.

You can also snorkel and skin-dive (see below) among the living reefs with lots of tropical fish. Offshore are coral formations and spectacular sea life—eels, octopuses, stingrays, tarpon, big puffer fish, turtles, nurse sharks, and squid, among other sea creatures.

SCUBA DIVING & SNORKELING

The best people to take you diving are at the **Dive Center** at the Westin Rio Mar Beach Resort, Country Club & Ocean Villas (© 787/888-6000). This is one of the largest dive centers in Puerto Rico, a PADI five-star facility with two custom-designed boats that usually take no more than 6 to 10 divers. Snorkeling and skin diving costs $65. The center also offers a full-day snorkeling trip, including lunch and drinks, for $89 per person. Boat tours are available daily from 9am to 4pm. For scuba divers, a two-tank dive costs $125.

WHERE TO STAY

Luquillo Beach Inn   This all-villa hotel has one-bedroom accommodations for up to four guests and two-bedroom villas that house six comfortably. Each unit has a full kitchen. By day the living room can be a social center, with the sofa bed converted to make it a bedroom in the evening. The inn is recommended for those who'd like to have a 2- or 3-day beach holiday at Luquillo, with visits to El Yunque. The room furnishings, although comfortable, evoke Miami motels in the 1950s. Units are spacious and graced with prints, but the aura is somewhat impersonal. The pool is small but is provided with chaise longues and tables. Because the beach is so close—and that's why guests flock here—the pool is little used. The hotel is ringed with balconies. Families are especially fond of the place because light meals can be prepared at any hour in the full kitchen in each unit.

Calle 701 Ocean Drive, Luquillo, PR 00773. © 787/889-3333. www.luquillobeachinn.com. 20 units. Year-round 1-bedroom apt for 2–4 persons $101.25 Sun–Thurs, $136.25 Fri–Sat; 2-bedroom apt for 4–6 $128.50 Sun–Thurs, $163.50 Fri–Sat. MC, V. **Amenities:** Summer snack bar; pool; babysitting; laundry. *In room:* A/C, TV, kitchen, coffeemaker, hair dryer.

Trinidad Guest House   Until recently, ever since the Martorell family arrived from Spain in 1800, this had been their family homestead. For decades it was one of the best-known paradores of Puerto Rico, called Parador Martorell. The location, a half block from Luquillo Beach, was its major asset. In 1999 the Martorells departed. The former parador is still basically the same place—only the name has changed. When you arrive, you enter an open courtyard, which suffices for alfresco outings because there are no grounds. Breakfast always features plenty of fresh-picked fruit and homemade breads and compotes. The main reason for staying here is its proximity to Luquillo Beach, which has shady palm groves, crescent beaches, coral reefs for snorkeling and scuba diving, and a surfing area. The in-room shower-only bathrooms are small but well kept, with tiled walls and just enough shelf space. There are also adequate bathrooms in the hallways for units that do not have private bathrooms.

6A Ocean Dr., Luquillo, PR 00773. (At km 36.2 along Rte. 3, turn toward the shore, then turn left and drive 4 short blocks.) © **787/889-2710.** Fax 787/889-0640. 10 units, 6 with bathroom. $69.55 double without bathroom; $85.60[nd]$107 double with bathroom. Rates include breakfast. AE, MC, V. **Amenities:** Horseback riding, kayaking, and snorkeling in nearby Fajardo can be arranged. *In room:* A/C, TV.

Westin Rio Mar Beach Resort, Country Club, & Ocean Villas ★★★
Marking Westin's debut in the Caribbean, this $180 million, 481-acre resort lies on a relatively uncrowded neighbor (Rio Mar Beach) of the massively popular Luquillo Beach, a 5-minute drive away. It was designed to compete with the Hyatt hotels at Dorado and El Conquistador, with which it's frequently compared. It's the newest, freshest, and best property in the area.

Landscaping includes several artificial lakes situated amid tropical gardens. More than 60% of the guest rooms look out over palm trees to the Atlantic. Other units open onto the mountains and forests of nearby El Yunque (just a 15-min. drive away). Throughout, the style is Spanish hacienda with nods to the surrounding jungle, incorporating unusual art and sculpture that alternates with dark woods, deep colors, rounded archways, big windows, and tile floors. In the bedrooms, muted earth tones, wicker, rattan, and painted wood furniture add to the ambience. Bedrooms are spacious, with balconies or terraces, and good mattresses, plus tub-and-shower combos in the spacious bathrooms.

The resort encompasses the Rio Mar Country Club, site of two important golf courses. The older of the two, the Ocean Course, was designed by George and Tom Fazio as part of the original resort, and it has been a staple on Puerto Rico's professional golf circuit since the 1960s. In 1997 Westin opened the property's second 18-holer, the slightly more challenging River Course, the first Greg Norman–designed course in the Caribbean.

For diversity of cuisine, the only hotel in Puerto Rico that outpaces it is the Wyndham El Conquistador Resort (see chapter 10). The resort also has a 6,500-square-foot casino.

6000 Rio Mar Blvd. (19 miles/31km east of Luis Muñoz Marín International Airport, with entrance off Puerto Rico Hwy. 3), Rio Grande, PR 00745. © **800/WESTIN-1** or 787/888-6000. Fax 787/888-6600. www.westin riomar.com. 694 units. Year-round $395–$675 double; from $900 suite. AE, DC, DISC, MC, V. **Amenities:** 8 restaurants, 6 bars, casino; 13 tennis courts; health club and spa; deep-sea game fishing, sailing; children's programs; 24-hour room service; laundry/dry cleaning; nearby horseback riding. *In room:* A/C, TV, minibar, coffeemaker, hair dryer, iron, safe.

WHERE TO DINE

Brass Cactus *Finds* AMERICAN   On a service road adjacent to Route 3 at the western edge of Luquillo, within a boxy-looking concrete building that's in need of repair, is one of the town's most popular bar/restaurants. Permeated with a raunchy, no-holds-barred spirit, this amiable spot has thrived since the early 1990s, when it was established by an Illinois-born bartender who outfitted the interior with gringo memorabilia. Drinks are stiff and the crowd looks tougher than it is, tending to calm down whenever food and drink are brought out. Menu items include king crab salad; tricolor tortellini laced with chicken and shrimp; several kinds of sandwiches and burgers; and platters of churrasco, T-bone steaks, chicken with tequila sauce, barbecued pork, and fried mahimahi.

In the Condominio Complejo Turistico, Rte. 3 Marginal. ℭ 787/889-5735. Reservations not necessary. Sandwiches $7.50–$10.75; main courses $15.75–$23.75. MC, V. Sun–Thurs 11am–11pm; Fri–Sat 11am–midnight.

Palio ⭐ ITALIAN   This richly decorated restaurant is the premier dining outlet of the region's largest and splashiest hotel. The Westin chain has poured time and energy into making this a showcase of the resort's creativity. Although most of the ingredients have to be flown in, the cuisine is excellent. A certain attachment to culinary tradition doesn't preclude a modern approach to the cookery. Dishes we've sampled have a superbly aromatic flavor and are beautifully presented and served. The sophisticated menu includes potato and sage gnocchi; rack of American lamb; fresh Maine lobster; center-cut veal chops stuffed with fresh mozzarella, tomatoes, and avocado and served with grappa-laced mashed potatoes; and baby free-range chicken, spit-roasted and served with rosemary jus.

In the Westin Rio Mar Beach Resort, Country Club & Ocean Villas. ℭ 787/888-6000. Reservations recommended. Main courses $28–$38. AE, DC, MC, V. Nov–May daily 6–11pm; June–Oct Tues–Sat 6–11pm.

Sandy's Seafood Restaurant & Steak House ⭐ *Value* SEAFOOD/STEAKS/PUERTO RICAN   The concrete-and-plate-glass facade is less obtrusive than that of other restaurants in town, and the cramped, Formica-clad interior is far from stylish. Nonetheless, Sandy's is one of the most famous restaurants in northeastern Puerto Rico, thanks to the wide array of luminaries—U.S. and Puerto Rican political figures, mainstream journalists, beauty pageant winners, and assorted slumming rich—who travel from as far away as San Juan to dine here. Set about a block from the main square of the seaside resort of Luquillo, it was founded in 1984 by Miguel Angel, a.k.a. Sandy.

Platters, especially the daily specials, are huge—so copious, in fact, that they're discussed with fervor by competitors and clients alike. The best examples include fresh shellfish, served on the half-shell; asopaos; four kinds of steak; five different preparations of chicken, including a tasty version with garlic sauce; four kinds of gumbos; paellas; a dozen preparations of lobster; and even jalapeño peppers stuffed with shrimp or lobster.

Calle Fernandez Garcia 276. ℭ 787/889-5765. Reservations recommended. Main courses $6–$20; lunch special Mon–Fri $5 11am–2:30pm. AE, DISC, MC, V. Daily 11am–between 9:30 and 11pm, depending on business.

8

Ponce, Mayagüez & San Germán

For those who want to see a less urban side of Puerto Rico, Ponce, on the south shore, and Mayagüez, on the west coast, make good centers for sightseeing. From either Ponce or Mayagüez you can take a side trip to historic San Germán, Puerto Rico's second-oldest city and site of the oldest church in the New World.

Founded in 1692, Ponce is Puerto Rico's second-largest city, and it has received much attention because of its inner-city restoration. It is home to the island's premier art gallery.

Puerto Rico's third-largest city, Mayagüez, is a port city on the west coast. It might not be as architecturally remarkable as Ponce, but it's a fine base for exploring and enjoying some very good beaches.

San Germán and Ponce are home to some of the finest Puerto Rican colonial architecture in the Caribbean.

Mayagüez and Ponce also attract beach lovers. Playa de Ponce, for example, is far less crowded than the beaches along San Juan's coastal strip. The area also lures hikers to Puerto Rico's government national forest reserves, the best of which lie outside Ponce and include Guánica State Forest, the Carite Forest Reserve, as well as the Toro Negro Forest Reserve.

One of the biggest adventure jaunts in Puerto Rico, a trip to Mona Island, can also be explored from the coast near Mayagüez.

1 Ponce ★★

75 miles (121km) SW of San Juan

"The Pearl of the South," Ponce was named after Loíza Ponce de León, great-grandson of Juan Ponce de León. Founded in 1692, Ponce is today Puerto Rico's principal shipping port on the Caribbean. The city is well kept and attractive. A suggestion of a provincial Mediterranean town lingers in the air.

Timed to coincide with 1992's 500th anniversary celebration of Christopher Columbus's voyage to the New World, a $440 million renovation began to bring new life to this once-decaying city. The streets are lit with gas lamps and lined with neoclassical buildings, just as they were a century ago. Horse-drawn carriages clop by, and strollers walk along sidewalks edged with pink marble. Thanks to the restoration, Ponce now recalls the turn of the 20th century, when it rivaled San Juan as a wealthy business and cultural center.

ESSENTIALS

GETTING THERE   Flying from San Juan to Ponce four times a day, **Cape Air** (© 800/352-0714), a small regional carrier, offers flights for $124 round-trip. Flight time is 35 minutes.

Ponce

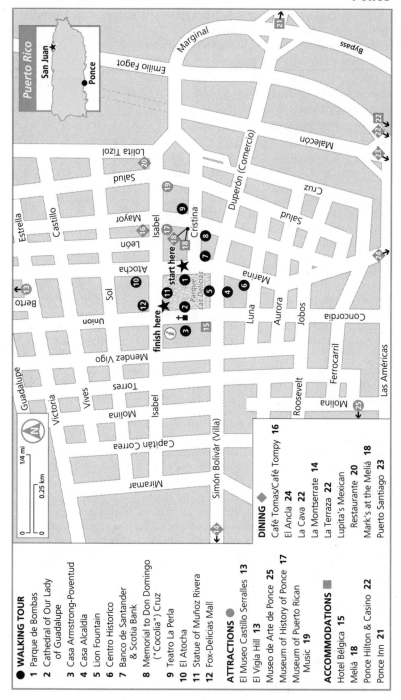

Puerto Rico

San Juan

Ponce

● WALKING TOUR

1 Parque de Bombas
2 Cathedral of Our Lady of Guadalupe
3 Casa Armstrong-Poventud
4 Casa Alcaldía
5 Lion Fountain
6 Centro Historico
7 Banco de Santander & Scotia Bank
8 Memorial to Don Domingo ("Cocolia") Cruz
9 Teatro La Perla
10 El Atocha
11 Statue of Muñoz Rivera
12 Fox-Delicias Mall

ATTRACTIONS ●

El Museo Castillo Serralles 13
El Vigía Hill 13
Museo de Arte de Ponce 25
Museum of History of Ponce 17
Museum of Puerto Rican Music 19

ACCOMMODATIONS ■

Hotel Bélgica 15
Meliá 18
Ponce Hilton & Casino 22
Ponce Inn 21

DINING ◆

Café Tomas/Café Tompy 16
El Ancla 24
La Cava 22
La Montserrate 14
La Terraza 22
Lupita's Mexican Restaurante 20
Mark's at the Meliá 18
Puerto Santiago 23

If you're driving, take Route 1 south to Highway 52, then continue south and west to Ponce. Allow at least 1½ hours.

GETTING AROUND The town's inner core is small enough that everything can be visited on foot. Taxis provide the second-best alternative.

VISITOR INFORMATION Maps and information can be found at the **tourist office,** Paseo del Sur Plaza, Suite 3 (*©* **787/843-0465**). It's open Monday to Friday from 8am to 5pm.

SEEING THE SIGHTS
ATTRACTIONS IN PONCE

Most visitors go to Ponce to see the city's architectural restoration. Calle Reina Isabel, one of the city's major residential streets, is a virtual textbook of the different Ponceño styles, ranging from interpretations of European neoclassical to Spanish colonial. The neoclassical style here often incorporates balconies, as befits the warm climate, and an extensive use of pink marble. The "Ponce Créole" style, a term for Spanish colonial, includes both exterior and interior balconies. The interior balconies have a wall of tiny windows that allows sunlight into the patio.

With partial funding from the governments of Puerto Rico and Spain, Ponce has restored more than 600 of its 1,000 historic buildings. Many are on streets radiating from the stately **Plaza Las Delicias** (Plaza of Delights). On calles Isabel, Reina, Pabellones, and Lolita Tizol, electrical and telephone wires have been buried, replica 19th-century gas lamps have been installed, and sidewalks have been trimmed with the distinctive locally quarried pink marble. Paseo Atocha, one of Ponce's main shopping streets, is now a delightful pedestrian mall with a lively street festival on the third Sunday of every month. Paseo Arias, or Callejon del Amor (Lover's Alley), is a charming pedestrian passage between two 1920s bank buildings, Banco Popular and Banco Santander, on Plaza Las Delicias, where outdoor cafe tables invite lingering. Two monumental bronze lions by Spanish sculptor Victor Ochoa guard the entrance to the old section of the city.

In addition to the attractions listed below, the **weekday marketplace,** open Monday through Friday from 8am to 5pm, at calles Atocha and Castillo is colorful. Perhaps you'll want to simply sit in the plaza, watching the Ponceños at one of their favorite pastimes—strolling about town.

Cathedral of Our Lady of Guadalupe In 1660 a rustic chapel was built on this spot on the western edge of the Plaza Las Delicias, and since then fires and earthquakes have razed the church repeatedly. In 1919 a team of priests collected funds from local parishioners to construct the Doric- and Gothic-inspired building that stands here today. Designed by architects Francisco Porrato Doría and Francisco Trublard in 1931, and featuring a pipe organ installed in 1934, it remains an important place for prayer for many. The cathedral, named after a famous holy shrine in Mexico, is the best-known church in southern Puerto Rico.

Calle Concordia/Calle Union. *©* 787/842-0134. Free admission. Mon–Fri 6am–2pm; Sat–Sun 6am–noon and 3–8pm.

El Museo Castillo Serralles *✶* Two miles (3km) north of the center of town is the largest and most imposing building in Ponce, constructed high on El Vigía Hill (see below) during the 1930s by the Serralles family, owners of a local rum distillery. One of the architectural gems of Puerto Rico, it is the best evidence of the wealth produced by the turn-of-the-20th-century sugar boom. Guides will escort you through the Spanish Revival house with Moorish and Andalusian details. Highlights include panoramic courtyards, a baronial dining room, a small cafe and souvenir shop, and a series of photographs showing the tons of earth that were brought in for the construction of the terraced gardens.

El Vigía 17. ℭ 787/259-1774. Admission $3 adults, $2 seniors over 62, $1.50 children under 16. Tues–Thurs 9:30am–5pm; Fri–Sun 9:30am–5:30pm. Free trolley leaving from Plaza Las Delicias de Ponce.

El Vigía Hill   The city's tallest geologic feature, El Vigía Hill (about 300 ft.) dominates Ponce's northern skyline. Its base and steep slopes are covered with a maze of 19th- and early 20th-century development. When you reach the summit, you'll see the soaring Cruz del Vigía (Virgin's Cross). Built in 1984 of reinforced concrete to replace a 19th-century wooden cross in poor repair, this modern 100-foot structure bears lateral arms measuring 70 feet long and an observation tower (accessible by elevator), from which you can see all of the natural beauty surrounding Ponce.

The cross commemorates Vigía Hill's colonial role as a deterrent to contraband smuggling. In 1801, on orders from Spain, a garrison was established atop the hill to detect any ships that might try to unload their cargoes tax-free along Puerto Rico's southern coastline.

At the north end of Ponce. Take a taxi from the Plaza Las Delicias; the ride will cost about $4.

Museo de Arte de Ponce ✮✮✮   Donated to the people of Puerto Rico by Luís A. Ferré, a former governor, this museum has the finest collection of European and Latin American art in the Caribbean. The building itself was designed by Edward Durell Stone (who also designed the John F. Kennedy Center for the Performing Arts in Washington, D.C.) and has been called the "Parthenon of the Caribbean." Its collection represents the principal schools of American and European art of the past 5 centuries. Among the nearly 400 works on display are exceptional pre-Raphaelite and Italian baroque paintings. Visitors will also see artworks by other European masters, as well as Puerto Rican and Latin American paintings, graphics, and sculptures. On display are some of the best works of the two "old masters" of Puerto Rico, Francisco Oller and José Campéche. The museum also contains a representative collection of the works of the old masters of Europe, including Gainsborough, Velázquez, Rubens, and Van Dyck. The museum is best known for its pre-Raphaelite and baroque paintings and sculpture—not only from Spain, but from Italy and France as well. Both the Whitney Museum in New York and the Louvre in Paris have borrowed from its collection. Temporary exhibitions are also mounted here.

Av. de Las Américas 25. ℭ 787/848-0505. www.museoarteponce.org. Admission $4 adults, $1 children under 12. Daily 10am–5pm. Follow Calle Concordia from Plaza Las Delicias 1½ miles (2.5km) south to Av. de Las Américas.

Museum of Puerto Rican Music   This museum showcases the development of Puerto Rican music, with displays of Indian, Spanish, and African musical instruments that were played in the romantic danza, the favorite music of 19th-century Puerto Rican society, as well as the more African-inspired bomba and plena styles. Also on view are memorabilia of composers and performers.

Calle Isabel 50. ℭ 787/848-7016. Admission $1. Tues–Sun 8:30am–4:30pm.

Museum of the History of Ponce (Casa Salazar)   Opened in the Casa Salazar in 1992, this museum traces the history of the city from the time of the Taíno peoples to the present. Interactive displays help visitors orient themselves and locate other attractions. The museum has a conservation laboratory, library, souvenir-and-gift shop, cafeteria, and conference facilities.

Casa Salazar ranks close to the top of Ponce's architectural treasures. Built in 1911, it combines neoclassical and Moorish details, while displaying much that is typical of the Ponce decorative style: stained-glass windows, mosaics, pressed-tin ceilings, fixed jalousies, wood or iron columns, porch balconies, interior patios, and the use of doors as windows.

Calle Reina Isabel 51–53 (at Calle Mayor). ℂ **787/844-7071.** Admission $3 adults, $1.50 seniors, $1 children. Mon and Wed–Fri 9am–5pm; Sat–Sun 10am–6pm.

Parque de Bombas   Constructed in 1882 as the centerpiece of a 12-day agricultural fair intended to promote the civic charms of Ponce, this building was designated a year later as the island's first permanent headquarters for a volunteer firefighting brigade. It has an unusual appearance—it's painted black, red, green, and yellow. A tourist-information kiosk is situated inside the building (see "Visitor Information" above).

Plaza Las Delicias. ℂ **787/284-4141.** Free admission. Wed–Mon 9:30am–6pm.

Teatro la Perla   This theater, built in the neoclassical style in 1864, remains one of the most visible symbols of the economic prosperity of Ponce during the mid-19th century. Designed by Juan Bertoli, an Italian-born resident of Puerto Rico who studied in Europe, it was destroyed by an earthquake in 1918, and rebuilt in 1940 according to the original plans; it reopened to the public in 1941. It is noted for acoustics so clear that microphones are unnecessary. After an extensive restoration completed in 1990, the theater is now the largest and most historic in the Spanish-speaking Caribbean. Everything from plays to concerts to beauty pageants takes place here.

At Calle Mayor and Calle Christina. ℂ **787/843-4080.**

NEARBY ATTRACTIONS

Hacienda Buena Vista   Built in 1833, this hacienda preserves an old way of life, with its whirring waterwheels and artifacts of 19th-century farm production. Once it was one of the most successful plantations on Puerto Rico, producing coffee, corn, and citrus. It was a working coffee plantation until the 1950s, and 86 of the original 500 acres are still part of the estate. The rooms of the hacienda have been furnished with authentic pieces from the 1850s.

Rte. 10, Barrio Magüeyes, km 16.8 (a 30-min. drive north of Ponce, in the small town of Barrio Magüeyes, between Ponce and Adjuntas). ℂ **787/848-7020** or 787/284-7020. Tours $5 adults, $2 children. Reservations required. 2-hr. tours Sat and Sun at 8:30am, 10:30am, 1:30pm, and 3:30pm (in English only at 1:30pm).

Tibes Indian Ceremonial Center   Bordered by the Río Portuguéz and excavated in 1975, this is the oldest cemetery in the Antilles. It contains some 186 skeletons, dating from A.D. 300, as well as pre-Taíno plazas from A.D. 700. The site also includes a re-created Taíno village, seven rectangular ball courts, and two dance grounds. The arrangement of stone points on the dance grounds, in line with the solstices and equinoxes, suggests a pre-Columbian Stonehenge. Here you'll also find a museum, an exhibition hall that presents a documentary about Tibes, a cafeteria, and a souvenir shop.

Rte. 503, Tibes., at km 2.2 (2 miles/3km north of Ponce). ℂ **787/840-2255.** Admission $2 adults, $1 children. Guided tours in English and Spanish are conducted through the grounds. Tues–Sun 9am–4:30pm.

HIKING & BIRD-WATCHING IN
GUANICA STATE FOREST 🎯🎯

Heading directly west from Ponce, along Route 2, you reach **Guánica State Forest** 🎯🎯 (ℂ **787/724-3724**), a setting that evokes Arizona or New Mexico.

Here you will find the best-preserved subtropical ecosystem on the planet. UNESCO has named Guánica a World Biosphere Reserve. Some 750 plants and tree species grow in the area.

The Cordillera Central cuts off the rain coming in from the heavily showered northeast, making this a dry region of cacti and bedrock, a perfect film location for old-fashioned western movies. It's also ideal country for birders. Some 50% of all of the island's terrestrial bird species can be seen in this dry and dusty forest. You might even spot the Puerto Rican emerald-breasted hummingbird. A number of migratory birds often stop here. The most serious ornithologists seek out the Puerto Rican nightjar, a local bird that was believed to be extinct. Now it's estimated that there are nearly a thousand of them.

To reach the forest, take Route 334 northeast of Guánica, to the heart of the forest. There's a ranger station here that will give you information about hiking trails. The booklet provided by the ranger station outlines 36 miles (58km) of trails through the four forest types. The most interesting is the mile-long (1.5km) **Cueva Trail,** which gives you the most scenic look at the various types of vegetation. You might even encounter the endangered bufo lemur toad, once declared extinct but found to still be jumping in this area.

Within the forest, El Portal Tropical Forest Center offers 10,000 square feet of exhibition space and provides information.

CARITE FOREST RESERVE ⍟

In southeastern Puerto Rico, lying off the Ponce Expressway near Cayey, **Carite Forest Reserve** ⍟ is a 6,000-acre reserve with a dwarf forest that was produced by the region's high humidity and moist soil. From several peaks there are panoramic views of Ponce and the Caribbean Sea. On one peak is Nuestra Madre, a Catholic spiritual meditation center that permits visitors to stroll the grounds. Fifty species of birds live in the Carite Forest Reserve, which also has a large natural pool called Charco Azul. A picnic area and campgrounds are shaded by eucalyptus and royal palms. The forest borders a lake of the same name. Entrances to the forest are signposted from the town of Cayey, which is reached after an hour's drive east of Ponce. Drive east from Ponce along Route 52, until you near the town of Cayey, where the entrance to the forest reserve is signposted.

TORO NEGRO FOREST RESERVE ⍟⍟⍟ & LAKE GUINEO ⍟

North of Ponce via Route 139, **Toro Negro Forest Reserve** ⍟⍟⍟ lies along the Cordillera Central, the cloud-shrouded panoramic route that follows the Cordillera Central as it goes from the southeast town of Yabucoa all the way to Mayagüez on the west coast. This 7,000-acre park, ideal for hikers, straddles the highest peak of the Cordillera Central in the very heart of Puerto Rico. A forest of lush trees, the reserve also contains the headwaters of several main rivers.

The lowest temperatures recorded on the island—some 40°F (4°C)—were measured at **Lake Guineo** ⍟, the island's highest lake, which lies within the reserve. The best trail to take here is a short, paved, and wickedly steep path on the north side of Route 143, going up to the south side of Cerro de Punta, which at 4,390 feet is the highest peak on Puerto Rico. Allow about half an hour for an ascent up this peak. Once at the top, you'll be rewarded with Puerto Rico's grandest view, sweeping across the lush interior from the Atlantic to the Caribbean coasts. Other peaks in the reserve also offer hiking possibilities.

Start:	East side of Plaza Las Delicias
Finish:	North side of Plaza Las Delicias
Time:	90 minutes, excluding coffee breaks, museum visits, and shopping stops

The downtown revitalization of Ponce has required more money and generated more publicity than that of any other city in Puerto Rico except San Juan. Your tour of this Caribbean showplace begins on the eastern edge of the town's main square, the Plaza Las Delicias (also known as Plaza Muñoz Rivera). Within the symmetrical borders of this main square, you'll see the red-and-black–striped clapboard facade of the town's most frequently photographed building. (Red and black, incidentally, are the colors of the city's flag.)

As you begin the tour, note the Victorian gingerbread and the deliberately garish colors of the:

❶ Parque de Bombas (Old Municipal Fire House)

This building housed the fire department before it moved into more modern quarters in another part of the city. You can still see a handful of bright red fire engines parked inside.

On the plaza's opposite side, adjacent to Calle Concordia/Calle Union, is the:

❷ Cathedral of Our Lady of Guadalupe

When you visit, there will almost certainly be parishioners at prayer inside this, the best-known church in southern Puerto Rico. Its alabaster altars were commissioned by an ex-governor of Puerto Rico in the late 1960s in Burgos, Spain.

As you leave the cathedral, notice the many impeccably clipped trees ringing the perimeter of the plaza. Identified as Indian laurels, they were planted between 1906 and 1908 and are one of the botanical triumphs of Ponce. Clipped manually into topiary forms and carefully groomed by a master gardener, they are well worth a second or third glance. The elaborate iron lampposts nearby date from 1916.

Across Calle Concordia from the main entrance to the cathedral is one of Ponce's most famous houses:

❸ Casa Armstrong-Poventud

This paneled and ornately crafted building was once the home of a wealthy Scottish-born banker. The Poventud family moved in after the Armstrongs. Today, it's a cultural center, and it's open Monday through Friday from 8am to noon and 1 to 4:30pm. Admission is free.

Note that at this western border of the Plaza Las Delicias, street signs might identify it as Plaza de Getou. Regardless of what the plaza is called, turn right upon exiting Casa Armstrong-Poventud and walk southward beneath the Indian laurels. On the square's southern edge, you'll see one of the most historic buildings of Ponce, restored to reflect its original function during Spanish colonial days:

❹ Casa Alcaldía (City Hall)

Standing on the site of an 18th-century monastery, this building was erected in 1840 as a general assembly, and then it served as the civic jail until 1905. Speeches by Theodore Roosevelt (in 1906), Herbert Hoover (in 1931), and Franklin D. Roosevelt (in 1934) were delivered from its central second-floor balcony to crowds assembled below. George Bush visited the building in 1987. The clock set into the tower was imported from London in 1877, and a tour of the baronial street-level interior reveals a memorial plaque dedicated to the fallen American dead (Second Wisconsin Regiment) during the Spanish-American

War. A few paces farther, you'll see a galleried courtyard that formerly served as prisoners' cells. The building's main courtyard was used for public executions. In City Hall, other plaques make clear that the city of Ponce was named not after Juan Ponce de León, but rather after de León's great-grandson, Loíza Ponce de León, one of the town's early civic leaders.

Across from the entrance to City Hall (in Plaza Las Delicias), you'll see one of the most beautiful fountains of Puerto Rico the:

⑤ Lion Fountain (Fuente de los Léones)

Crafted from marble and bronze, the Lion Fountain was modeled after a famous fountain in Barcelona, Spain. It was made for the 1939 New York World's Fair and later purchased by the mayor of Ponce.

Continue your walk along the southern edge of the square. Note the way the plaza has "chopped corners" (broadly rounded 45-degree corners rather than 90-degree perpendicular corners). They were designed this way for increased visibility by the Spanish armies as a deterrent to civil unrest and the contraband trade that flourished here during their regime. Ponce is said to have the only large square on Puerto Rico designed with such a feature.

When you reach the corner of Calle Marina and Calle Duperón (Comercio), head south (to your right) for 1 block until you come to the landmark:

⑥ Centro Historíco

Originally built in 1922, this landmark served as the town's casino until it was closed in the mid-1960s. Today it houses government agencies and is not open to the public, although it can be admired from the outside.

After admiring the facade of the Centro Histórico, backtrack along Calle Marina (that is, walk north again) until you again come to the intersection with Calle Duperón (Comercio). On the far right (east) of this intersection loom the:

⑦ Banco de Santander & Scotia Bank

These two banks are both adorned with intricate stained-glass windows, Art Nouveau detailing, and dozens of unusual architectural features. The alleyway separating the two banks, Callejon Amor, is lined with African tulip trees planted to evoke the romantic spirit of a couple in love. This is also the site of public concerts that are held every Sunday between 8 and 9pm by classical orchestras or dance bands.

Proceed eastward along Calle Cristina. Behind you, you should see the red-and-black–sided fire station at Plaza Las Delicias. At the next cross street, Calle Mayor, diagonal to where you're standing, you'll see the:

⑧ Memorial to Don Domingo

This statue is dedicated to Don Domingo ("Cocolia") Cruz, longtime leader of Ponce's municipal band and one of the best-known musicians from Ponce. He died in 1934.

Turn left on Calle Mayor and admire:

⑨ Teatro La Perla

The neoclassical facade of this, the largest and most historic theater in the Caribbean, is graced by six classical columns (see "Seeing the Sights" above). Depending on the time of day and the season, the lobby of this theater might be open for a quick look at the interior decoration.

Continue walking northward along Calle Mayor to the first intersection (Calle Isabel). To your right stands a Moorish-inspired building known as the Casa Salazar (Salazar House), which accommodates a branch of the Puerto Rican Museum of History.

TAKE A BREAK
Stop for a cup of coffee, an ice cream, or a sandwich at the **Café Tomas/Café Tompy**, Calle Isabel at Calle Mayor (℃ 787/840-1965). Divided into less formal and more formal sections, it is open daily from 7am to midnight. For more information, see "Where to Dine" below.

Walk westward along Calle Isabel until you reach the edge of the previously explored Plaza Las Delicias. From the square's north-eastern corner stretches:

⑩ El Atocha

El Atocha is the city's main shopping street. Stroll along its broad borders, noting the Spanish-inspired turn-of-the-20th-century architecture, the cast-iron benches, and the many police guards who ensure the street's tranquillity.

After your shopping, return to the Plaza Las Delicias and walk westward along its northern edge. Note that within the confines of the square is the:

⑪ Statue of Muñoz Rivera

This statue is a memorial to Luis Muñoz Rivera (1898–1980), one of Puerto Rico's best-known politicians. He helped Puerto Ricans become U.S. citizens after a career of political lobbying.

Proceeding west along the edge of the square, note the:

⑫ Fox-Delicias Mall

Originally built in 1931 as a movie theater, this is one of the city's most alluring watering holes and shopping enclaves. Its pink walls are excellent examples of Art Deco architecture in Puerto Rico. In crumbling disrepair, the theater was transformed into a disco during the 1960s. In 1989 the government of Spain earmarked funds for the restoration of this building to its original celluloid glamour. Today this mall contains an array of shops, nightclubs, and cafes, a good place for refreshment at the end of your stroll.

After exploring the mall, you can walk out and cross Calle Isabel, heading south. You will once again be at Plaza Las Delicias.

BEACHES & OUTDOOR ACTIVITIES

Ponce is a city—not a beach resort—and should be visited mainly for its sights. There is little here in the way of organized sports, but a 10-minute drive west of Ponce will take you to **Playa de Ponce** ★★, a long strip of white sand opening onto the tranquil waters of the Caribbean. This beach is usually better for swimming than the Condado in San Juan.

Because the northern shore of Puerto Rico fronts the often-turbulent Atlantic, many snorkelers prefer the more tranquil southern coast, not only off Ponce, but also off **La Parguera** (see "The Southwest Coast" in chapter 9). On the beaches around Ponce, water lovers can go snorkeling right off the beach, and it isn't necessary to take a boat trip. Waters here are not polluted, and visibility is usually good, unless there are heavy winds and choppy seas.

La Guancha is a sprawling compound of publicly funded beachfront, located 3 miles (5km) south of Ponce's cathedral. It has a large parking lot, a labyrinth of boardwalks, and a saltwater estuary with moorings for hundreds of yachts and pleasure craft. A tower, which anyone can climb free of charge, affords high-altitude vistas of the active beach scene. La Guancha is a relatively wholesome version of Coney Island, with a strong Hispanic accent and vague hints of New England. On hot weekends, the place is mobbed with thousands of families who listen to recorded merengue and salsa. Lining the boardwalk are at least a dozen emporiums purveying beer, party-colored drinks, high-calorie snacks, and souvenirs. Weather permitting, this free beach is good for a few hours' diversion at any time of the year.

Although snorkeling is good off the beaches, the best snorkeling is reached by boat trip to the offshore island of **Caja de Muertos,** or **Coffin Island,** an uninhabited key that's covered with mangrove swamps and ringed with worthwhile beaches. A government ferry used to take beach buffs to the wild beaches here, but it was needed for passenger service between Fajardo and Vieques. Today, a

private outfitter, **Island Adventures,** c/o Rafi Vega, La Guancha (© 787/
842-8546), will haul day-trippers there for a full-day beachgoers' outing ($20
per person without snorkeling equipment; $35 per person with snorkeling
equipment). Advance reservations (which you can make yourself, or leave to the
desk staff of whatever hotel you opt for in Ponce) are necessary, as most of this
outfit's excursions don't leave unless there are a predetermined number of
participants.

The city owns two **tennis complexes,** one at Poly Deportivos, with nine hard
courts, and another at Rambla, with six courts. Both are open from 9am to
10pm daily and are lighted for night play. You can play for free, but you must
call to make a reservation. For information, including directions on how to get
there, call the **Secretary of Sports** at © 787/840-4400.

To play golf, you can go to **Aguirre Golf Club,** Route 705, Aguirre (© 787/
853-4052), 30 miles (48km) east of Ponce (take Hwy. 52). This nine-hole
course, open from 7:30am to sunset daily, charges $15 greens fees Monday
through Friday, and $18 on weekends and holidays. Another course, **Club
Deportivo,** Carretera 102, km 15.4, Barrio Jogudas, Cabo Rojo (© 787/
254-3748), lies 30 miles (48km) west of Ponce. This course is a nine-holer, open
daily from 7am to 5pm. Greens fees are $30 daily.

SHOPPING

If you feel a yen for shopping in Ponce, head for the Fox-Delicias Mall, at the
intersection of Calle Reina Isabel and Calle Union, the city's most innovative
shopping center. Among the many interesting stores is **Regalitos y Algo Mas**
(no phone), located on the upper level. It specializes in unusual gift items from
all over Puerto Rico. Look especially for the Christmas tree ornaments, crafted
from wood, metal, colored porcelain, or bread dough, and for the exotic dolls
displayed by the owners. Purchases can be shipped anywhere in the world.

At the mall, the best outlet for souvenirs and artisans' work is **El Palacio del
Coquí Inc.** (© 787/841-0216), whose name means "palace of the tree frog."
This is the place to buy the grotesque masks (viewed as collectors' items) that are
used at Carnival time. Ask the owner to explain the significance of these masks.

Utopía, Calle Isabel 78 (© 787/845-8742), conveniently located in Plaza
Las Delicias, has the most imaginative and interesting selection of gift items and
handcrafts in Ponce. Prominently displayed are *vegigantes,* brightly painted carnival masks inspired by carnival rituals and crafted from papier-mâché. In
Ponce, where many of these masks are made, they sell at bargain prices of
between $5 and $500, depending on their size. Other items include cigars, pottery, clothing, and jewelry; gifts imported from Indonesia, the Philippines, and
Mexico; and rums from throughout the Caribbean. Julio and Carmen Aguilar
are the helpful and enthusiastic owners, who hail from Ecuador and Puerto
Rico, respectively.

WHERE TO STAY
EXPENSIVE
Ponce Hilton & Casino ★★   On an 80-acre tract of land right on the beach
at the western end of Avenida Santiago de los Caballeros, about a 10-minute
drive from the center of Ponce, this is the most glamorous hotel in southern
Puerto Rico. Designed like a miniature village, with turquoise-blue roofs, white
walls, and lots of tropical plants, ornamental waterfalls, and gardens, it welcomes
conventioneers and individual travelers alike. Each unit has tropically inspired
furnishings, ceiling fans, and a terrace or balcony. All the rooms are medium-size

to spacious, with adequate desk and storage space, tasteful fabrics, good uphol-stery, and fine linens. Each is equipped with a generous tiled bathroom with a tub-and-shower combo. The ground-floor rooms are the most expensive.

The food at one of the hotel's restaurants, La Cava, is the most sophisticated and refined on the south coast of Puerto Rico. All the waiters seem to have an extensive knowledge of the menu and will guide you through some exotic dishes—of course, you'll find familiar fare, too. For less expensive buffet dining, you can also patronize La Terraza, which serves the best lunch buffet in Ponce (see "Where to Dine" below).

Av. Caribe 1150 (P.O. Box 7419), Ponce, PR 00732. © **800/HILTONS** or 787/259-7676. Fax 787/259-7674. www.hilton.com. 153 units. Year-round $185–$280 double; $475 suite. AE, DC, DISC, MC, V. Self-parking $5; valet parking $10. **Amenities:** 2 restaurants, 3 bars, casino; lagoon-shaped pool ringed with gardens; 4 tennis courts; fitness center; watersports; bike rentals; playground; children's program; business center; room service (7am–midnight); babysitting; laundry/dry cleaning. *In room:* A/C, TV, minibar, coffeemaker, hair dryer, safe.

MODERATE

Meliá *(Value* This city hotel with southern hospitality, which has no connec-tion with the international hotel chain, attracts businesspeople. It is located a few steps from the Cathedral of Our Lady of Guadalupe and from the Parque de Bombas (the red-and-black firehouse). Although this old and somewhat tat-tered hotel was long ago outclassed by the more expensive Hilton, many people who can afford more upscale accommodations still prefer to stay here for the old-time atmosphere. The lobby floor and all stairs are covered with Spanish tiles of Moorish design. The desk clerks speak English. The small rooms are com-fortably furnished and pleasant enough, and most have balconies facing either busy Calle Cristina or the old plaza. The shower-only bathrooms are tiny. Break-fast is served on a rooftop terrace with a good view of Ponce, and Mark's at the Meliá thrives under separate management (see "Where to Dine" below). *Note:* There's no pool here.

Calle Cristina 2, Ponce, PR 00731. © **800/742-4276** or 787/842-0260. Fax 787/841-3602. 75 units (shower only). Year-round $82–$131 double; $120 suite. Rates include continental breakfast. AE, DC, MC, V. Parking $3. **Amenities:** Restaurant, bar; room service; babysitting; laundry/dry cleaning. *In room:* A/C, TV, hair dryer, iron, safe.

Ponce Inn *(Kids* This hotel, a 15-minute drive east of Ponce, opened in 1989. Its modest bedrooms are conservative and comfortable, equipped with contem-porary furnishings. Each unit has a small tiled bathroom with tub-and-shower combination. The prices appeal to families with children.

Turpo Industrial Park 103, Mercedita, Ponce, PR 00715. (East of Ponce on Hwy. 52, opposite the Interameri-can University.) © **866/668-4577.** Fax 787/841-2560. www.hidpr.com. 120 units. $99.50–$108.46 double; $129 suite. AE, DC, MC, V. Free parking. **Amenities:** Restaurant, bar/disco; pool, children's wading pool; gym; whirlpool; room service; babysitting; laundry/dry cleaning. *In room:* A/C, TV, coffeemaker, hair dryer, safe.

INEXPENSIVE

Hotel Bélgica   In the hands of a skilled decorator with a large bankroll, this Spanish colonial mansion from around 1911 could be transformed into a very chic bed-and-breakfast. Until then, however, you'll be faced with a combination of historic charm and modern junkiness, overseen by a brusque staff. You might find this cost-conscious spot wonderful or horrible, depending on your point of view and room assignment. The most appealing accommodations are nos. 8, 9, and 10; these rooms are spacious and have balconies that hang over Calle Villa, a few steps from Plaza Las Delicias. Each unit has a small tiled shower-only bath-room. This venue is for roughing it, backpacker style. The hotel is devoid of the standard amenities, and no meals are served, but there are several cafes in the area.

Calle Villa 122 (at Calle Union/Concordia), Ponce, PR 00731. ℭ **787/844-3255**. Fax 787/844-6149. http://hotelbelgica.somewhere.net. 21 units (shower only). $60–$75 double. MC, V. *In room:* A/C, TV.

WHERE TO DINE
EXPENSIVE

La Cava ✿✿ INTERNATIONAL   Designed like a hive of venerable rooms within a 19th-century coffee plantation, this is the most appealing and elaborate restaurant in Ponce. It has a well-trained staff, a sense of antique charm, well-prepared cuisine, and a champagne-and-cigar bar where the bubbly sells for around $6 a glass. Menu items change every 6 weeks but might include duck foie gras with toasted brioche, Parma ham with mango, cold poached scallops with mustard sauce, fricassee of lobster and mushrooms in a pastry shell, and grilled lamb sausage with mustard sauce on a bed of couscous. Dessert could be a black-and-white soufflé or a trio of tropical sorbets.

In the Ponce Hilton, Av. Caribe 1150. ℭ **787/259-7676**. Reservations recommended. Main courses $24–$30. AE, DC, DISC, MC, V. Mon–Sat 6:30–10:30pm.

Mark's at the Meliá ✿✿✿ INTERNATIONAL   Mark French (isn't that a great name for a chef?) elevates Puerto Rican dishes into haute cuisine at this eatery. You'd think he'd been entertaining the celebs in San Juan instead of cooking at what is somewhat of a Caribbean backwater. French was hailed as "Chef of the Caribbean 2000" in Fort Lauderdale. With his constantly changing menus and his insistence that everything be fresh, he's still a winner. You'll fall in love with this guy when you taste his tamarind barbecued lamb with yucca mojo. Go on to sample the lobster pionono with tomato-and-chive salad or the freshly made sausage with pumpkin, cilantro, and chicken. All over Puerto Rico you get fried green plantains, but here they come topped with sour cream and a dollop of caviar. The corn-crusted red snapper with yucca purée and tempura jumbo shrimp with Asian salad are incredible. The desserts are spectacular, notably the vanilla flan layered with rum sponge cake and topped with a caramelized banana, as well as the award-winning bread pudding soufflé with coconut vanilla sauce.

In the Meliá Hotel, Calle Cristina. ℭ **787/284-6275**. Reservations recommended. Main courses $14–$30. AE, MC, V. Wed–Sat noon–3pm and 6–10:30pm; Sun noon–5pm.

MODERATE

El Ancla ✿✿ PUERTO RICAN/SEAFOOD   This is one of Ponce's best restaurants, with a lovely location 2 miles (3km) south of the city center, on soaring piers that extend from the rocky coastline out over the surf. As you dine, the sound of the sea rises literally from beneath your feet.

Menu items are prepared with real Puerto Rican zest and flavor. A favorite here is red snapper stuffed with lobster and shrimp, served either with fried plantain or mashed potatoes. Other specialties are filet of salmon in caper sauce and a seafood medley of lobster, shrimp, octopus, and conch. Most of the dishes are reasonably priced, especially the chicken and conch. Lobster tops the price scale. The side orders, including crabmeat rice and yucca in garlic, are delectable.

Av. Hostos 805, Playa Ponce. ℭ **787/840-2450**. Main courses $13–$36. AE, DC, MC, V. Sun–Thurs 11am–9:30pm; Fri–Sat 11am–11pm.

La Montserrate PUERTO RICAN/SEAFOOD   Beside the seafront, in a residential area about 4 miles (6.5km) west of the town center, this restaurant draws a loyal following from the surrounding neighborhood. A culinary institution in Ponce since it was established 20 years ago, it occupies a large, airy, modern building divided into two different dining areas. The first of these is slightly more formal than the other. Most visitors head for the less formal, large room in back, where windows on three sides encompass a view of some offshore islands. Specialties, concocted from the catch of the day, might include octopus salad, several different kinds of asopao, a whole red snapper in Creole sauce, or a selection of steaks and grills. Nothing is innovative, but the cuisine is typical of the south of Puerto Rico, and it's a family favorite. The fish dishes are better than the meat selections.

Sector Las Cucharas, Rte. 2. ✆ **787/841-2740.** Main courses $15–$25. AE, DC, DISC, MC, V. Daily 11am–10pm.

La Terraza 🍷 INTERNATIONAL   During the design phase of the Ponce Hilton, a team of architects devoted one of its biggest, sunniest, and most interesting interior spaces to this dramatic-looking restaurant, where two-story walls of windows sweep the eye out over the greenery of the hotel's garden. Lunchtimes focus on a well-stocked buffet that dominates rooms off to the side of the eating area. At nighttime, except for a sprawling soup-and-salad bar (access to which is included in the price of any main course), the buffet is eliminated in favor of a la carte dining that's choreographed by a carefully trained staff. Menu items change with the seasons but are likely to include grilled grouper with either lemon butter or criolla sauce; T-bone steaks with béarnaise, red wine, or mushroom sauce; a succulent chateaubriand that's prepared for two diners at a time; and lobster that's available in several different ways.

In the Ponce Hilton, Av. Caribe 1150. ✆ **787/259-7676.** Breakfast $4–$17; lunch buffet $14; dinner main courses $13–$30. AE, DC, DISC, MC, V. Daily noon–3pm and 6:30–10:30pm.

Puerto Santiago 🍷 *Finds* INTERNATIONAL/SEAFOOD   This is the best restaurant at La Guancha. Occupying the ground floor of the compound's most impressive tower, this spot is immediately adjacent to the longest stretch of boardwalk. Here, within a nautical-style room reminiscent of a seaside bar on Cape Cod, you can order a well-prepared seafood meal with all the fixings. Shrimp comes with garlic or saffron-flavored butter sauce, or in crepes covered in melted mozzarella cheese; lobster can be served in at least seven different ways; and virtually any seafood can be ladled over heaping platters of pasta. Local fish comes Louisiana-style (blackened), with crabmeat sauce or beurre blanc (white butter) sauce, or simply grilled with lemon. There's a limited list of beef and chicken dishes, but in light of the many varieties of fish and shellfish, almost everyone orders seafood. Either before or after your meal, consider a trek upstairs to La Terrazza, our favorite music bar (recommended below).

Paseo Tablado, La Guancha. ✆ **787/840-7313.** Reservations not necessary. Main courses $18–$26. MC, V. Tues–Sun noon–10:30pm.

INEXPENSIVE

Café Tomas/Café Tompy *Value* PUERTO RICAN   The more visible and busier section of this establishment functions as a simple cafe for neighbors and local merchants. At plastic tables often flooded with sunlight from the big windows, you can order coffee, sandwiches, or cold beer, perhaps while relaxing after a walking tour of the city.

The family-run restaurant part of this establishment is more formal. The discreet entrance is adjacent to the cafe on Calle Isabel. Here, amid a decor reminiscent of a Spanish *tasca* (tapas bar), you can enjoy such simply prepared dishes as salted filet of beef, beefsteak with onions, four kinds of asopao, buttered eggs, octopus salads, and yucca croquettes.

Calle Isabel at Calle Mayor. © **787/840-1965.** Breakfast $2.25–$4; main courses lunch and dinner $4.50–$10. AE, MC, V. Restaurant daily 11:30am–midnight; cafe daily 7am–midnight.

Lupita's Mexican Restaurante MEXICAN   Lending a note of lighthearted fun to the city, this is the only Mexican restaurant in Ponce. Set in a 19th-century building and its adjoining courtyard, a short walk from Ponce's main square, it's the creative statement of Hector de Castro, who traveled throughout Mexico to find the elaborate fountains and the dozens of chairs and decorative accessories. The trompe l'oeil murals on the inside (featuring desert scenes in an amusing surrealism) were painted by the owner's sister, Flor de Maria de Castro.

A well-trained staff serves blue and green margaritas (frozen or unfrozen) and a wide array of other tropical drinks. These can be followed by Mexican dishes such as tortilla soup, taco salads, grilled lobster tail with tostones, seafood fajitas, and burritos, tacos, or enchiladas with a wide choice of fillings. A mariachi band plays on Friday. Lupita is an affectionate nickname for Guadalupe, the patron saint of both Mexico and the city of Ponce.

Calle Reina Isabel 60. © **787/848-8808.** Reservations recommended. Main courses $8–$15; platters for 2 $12–$30. AE, DC, MC, V. Sun–Thurs 11am–11pm; Fri–Sat 11am–2am.

PONCE AFTER DARK

La Terrazza, above the Puerto Santiago Restaurant, Paseo Tablado, La Guancha (© **787/840-7313**), is the most whimsical bar at La Guancha, the board-laced beachfront of Ponce. Part of the appeal is its location at the top of an open-sided watchtower. The owners define it as "a music pub," and as such, its collection of CDs rivals that of a sophisticated dance club in New York. Come here for an insight into what's hip with the young and restless of Puerto Rico's "second city." The venue is friendly, the drinks stiff, and if you're hungry, you can select from a short list of food items, including fried calamari and lobster empanadas. Hours are Wednesday, Thursday, and Sunday from noon to 10pm, Friday and Saturday from noon to 2am. There is no cover charge.

2 Mayagüez ⟨★⟩

98 miles (158km) W of San Juan, 15 miles (24km) S of Aguadilla

The largest city on the island's west coast, Mayagüez is a port whose elegance and charm reached its zenith during the mercantile and agricultural prosperity of the 19th century. Most of the town's stately buildings were destroyed in an earthquake in 1918, and today the town is noted more for its industry than its aesthetic appeal.

Although it's a commercial city, Mayagüez is a convenient stopover for those exploring the west coast. If you want a windsurfing beach, you can head north of Rincón, and if you want a more tranquil beach, you can drive south from Mayagüez along Route 102 to Boquerón. See chapter 9.

Although the town itself dates from the mid-18th century, the area around it has figured in European history since the time of Christopher Columbus, who landed nearby in 1493. Today, in the gracious plaza at the town's center, a bronze statue of Columbus stands atop a metallic globe of the world.

Famed for the size and depth of its **harbor** (the second-largest on the island, after San Juan's harbor), Mayagüez was built to control the **Mona Passage,** a route essential to the Spanish Empire when Puerto Rico and the nearby Dominican Republic were vital trade and defensive jewels in the Spanish crown. Today this waterway is notorious for the destructiveness of its currents, the ferocity of

---

Fun Fact **A History of Honeymooning**

Mayagüez is still identified by some as "the honeymoon capital of Puerto Rico," partly because of the lush and beautiful vegetation that grows here and partly because of a peculiarly romantic 16th-century legend. It is said that local farmers often kidnapped young Spanish sailors who had stopped at Mayagüez for provisions en route to South America. There was a scarcity of eligible bachelors in Mayagüez, and the farmers kidnapped the young sailors in hopes of providing their daughters with husbands and their farms with overseers. However, it's anyone's guess whether this was good or bad luck.

Many tradition-minded Puerto Rican couples still come here on their honeymoons. But for most international visitors, Mayagüez would rank low as a honeymoon retreat.

---

its sharks, and the thousands of boat people who arrive illegally from either Haiti or the Dominican Republic, both on the island of Hispaniola.

Queen Isabel II of Spain recognized Mayagüez's status as a town in 1836. Her son, Alfonso XII, granted it a city charter in 1877. Permanently isolated from the major commercial developments of San Juan, Mayagüez, like Ponce, has always retained its own distinct identity.

Today the town's major industry is tuna packing. In fact, 60% of the tuna consumed in the United States is packed here. This is also an important departure point for deep-sea fishing and is the bustling port for exporting agricultural produce from the surrounding hillsides.

ESSENTIALS

GETTING THERE **American Eagle** (© 800/433-7300) flies from San Juan to Mayagüez twice daily Monday through Friday, three times a day on weekends (flying time: 40 min.). Depending on restrictions, round-trip passage ranges from $99 to $242 per person.

If you're driving from San Juan, head either west on Route 2 (trip time: 2½ hr.) or south from San Juan on the scenic Route 52 (trip time: 3 hr.). Route 52 offers easier travel.

GETTING AROUND **Taxis** meet arriving planes. If you take one, negotiate the fare with the driver first because cabs are unmetered here.

There are branches of **Avis** (© 787/833-7070), **Budget** (© 787/832-4570), and **Hertz** (© 787/832-3314) at the Mayagüez airport.

VISITOR INFORMATION Mayagüez doesn't have a tourist-information office. If you're starting out in San Juan, inquire there before you set out (see "Visitor Information" under "Orientation" in chapter 3).

EXPLORING THE AREA: SURFING BEACHES & TROPICAL GARDENS

Along the western coastal bends of Route 2, north of Mayagüez, lie the best **surfing beaches** in the Caribbean. Surfers from as far away as New Zealand come to ride the waves. You can also check out panoramic **Punta Higüero** beach, nearby on Route 413, near Rincón. For more information see "Rincón" in chapter 9.

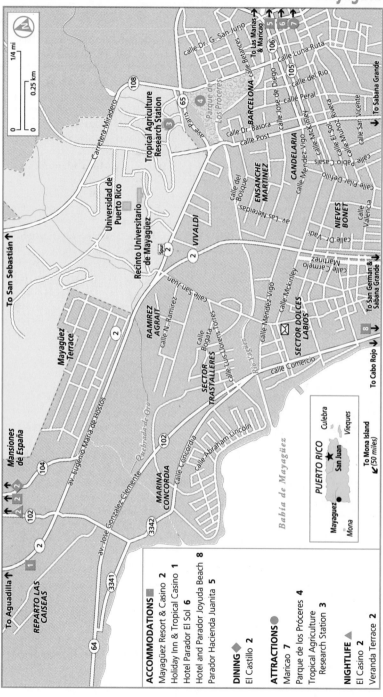

Mayagüez

To Aguadilla

To San Sebastián

REPARTO LAS CAISEAS

Mansiones de España

Mayagüez Terrace

Universidad de Puerto Rico

Recinto Universitario de Mayagüez

Tropical Agriculture Research Station

Parque de los Próceres

To Las Marías & Maricao

To Sabana Grande

calle Dr. G. San Junio

calle Betances

ave. paris 65

108

calle Dr. Basora

calle Post

calle José de Diego

calle Luna Ruta

calle del Río

calle Peral

BARCELONA

CANDELARIA

ENSANCHE MARTINEZ

NIEVES BONET

calle del Bosque

calle Méndez Vigo

calle Pablo Casals

calle Pilar Defilló

calle El Sol

calle Muñoz Rivera

calle San Vicente

calle Valencia

av. Las Nereidas

calle Dr. Vadi

VIVALDI

RAMIREZ AGRAIT

calle San Juan

calle N. Ramírez

SECTOR TRASTALLERES

calle Bogata

calle Luis Llorens-Torres

calle McKinley

calle Carmelo Martínez

calle Méndez Vigo

SECTOR DOLCES LABIOS

calle Comercio

calle Concordia

calle Abraham Lincoln

MARINA CONCORDIA

Bahía de Mayagüez

av. Eugenio María de Hostos

av. José González Clemente

Quebrada de Oro

Río Yaguez

Carretera Miradero

104

102

3342

3341

64

To Cabo Rojo

To San Germán & Sabana Grande

To Mona Island (50 miles)

PUERTO RICO

San Juan ★

Mayagüez ●

Mona

Culebra

Vieques

1/4 mi

0.25 km

N

ACCOMMODATIONS ■
Mayagüez Resort & Casino **2**
Holiday Inn & Tropical Casino **1**
Hotel Parador El Sol **6**
Hotel and Parador Joyuda Beach **8**
Parador Hacienda Juanita **5**

DINING ◆
El Castillo **2**

ATTRACTIONS ●
Maricao **7**
Parque de los Próceres **4**
Tropical Agriculture
  Research Station **3**

NIGHTLIFE ▲
El Casino **2**
Veranda Terrace **2**

South of Mayagüez is **Boquerón Beach** ⭐⭐, one of the island's best, with a wide strip of white sand and good snorkeling conditions.

The chief attraction in Mayagüez is the **Tropical Agriculture Research Station** (Estación Experimental Agrícola Federal) ⭐ (📞 **787/831-3435**). It's located on Route 65, between Post Street and Route 108, adjacent to the University of Puerto Rico at Mayagüez campus and across the street from the **Parque de los Próceres** (Patriots' Park). At the administration office, ask for a free map of the tropical gardens, which have one of the largest collections of tropical plant species intended for practical use, including cacao, fruit trees, spices, timbers, and ornamentals. The grounds are open Monday through Friday from 7am to 5pm, and there is no admission fee.

Mayagüez is the jumping-off point for visits to unique **Mona Island** ⭐⭐⭐, the "Galápagos of the Caribbean." See the box below for details.

Not far from Mayagüez is **Maricao.** You can reach Maricao from Mayagüez by heading directly east along Route 105, which will take you across mountain scenery and along fertile fields until you reach the village.

From Maricao, you can take Route 120 south to km 13.8, or from Mayagüez you can take Route 105 east to the **Maricao State Forest** ⭐ picnic area, located 2,900 feet above sea level. The observation tower here provides a panoramic view across the green mountains up to the coastal plains. Trails are signposted here, and your goal might be the highest peak in the forest, Las Tetas de Cerro Gordo, at 2,625 feet. A panoramic view unfolds from here, including a spotting of the offshore island of Mona. Nearly 50 species of birds live in this forest, including the Lesser Antillean pewee and the scaly naped pigeon. Nature watchers will delight to know that there are some 280 tree species in this reserve, 38 of which are found only here.

WHERE TO STAY

Holiday Inn & Tropical Casino   This six-story hotel competes with the Mayagüez Resort & Casino, which we like better. However, the Holiday Inn is well maintained, contemporary, and comfortable. It has a marble-floored, high-ceilinged lobby, an outdoor pool with a waterside bar, and a big casino, but its lawn simply isn't as dramatically landscaped as the Mayagüez Resort's surrounding acreage. Bedrooms here are comfortably but functionally outfitted in motel style; they've recently been refurbished. Each unit is equipped with a tiled bathroom with a tub-and-shower combo.

2701 Rte. 2, km 149.9, Mayagüez, PR 00680-6328. 📞 800/HOLIDAY or 787/833-1100. Fax 787/833-1300. www.holiday-inn.com. 142 units. Year-round $99.50–$130.50 double; $210–$260 suite. AE, DC, MC, V. **Amenities:** Restaurant, 2 bars, casino; pool; gym; room service; laundry. *In room:* A/C, TV, coffeemaker, hair dryer, safe.

Hotel Parador El Sol   This parador from around 1970 provides some of the most reasonable and hospitable accommodations in this part of Puerto Rico, although it's far more geared to the business traveler than to the tourist, with no-frills furnishings. Each unit has a small bathroom with tub and shower. This six-floor restored hotel is central to the shopping district and to all highways, 2 blocks from the landmark Plaza del Mercado in the heart of the city. (For the location of this parador, see the map "Paradores & Country Inns of Puerto Rico" on p. 69.)

Calle Santiago Riera Palmer, 9 Este, Mayagüez, PR 00680. 📞 787/834-0303. Fax 787/265-7567. www.plazapop.com. 52 units. $60–$70 double; $70–$80 triple. Rates include continental breakfast. AE, DC, MC, V. Free parking. **Amenities:** Restaurant; pool; babysitting. *In room:* A/C, TV, hair dryer.

Mona Island: The Galápagos of Puerto Rico

Off Mayagüez, the unique island of **Mona** ✹✹✹ teems with giant iguanas, three species of endangered sea turtles, red-footed boobies, and countless other sea birds. It features a tabletop plateau with mangrove forests and cacti, giving way to dramatic 200-foot-high limestone cliffs that rise above the water and encircle much of Mona.

A bean-shaped pristine island with no hotels, Mona is a destination for the hardy pilgrim who seeks the road less traveled. A pup tent, backpack, and hiking boots will do fine if you plan to forego the comforts of civilization and immerse yourself in nature. Snorkelers, spelunkers, biologists, and eco-tourists find much to fascinate them in Mona's wildlife, mangrove forests, coral reefs, and complex honeycomb, which is the largest marine-originated cave in the world. There are also miles of secluded white-sand beaches and palm trees.

Uninhabited today, Mona was for centuries the scene of considerable human activity. The pre-Columbian Taíno Indians were the first to establish themselves here. Later, pirates used it as a base for their raids, followed by guano miners, who removed the rich crop fertilizer from Mona's caves. Columbus landed in Mona during his 1494 voyage, and Ponce de León spent several days here en route to becoming governor of Puerto Rico in 1508. The notorious pirate Captain Kidd used Mona as a temporary hideout.

Mona can be reached by organized tour from Mayagüez. Camping is available at $4 per night. Everything needed, including water, must be brought in, and everything, including garbage, must be taken out. For more information, call the **Puerto Rico Department of Natural Resources** at ✆ **787/721-5495.**

Encantos Ecotours (✆ **787/272-0005** or **787/808-0005**) offers barebones but ecologically sensitive tours to Mona Island at sporadic intervals that vary according to the interest of clients. The experience includes ground transport to and from San Juan, sea transport departing from Cabo Rojo (a few miles south of Mayagüez), plus a half-day tour of the island. The tour costs $50 per person (including travel expenses) and takes approximately 4 hours (not including travel time).

Mayagüez Resort & Casino ✹ Except for the ritzy Horned Dorset Primavera (p. 212), this is the largest and best general hotel resort in western Puerto Rico, appealing equally to business travelers and vacationers. In 1995 local investors took over what was then a sagging Hilton and radically renovated it, to the tune of $5 million. The hotel benefits from its redesigned casino, country-club format, and 20 acres of tropical gardens. The landscaped grounds have been designated an adjunct to the nearby Tropical Agriculture Research Station. Five species of palm trees, eight kinds of bougainvillea, and numerous species of rare flora flourish here, adjacent to the institute's collection of tropical plants, including a pink torch ginger and a Sri Lankan cinnamon tree.

The hotel's well-designed bedrooms open onto views of the pool, and many units have private balconies. Units tend to be small, but they have good beds.

Some units are designated as nonsmoking rooms, and others are accessible for people with disabilities. The restored bathrooms are well equipped with makeup mirrors, scales, and tub-and-shower combos.

For details about El Castillo, the hotel's restaurant, see "Where to Dine" below. The hotel is the major entertainment center of Mayagüez. Its casino is open daily from noon to 4am. You can also drink and dance at the Victoria Lounge.

Rte. 104 (P.O. Box 3781), Mayagüez, PR 00709. ℂ **888/689-3030** or 787/832-3030. Fax 787/834-3475. www.mayaguezresort.com. 140 units. Year-round $169–$189 double; $260 suite. AE, DC, DISC, MC, V. Parking $5. **Amenities:** Restaurant, 3 bars, nightclub, casino; Olympic-size pool; children's pool; 3 tennis courts; small fitness room; Jacuzzi; deep-sea fishing, skin-diving, surfing, scuba diving; playground; room service (6:30am–10:30pm); babysitting; laundry. *In room:* A/C, TV, minibar, coffeemaker.

NEARBY PLACES TO STAY

For the location of the paradores described here, see the map "Paradores & Country Inns of Puerto Rico" on p. 69.

Hotel and Parador Joyuda Beach Built on the beach in scenic Cabo Rojo in 1989, this is little more than an average motel with standard furnishings, but it's a convenient and reasonably priced stopover nevertheless. Each of the simply furnished, yet comfortable units has a small tiled bathroom with tub and shower. From here you can easily head to El Combate Beach and the Cabo Rojo Wildlife Refuge. Tennis and golf are just 5 minutes away, and sport-fishing charters, as well as windsurfing and canoeing, can also be arranged. The hotel is often a favorite of Puerto Rican honeymooners.

Rte. 102, km 11.7, Cabo Rojo, PR 00623. (Follow Rte. 102 south of Mayagüez to Joyuda.) ℂ **787/851-5650.** Fax 787/255-3750. www.joyudabeach.com. 41 units. $70–$91 double. 2 children 11 and under stay free in parents' room. AE, MC, V. **Amenities:** Restaurant, bar; pool; room service. *In room:* A/C, TV.

Parador Hacienda Juanita Named after one of its long-ago owners, a matriarch named Juanita, this pink stucco building dates from 1836, when it was a coffee plantation. Situated 2 miles (3km) west of the village of Maricao, beside Route 105 heading to Mayagüez, it has a long veranda and a living room furnished with a large-screen TV and decorated with antique tools and artifacts of the coffee industry. Relatively isolated, it's surrounded by only a few neighboring buildings and the jungle. The Luis Rivera family welcomes visitors and

---

A Wildlife Refuge for Bird Fanciers

The area around Cabo Rojo, the **Refugio Nacional Cabo Rojo** (Red Cape National Refuge; ℂ **787/851-7297**) attracts serious bird-watchers to its government-protected sector. The refuge is on Route 301 at km 5.1, a mile (1.5km) north of the turnoff to El Combate. At the entrance to the refuge is a visitor center. The only time you can visit the refuge is from 7:30am to 4pm Monday to Friday; admission is free.

Migratory birds, especially ducks and herons but also several species of songbirds, inhabit this refuge. Birders have reported seeing at least 130 species. Trails for bird-watchers have been cut through the reserve. The best time to observe the birds is during the winter months, when they have fled from their cold homelands in the north.

serves drinks and meals in their restaurant. There's a swimming pool, billiards table, and Ping-Pong table on the premises. The bedrooms are simple and rural, with ceiling fans, rocking chairs, and rustic furniture, plus small tub-and-shower bathrooms. None of the rooms has air-conditioning (ceiling fans suffice in the cool temperatures of this high-altitude place).

Rte. 105, km 23.5 (P.O. Box 777), Maricao, PR 00606. ✆ 800/443-0266 for reservations only, or 787/838-2550. Fax 787/838-2551. www.haciendajuanita.com. 21 units. $64–$86 double without breakfast and dinner; $104–$126 double with breakfast and dinner. Children 11 and under stay free in parents' room. AE, MC, V. Free parking. **Amenities:** Restaurant, bar; pool; tennis; babysitting; laundry/dry cleaning. *In room:* TV, no phone.

WHERE TO DINE

El Castillo ✿ INTERNATIONAL/PUERTO RICAN This is the best-managed large-scale dining room in western Puerto Rico, as well as the main restaurant for the largest hotel and casino in the area. Known for its generous lunch buffets, El Castillo serves only a la carte items at dinner, including seafood stew served on a bed of linguine with marinara sauce, grilled salmon with mango-flavored Grand Marnier sauce, and filets of sea bass with cilantro, white wine, and butter sauce. Steak and lobster can be served on the same platter. The food has real flavor and flair, and it isn't the typical bland hotel fare so often dished up.

In the Mayagüez Resort & Casino, Rte. 104. ✆ 787/832-3030. Breakfast buffet $11.25; Mon–Fri lunch buffet $14; Sat–Sun brunch buffet $25; main courses $13.50–$32. AE, MC, V. Daily 6:30am–11pm.

MAYAGÜEZ AFTER DARK

El Casino At the completely remodeled casino at the Mayagüez Resort & Casino, with the adjoining Player's Bar you can try your luck at blackjack, dice, slot machines, roulette, and minibaccarat. At the Mayagüez Resort & Casino, Rte. 104. ✆ 787/832-3030. Daily noon–4am.

Veranda Terrace On a large and airy covered terrace that opens to a view of a manicured tropical garden, this is a relaxing and soothing place for a cocktail. The bartenders specialize in rum-based concoctions that go well with the hibiscus-scented air. In the Mayagüez Resort & Casino, Rte. 104. ✆ 787/831-7575. Daily 10:30am–1am.

3 San Germán ✿✿

104 miles (167km) SW of San Juan, 34 miles (55km) W of Ponce

Only an hour's drive from Ponce or Mayagüez and the beaches of the southern coast, and just over 2 hours from San Juan, San Germán, Puerto Rico's second-oldest town, is a little museum piece. It was founded in 1512 and destroyed by the French in 1528. Rebuilt in 1570, it was named after Germain de Foix, the second wife of King Ferdinand of Spain. Once the rival of San Juan, San Germán harbored many pirates who pillaged the ships that sailed off the nearby coastline. Indeed, many of today's residents are descended from the smugglers, poets, priests, and politicians who once lived here.

The pirates and sugar plantations are long gone, but the city retains colorful reminders of its Spanish colonial past. Flowers brighten some of the patios here as they do in Seville. Also, as in a small Spanish town, many of the inhabitants stroll through the historic zone in the early evening. Nicknamed *Ciudad de las Lomas* (City of the Hills), San Germán boasts verdant scenery that provides a pleasant backdrop to a variety of architectural styles—Spanish colonial (1850s), criollo (1880s), neoclassical (1910s), Art Deco (1930s), and international

(1960s)—depicted in the gracious old-world buildings lining the streets. So significant are these buildings that San Germán is only the second Puerto Rican city (the other is San Juan) to be included in the National Register of Historic Places.

The city's 249 historical treasures are within easy walking distance of one another. Regrettably, you must view most of them from the outside. If some of them are actually open, count yourself fortunate, as they have no phones, keep no regular hours, and are staffed by volunteers who rarely show up. Also, be aware that the signage for the historic buildings can be confusing, and many of the streets in the old town tend to run one way. Most of the city's architectural treasures lie uphill from the congested main thoroughfare (Calle Luna). We usually try to park on the town's main street (Carretera 102, which changes its name within the borders of San Germán to Calle Luna), and then proceed on foot through the city's commercial core before reaching the architectural highlights described below.

One of the most noteworthy churches in Puerto Rico is **Iglesia Porta Coeli** (Gate of Heaven) ⚜ (© **787/892-0160**), which sits atop a knoll at the eastern end of a cobble-covered square, the Parque de Santo Domingo. Dating from 1606 and built in a style inspired by the Romanesque architecture of northern Spain, this is the oldest church in the New World. Restored by the Institute of Puerto Rican Culture, and sheathed in a layer of salmon-colored stucco, it contains a museum of religious art with a collection of ancient *santos,* the carved figures of saints that have long been a major part of Puerto Rican folk art. Look for the 17th-century portrait of St. Nicholas de Bari, the French Santa Claus. Inside, the original palm-wood ceiling and tough ausobo-wood beams draw the eye upward. Other treasures include early choral books from Santo Domingo, a primitive carving of Jesus, and 19th-century Señora de la Monserrate Black Madonna and Child statues. Admission is $1 for both adults and children. The church is open Wednesday through Sunday from 8:30am to noon and 1 to 4:30pm.

Less than 100 feet downhill from Iglesia Porta Coeli, at the bottom of the steps that lead from its front door down to the plaza below, is the **Casa Morales** (also known as the **Tomás Vivoni House,** after its architect), San Germán's most photographed and widely recognized house. Designed in the Edwardian style, with wraparound porches, elaborate gables, and elements that might remind you of a Swiss chalet, it was built in 1913, reflecting the region's turn-of-the-century agrarian prosperity. (Note that it is a private residence and can be admired only from the outside.)

The long and narrow, gently sloping plaza that prefaces Iglesia Porta Coeli is the Parque de Santo Domingo, one of San Germán's two main plazas. Street signs also identify the plaza as the Calle Ruiz Belvis. Originally a marketplace, the plaza is paved with red and black cobblestones, and it's bordered with cast-iron benches and portrait busts of prominent figures in the town's history. This plaza merges gracefully with a second plaza, which street signs and maps identify as the Plaza Francisco Mariano Quiñones, the Calle José Julian Acosta, and the Plaza Principal. Separating the two plazas is the unused (and closed to the public) **Vieja Alcaldía** (Old Town Hall). Built late in the 19th century, it's awaiting a new vision, perhaps as a museum or public building.

San Germán's most impressive church—and the most monumental building in the region—is **San Germán de Auxerre** (© **787/892-1027**), which rises majestically above the western end of the Plaza Francisco Mariano Quiñones. Designed in the Spanish baroque style, it was built in 1573 in the form of a simple chapel with a low-slung thatch roof. Its present grandeur is the result of at least five subsequent enlargements and renovations. Much of what you see today is the result of a rebuilding in 1688 and a restoration in 1737 that followed a disastrous earthquake. Inside are 3 naves, 10 altars, 3 chapels, and a belfry that was rebuilt in 1939, following an earthquake in 1918. The central chandelier, made from rock crystal and imported from Barcelona in 1866, is the largest in the Caribbean. The pride of the church is the trompe l'oeil ceiling, which was elaborately restored in 1993. A series of stained-glass windows with contemporary designs were inserted during a 1999 restoration. The church can be visited daily from 7am to 7:30pm.

A few lesser sights are located near the town's two main squares. **Farmacia Martin,** a modern pharmacy, is incongruously set within the shell of a graceful but battered Art Deco building at the edge of the Parque Santo Domingo (22 Calle Ruiz Belvis; ℭ **787/892-1122**). A cluster of battered and dilapidated clapboard-sided houses line the southern side of the Calle Dr. Ueve, which rambles downhill from its origin at the base of the Iglesia Porta Coeli. The most important house is no. 66, the **Casa Acosta y Fores.** Also noteworthy is **Casa Juán Perichi,** a substantial-looking structure at the corner of Calle Dr. Ueve and Parque Santo Domingo, nearly adjacent to the Iglesia Porta Coeli. Both houses were built around 1917, of traditional wood construction, and are viewed as fine examples of Puerto Rican adaptations of Victorian architecture. Regrettably, both are seriously dilapidated, although that might change as San Germán continues the slow course of its historic renovations.

To the side of the Auxerre church is the modern, cement-sided **Public Library,** Calle José Julia Acosta (ℭ **787/892-3240**), where you might be tempted to duck into the air-conditioned interior for a glance through the stacks and periodical collection. It's open Monday through Thursday from 8am to 8:30pm, Friday from 8am to 6pm, and Saturday from 8am to 1pm and 2 to 4:30pm. Behind the Auxerre church is at least one masonry-fronted town house whose design might remind you of southern Spain (Andalusia), especially when the flowers in the window boxes add splashes of color.

WHERE TO STAY & DINE

For the location of the parador described here, see the map "Paradores & Country Inns of Puerto Rico" on p. 69.

Parador El Oasis   Although it's not state of the art, this hotel has a hardworking staff and Spanish colonial charm. As an anchor in this quaint old town, far removed from the beaches, it's a fine place to stay. A three-story building constructed around a pool and patio area, the hotel originated in the late 1700s as a privately owned mansion. With its mint green walls and white wicker furniture, some of the grace remains. The older rooms, positioned close to the lobby, show the wear and tear of the years but are still preferred by some. More modern rooms, located in the back, are plain and functional yet clean and more spacious than the older units. Three of the units have private balconies, and all units have small shower-only bathrooms.

The in-house restaurant is not the most imaginative choice in town, but it emerges year after year as the most reliable and consistent. It's open Tuesday through Sunday from 11am to 2:30pm and 6 to 10pm. Main courses ($12–$18) include empañadillas, platters of Creole-style corn sticks and cheese balls, tenderloin wrapped in bacon, and combination platters of steak and red snapper.

Calle Luna 72, San Germán, PR 00683. ℭ **787/892-1175.** Fax 787/892-4546. paradoroasis@prtc.net. 52 units (shower only). $73–$75 double. Children 11 and under stay free in parents' room. Extra person $10. AE, DC, DISC, MC, V. Free parking. **Amenities:** Restaurant, bar; pool; babysitting. *In room:* A/C, TV, hair dryer.

9

Western Puerto Rico

The scenery of western Puerto Rico varies from a terrain evoking the Arizona desert to a dense blanket of green typical of Germany's Black Forest. The interior has such attractions as the Taíno Indian Ceremonial Park, Río Camuy Cave Park, Arecibo Observatory, and the Karst Country (see chapter 7). Along the west and south coasts, you'll find white sandy beaches, world-class surfing conditions, and numerous towns and attractions. There are modest hotels from which to choose, as well as a few noteworthy paradores, a chain of government-sponsored, privately operated country inns.

The waters of the Atlantic northwest coast tend to be rough—ideal for surfers but not always good for swimming.

Some 8 centuries ago, the Taíno Indians inhabited this western part of Puerto Rico, using it as a site for recreation and worship. Stone monoliths, some decorated with petroglyphs, remain as evidence of that long-ago occupation.

There is a tremendous difference between a holiday on the east coast of Puerto Rico (see chapter 10) and one on the west coast. Nearly all visitors from San Juan head east to explore the El Yunque rain forest (see chapter 7). After that, and perhaps a lazy afternoon on Luquillo Beach, they head back to San Juan and its many resorts and attractions. Others who remain for a holiday in the east are likely to do so because they want to stay at one of the grand resorts such as Doral Palmas del Mar or Wyndham El Conquistador (see chapter 10).

Western Puerto Rico, particularly its southwestern sector, is where the Puerto Ricans themselves go for holidays by the sea. The only pocket of posh here is the Horned Dorset Primavera Hotel at Rincón (see "Rincón" below). Rincón is also the beach area most preferred by windsurfers.

Other than that, most locals and a few adventurous visitors seeking the offbeat and charming head for the southwestern sector of the island. This is the real Puerto Rico; it hasn't been taken over by high-rise resorts and posh restaurants.

Puerto Rico's west coast has been compared to the old U.S. Wild West. There is a certain truth to that. The cattle ranches on the rolling upland pastures south of the town of Lajas will evoke home for those who come from northwest Texas. Others have compared the peninsula of Cabo Rojo in Puerto Rico to Baja, California.

This western part of Puerto Rico also contains the greatest concentration of paradores, attracting those who'd like to venture into the cool mountainous interior of the west, a wonderful escape from pollution and traffic on a hot day.

1 Rincón

100 miles (161km) W of San Juan, 6 miles (9.5km) N of Mayagüez

North of Mayagüez, on the westernmost point of the island, lies the small fishing village of Rincón, in the foothills of La Cadena mountains. It's not a sightseeing destination unto itself, but surfers from as far away as New Zealand say the area's reef-lined beaches, off Route 2 between Mayagüez and Rincón, are the best in the Caribbean. Surfers are particularly attracted to **Playa Higüero** ★★★ , the beach at Punta Higüero, on Route 413, which ranks among the finest surfing spots in the world. During winter, uninterrupted swells from the North Atlantic form perfect waves, averaging 5 to 6 feet in height, with ridable rollers sometimes reaching 15 to 25 feet.

The best snorkeling is at a beach gringos have labeled **"Steps."** The waters here are more tranquil than at the beaches attracting surfers. Steps lies right off Route 413, just north of the center of Rincón.

Endangered humpback whales winter here, attracting a growing number of whale-watchers from December to March. The lighthouse at El Faro Park is a great place to spot these mammoth mammals.

Many nonsurfers visit Rincón for only one reason: the Horned Dorset Primavera Hotel, not only one of the finest hotels in Puerto Rico, but one of the best in the entire Caribbean.

ESSENTIALS

GETTING THERE & GETTING AROUND   **American Eagle** (© **800/ 352-0714** or 787/749-1747) flies from San Juan to Mayagüez, the nearest airport, four times daily (flying time: 40 min.).

Taxis meet planes arriving from San Juan. Because the taxis are unmetered, you should negotiate the fare with your driver at the outset.

There are branches of **Avis** (© **787/833-7070**), **Budget** (© **787/832-4570**), and **Hertz** (© **787/832-3314**) at the Mayagüez airport.

If you're driving from San Juan, either travel west on Route 2 (trip time: 2 hr.) or travel south on scenic Route 52 (trip time: 3½ hr.).

VISITOR INFORMATION   There is no tourist-information office in Rincón. Inquire in San Juan before heading here (see "Visitor Information" under "Orientation" in chapter 3).

SURFING & OTHER OUTDOOR PURSUITS

Despite its claim as the windsurfing capital of the Caribbean, there are very definite dangers in the waters off Rincón. In November 1998 three surfers (two from San Juan, one from the U.S. mainland) drowned in unrelated incidents offshore at Maria's Beach. These deaths are often cited as evidence of the dangerous surf that has misled some very experienced surfers. Local watersports experts urge anyone who's considering surfing at Rincón to ask a well-informed local for advice. When the surf is up and undertows and riptides are particularly strong, losing a surfboard while far offshore seems to be one of the first steps to eventually losing your life.

Windsurfing is best from November to April. The best beaches for surfing lie from Borinquén Point south to Rincón. There are many surfing outfitters along this strip, the best of which is **West Coast Surf Shop,** 2 E. Muñoz Rivera at Rincón (© **787/823-3935**), open Monday to Saturday from 9am to 6pm.

The windsurfers who hang out here like **Sandy Beach** because it does not have the stone and rocks found on some of the other beaches in the area. Also, from December to February it gets almost constant winds every day. Windsurfers wait on the terrace of Tamboo Tavern (see "Where to Dine" below) for the right wind conditions before hitting the beach.

West Coast Charters, located in the Marina at Rincón (© **787/823-4114**), offers a number of options for fun in the water, ranging from whale-watching (Dec–Mar) and other fun cruises to renting diving or fishing equipment. Expeditions are arranged to Desecho Island Reef, one of the best reefs in the Caribbean for snorkeling and diving. Desecho Island is an uninhabited island 13½ miles (22km) offshore. A Federal Wildlife Preserve, it consists of 360 acres. The highest point rises 715 feet. West Coast Charters also attracts sports fishermen in search of tuna, grouper, marlin, wahoo, and dolphin (the fish, not the mammal). Fishermen are taken out for a half day aboard a fully equipped boat, with a licensed and experienced charter captain. A snorkeling trip costs $35, a one-tank scuba dive $85. A half-day fishing charter is $450 per boat, including the guide.

Another good scuba outfitter is **Taíno Divers,** Black Eagle Marina at Rincón (© **787/823-6429**), which offers local boat charters along with scuba and snorkeling trips. Other activities include whale-watching expeditions and sunset cruises. Fees are $95 for a one-tank dive, $475 for a half-day fishing-boat rental, and $45 for snorkeling.

The most visible and sought-after whale-watching panorama in Rincón is **Parque El Faro de Rincón (Rincón's Lighthouse Park),** which lies on El Faro Point peninsula at the extreme western tip of town. Within its fenced-in perimeter are pavilions that sell souvenirs and snack items, rows of binoculars offering 25¢ views, and a stately looking lighthouse built in 1921. The park is at its most popular from December to March for whale-watching and in January and February for surfer gazing. The park is locked every evening between midnight and 7am. Otherwise, you're free to promenade with the locals any time you like.

The park's snack bar is called **Restaurant El Faro,** Barrio Puntas, Carretera 413, km 3.3 (no phone). Platters of American and Puerto Rican food, including mofongos, steaks, and burgers, cost from $13 to $19. When is it open? The owner told us, "I open whenever I want to. If I don't want to, I stay home."

Punta Borinquén Golf Club, Route 107 (© **787/890-2987**), 2 miles (3km) north of Aquadilla's center, across the highway from the city's airport, was originally built by the U.S. government as part of Ramey Air Force Base. Today, it is a public 18-hole golf course, open daily from 7am to 6:30pm. Greens fees are $20 for an all-day pass; a golf cart that can carry two passengers rents for $26 for 18 holes. A set of clubs can be rented for $10. The clubhouse has a bar and a simple restaurant.

WHERE TO STAY
VERY EXPENSIVE

Horned Dorset Primavera Hotel ★★★ This is the most sophisticated hotel on Puerto Rico, and it's one of the most exclusive and elegant small properties anywhere in the Caribbean. It was built on the massive breakwaters and seawalls erected by a local railroad many years ago. Guests here enjoy a secluded, semiprivate beach; this narrow strip of golden sand is choice, if small.

The hacienda evokes an aristocratic Spanish villa, with wicker armchairs, hand-painted tiles, ceiling fans, seaside terraces, and cascades of flowers. This is really a restful place. Accommodations are in a series of suites that ramble uphill amid lush gardens. The decor is tasteful, with four-poster beds and brass-footed tubs in marble-sheathed bathrooms. Rooms are spacious and luxurious, with

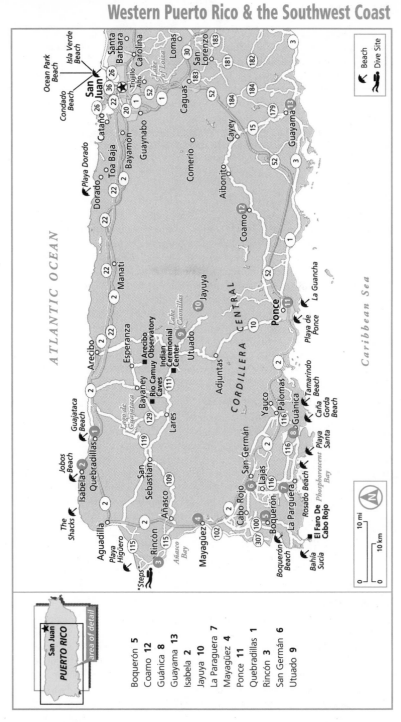

Western Puerto Rico & the Southwest Coast

Boquerón **5**
Coamo **12**
Guánica **8**
Guayama **13**
Isabela **2**
Jayuya **10**
La Paraguera **7**
Mayagüez **4**
Ponce **11**
Quebradillas **1**
Rincón **3**
San Germán **6**
Utuado **9**

San Juan
PUERTO RICO

area of detail

Beach
Dive Site

ATLANTIC OCEAN

Caribbean Sea

CORDILLERA CENTRAL

Persian rugs over tile floors, queen sofa beds in sitting areas, and fine linen. Bathrooms are equally roomy and luxurious, with tub-and-shower combinations. Eight suites are located in the separate Casa Escondida villa, set at the edge of the property. Some of these units have private pools; others offer private verandas or sundecks.

The hotel's restaurant, Horned Dorset Primavera, is one of the finest on Puerto Rico (see "Where to Dine" below).

Hotel Rte. 429 (P.O. Box 1132), Rincón, PR 00677. ℂ **800/633-1857** or 787/823-4030. Fax 787/823-5580. www.horneddorset.com. 31 units. Winter $380–$440 double; $540–$800 suite for 2. Off-season $280–$340 double; $420–$650 suite for 2. MAP (breakfast and dinner) $82 per person extra. AE, MC, V. Children under age 12 not accepted. **Amenities:** 2 restaurants, bar; 2 pools; tennis court; fitness center; deep-sea fishing; room service (breakfast and lunch); massage; laundry; library. *In room:* A/C, minibar, hair dryer, iron, safe, no phone.

MODERATE

Casa Isleña Inn ⭐ *(Finds*   "Island House" is created from a simple oceanfront former home right on the beach. Behind its gates, away from the water, is a private and tranquil world that offers a series of medium-size and comfortably furnished bedrooms decorated in bright Caribbean colors and designs. Each room has a neatly maintained shower-only bathroom. A natural tidal pool formed by a reef is an 8-minute stroll from the inn. At the tidal pool and from the inn's terraces guests can enjoy views of Aguadilla Bay and Mona Passage. In winter, while standing on the terraces, you can often watch the migration of humpback whales.

Barrio Puntas Carretera Int. 413 km 4, Rincón, PR 00677. ℂ **888/289-7750** or 787/823-1525. Fax 787/823-1530. www.casa-islena.com. 9 units (shower only). Year-round $125–$135 double. AE, MC, V. **Amenities:** Restaurant for breakfast and lunch, bar. *In room:* A/C, TV, no phone.

Lemontree Waterfront Cottages ⭐ *(Finds*   Right on a good, sandy beach, these spacious apartments with kitchenettes are for those who don't want to limit themselves to hotel rooms and meals. With the sound of the surf just outside your private back porch, these well-furnished seaside units can provide a home away from home, with everything from ceiling fans to air-conditioning, from paperback libraries to custom woodworking details. The property is well maintained. Families enjoy the three-bedroom, two-bathroom oceanfront suite called "Papaya" and "Mango" and "Pineapple" are ideal for two persons. Each unit contains a midsize shower-only bathroom. The least expensive units, "Banana" and "Coconut," are studio units for those who want a kitchen but don't require a living room. The cottages lie a 10-minute drive west of Rincón.

Rte. 4290 (P.O. Box 3200), Rincón, PR 00677. ℂ **787/823-6452.** Fax 787/823-5821. www.lemontreepr.com. 6 units (shower only). Winter $110–$140 double; $165 quad; $185 for 6. Off-season $95–$125 double; $145 quad; $165 for 6. AE, MC, V. **Amenities:** Laundry. *In room:* A/C, TV, kitchenette, coffeemaker.

INEXPENSIVE

Lazy Parrot   Set within an unlikely inland neighborhood, far from any particular view of the sea, this place has a better-than-average restaurant and clean, well-organized bedrooms. Each unit is comfortable, even if not overly large, with light-grained and durable furnishings that might seem appropriate for the bedroom of a high-school senior in a suburb on the U.S. mainland. Bathrooms are simple, functional, and workable, each with a shower, but not at all plush. Lazy Parrot was built as a private home in the 1970s, and then transformed into the inn you see today. The place is just as well known for its restaurant as it is for its rooms. Meals are served in an open-sided aerie on the building's uppermost floor.

Rd. 413, km 4.1. Barrio Puntas, Rincón, PR 00677. © **800/294-1752** or 787/823-5654. Fax 787/823-0224. www.lazyparrot.com. 11 units. Winter $95–$125 double; off-season $75–$95 double. AE, MC, V. **Amenities:** Restaurant, bar; pool; room service; babysitting. *In room:* A/C, TV.

Parador Villa Antonio Ilia and Hector Ruíz offer apartments by the sea in this privately owned and run parador. The beach outside is nice, but the local authorities don't keep it as clean as they ought to. Surfing and fishing can be enjoyed just outside your front door, and you can bring your catch right into your cottage and prepare a fresh seafood dinner in your own kitchenette (there's no restaurant). This is a popular destination with families from Puerto Rico, who crowd in on the weekends to occupy the motel-like rooms with balconies or terraces. Furnishings are well used but offer reasonable comfort, and the shower-only bathrooms are small.

Rte. 115, km 12.3 (P.O. Box 68), Rincón, PR 00677. © **787/823-2645**. Fax 787/823-3380. www.villa-antonio.com. 61 units (shower only). Year-round $85–$117.50 double; $120 suite. AE, DISC, MC, V. **Amenities:** Pool; 2 tennis courts; playground; babysitting; laundry. *In room:* A/C, TV, coffeemaker, iron, safe.

Villa Cofresi Set about a mile (1.5km) south of Rincón's center, this is a clean, family-run hotel with a view of the beach. Thanks to the three adult children of the Caro family, the place is better managed than many of its competitors. Bedrooms are comfortable and airy, with well-chosen furniture that might remind you of something in southern Florida. Each unit has a white tile floor and a small bathroom with a tub and shower. Most rooms have two double beds; some have two twin beds. The two units that tend to be reserved out long in advance are nos. 47 and 55, which have windows opening directly onto the sea.

The in-house restaurant, La Ana de Cofresi, is named after the ship that was captained by the region's most famous 18th-century pirate, Roberto Cofresi. Hand-painted murals highlight some of his adventures. Open Monday through Friday from 5 to 10pm, Saturday and Sunday from noon to 10pm; it charges $8 to $30 for well-prepared main courses that are likely to include fish consommé, four kinds of mofongo, breaded scampi served either with Creole sauce or garlic, and very good steaks, including a 12-ounce New York sirloin.

Rd. 115, km 12.3, Rincón, PR. 00677. © **787/823-2450**. Fax 787/823-1770. www.villacofresi.com. 70 units. Winter $105 double; $135 suite. Off-season $95 double; $115 suite. AE, DC, MC, V. **Amenities:** Restaurant, bar; pool; room service; babysitting; laundry/dry cleaning. *In room:* A/C, TV, fridge, hair dryer, iron.

WHERE TO DINE
VERY EXPENSIVE

Horned Dorset Primavera ★★ FRENCH/CARIBBEAN This is the finest restaurant in western Puerto Rico—so romantic that people sometimes come from San Juan just for an intimate dinner. A masonry staircase sweeps from the garden to the second floor, where soaring ceilings and an atmosphere similar to that in a private villa awaits you.

The menu, which changes virtually every night, based on the inspiration of the chef, might include chilled parsnip soup, a fricassee of wahoo with wild mushrooms, grilled loin of beef with peppercorns, and medallions of lobster in an orange-flavored beurre-blanc sauce. The grilled breast of duckling with bay leaves and raspberry sauce is also delectable. Mahimahi is grilled and served with ginger-cream sauce on a bed of braised Chinese cabbage. It's delicious.

In the Horned Dorset Primavera Hotel, Rte. 429. © **787/823-4030**. Reservations recommended. Lunch $8–$20; fixed-price dinner $68–$72 for 5 dishes, $92 for 8 dishes. AE, MC, V. Daily noon–2pm and 7–9pm.

MODERATE

The Landing ★★ INTERNATIONAL   This is the most substantial of the many bars in Rincón, with a popularity so widespread that it's likely to attract as many as 800 customers on a Friday or Saturday night. The restaurant, which looks like a stylish private house, is adjacent to a beach favored by a cadre of devoted surfers. Its focal point is a sprawling bar where popular drinks include an M&M ($5.50 each)—loosely defined as a piña colada capped with layers of both light and dark rum. Edwin Nault, a former dental technician from Boston, is the competent entrepreneur who runs this place. Menu items include fried calamari, scampi, T-bone steaks, jerk chicken, churrasco, barbecued ribs, stuffed chicken breast, and lobster kebabs. The view of Rincón's legendary surf, complete with dozens of surfers trying their luck on the deep blue, is panoramic.

Carretera 413 (Interior), Barrios Puntas/Playa Antonio. ✆ 787/823-3112. Reservations recommended for dinner Fri–Sat. Burgers and sandwiches $6.75–$9.75; platters $16–$33. AE, MC, V. Fri–Sat and Mon 11am–2am.

INEXPENSIVE

Calypso Café AMERICAN   Set on a bend in the road between the Black Eagle Marina and the lighthouse (El Faro de Rincón), this sometimes-charming bar attracts many of Rincón's young singles. One of the simplest drinking emporiums in the region, it consists of a roof, a fiesta-colored balustrade, and a collection of surfers, many from New York, New Jersey, and Florida. Maria's Beach, a well-known surfer's hangout, is a few steps away. A deejay or live band performs every Friday and Saturday night. The ambience might remind you of a latter-day remake of *The Endless Summer.*

Maria's Beach. No phone. Reservations not accepted. Burgers and simple platters $6–$8. No credit cards. Daily noon–2am.

Panaderia/Cafeteria Calvache AMERICAN/PUERTO RICAN   The food-service area of this place occupies one end of a store otherwise devoted to the sale of rum, baked goods, and hardware. But it's so friendly and the counter setting is so appropriate for the food (bacon and eggs, hamburgers, spaghetti with sausage, and such local fare as rice with seafood) that we wanted to add it to our listings. In the evening, the staff offers only sandwiches, no hot food. You'll find this Formica-clad heaven about 1½ miles (2.5km) south of the center of Rincón.

Rte. 115, km 9. ✆ 787/823-6658. Reservations not necessary. Breakfast and sandwiches $2–$6; fixed-price lunch $3.50. MC, V. Daily 5am–10pm.

Tamboo Tavern AMERICAN   The allure of this place derives from the crowd of surfing enthusiasts who gather here for drinks and fuel before braving the sometimes-treacherous waters at Sandy Beach. The staff prides themselves on knowing the latest surfing conditions. Burgers and sandwiches are the most frequently ordered items, and rum-and-Cokes and piña coladas are enduringly popular, too.

Sandy Beach. ✆ 787/823-8550. Reservations not accepted. Main courses $5–$9 lunch, $7–$18 dinner. MC, V. Bar daily 11am–midnight. Restaurant Apr–Nov 15 Thurs–Sun 11am–midnight; Nov 16–Mar daily 11am–midnight.

A NEARBY PLACE TO STAY & DINE IN AGUADA

For the location of the parador described here, see the map "Paradores & Country Inns of Puerto Rico" on p. 69.

J. B. Hidden Village Hotel ⭐ Named using the initials of its owners (Julio Bonilla, his wife, Jinnie, and their son, Julio, Jr.), this is a well-maintained and isolated hotel launched in 1990. Half a mile (1km) east of Aguada, on a side street that runs off Route 4414, it's nestled in a valley between three forested hillsides, almost invisible from the road. The hotel is a quiet and simple refuge to vacationers who enjoy exploring the area's many beaches. There are two restaurants on the premises (one with a view of a neighboring ravine). Each comfortable bedroom offers views of the pool and has a small tiled bathroom with tub-and-shower combination.

Carretera 2, Intersection 4416, km 1, Punta Nueve, Barrio Piedras Blancas, Sector Villarrubia, Aguada, PR 00602. ℂ 787/868-8686. Fax 787/868-8701. 40 units. $75–$94 double; $112–$134 suite. AE, MC, V. **Amenities:** Restaurant, bar; pool; babysitting. *In room:* A/C, TV, no phone.

2 The Southwest Coast

The true native of Puerto Rico heads not to the fancy resorts along the north coast near San Juan, but instead to the southwestern corner, a region with a distinctly island flavor. Here are some of Puerto Rico's great beaches, notably **Boquerón Beach** ⭐⭐, and a lot of mom-and-pop operations that offer nightly rentals and good seafood dinners.

Southern Puerto Rico is increasingly gaining a reputation among **scuba divers,** although the outfitters are a bit lean here and not as well organized or plentiful as in the Cayman Islands. The attraction is the continental shelf that drops off a few miles off the southern coast. Within this watery range is a towering wall that is some 20 miles (32km) long and filled with one of the best assortments of marine life in the West Indies. Diving is possible from the town of La Parguera in the west all the way to Ponce in the east. The wall drops from 60 to 120 feet before it "vanishes" into 1,500 feet of sea. With a visibility of around 100 feet, divers experience the beautiful formations of some of Puerto Rico's most dramatic coral gardens.

Bird-watchers should head to the **Guánica State Forest,** which is the sanctuary that has the greatest number of birds on the island. For beachcombers, there are many hidden places, such as Gilligan's Island off the coast of the little village of Guánica. For snorkelers, there are miles of coral reefs, awash with tropical fish and coral and marine life. The Cabo Rojo lighthouse, south of Boquerón, offers views of the rocky coastline and a panoramic sweep of the Caribbean.

BOQUERON

Lying 85 miles (137km) southwest of San Juan and 33 miles (53km) west of Ponce is the little beach town of Boquerón. It is just south of Cabo Rojo, west of the historic city of San Germán, and near the western edge of the Boquerón Forest Preserve.

What puts sleepy Boquerón on the tourist map is its lovely public beach, one of the island's finest for swimming. It is also known for the shellfish found offshore. The beach has facilities, including lockers and changing places, plus kiosks that rent watersports equipment. Parking costs $2. On weekends the resort tends to be crowded with families driving down from San Juan.

The outfitter that offers the best scuba diving and snorkeling in the area is **Mona Aquatics,** on Calle José de Diego, directly west of the heart of town (ℂ 787/851-2185). It can arrange special trips to Mona Island some 50 miles (81km) out to sea, a sanctuary known for its spectacular dive opportunities. The company also rents snorkeling gear and, if enough people are interested, conducts boat tours of the Bahía de Boquerón.

From Boquerón you can head directly south to **El Faro de Cabo Rojo** at the island's southernmost corner. The century-old Cabo Rojo Lighthouse lies on Route 301, along a spit of land between Bahia Sucia and Bahia Salinas. Looking down from the lighthouse, you'll see a 2,000-foot drop along jagged limestone cliffs. The lighthouse dates from 1881, when it was constructed under Spanish rule. The famous pirate Roberto Cofresi used to terrorize the coast along here in the 19th century and was said to have hidden out in a cave nearby.

WHERE TO STAY

Cofresi Beach Hotel Set across from one of the area's best dive shops, this is a choice for clients who can live without maid service and other resort-oriented amenities—there is no full-time reception or concierge staff. The apartments here have kitchens with cutlery, plates, and cooking equipment, durable furniture, and comfortable beds; each has a small tiled bathroom with a tub and shower. It's about as laissez-faire as they come.

Calle Muñoz Rivera 58, P.O. Box 910, Boquerón, PR 00622. ℂ 787/254-3000. Fax 787/254-1048. www.cofresibeach.com. 12 units. Winter $119 1-bedroom; $159 2-bedroom; $199 3-bedroom. Off-season $69 1-bedroom; $143.10 2-bedroom; $179.10 3-bedroom. AE, MC, V. **Amenities:** Pool. *In room:* A/C, TV, kitchenette, coffeemaker, hair dryer, iron.

Parador Boquemar The pink-walled Parador Boquemar is a late-1980s inn that lies a block or so from Boquerón Beach. Rooms are at the end of long corridors that evoke a college dormitory or an anonymous office building. Despite the small units here, Puerto Rican families like this place a lot, causing readers to complain that children sometimes run up and down the corridors. Rooms are simple, stripped down to the bare essentials, although each has a small tiled shower-only bathroom. The place is a little too rustic and not maintained well enough for our tastes, but the beach somehow compensates. Stay here only if you plan to spend most of your time outside the hotel. Surprisingly, the hotel has one of the best restaurants in the area, Las Cascadas (see "Where to Dine" below).

Carretera 101, Poblado de Boquerón, Cabo Rojo, PR 00622. ℂ 787/851-2158. Fax 787/851-7600. www.boquemar.com. 75 units (shower only). Year-round $80 double; $92 junior suite. AE, DC, MC, V. **Amenities:** Restaurant, bar; pool; babysitting. *In room:* A/C, TV.

WHERE TO DINE

For some reason, Boquerón has more shellfish vendors than any other area in western Puerto Rico. They display their bounty on wooden tabletops along the town's main street. Most of the shellfish is not refrigerated, and as such, we cannot vouch for its safety. But if you're adventurous, you might want to give it a try. Most vendors offer a selection of spicy sauces to accompany the shellfish.

Las Cascadas ★ CREOLE/CONTINENTAL One of the best restaurants in the area, this popular bar and restaurant is the only mesónes gastronómicos in Boquerón. On the second floor of Parador Boquemar, it has a waterfall in its interior. The bartenders are the best in the area and seem to know how to whip up any kind of drink. The day begins early here. The chef's breakfast specialty is an omelet Cascada, with ham, tomatoes, onions, peppers, and cheese. At dinner many Creole recipes appear, such as *fomongo de yucca relleno* (stuffed mashed plantains); the plantains can be stuffed with lobster, shrimp, octopus, or conch.

The meats such as filet mignon are imported but tasty. Lobster can be served with five different sauces. Other specialties of the chef include chicken breast stuffed with lobster or shrimp. The tastiest appetizers are fish and cheese balls.

In the Parador Boquemar, Carretera 101, Poblado de Boquerón, Cabo Rojo. ℂ **787/851-2158.** Reservations not necessary. Breakfast $4–$5; main courses $13–$22. AE, MC, V. Daily 7:30–11:30am; Thurs–Tues 6–10pm.

Roberto's Fish Net PUERTO RICAN   This is one of two restaurants, both named "Roberto," on the same sleepy street in the center of Boquerón. Both belong to Roberto Aviles and offer roughly equivalent versions of the same food. We prefer this spot to Roberto's Restaurant Villa Playera (ℂ **787/254-3163**). However, the Villa Playera is still a good choice, particularly on Monday and Tuesday, when the Fish Net is closed. Within the Fish Net's simple environment, a cross between a luncheonette and a bar, you can order tender beefsteaks, well-flavored chicken breasts, or fresh fish, any of which comes with rice and beans. More unusual are the *pilones,* a combination of mashed plantains flavored with your choice of shrimp, conch, or octopus, usually served with salsa, that come in tall wooden cups with old-fashioned mortars.

Calle José de Diego s/n (without number). ℂ **787/851-6009.** Reservations not necessary. Main courses $4–$19. AE, MC, V. Wed–Sun 11am–10pm.

LA PARGUERA ★
This charming fishing village lies 78 miles (126km) southwest of San Juan and 26 miles (42km) west of Ponce, just south of San Germán. From San Germán, take Route 320 directly south and follow the signposts. Note that this route changes its name several times along the way, becoming Route 101, 116, 315, 305, and then 304 before reaching La Parguera—even though it's all the same highway.

The name of the village comes from *pargos,* meaning snapper. Its main attraction, other than its beaches and diving, is **Phosphorescent Bay,** which contains millions of luminescent dinoflagellates (microscopic plankton). A disturbance causes them to light up the dark waters. For dramatic effect, they are best seen on a moonless night. Boats leave for a troll around the bay nightly from 7:30pm to 12:30am from La Parguera pier, depending on demand. The trip costs $5 per person.

Offshore are some 12 to 15 reefs with a variety of depths. The Beril reef goes down to 60 feet, then drops to 2,000 feet. This wall is famous among divers, and visibility ranges from 100 to 120 feet. These reefs also provide some of the best snorkeling possibilities in Puerto Rico. Marine life is both abundant and diverse, including big morays, sea turtles, barracudas, nurse sharks, and manatees. **Paradise Scuba Center,** Hotel Casa Blanca Building, at La Parguera (ℂ **787/899-7611**), offers the best diving and snorkeling. A two-tank dive costs $70, a night dive $50; a 3-hour snorkeling jaunt goes for $35 per person. Full equipment can be rented.

WHERE TO STAY
La Jamaka   Set on a low but breezy hillside, a 10-minute hike from the town's congested center, this is a tasteful vacation compound in a verdant setting of bougainvillea and flowering shrubs. Guests here are pulled into the gregarious life of the establishment simply by the warmth of the owners, Elsie Cintron and Carlos Rosado. La Jamaka has a small swimming pool, a communal kitchen, and a garden-style setting for relaxation. Bedrooms are small—almost to the point of being a bit claustrophobic—but they're well maintained and filled in midsummer with holidaymakers from other parts of Puerto Rico. Each unit has a small, tiled shower-only bathroom.

Colinas de la Parguera, P.O. Box 303, Lajas, La Parguera PR 00667. (From La Parguera, head north on Rte. 304 until you reach the junction with Rte. 116. Continue north on 116 until you see the sign for the resort.) ℂ and fax **787/899-6162**. 9 units (shower only). $60–$71 double. AE, MC, V. **Amenities:** Restaurant, bar; pool; room service; babysitting. *In room:* A/C, no phone.

Parador Posada Porlamar   Developed by the Pancorbo family in 1967 as one of the first full-service hotels in town, this parador evokes life in a simple fishing village. A horseshoe-shaped compound that overlooks a narrow channel flanked by mangroves, it conducts an ongoing business with dive enthusiasts, thanks to its on-site scuba shop. Bedrooms are plain and neat but don't invite lingering. Some have balconies, minibars, and small sitting rooms, and each has a small, tiled shower-only bathroom. The social center here is a patio overlooking the channel. The restaurants and bars of La Parguera are within a short walk of this centrally located place. On the premises is a rather formal restaurant, La Pared. Specialties include seafood in Creole sauce, lamb chops in Dijon mustard, and sautéed shrimp in soursop-flavored butter sauce.

Rte. 304 (P.O. Box 3113), La Parguera, Lajas, PR 00667. (Drive west along Rte. 2 until you reach the junction of Rte. 116; then head south along Rte. 116 and Rte. 304.) ℂ **787/899-4015.** Fax 787/899-5558. www.posadaporlamar.com. 40 units (shower only). Winter $90–$127 double; off-season $60–$91 double. AE, MC, V. **Amenities:** Restaurant, bar; pool; room service; babysitting. *In room:* A/C, TV, minibar, coffeemaker, hair dryer, safe.

Parador Villa Parguera *Kids*   Although the water in the nearby bay is too muddy for swimming, guests can enjoy a view of the harbor and take a dip in the swimming pool. Situated on the southwestern shore of Puerto Rico, this parador is favored by *Sanjuaneros* for weekend escapes. It's also known for its seafood dinners (the fish are not caught in the bay), comfortable and uncomplicated bedrooms, and location next to the bay's famous phosphorescent waters. Each unit has either a balcony or a terrace. Bathrooms are rather cramped but well maintained, and each has either a shower or a tub. This place is more gregarious and convivial, and usually more fun, than the Porlamar, a few steps away.

The spacious, air-conditioned restaurant, where the occasionally slow service might remind you of Spain in a bygone era, offers traditional favorites, such as filet of fish stuffed with lobster and shrimp. Nonguests are welcome here, and there's a play area for children.

Because the inn is popular with Puerto Rican families, especially on weekends, there's a special weekend package for a 2-night minimum stay; $350 to $375 (depending on the exposure of your room) covers the price of a double room, welcome drinks, breakfasts, dinners, flowers, and dancing, along with a free show. However, we prefer to stay here during the week, when it's more tranquil.

304 Main St. (P.O. Box 273), Carretera 304, km 303, La Parguera, Lajas, PR 00667. (Drive west along Rte. 2 until you reach the junction with Rte. 116; then head south along Rte. 116 and Rte. 304.) ℂ **787/899-7777.** Fax 787/899-6040. www.elshop.com. 70 units (all with either shower or tub). Sun–Thurs $81–$90 double; Fri–Sat $100–$112 double. 2 children 9 or under stay free in parents' room. AE, DC, DISC, MC, V. **Amenities:** Restaurant, 2 bars; pool; babysitting. *In room:* A/C, TV.

WHERE TO DINE

Besides the following recommendation, **La Jamaka** (see "Where to Stay" above) also serves excellent cuisine.

La Casita SEAFOOD   This is the town's most consistently reliable and popular restaurant. It's flourished here since the 1960s, in a simple wooden building. Inside, lots of varnished pine acts as a decorative foil for platters of local and imported fish and shellfish. Filets of fish can be served in any of seven different styles; lobster comes in five. Even the Puerto Rican starchy staple of mofongo comes in versions stuffed with crab, octopus, shrimp, lobster, and assorted shellfish. Begin with fish chowder, a dozen cheese balls, or fish croquettes. End with coconut-flavored flan. Don't expect grand service or decor, but rather a setting where food is the focus.

Calle Principal 304. (*C*) 787/899-1681. Reservations not necessary. Main courses $4.50–$25. AE, DC, MC, V. Tues–Sun 11am–10:30pm. Closed 2 weeks in Sept.

GUANICA

Guánica, on the Caribbean Sea, lies 73 miles (118km) southwest of San Juan and 21 miles (34km) west of the city of Ponce. Part of the area is a UNESCO-designated world biosphere reserve, adjacent to the famed Guánica dry forest, home to more than 100 species of migratory and resident birds, the largest number in Puerto Rico.

The beach at Guánica is pristine and the crystal clear water is ideal for swimming, snorkeling, and diving. Directly offshore is the famed Gilligan's Island, plus six of Puerto Rico's best sites for night or day dives.

The area was once known for its leaping bullfrogs. The Spanish conquerors virtually wiped out this species. But the bullfrogs have come back and live in the rolling, scrub-covered hills that surround the 18-acre site of the Copamarina Beach Resort, the area's major hotel (see below.)

Guánica is adjacent to the unique "Dry Forest" and experiences very little rainfall. Nearby mountains get an annual rainfall of 15 feet, but Guánica receives only about 15 inches. This is the world's largest dry coastal forest region. The upper hills are ideal for hiking.

Guánica was once the haunt of the Taíno Indians, and it was the place where Ponce de León first explored Puerto Rico in 1508. One of his descendants later founded the nearby city of Ponce in 1692.

SCUBA DIVING, SNORKELING & OTHER OUTDOOR PURSUITS

The best dive operation in Guánica is **Dive Copamarina** ((*C*) 787/821-0505), part of the Copamarina Beach Resort. Copamarina has a long pier where fishing is permitted and a 42-foot Pro Jet dive boat. Guánica is one of the Caribbean's best areas for day and night dives. A two-tank dive costs $75, and full diving equipment can be rented for $20. You can also rent snorkeling gear. Whale-watching excursions can be arranged from January to March at the hotel's tour desk, which also offers ecotours, kayaking, deep-sea fishing, and sunset sails. Horseback riding and sunset biking are also available.

At one of the local beaches, **Playa Santa,** west of town, **Pino's Boat & Water Fun** ((*C*) 787/821-6864) will rent you a paddleboat or kayak for $15 an hour.

One of the most visited sites is **Gilligan's Island,** a series of mangrove and sand cays near the Caña Gorda peninsula. Part of the dry forest reserve, it is set aside for recreational use. A small ferry departs from in front of Restaurant San Jacinto, just past Copamarina Beach Resort, every hour daily from 10am to 5pm, weather permitting; round-trips cost $5.

WHERE TO STAY

Copamarina Beach Resort ★★ *Value*   In the 1950s Copamarina was the private vacation retreat of the de Castro family, Puerto Rican cement barons. In 1991 it was enlarged and upgraded by talented entrepreneurs. Today, charming,

Finds **Puerto Rico's Secret Beaches**

Some of Puerto Rico's most beautiful and isolated beaches lie on the island's southwestern coast, on the Caribbean Sea, far from major highways. Stretching between Ponce in the east and Cabo Rojo on Puerto Rico's extreme southwestern tip, these beaches flank some of the least densely populated parts of the island. And because the boundaries between them are relatively fluid, only a local resident (or perhaps a professional geographer) could say for sure where one ends and the other begins.

If you consider yourself an aficionado of isolated beaches, it's worth renting a car and striking out for these remote locales. Drive westward from Ponce along Highway 2, branching south along Route 116 to **Guánica,** the self-anointed gateway and capital of this string of "secret beaches."

By far the most accessible and appealing beach is **Caña Gorda** 𝄐. Set about a quarter-mile (.5km) south of Guánica, at the edge of a legally protected marsh that's known for its rich bird life and thick reeds, Caña Gorda is a sprawling expanse of pale beige sand that's dotted with ramshackle-looking *bohios* (huts) crafted from tree branches and palm fronds. Despite its rusticity, it's a site that's been improved and developed by the local authorities. The centerpiece here is a well-recommended hotel, the **Copamarina** (𝄐 **800/468-4553** or 787/821-0505). You can check in for a night or two of sun-flooded R&R (see "Where to Stay" below). Even if you're not staying at the hotel, consider dropping in for a *cuba libre,* a margarita, or a meal.

In the very southwest sector of Puerto Rico are some relatively hidden and very secluded beaches, although getting to them is a bit difficult along some potholed roads. From Boquerón head east on Route 101, cutting south at the junction with Route 301 which will carry you to the one of the most westerly beaches in Puerto Rico, Playa Sucia. The beach opens onto **Bahia Sucia** 𝄐, whose name rather unappetizingly translates as "Dirty Bay." Actually it isn't dirty, and it's a lovely spot.

From Bahia Sucia, you can head east to discover other secret beaches, which are reached along various signposted roads: 324, 304, and 323. The finest beaches, moving toward Ponce, are **Rosado Beach** 𝄐, **Playa Santa** 𝄐, and **Playa Tamarindo** 𝄐.

All these beaches might be hard to reach, but persevere and you'll be met with warm water and long, uncrowded stretches of sand, where towering king palms and salt-tolerant sea grapes provide an idyllic tropical backdrop for sun and surf. Keep in mind that with the exception of Caña Gorda, the beaches mentioned here have virtually no services and public utilities. Pack what you'll need for the day— food, water, sunscreen, and so forth.

low-key, and discreetly elegant, it stands head and shoulders above everything else along Puerto Rico's western coast, except for the regal Horned Dorset Primavera (its strongest competitor). Situated beside a public beach (the best in the area), amid a landscaped palm grove, the resort is airy and relaxing. A favorite destination of *Sanjuaneros,* it also draws a well-heeled crowd of clients from Europe and North America, who know good value when they see it.

The accommodations are in one- and two-story wings that radiate from the resort's central core. The attractively decorated units have tile floors, lots of exposed wood, and louvered doors with screens that open onto large verandas or terraces. Everything is airy and comfortable. Bathrooms are larger than you might expect, and up-to-date, some with shower, others with tub.

The resort houses two restaurants, one of which reigns as one of the finest in western Puerto Rico: Copamarina Coastal Cuisine is a destination for clients from as far away as San Juan (see "Where to Dine" below). Less formal, and staffed with a hardworking crowd of young people, is Las Palmas, which is set in the open air beneath a canopy.

The dive facilities here are the best and most varied in western Puerto Rico, attracting divers of all levels of expertise.

Rte. 333, km 6.5, Caña Gorda (P.O. Box 805), Guánica, PR 00653. (From Ponce, drive west along Rte. 2 to Rte. 116 and go south to Rte. 333, then head east.) © **800/468-4553** or 787/821-0505. Fax 787/821-0070. www.copamarina.com. 106 units. Year-round $165–$260 double; $400 suite. AE, DC, DISC, MC, V. **Amenities:** 2 restaurants, bar; 2 pools; health club; babysitting; laundry/dry cleaning. *In room:* A/C, TV, coffeemaker, hair dryer.

Mary Lee's by the Sea *Finds*   Owned and operated by Michigan-born Mary Lee Alvarez, a former resident of Cuba and a self-described "compulsive decorator," this is an informal collection of cottages, seafront houses, and apartments, located 4 miles (6.5km) east of Guánica. Five California-style houses are subdivided into eight living units, each suitable for one to three couples. Rooms are whimsically decorated in an airy, somewhat bohemian way, with a sense of 1960s comfort and a sometimes soothing sense of clutter. Each unit has a small, tiled bathroom with tub. The entire compound, which grew in an artfully erratic way, is landscaped with flowering shrubs, trees, and vines. Overall, the ambience is kind and low-key.

There aren't any formally organized activities here, but the hotel sits next to sandy beaches and a handful of uninhabited offshore cays. The management maintains rental boats with motors, two waterside sundecks, and several kayaks for the benefit of active guests. Hikers and bird-watchers can go north to the Guánica State Forest.

Don't come here looking for nighttime activities or enforced conviviality. The place is quiet, secluded, and appropriate for low-key vacationers looking for privacy. There isn't a bar or restaurant here, but each unit has a modern kitchen and an outdoor barbecue pit. The rooms are serviced weekly, although guests can arrange daily maid service for an extra fee.

Rte. 333, km 6.7 (P.O. Box 394), Guánica, PR 00653. (From Ponce, take Rte. 2. When you reach Rte. 116, head south toward Gúanica. The hotel is signposted from the road.) © **787/821-3600.** Fax 787/821-0744. www.maryleesbythesea.com. 11 units. Year-round $89 double; $100–$140 studio and 1-bedroom apt; $160–$170 2-bedroom apt; $250 3-bedroom house. MC, V. **Amenities:** Laundry/dry cleaning. *In room:* A/C, kitchen, coffeemaker, iron, safe, no phone.

WHERE TO DINE

Copamarina Coastal Cuisine ⭐ INTERNATIONAL   This is a genuinely excellent restaurant whose culinary inspiration originated with Puerto Rico's most celebrated chef, Wilo Benet. Despite Benet's departure, a team of disciples continues, with delectable dishes that include fried red snapper with Creole sauce, filet of mahimahi with pigeon peas, garlic shrimp with local rice, and beef parmigiana with red wine sauce. The interior is air-conditioned but tropical in its feel, providing a welcome dose of relaxed glamour.

In the Copamarina Beach Resort, Rte. 333, km 6.5, Caña Gorda (P.O. Box 805), Guánica. ℂ **787/821-0505.** Reservations recommended. Main courses $19–$34. AE, DC, DISC, MC, V. Sun–Thurs 6–10:30pm; Fri–Sat 6–11pm.

3 Paradores of Western Puerto Rico

One program that has helped the Puerto Rico Tourism Company successfully promote the commonwealth as "The Complete Island"—the paradores puertorriqueños—will help make your travels even more enjoyable.

The *paradores puertorriqueños* (see chapter 2 for more details about these government-sponsored inns and a map pinpointing their locations) are a chain of privately owned and operated country inns under the auspices and supervision of the Commonwealth Development Company. These hostelries are easily identified by the Taíno grass hut that appears in the signs and logos of each one. The Puerto Rico Tourism Company started the program in 1973, modeling it after Spain's parador system, although many of the paradores here are mere shanties compared to some of the deluxe Spanish hostelries. Each parador is situated in a historic or particularly beautiful spot. They vary in size, but most share the virtues of affordability, hospitable staffs, and high standards of cleanliness. Most but not all of their rooms are air-conditioned, and each room has a bathroom.

For reservations or further information, contact the **Paradores Puertorriqueños Reservation Office,** P.O. Box 9023960, San Juan, PR 00902 (ℂ **800/ 443-0266**).

JAYUYA

The village of Jayuya, southwest of San Juan and north of Ponce, lies in the middle of the Cordillera Central, a mountain massif. From San Juan, travel west along Highway 22, going past the town of Barceloneta until you come to the junction of Route 140; head south to the town of Florida, passing through some of the most dramatic scenery in Puerto Rico. Continue along Route 140 until you come to the junction of Route 141, signposted southwest into Jayuya.

Jayuya is a small town that still retains strong Taíno cultural influences, particularly in the language. At the Jayuya Indian Festival in mid-November, you'll see craft markets, parades, and displays of Taíno dances. The festival honors the patron saint of the town, Nuestra Señora la Monserrate.

Here you'll also find the Parador Hacienda Gripiñas (see below), a former coffee plantation, where you can glimpse the good old days on Puerto Rico. In 1950 Jayuya received worldwide attention when *independentistas* proclaimed the "Republic of Puerto Rico" and held the town under siege until the National Guard was called in.

WHERE TO STAY & DINE

Parador Hacienda Gripiñas ⭐   A former coffee plantation about 2½ hours from San Juan, Parador Hacienda Gripiñas is reached via a long, narrow, and

---

(*Tips* Mesónes Gastronómicos

Except for those in major hotels, you'll find few well-known restaurants as you tour the western part of the island. However, there are plenty of roadside places and simple taverns. For authentic island cuisine, you can rely on the *mesónes gastronómicos* (gastronomic inns). This established dining network, sanctioned by the Puerto Rico Tourism Company, highlights restaurants recognized for excellence in preparing and serving Puerto Rican specialties at modest prices.

Mesón gastronómico status is limited to restaurants outside the San Juan area that are close to major island attractions. Membership in the program requires that restaurants have attractive surroundings and comply with strict standards of service. Members must specialize in native foods, but if you order fresh fish, chances are you'll be pleased. Regrettably, there are no maps listing these myriad restaurants, but their signs are easy to spot as you drive around the island.

---

curvy road. This home-turned-inn is a delightful blend of old-world hacienda and modern conveniences. The plantation ambience is created by ceiling fans, splendid gardens, porch hammocks, and more than 20 acres of coffee bushes. You'll taste the homegrown product when you order the inn's aromatic brew.

The modest rooms vary in size and all are kept very tidy. Each unit has a small, tiled shower-only bathroom. For meals, we suggest the restaurant's Puerto Rican dishes rather than the international cuisine. You can swim in the two chilly mountain pools, soak up the sun, or enjoy the nearby sights, such as the Taíno Indian Ceremonial Park at Utuado. Boating and plenty of fishing are just 30 minutes away, at Lake Caonillas. The parador is also near the Río Camuy Caves.

Rte. 527, km 2.5 (P.O. Box 387), Jayuya, PR 00664. (From Jayuya, head east via Rte. 144; at the junction with Rte. 527, go south 1½ miles/2.5km.) © 787/828-1717. 20 units (shower only). Year-round $125 double. Rates include 2 meals a day. AE, MC, V. **Amenities:** Restaurant; pool. *In room:* A/C, TV.

UTUADO

Another good base in the Cordillera Central massif is the little mountain town of Utuado, which lies northwest of Jayuya (see above). This is the heartland of karst, an irregular limestone terrain with sinkholes, underground streams, and caverns. This unique landscape was created over several millennia by heavy rainfall (see chapter 7). Utuado is a stronghold of *jíbaro* ("hillbilly") culture, reflecting the mountain life of the island as few other settlements do.

Petroglyphs left over from the Taíno civilization have been found in the area. One depicted an Indian woman with frog legs and an elaborate headdress. From Utuado, you can continue west for 20 miles (32km) on Route 111 to km 12.3, to reach the Taíno Indian Ceremonial Center (see "Life After Death" below).

WHERE TO STAY & DINE

Hotel La Casa Grande ✦ This parador, situated on 107 acres of a former coffee plantation in the Caonillas Barrios district, about 1½ hours from San Juan, has been vastly improved since its takeover by Steven Weingarten and his wife, Marlene, a gourmet cook. Steven is still a practicing attorney in New York City, commuting to Puerto Rico on a regular basis. All the comfortably but simply furnished bedrooms have ceiling fans in lieu of air-conditioning, which is hardly needed during the cool nights here. Each room has a balcony, a hammock, a mountain view, and a small bathroom with shower. Nature trails are carved out of the jungle.

Marlene presides over Jungle Jane's Restaurant, which serves an array of delectably prepared international and Puerto Rican dishes. Even if you're not a guest, you can feast here daily from 7:30am to 9:30pm. It might make an ideal luncheon stopover if you're touring in the area.

P.O. Box 1499, Caonillas, Utuado, PR 00641. (From Arecibo, take Rte. 10 south to Utuado; then head east on Rte. 111 to Rte. 140; head north on Rte. 140 to Rte. 612 for ¼ mile/.5km.) (C) **888/343-2272** or 787/894-3900. Fax 787/894-3939. www.hotelcasagrande.com. 20 units. Year-round $70–$90 double. AE, MC, V. **Amenities:** Restaurant, bar; pool; room service. *In room:* No phone.

QUEBRADILLAS

Quebradillas is one of the sleepy municipalities of northwest Puerto Rico. With its flamboyantly painted houses, narrow streets, and spiritualist herb shops, it is like a town of long ago. Quebradillas lies 70 miles (113km) west of San Juan, only about a 15-mile (24km) trip from the city of Arecibo along Route 2.

The Atlantic waters along the northwest coast of Puerto Rico tend to be rough, with the rugged coastline seemingly plunging right into the ocean. Both snorkelers and scuba divers are drawn to a protected beach area known as **"The Shacks,"** close to the town of Isabela, northwest of Quebradillas. The reefs and coral caverns here are some of the most dramatic in Puerto Rico. Surfers also flock to Isabela's Jobos Beach. Neither beach, however, is ideal for swimming.

Also northwest of Quebradillas lies beautiful **Guajataca Beach,** with its white sands, raging surf, and turbulent, deep waters. This is a fine beach for sunning and collecting shells, but it's a *playa peligrosa* (dangerous beach) unless you're a skilled swimmer. You can also visit **Lago de Guajataca,** another beautiful spot, by heading south for 7 miles (11km) on Route 113. This man-made lake is a lovely place for hiking, and it's the site of two paradores (see below). The staff at these government-sponsored inns will give you advice about jaunts in the **Guajataca Forest Reserve** to the immediate west.

WHERE TO STAY & DINE

Parador El Guajataca   You'll find this place on a rolling hillside reaching down to a surf-beaten beach along the north coast. Stay here for the stunning natural setting and don't expect too much, because the hotel itself is somewhat seedy. Each room is rather standard and has its own entrance and private balcony opening onto the turbulent Atlantic. Bathrooms are slightly battered but functional, each with a tub.

Served in a glassed-in dining room where all the windows face the sea, the cuisine isn't much more memorable than the accommodations, with little care going into the preparation of the often-canned ingredients. A local musical group plays for dining and dancing on Friday and Saturday evenings. There are two swimming pools (one for adults, another for children), plus a playground for children.

Rte. 2, km 103.8 (P.O. Box 1558), Quebradillas, PR 00678. (From Quebradillas, continue northwest on Rte. 2 for 1 mile/1.5km; the parador is signposted.) (C) **800/964-3065** or 787/895-3070. Fax 787/895-3589. www.elguajataca.com. 38 units. $89–$96 double. AE, DISC, MC, V. **Amenities:** Restaurant, bar; 2 pools; room service; babysitting; laundry/dry cleaning. *In room:* A/C, TV, coffeemaker, iron.

Parador Vistamar   In the Guajataca area, this parador, one of the largest in Puerto Rico, sits like a sentinel surveying the scene from high atop a mountain overlooking greenery and a seascape. There are gardens and intricate paths carved into the side of the mountain, where you can stroll while enjoying the

Life After Death

The Taíno Indians who lived in Puerto Rico before Europeans came here were ruled by *caciques*, or chiefs, who controlled their own villages and several others nearby. The Taínos believed in life after death, which led them to take extreme care in burying their dead. Personal belongings of the deceased were placed in the tomb with the newly dead, and bodies were carefully arranged in a squatting position. Near Ponce, visitors can see the oldest Indian burial ground uncovered in the Antilles, Tibes Indian Ceremonial Center (p. 192).

Even at the time of the arrival of Columbus and the conquistadores who followed, the Taínos were threatened by the warlike and cannibalistic Carib Indians coming up from the south. But though they feared the Caribs, they learned to fear the conquistadores even more. Within 50 years of the Spanish colonization, the Taíno culture had virtually disappeared, the Indians annihilated through either massacres or due to European diseases.

But Taíno blood and remnants of their culture live on. The Indians married with Spaniards and Africans, and their physical characteristics—straight hair, copper-colored skin, and prominent cheekbones—can still be seen in some Puerto Ricans today. Many Taíno words became part of the Spanish language that's spoken on the island even today. Hammocks, the weaving of baskets, and the use of gourds as eating receptacles are part of the heritage left by these ill-fated tribes.

Still standing near Utuado, a small mountain town, **Parque Ceremonial Indígena-Caguaña (Indian Ceremonial Park at Caguaña),** Route 111, km 12.3 (© **787/894-7325**), was built by the Taínos for recreation and worship some 800 years ago. Stone monoliths, some etched with petroglyphs, rim several of the 10 *bateyes* (playing fields) used for a ceremonial game that some historians believe was a forerunner to soccer. The monoliths and petroglyphs, as well as the *dujos* (ceremonial chairs), are existing examples of the Taínos' skill in carving wood and stone.

Archaeologists have dated this site to approximately 2 centuries before Europe's discovery of the New World. It is believed that the Taíno chief Guarionex gathered his subjects on this site to celebrate rituals and practice sports. Set on a 13-acre field surrounded by trees, some 14 vertical monoliths with colorful petroglyphs are arranged around a central sacrificial stone monument. The ball complex also includes a museum, which is open daily from 8:30am to 4pm; admission is free.

There is also a gallery called Herencia Indígena, where you can purchase Taíno relics at reasonable prices, including the sought-after *Cemis* (Taíno idols) and figures of the famous little frog, the coquí. The Taínos are long gone, and much that was here is gone, too. This site is of special interest to those with academic pursuits, but of only passing interest to the lay visitor.

fragrance of the tropical flowers. Or you might choose to search for the calcified fossils that abound on the carved mountainside. For a unique experience, visitors can try their hand at freshwater fishing just down the hill from the hotel (bring your own gear). Flocks of rare tropical birds are frequently seen in the nearby mangroves.

Bedrooms are comfortably furnished in a rather bland motel style. Bathrooms with either shower or tub are functional, but without much decorative zest. There's a dining room with an ocean view where you can have a typical Puerto Rican dinner or choose from the international menu.

A short drive from the hotel will bring you to the Punta Borinquén Golf Course. Tennis courts are just down the hill from the inn itself. Sightseeing trips to the nearby Arecibo Observatory (see chapter 7)—the largest radar/radio-telescope in the world—and to Monte Calvario (a replica of Mount Calvary) are available. Another popular visit is to the plaza in the town of Quebradillas.

6205 Rte. 113N (P.O. Box T-38), Quebradillas, PR 00678. (At Quebradillas, head northwest on Rte. 2, then go left at the junction with Rte. 113 and continue for a half mile/1km.) ✆ **787/895-2065.** Fax 787/895-2294. www.paradorvistamar.com. 55 units (each with either shower or tub). Year-round $71–$95 double. Up to 2 children under 12 stay free in parents' room. AE, DC, MC, V. **Amenities:** Restaurant, bar; pool; room service; laundry/dry cleaning. *In room:* A/C, TV, coffeemaker (in some), hair dryer (in some), iron.

ISABELA

On the northwestern coast, a 1½-hour drive west of San Juan, the town of Isabela captures the flavor of the west, although it's far less known by visitors than Rincón and Mayagüez. Its pastel-colored, whitewashed houses border the sea, known for its surfing and swimming beaches.

The locals don't survive on tourism, but on such industries as shoemaking and textiles. In spite of manufacturing, many small farms still dot the area.

Tragedy has struck repeatedly in the area because of the geographical location of Isabela, which has made it the victim of both tidal waves and earthquakes since it was first settled.

Isabela enjoys a reputation for horse breeding. This activity is centered around Arenales, south of the town, where a number of horse stables are located.

The area abounds in good beaches, including Jobos Beach, directly west of Isabela on Route 466. The beach is set against a backdrop of cliffs, the most dramatic of which is El Pozo de Jacinto. Nearby at a beach called "The Shacks," both snorkelers and scuba divers enjoy swimming among the reefs, teeming with rainbow-hued fish and the coral caverns.

WHERE TO STAY & DINE

Villas del Mar Hau 🏅 *Kids*   Opening onto a long private beach, this family-friendly parador complex is peppered with West Indian–style cottages in vivid Caribbean pastels with Victorian wood trim. The location is midway between the west coast cities of Arecibo in the east and Aguadilla in the west, right outside the smaller town of Isabela. Under the shelter of Causuarina pine trees, most guests spend their days lying on Playa Montones. The huge tidal "wading" pool is ideal for children. The place is unpretentious but not completely back to nature, as the beachfront cottages are well furnished and equipped, each with a balcony and with capacities for two to six guests. Some have ceiling fans, others have air-conditioning, and all units are equipped with small, tiled, shower-only bathrooms. Since 1960 the Hau family has run this little beach inn. The on-site restaurant is well known in the area for its creative menu featuring fresh fish, shellfish, and meats.

Carretera 466, km 8.3, Playa Montones, Isabela, PR 00662. (From the center of Isabella, take Rte. 466 toward Aguadilla.) ℂ **787/872-2045.** Fax 787/830-2490. www.villahau.com. 38 units (shower only). Year-round $95 for 2; $137.75 for 4; $155 for 6. **Amenities:** Restaurant, bar; pool with snack bar, BBQ area; tennis; beach toy rental; photocopy and fax; convenience store; babysitting; laundry; horseback riding; volleyball court. *In room:* A/C, TV (in most rooms), kitchenette, coffeemaker.

COAMO

Legend has it that the hot springs in this town, located inland on the south coast about a 2-hour drive from San Juan, were the Fountain of Youth sought by Ponce de León. It is believed that the Taíno peoples, during pre-Columbian times, held rituals and pilgrimages here as they sought health and well-being. Between 1847 and 1958, the site was a center for rest and relaxation for Puerto Ricans and others, some on their honeymoons, others in search of the curative powers of the geothermal springs, which lie about a 5-minute walk from **Parador Baños de Coamo.** Nonguests can come here to use the baths, but the experience is hardly special today. The baths are in poor condition.

South of Coamo you can get on the expressway (no. 52) and head east for a 40-minute drive to **Guayama,** a green and beautiful small town with steepled churches, and the Casa Cautiño Museum on the main plaza of town (ℂ **787/864-0600**). It is open Tuesday through Sunday from 10am to 4pm. Admission is $1 for adults and 50¢ for seniors, students, and children 7 to 12 (free for children 6 and under). This museum is in a turn-of-the-20th-century mansion that once was occupied by the Cañuelo family. It contains all of the family's original belongings and is a showplace for fine turn-of-the-century furnishings and pictures of the prize horses for which Guayama is famous. Just minutes from town is Arroyo Beach, a tranquil place to spend an afternoon, but lacking facilities.

WHERE TO STAY & DINE

Parador Baños de Coamo   The spa at Baños de Coamo features this parador, offering hospitality in traditional Puerto Rican style. The Baños has welcomed many notable visitors over the years, including Franklin D. Roosevelt, Frank Lloyd Wright, Alexander Graham Bell, and Thomas Edison, who came here to swim in the on-site hot springs, said to be the most radioactive in the world. Since those days and since those long-departed visitors, the spa world is now state-of-the-art in many places, including San Juan and some nearby resorts. Such is not the case here; maintenance is poor, and the baths show signs of aging. (Locals sometimes purchase a day pass and use the pool, which leads to noise, confusion, and overcrowding on weekends.)

The buildings range from a lattice-adorned two-story motel unit with wooden verandas to a Spanish colonial pink stucco building, which houses the restaurant. The bedrooms draw a mixed reaction from visitors, so ask to see your prospective room before deciding to stay here. Many of the often-dark rooms are not well maintained, and the bathrooms seem more appropriate for a campsite. Mildew is also evident. The cuisine here is both Creole and international, and the coffee Baños-style is a special treat.

P.O. Box 540, Coamo, PR 00769. (From Rte. 1, turn onto Rte. 153 at Santa Isabel; then turn left onto Rte. 546 and drive west 1 mile/1.5km.) ℂ **787/825-2186.** Fax 787/825-4739. www.banosdecoamo.com. 48 units. Year-round $81 double. AE, DC, DISC, MC, V. **Amenities:** Restaurant, bar; pool; laundry/dry cleaning. *In room:* A/C, TV.

10

Eastern Puerto Rico

The northeast corner of the island, only about 45 minutes from San Juan, contains the island's major attractions, El Yunque rain forest and Luquillo Beach (see chapter 7), as well as a variety of landscapes, ranging from miles of forest to palm groves and beachside settlements. Here you will find two of the best resorts on the island, Wyndham El Conquistador Resort and Doral Palmas del Mar Resort.

This is also the site of Fajardo, a preeminent sailor's haven, where you can catch ferries to the islands of Vieques and Culebra (see chapter 11).

1 Las Croabas

35 miles (56km) E of San Juan

Las Croabas, near Fajardo, is the site of the Wyndham El Conquistador Resort. El Conquistador was the leader in luxury resorts in the Caribbean from the 1960s through the late 1970s. Celebrities Elaine May, Jack Gilford, Celeste Holm (with her husband and two poodles), Elaine Stritch (and her dog), Amy Vanderbilt, Jack Palance, Burt Bacharach, Angie Dickinson, Omar Shariff, Marc Connelly, Maureen O'Sullivan, and Xavier Cugat attended its grand inaugural festivities in 1968. Later, its circular casino, in black and stainless steel, appeared in the James Bond movie *Goldfinger.* The original hotel closed in 1980, but it was reborn in 1993 as the distinctive $250 million El Conquistador we have today.

GETTING THERE

Wyndham El Conquistador staff members greet all guests at the San Juan airport and transport them to the resort. Guests at the resort can take a taxi or a hotel courtesy car, or they can drive a rental car to Luquillo Beach.

The cost of a taxi from the San Juan airport averages around $60.

If you're driving from San Juan, head east on Route 3 toward Fajardo. At the intersection, cut northeast on Route 195 and continue to the intersection with Route 987, at which point you turn north.

OUTDOOR ACTIVITIES

In addition to the lovely beach and the many recreational facilities that are part of the Wyndham El Conquistador (p. 232), there are other notable places to play in the vicinity. Don't forget that not far from Las Croabas is **Luquillo Beach,** one of the island's best stretches of sand (see chapter 7).

WATERSPORTS For a cruise, your best bet in Las Croabas is **Erin Go Bragh Charters** (© 787/860-4410). The 50-foot ketch is operated by Capt. Bill Henry, who is licensed to carry six passengers. The boat is available for day charters and sunset and evening cruises, and it has equipment for watersports, including Windsurfers and masks and fins. A full-day tour costs $75 per person, including a barbeque lunch.

To the Lighthouse: Exploring Las Cabezas de San Juan Nature Reserve

Las Cabezas de San Juan Nature Reserve is better known as El Faro, or "The Lighthouse." In the northeastern corner of the island, it is one of the most beautiful and important areas in Puerto Rico. Here you'll find seven ecological systems and a restored 19th-century Spanish colonial lighthouse. From the lighthouse observation deck, majestic views extend to islands as far off as St. Thomas in the U.S. Virgin Islands.

Surrounded on three sides by the Atlantic Ocean, the 316-acre site encompasses forestland, mangroves, lagoons, beaches, cliffs, offshore cays, and coral reefs. Boardwalk trails wind through the fascinating topography. Ospreys, sea turtles, and an occasional manatee are seen from the windswept promontories and rocky beach.

The nature reserve is open Wednesday through Sunday. Reservations are required; for reservations during the week, call (©) **787/722-5882,** and for reservations on weekends, (©) **787/860-2560** (weekend reservations must be made on the day of your visit). Admission is $5 for adults, $2 for children under 13, and $2.50 for seniors. Guided 2½-hour tours are conducted at 9:30am, 10am, 10:30am, and 2pm (in English at 2pm).

For scuba divers, the best deal is offered by the PADI outfit **La Casa del Mar,** at the Puerto del Rey marina, the lowest level of the Wyndham El Conquistador (© **787/863-1000,** ext. 7917). You can go for ocean dives on the outfitter's boats, a one-tank dive costing $69 or a two-tank dive for $99, including tanks and weight belt. A PADI snorkel program, at $50 per person, is also available.

In Fajardo, the Caribbean's largest and most modern marina, **Puerto del Rey** (© **787/860-1000**), has facilities for 70 boats, including docking and fueling for yachts up to 200 feet and haul-out and repair for yachts up to 90 feet. The marina has boat rentals, yacht charters, and watersports, plus shops and a restaurant.

Some of the best snorkeling in Puerto Rico is in and around Fajardo. Its beach, **Playa Seven Seas,** is not as hotsy-totsy as Luquillo Beach, but is an attractive and sheltered strip of sand. The beach lies on the southwestern shoreline of Las Cabezas peninsula and is crowded on weekends. For even better snorkeling, walk along this beach for about half a mile (1km) to another beach, called **Playa Escondido** ("Hidden Beach"). Coral reefs in clear waters lie right off this beach. We'll let you in on a secret: East from Las Cabezas is a marine wildlife refuge known as **La Cordillera,** or "The Spine." Off the mainland of the island, these are the most gin-clear and tranquil waters we have found to date in Puerto Rico. They are teeming with wildlife, including several species of fish such as grouper, but also lobster, moray eels, and sea turtles. On these islets you might even see a rare crested iguana. **Aqua Sports** in Fajardo (© **787/888-8841**) will take you there.

TENNIS   The seven Har-Tru courts at the **Wyndham El Conquistador** ✿✿ are among the best tennis courts in Puerto Rico, rivaling those at Palmas del

Mar. The staff at the pro shop is extremely helpful to beginning players. Courts are the least crowed during the hottest part of the day, around the lunch hour. If you're a single traveler to the resort and in search of a player, the pro shop will try to match you up with a player of equal skill.

WHERE TO STAY

Wyndham El Conquistador Resort & Country Club ★★★ *Kids*   One of the most impressive resorts in the Caribbean, with a flash and glitter that remains supremely tasteful, El Conquistador has an incredible array of facilities. Rebuilt in 1993 at a cost of $250 million, it encompasses 500 acres of forested hills sloping to the sea. Accommodations are divided into five separate sections that share the common themes of Mediterranean architecture and lush landscaping. A replica of an Andalusian hamlet, Las Casitas Village seems straight out of the south of Spain; each of the plush, pricey units here has a full kitchen. A short walk downhill takes you to Las Olas Village, a cluster of tastefully modern accommodations. At sea level, adjacent to an armada of pleasure craft bobbing at anchor, is La Marina Village, whose balconies seem to hang directly over the water. All the far-flung elements of the resort are connected by serpentine, landscaped walkways and by a railroad-style funicular that makes frequent trips up and down the hillside. The accommodations are outfitted with comfortable and stylish furniture, soft tropical colors, and robes.

The resort has an array of restaurants and lounges; you could live here for a month and always sample something new and different. One of the most comprehensive spas in the world, The Golden Door, maintains a branch in this resort (see "Portal of Luxury" below). The hotel is sole owner of a "fantasy island" (Palomino Island), with caverns, nature trails, horseback riding, and watersports such as scuba diving, windsurfing, and snorkeling. About half a mile (1km) offshore, the island is connected by free ferries to the main hotel at frequent intervals. Camp Coquí on Palomino Island is for children 3 to 12 years old.

Av. Conquistador 1000, Las Croabas, Fajardo, PR 00738. ✆ 800/468-5228 or 787/863-1000. Fax 787/863-6500. www.wyndham.com. 915 units. Winter $455–$765 double; from $1,375 suite for 1–4; from $1,195 casita, with kitchen, for 1–6. Off-season $295–$525 double; from $1,125 suite for 1–4; $325–$1,025 casita, with kitchen, for 1–6. MAP (breakfast and dinner) $92 extra per adult per day, $46 extra per child age 12 and under. Children age 15 and under stay free in parents' room. AE, DC, DISC, MC, V. Parking $10 per day. **Amenities:** 6 restaurants, 7 bars, nightclub, casino; 6 pools; golf course; 7 Har-Tru tennis courts; health club and spa; watersports; 25-slip marina; fishing; sailing; dive shop; children's programs; room service; massage; laundry/dry cleaning. *In room:* A/C, TV, minibar, coffeemaker, hair dryer, iron, safe.

WHERE TO DINE
VERY EXPENSIVE

Isabela's Grill ✪   AMERICAN/STEAK   If Dwight Eisenhower were to miraculously return, he'd feel comfortable with this 1950s American menu. The massive gates are among the most spectacular pieces of wrought iron in Puerto Rico. The service is impeccable, the steaks are tender, and the seafood is fresh. You can begin with the lobster bisque or French soup, then move on to the thick cut of veal chop or the perfectly prepared rack of lamb. Prime rib of beef is a feature, as are the succulent steaks, especially the New York strip and porterhouse.

In the Wyndham El Conquistador Resort. ✆ 787/863-1000. Reservations recommended. Main courses $24–$35. AE, DISC, MC, V. Mon–Sat 6–10pm; Sun 6pm–midnight. Parking $2.50–$15.

Map labels:

ATLANTIC OCEAN

Condado Beach
Ocean Park Beach
Isla Verde Beach
San Juan
Loiza
Luquillo Beach
Cabezas de San Juan Nature Reserve

165
Cataño
26
22
36
26
Santa Barbara
Las Croabas
7
8
6

Bayamón
20
Guaynabo
1
18
Carolina
Río Grande
3
194
Fajardo
5
Fajardo Beach

Trujillo Alto
Lake of Loiza
186
191

To Culebra

Lomas
191
Ceiba

Comerío
Caguas
30
Juncos
Rio Blanco
Daguao

San Lorenzo
183
La Permina
Naguabo
31
192
4
Naguabo Beach

52
183
30
Punta Santiago

Cayey
184
181
Humacao
2
Cayo Santiago

179
3
Playa de Humacao

15
184
182
Pasaje de Vieques
To Vieques

179
3
Yabucoa

Guayama
3
3

0   10 mi
0   10 km
N
Caribbean Sea

El Yunque **1**
Fajardo **5**
Humacao **2**
Las Cabezas de San Juan
    Nature Reserve **7**
Las Croabas **6**
Luquillo Beach **8**
Naguabo **4**
Palmas del Mar **3**

EXPENSIVE

Blossoms ★★ CHINESE/JAPANESE   Blossoms boasts some of the freshest seafood in eastern Puerto Rico. Sizzling delights are prepared on teppanyaki tables, and there's a zesty selection of Hunan and Szechwan specialties. On the teppanyaki menu, you can choose dishes ranging from chicken to shrimp, from filet mignon to lobster. Sushi bar selections range from eel and squid to salmon roe and giant clams.

In the Wyndham El Conquistador Resort. ✆ **787/863-1000.** Reservations recommended. Main courses $19–$40. AE, DC, MC, V. Daily 6–11:30pm.

Otello's ★ NORTHERN ITALIAN   Here you can dine by candlelight in the old-world tradition, with a choice of indoor or outdoor seating. You might begin with one of the soups, perhaps pasta fagioli, or select one of the zesty Italian appetizers, such as excellently prepared clams Posillipo. Pastas can be ordered as a half-portion appetizer or as a main dish, and they include the likes of home-made gnocchi and fettuccine with shrimp. The chef is known for his superb veal dishes. A selection of poultry and vegetarian food is offered, as are shrimp and fish dishes.

In the Wyndham El Conquistador Resort. ✆ **787/863-1000.** Reservations required in winter, recommended off-season. Main courses $20–$37. AE, DISC, MC, V. Daily 6–11pm.

Portal of Luxury

Perched atop a stunning 300-foot bluff overlooking the Caribbean Sea and the Atlantic Ocean, the **Golden Door,** in Las Casitas Village complex at the Wyndham El Conquistador Hotel (℃ **787/863-1000**), is the most sophisticated, well-managed, and comprehensive spa in the Caribbean, and it is one of the finest in the world. One of only three branches of a spa founded in Escondido, California, and today administered by the Wyndham group, it's devoted to the relaxation and healing of body, soul, and mind. Spa rituals are taken seriously; New Age mysticism is gracefully dispensed within a postmodern setting that's a cross between a Swiss clinic, a state-of-the-art health club, and a Buddhist monastery.

Spa treatments begin at $150 for 80 minutes. You can exercise here for a fee of $15 per day. The spa is open daily from 6:30am to 8:30pm. American Express, MasterCard, and Visa are accepted.

2 Palmas del Mar

46 miles (74km) SE of San Juan

An hour east of San Juan, the residential resort community of Palmas del Mar lies near Humacao. Here you'll find one of the most action-packed sports programs in the Caribbean, offering golf, tennis, scuba diving, sailing, deep-sea fishing, and horseback riding. Palmas del Mar's location is one of its greatest assets. The pleasing Caribbean trade winds steadily blow across this section of the island, stabilizing the weather and making Palmas del Mar ideal for many outdoor sports.

The resort is no longer what it was in its heyday in the early 1990s. Today it is a real estate conglomerate that promotes vacation properties to investors, although outsiders can stay here as well. Many of the occupants are residents of San Juan who come here on weekends. Tourists are welcome, but most first-time visitors will find better accommodations up the coast, at the Westin Rio Mar (p. 186) or the Wyndham El Conquistador (p. 232).

GETTING THERE

Humacao Regional Airport is 3 miles (5km) from the northern boundary of Palmas del Mar. It accommodates private planes; no regularly scheduled airline currently serves the Humacao airport. Doral Palmas del Mar Resort will arrange minivan or bus transport from Humacao to the San Juan airport for $36 per person for two passengers or $24 per person for four passengers. For reservations, call ℃ **787/285-4323.** Call the resort if you want to be met at the airport.

If you're driving from San Juan, take Highway 52 south to Caguas, then take Highway 30 east to Humacao. Follow the signs from there to Palmas del Mar.

BEACHES & OUTDOOR ACTIVITIES

Doral Palmas del Mar Resort offers a variety of choices to keep active vacationers in shape (many are also open to the public, with prior reservation). Following are details on some of the most popular, along with a few other offerings in the area that are not connected with the resort complex.

BEACHES   Doral Palmas del Mar Resort has 3 exceptional miles (5km) of white-sand beaches (all open to the public). Nonguests pay a $1 charge for parking and 25¢ for a changing room and a locker. The waters here are calm year-round, and there's a watersports center and marina (see "Scuba Diving & Snorkeling" below).

FISHING   Some of the best year-round fishing in the Caribbean is found in the waters just off Palmas del Mar. **Capt. Bill Burleson,** based in Humacao (© **787/850-7442**), operates charters on his customized, 46-foot sport-fisherman, *Karolette,* which is electronically equipped for successful fishing. Burleson prefers to take fishing groups to Grappler Banks, 18 nautical miles away, which lie in the migratory paths of wahoo, tuna, and marlin. A maximum of six people are taken out, costing $500 for 4 hours, $600 for 4½ hours, or $750 for 6 hours. Burleson also offers snorkeling expeditions to Vieques at $95 per person for up to 5 hours. He can also take you to other snorkeling locations as well.

GOLF   Few other real-estate developments in the Caribbean devote as much attention and publicity to their golf facilities as the **Palmas del Mar Golf Club** ★★ (© **787/285-2256**). Today, both the older course, the Gary Player–designed Palm course, and the newer course, the Reese Jones–designed Flamboyant course, have pars of 72 and layouts of around 6,800 feet each. Crack golfers consider holes 11 to 15 of the Palm course among the toughest five successive holes in the Caribbean. The pro shop that services both courses is open daily from 7am to 5:30pm. The Flamboyant course costs $176 for 18 holes; the Palm Course costs $160 for 18 holes.

HIKING   Palmas del Mar's land is an attraction in its own right. Here you'll find more than 6 miles (9.5km) of Caribbean ocean frontage—3½ (5.5km) miles of sandy beach amid rocky cliffs and promontories. Large tracts of the 2,700-acre property have harbored sugar and coconut plantations over the years, and a wet tropical forest preserve with giant ferns, orchids, and hanging vines covers about 70 acres near the resort's geographic center.

SCUBA DIVING & SNORKELING   Some of the best dives in Puerto Rico are right off the eastern coast. Two dozen dive sites south of Fajardo are within a 5-mile (8km) radius offshore. Refer to "The Best Scuba Diving" in chapter 1.

Set adjacent to a collection of boutiques, bars, and restaurants at the edge of Palmas del Mar's harbor, **Palmas Dive Center** ★, Anchors Village, 110 Harbor Drive (© **787/633-7314** or cellphone 787/504-7333), owns a 44-foot-long diveboat with a 16-foot beam to make it stable in rough seas. Pennsylvania-born Bill Winnie, a 5-year veteran of other dive operations in and around Palmas del Mar, offers $120 full-day "Discover Scuba" resort courses that are geared to beginners. They include classroom testing, presentation of a video on water safety, a practice session in a swimming pool, and a one-tank afternoon dive in the open sea. Also available are both morning and afternoon sessions of two-tank dives that are available only to experienced and certified divers, priced at $95 each. Half-day snorkeling trips, priced at $55 per participant and departing for both morning and afternoon sessions, go whenever there's demand to the fauna-rich reefs that encircle Monkey Island, an offshore uninhabited cay.

TENNIS   The **Tennis Center at Palmas del Mar** ★★ (© **787/852-6000**, ext. 51), the largest in Puerto Rico, features 15 hard courts and 5 clay courts, open to hotel guests and nonguests. Fees for hotel guests are $20 per hour during the day and $25 per hour at night. Fees for nonguests are $24 per hour during the day and $29 per hour at night. Tennis packages, including accommodations, are available. Within the resort's tennis compound is a **fitness center,** which has the best-equipped gym in the region; open daily from 7am to 9pm. The center is free for guests of the resort; nonguests can use the center for $7 per day.

WHERE TO STAY

Doral Palmas del Mar Resort ★★ *Kids*   Although the acreage within the Palmas del Mar development contains thousands of privately owned villas, many of which can be rented or purchased outright, this is the only conventional, full-service hotel in Palmas del Mar. At least some of its business derives from new-comers who want to experience firsthand what Palmas del Mar is like before buying a villa. It was radically renovated in 1997, and again in 1999. None of the well-furnished bedrooms overlook the sea, but many have private patios or verandas, and most are roomier than you might expect. Each room has tile floors, tropical furnishings, large closets, fine linens, and either a king- or two queen-sized beds, plus a tiled bathroom with a tub-and-shower combo.

The resort has an Adventure Club for children ages 3 to 13. Supervised activities include crafts and sports, plus horseback riding for older children. For nonguests, the cost is $30 per half day or $35 per day, including lunch; it's free for guests. The beach, tennis center, and golf courses are close at hand. Palma's Café (see "Where to Dine" below) is one of the panoply of dining options here.

170 Candalero Dr., Palmas del Mar, Humacao, PR 00791. ℗ **800/725-6273** or 787/852-6000. Fax 787/852-6320. www.palmasdelmar.com. 102 units. Winter $225–$260 double; off-season $160–$195 double. MAP (breakfast and dinner) $45 per person extra. AE, DC, MC, V. **Amenities:** Restaurant, 2 bars, casino; pool; 2 18-hole golf courses; 20 tennis courts (7 lit); health club; dive shop; fishing; bikes; children's program; car rental; room service (6am–10pm); babysitting; laundry/dry cleaning; horseback riding. *In room:* A/C, TV, hair dryer.

The Villas at Palmas ★ *Kids*   Set almost adjacent to Doral Palmas del Mar Resort, this complex of red-roofed, white-walled town houses is a good choice for a family vacation. Divided into five separate clusters and carefully landscaped with tropical plants, the units are furnished and decorated according to the tastes of their individual owners. Each contains a working kitchen, a sense of privacy, views of either the ocean or the gardens, and a midsize and comfortable private bathroom with tub-and-shower combo. Rental fees depend on the unit's proximity to the beachfront or golf course. A handful of villas built against a steep hillside overlook the Palmas del Mar tennis courts.

170 Candalero Dr., Palmas del Mar, Humacao, PR 00792. ℗ **800/725-6273** or 787/852-6000. Fax 787/852-6320. 135 town house–style suites. Winter $400–$560 1-bedroom suite; $600–$760 2-bedroom suite; $800–$960 3-bedroom suite. Off-season $280–$380 1-bedroom suite; $380–$480 2-bedroom suite; $480–$580 3-bedroom suite. Minimum bookings ranging from 3–7 nights required during some peak seasons, depending on the accommodation. AE, DC, MC, V. **Amenities:** Bar; pool; gym; babysitting. *In room:* A/C, TV, kitchen, coffeemaker, hair dryer, iron, safe, washing machine/dryer.

WHERE TO DINE

Thanks to the kitchens that are built into virtually every unit in Palmas del Mar, many guests prepare at least some of their meals "at home." This is made relatively feasible thanks to the on-site general store at the Palmanova Plaza, which sells everything from fresh lettuce and sundries to liquor and cigarettes. In addition, there are several other dining options in the Doral Palmas del Mar complex.

Barracuda Bistro ★ PUERTO RICAN/INTERNATIONAL   The most active bar scene in the early evening takes place here, as yachters gather to talk about the adventures of the day. The sautéed mahimahi in tequila butter and lime

> **Finds** **Where the Locals Go for Soul Food**
>
> To escape the confines of the resort for the evening, drive over to a local dive, **Trulio's Sea Food** (© **787/850-1840**), just off Route 3 on Calle Isidro Andreux Andreu in the hamlet of Punta Santiago. This is strictly no-frills. Though very low in cost, the food is top-notch and even memorable, especially the fried plantain filled with sea conch. The shrimp in garlic sauce will have you asking for more, and you can also order perfectly baked lobster in garlic sauce. Also try the grilled whole red snapper in garlic and onions. You get the point now: Garlic is king here. Puerto Ricans rave about the chef's dessert specialty, which is pound cake soaked in sweet milk. It tastes better than it sounds and is like soul food to the locals because it's just like Mom used to make.

sauce alone is worth the trip. Fresh red snapper is sautéed in butter and lemon zest, and you can also count on the chef throwing a T-bone steak on the grill. You can also order both Mexican and Creole specialties, including roast pork and fajitas with either chicken or beef. If you're visiting at lunch or during the afternoon, you can also order fast food, including hot dogs, sandwiches, and burgers.

La Marina. © **787/850-4441**. Reservations recommended. Main courses $5–$30. DC, MC, V. Daily noon–10pm.

Blue Hawaiian CHINESE   This is the best Chinese restaurant in the region. It combines Polynesian themes (similarly to a toned-down Trader Vic's) with an Americanized version of Chinese food that's flavorful and well suited to Puerto Rico's hot, steamy climate. Menu items include lobster with garlic-flavored cheese sauce; blackened salmon or steaks reminiscent of styles in New Orleans; and a superb house version of honey chicken. You'll find the place within the dignified courtyard of the resort's shopping center, with tables for alfresco dining. Your host is Tommy Lo, former chef aboard the now-defunct ocean liner SS *United States.*

In the Palmanova Shopping Center. © **787/852-0897**. Reservations recommended. Main courses $11–$25. AE, MC, V. Daily noon–10:30pm.

Chez Daniel/Le Grill ★ FRENCH   It's French and it's the favorite of the folks who tie up their yachts at the adjacent pier. Normandy-born Daniel Vasse, the owner, along with his French Catalonian wife, Lucette, maintain twin dining rooms that in their way are the most appealing in Palmas del Mar. Le Grill is a steakhouse with a Gallic twist and lots of savory flavor in the form of béarnaise, garlic, peppercorn sauce, or whatever else you specify. Chez Daniel shows a more faithful allegiance to the tenets of classical French cuisine, placing emphasis on such dishes as bouillabaisse, onion soup, and snails, as well as lobster and chicken dishes. For dessert, consider a soufflé au Cointreau.

Marina de Palmas del Mar. © **787/852-6000**. Reservations required. Main courses $8–$12 at lunch, $22–$35 at dinner. AE, MC, V. Wed–Sun noon–3pm; Wed–Mon 6:30–10pm. Chez Daniel open only Dec–Apr; Le Grill closed June.

Palma's Café INTERNATIONAL   Cooled by trade winds, this restaurant overlooking a courtyard and pool is an ideal choice for a casual meal. Lunch includes sandwiches and burgers; if you want heartier fare, ask for the Puerto Rican specialty of the day, perhaps red snapper in garlic butter, preceded by black-bean soup. Dinner is more elaborate. Begin with stuffed jalapeños or chicken tacos, followed by Caribbean lobster, New York sirloin, paella, or the catch of the day. The hearty cooking, although of a high standard, is never quite gourmet.

In Doral Palmas del Mar Resort. (*C* 787/852-6000, ext. 50. Reservations required only for groups of 6 or more. Main courses $5–$11 breakfast, $12–$17 lunch and dinner. AE, DC, DISC, MC, V. Daily 6:30–11am, noon–5pm, and 6–10:30pm.

PALMAS DEL MAR AFTER DARK

The **casino** in the Palmas del Mar complex (*C* **787/852-6000,** ext. 10142), has 12 blackjack tables, 2 roulette wheels, a craps table, and dozens of slot machines. The casino is open daily year-round, Sunday through Thursday from 4pm to 2am and Friday and Saturday from 6pm to 3am. Under Puerto Rican law, alcoholic beverages cannot be served in a casino.

3 Paradores of Eastern Puerto Rico

Most of the government-certified inns called paradores are found in western Puerto Rico (see "Paradores of Western Puerto Rico" in chapter 9). However, we have recently discovered two paradores along the eastern coast. Either of these inns would be an ideal retreat for escapists. For the locations of these paradores, see the map "Paradores & Country Inns of Puerto Rico" on p. 69.

The Fajardo Inn ★ *Finds* A good base for those visiting El Yunque, this inn is ideal for those who are seeking a location in the east and don't want to pay the prices charged at the Wyndham El Conquistador (p. 232). Lying on a hilltop overlooking the port of Fajardo, this parador evokes a Mediterranean villa with its balustrades and grand staircases. The midsize bedrooms, most of which open onto good views, are spotless, and each has a small shower-only bathroom. The inn and its pool are handsomely landscaped. A few steps from the inn is an older building, The Scenic Inn, which offers access to all of Fajardo Inn's facilities at lower rates—$60 per night—for a double, for those who don't mind a room without phone or view. The Fajardo Inn's restaurant specializes in Creole and continental cuisine, especially fresh fish, with indoor and outdoor dining.

52 Parcela Beltrán, Fajardo, PR 00740. (A 15-min. walk east of the center of Fajardo.) (*C* 787/860-6000. Fax 787/860-5063. www.fajardoinn.com. 75 units (shower only). Year-round $85–$95 double. AE, DISC, MC, V. **Amenities:** 2 restaurants, 2 bars; pool; snorkeling and diving arranged; business services; room service. *In room:* A/C, TV, hair dryer, iron.

Hotel Parador Palmas de Lucía ★ *Finds* In the southwestern corner of Puerto Rico, where accommodations are scarce, this government-affiliated parador is a knockout discovery. It lies at the eastern end of Ruta Panorámica, a network of scenic, winding roads along which you can take in some of the finest views in the Caribbean before coming to rest at Palmas de Luca, just steps from the pleasant sands of Playa Lucüa. This is one of the newest hotels in eastern Puerto Rico, filling a vast gap in accommodations in this remote part of the island. The Lopez family are your hosts, and their complex combines colonial styling with tropical decoration. Each midsize bedroom is well furnished and has a pool-view balcony and an efficiently organized, tiled shower-only bathroom.

Palmas de Lucía, Routes 901 and 911, Camino Nuevo, Yabucoa, PR 00767. (From Humacao, take Rte. 53 south to Yabucoa, to the end of the highway, where you connect with Rte. 901 to Maunabo. After a 2-min. drive, turn left at the signposted Carretera 9911, which leads to Playa Lucía.) (*C* 787/893-4423. Fax 787/893-0291. www.palmasdelucia.com. 29 units (shower only). $84 double; $102 suite. AE, MC, V. **Amenities:** Restaurant, bar; pool; basketball court. *In room:* A/C, TV.

11

Vieques & Culebra

Vieques and Culebra are where Puerto Ricans go for their own vacations. Sandy beaches and low prices are the powerful attractions of both islands. Culebra still slumbers in the early 1950s, but Vieques is fast becoming one of the hottest tropical destinations in the Caribbean. The unspoiled beaches and stylish inns have created quite a buzz. When you spot Sandra Bernhard on the beach, you know the times are changin'.

Vieques, which has more tourist facilities than Culebra, lies 7 miles (11km) off the eastern coast of the Puerto Rican "mainland." It is visited mainly for its 40-odd white-sand beaches. Vieques was occupied at various times by the French and the British before Puerto Rico acquired it in 1854. The ruins of many sugar and pineapple plantations testify to its once-flourishing agricultural economy.

The U.S. military took control of two-thirds of the island's 26,000 acres in 1941 and still uses the area for military training with live-fire maneuvers. However, the fact that the island is a military base should not deter a visit. It is unlikely that you'll hear planes flying low overhead, and it's very rare to hear test bombs exploding, as you might have a few years ago. You probably won't be aware of any military equipment or personnel when you visit.

Culebra, 18 miles (29km) east of the Puerto Rican "mainland" and 14 miles (23km) west of St. Thomas in the U.S. Virgin Islands, is surrounded by coral reefs and edged with nearly deserted, powdery white-sand beaches. Much of the island has been designated a wildlife refuge by the U.S. Fish and Wildlife Service.

1 Vieques ⓧ

41 miles (66km) E of San Juan, 7 miles (11km) SE of Fajardo

About 7 miles (11km) east of the big island of Puerto Rico lies Vieques (Bee-*ay*-kase"), an island about twice as large as New York's Manhattan, with about 9,300 inhabitants and some 40 palm-lined white-sand beaches.

Although Vieques remains a bit primitive—you can still hear wild horses galloping in the middle of the night—change is on the way, with the opening of some of the most sophisticated inns in the Caribbean. The kind of trendsetters who discovered St. Barts and Anguilla years ago are now showing up here.

Since World War II, about two-thirds of the 21-mile (34km) long island has been controlled by U.S. military forces. Much of the government-owned land is now leased for cattle grazing, and when there are no military maneuvers, the public can visit the beaches, although you might be asked to produce a photo ID. Freedom to use the land has not, however, totally defused local discontent at the presence of Navy and Marine Corps personnel. In fact, the military has come under increased attack by Vieques's residents and top-ranking members of the Puerto Rican government. Some claim that the Navy's presence is strangling economic development; others cite potential dangers such as accidental deaths.

The Bush administration, facing mounting opposition, announced in 2002 that it plans to withdraw the Navy from the Puerto Rican island and seek another spot to conduct its Atlantic fleet's bombing exercises. Navy Secretary Gordon England said that a panel is searching for a new training site, with the goal of ending exercises in Vieques sometime in 2003. But there has been, as yet, no exact announcement. If the Navy pulls out, major changes will be in store for Vieques.

Unlike the military, the Spanish conquistadores didn't think much of Vieques. They came here in the 16th century but didn't stay long, reporting that the island and neighboring bits of land held no gold and were, therefore, *las islas inutiles* (the useless islands). The name Vieques comes from the native Amerindian word *bieques* meaning "small island."

The Spaniards later changed their minds and founded the main town, **Isabel Segunda,** on the northern shore. Construction on the last Spanish fort built in the New World began here around 1843, during the reign of Queen Isabella II, for whom the town was named. The fort, never completed, is not of any special interest. The island's fisherfolk and farmers conduct much of their business here. The **Punta Mula lighthouse,** north of Isabel Segunda, provides panoramic views of the land and sea.

On the south coast, **Esperanza,** once a center for the island's sugarcane industry and now a pretty little fishing village, lies near **Sun Bay (Sombe) public beach** ✿. Sun Bay, a government-run, panoramic crescent of sand, is the beach to visit if you have only 1 day to spend on the island. The fenced area has picnic tables, a bathhouse, and a parking lot. A recently built resort, marina, and other facilities add to the allure of the many scalloped stretches of sandy waterfront.

ESSENTIALS

GETTING THERE   Flights to Vieques leave from Isla Grand Airport near the heart of San Juan—not to be confused with the main Luis Muñoz Marín International Airport near Isla Verde. **Vieques Air Link** (© 787/253-3644) operates four daily flights from San Juan. **Isla Nena** (© 787/741-1577) also flies to Vieques from San Juan three times daily. One-way fares cost around $65.

The **Puerto Rico Port Authority** operates two **ferries** a day to Vieques from the eastern port of Fajardo; the trip takes about an hour. The round-trip fare is $4 for adults, $2 for children. Tickets for the morning ferry that leaves Saturday and Sunday sell out quickly, so you should be in line at the ticket window in Fajardo before 8am to be certain of a seat on the 9:30am boat. Otherwise, you'll have to wait until the 1 or 4:30pm ferry. For more information about these sea links, call © 787/723-2260. For reservations, call © 787/863-0705 or 787/863-0852.

GETTING AROUND   Public cabs or vans called públicos transport people around the island. We recommend that you rent a car for at least some of the time, just for the purpose of seeing the layout of the island. To do this, contact **Island Car Rental** (© 787/741-1666), in the hamlet of Florida, about a 12-minute ride southwest of Isabel Segunda, 5 minutes from the airport. The office is next door to the Crow's Nest hotel (p. 245). The cost of the local vehicles begins at $55 per day, plus another $10 for collision-damage-waiver insurance. American Express, MasterCard, and Visa cards are accepted.

Vieques & Culebra

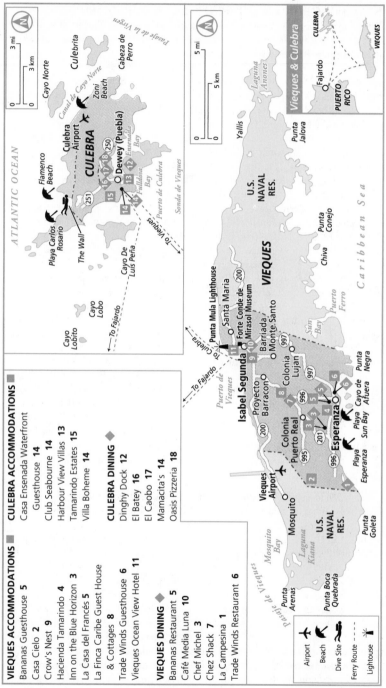

VIEQUES ACCOMMODATIONS ■

Bananas Guesthouse **5**
Casa Cielo **2**
Crow's Nest **9**
Hacienda Tamarindo **4**
Inn on the Blue Horizon **3**
La Casa del Francés **5**
La Finca Caribe Guest House
  & Cottages **8**
Trade Winds Guesthouse **6**
Vieques Ocean View Hotel **11**

VIEQUES DINING ◆

Bananas Restaurant **5**
Café Media Luna **10**
Chef Michel **3**
Chez Shack **7**
La Campesina **1**
Trade Winds Restaurant **6**

CULEBRA ACCOMMODATIONS ■

Casa Ensenada Waterfront
  Guesthouse **14**
Club Seabourne **14**
Harbour View Villas **13**
Tamarindo Estates **15**
Villa Boheme **14**

CULEBRA DINING ◆

Dinghy Dock **12**
El Batey **16**
El Caobo **17**
Mamacita's **14**
Oasis Pizzeria **18**

Airport ✈
Beach ⌇
Dive Site ◆
Ferry Route - - - - -
Lightouse ☆

BEACHES, DIVING & OTHER OUTDOOR PURSUITS

Few of the beaches on Vieques have been named, but most have loyal support-ers—loyal, that is, until too many people learn about them, in which case the devotees can always find another good spot.

The U.S. Navy named some of the beaches, such as **Green Beach,** a beauti-ful, clean stretch at the island's west end. **Red and Blue Beaches** are great jump-ing-off points for snorkelers. **Sun Bay** (Sombe) ✪ is also a very beautiful white-sand beach, which offers picnic tables, a bathhouse, tent sites, and good snorkeling offshore. Other popular beaches are **Navia, Half Moon, Orchid,** and **Silver,** but if you continue along the water, you might find your own nameless secluded cove with a fine strip of sand.

Playa Esperanza ✪ is one of the most frequented beaches on Vieques. It's best for snorkeling, not for beaching it. The beach opens onto the little fishing village of Esperanza on the south coast.

Overlooking the harbor at Esperanza is **Cayo de Afuera** ✪, an islet so small you could build a big house and occupy the whole site. Snorkelers, including Navy SEALs, seek out Cayo de Afuera for its gin-clear waters that reveal a stun-ning collection of antler coral. Some days you can see nurse sharks swim by, and occasionally you can see the increasingly elusive manatee.

The best dive outfitter is **Blue Caribe Dive Center,** Esperanza Beach (© 787/741-2522). It offers full PADI instruction and certification. A morn-ing two-tank dive goes for $70, and you can also take bioluminescent bay tours by kayak for $25 per person. Your instructor is Denny Johnson, a retired U.S. Navy SEAL.

A well-rehearsed outfit that's good at leading newcomers into the island's most savage landscapes is **La Dulce Vita Mountain Bike and Adventure Com-pany,** c/o La Finca Caribe Guest House & Cottages, Rte. 995, km 1.2 (P.O. Box 1332), Vieques, PR 00765 (© 787/741-0495; www.bikevieques.com). Karl Husson and members of his staff lead mountain bikers on half-day ($30 per per-son) and full-day ($50–$65 per person) tours of obscure trails that are note-worthy for their panoramas and technical difficulties. Use of a mountain bike, usually an aluminum-framed 28-speed state-of-the-art model, is included in the price. You can rent one of these bikes, without the services of a trail guide, for $20 per day.

THE LUMINOUS WATERS OF PHOSPHORESCENT BAY ✪

One of the major attractions on the island is **Mosquito Bay** ✪, also called **Phos-phorescent Bay,** with its glowing waters produced by tiny bioluminescent organisms. These organisms dart away from boats, leaving eerie blue-white trails of phosphorescence. The *Vieques Times* wrote: "By any name the bay can be a magical, psychedelic experience and few places in the world can even come close to the intensity of concentration of the dinoflagellates called pyrodiniums (whirling fire). They are tiny (⅕₀₀-inch) swimming creatures that light up like fireflies when disturbed but nowhere are there so many fireflies. Here a gallon of bay water may contain almost three-quarters of a million." The ideal time to tour is on a cloudy, moonless night. You should wear a bathing suit because it's possible to swim in these glowing waters.

Shannon Grasso (© 787/741-0720) operates trips in Phosphorescent Bay aboard her *Luminosa* from La Casa del Francés (see "Where to Stay" below). These trips are not offered around the time of the full moon. The charge is $23, and most jaunts last about 90 minutes. A similar tour on a kayak that also costs $23 is offered by **Blue Caribe Dive Center** (© 787/741-2522 for details).

SEEING THE SIGHTS

The **Fort Conde de Mirasol Museum,** Barrio Fuente at Magnolia 471 (✆ 787/
741-1717), is the major man-made attraction on the island. In the 1840s,
Count Mirasol convinced the Spanish government to build a defensive fortress
here. Today the carefully restored fort houses a museum of art and history cele-
brating the story of Vieques. There are Indian relics, displays of the Spanish conquest, and old flags of the Danes, British, and French. The French sugarcane
planters and their African slaves are depicted, and there's even a bust of the great
liberator Simón Bolívar, who once visited Puerto Rico. A unique collection of
maps shows how the world's cartographers envisioned Vieques. Because the U.S.
Navy occupies more than two-thirds of the island, its presence and controversial
role are chronicled. The museum and fort are open Wednesday through Sunday
from 10am to 4pm. Admission is $2; free for ages 11 and under.

WHERE TO STAY

Many in-the-know guests, including repeat visitors who fall in love with the
island, rent private villas by the week. Two-, three-, and four-bedroom houses
are available at moderate rates, and some have pools or are by the ocean. One of
the most spectacular is **Glass House** at Puerto Real (✆ 310/558-7100), which
costs $5,000 a week; it's a stunning bit of modern architecture with two bed-
rooms and a pool. More modest in price is **Cane Garden,** also at Puerto Real
(✆ 207/338-3618), a pair of two-bedroom cottages, each costing $1,600
weekly. You could instead check out **Casa Dos Cuervos,** La Llave (✆ 314/
533-9995), for a small palazzo that sleeps four. It's a bit minimalist, and the cost
is $1,600 a week.

EXPENSIVE

Casa Cielo ⭐   In 1997 an architect/investor (Steve Mensch) from Rhinebeck,
New York, bought a conventional-looking preexisting house and radically transformed it into a startling piece of postmodern architecture. Perched on a high-
altitude ridge midway between the Caribbean coast and the Atlantic coast of
Vieques, it enjoys sweeping panoramas in both directions from decks and terraces that seem to be suspended over the rock and scrub-covered landscapes.
Joanne Hamilton and Jim Ducharme are the polite, hardworking managers,
welcoming visitors to this lair that indeed seems perched high in the *cielo* (sky).
Expect the most from your car's transmission as you bump and jog across impos-
sibly rutted roads to reach it. Once here, the venue is pure *Architectural Digest,*
thanks to big windows, large rectangular indoor/outdoor spaces, and a sense that
some very high-powered members of the fashion world have checked in here
before you. The rooms are airy and have white walls, floors made of either white
glazed tiles or terra-cotta, rattan furniture, and unbelievable views.

On this 6-acre retreat, you can lounge poolside or take a cool drink in the
gazebo bar. All rooms are nonsmoking and have a light, breezy decor and ceiling fans. Each has either one king or two full-size beds. Each unit has a private
balcony from which you can take in the ocean views, and a tiled, shower-only
bathroom. The staff can arrange scuba diving, horseback riding, snorkeling, hiking, biking, kayaking, day sailing, and charter fishing.

Calle 995, km 1.1, Vieques, PR 00765. ✆ and fax 787/741-2403. cielo@coqui.net. 9 units (shower only).
Winter $125–$200 double; off-season $100 double. Discounts negotiated for stays of more than 5 nights.
Rates include continental breakfast. MC, V. Closed Sept. **Amenities:** Bar; pool; laundry. *In room:* A/C (in 5
units), coffeemaker (upon request), hair dryer (upon request), iron (upon request).

Inn on the Blue Horizon ✫✫✫   Set on the island's southern coastal road, less than a mile west of Esperanza, this is the most charming hotel on Vieques, and it's the one that has repeatedly earned the highest accolades from the international press. In winter, it reigns as the most hip and stylish gathering place in the Caribbean for the low-key rendezvous of North America's fashion photographers and supermodels, who appreciate its offbeat glamour and urban sophistication. Its centerpiece is an airy seafront house, built in a Mediterranean style in 1975, whose soaring living area opens onto a view of the blue horizon.

In the mid-1990s, the site was transformed into an inn by hotel and restaurant entrepreneurs William Knight and James Weis, refugees from the New York fashion world. Three of the bedrooms are in the main house; a half-dozen others are in a trio of bungalows, each of which contains two spacious and comfortable units, each with a private balcony and sea view. Airy and clean, they're outfitted with early 19th-century North American antiques and eclectic art from a variety of artists. Two units contain tubs, and the rest are equipped with showers.

Symmetrically positioned arbors are covered with cascades of bougainvillea, with a pool and lawns that slope gracefully down to cliffs at the edge of the sea. The sea adjacent to the hotel has a rocky coastline, but the staff will direct you to the dozens of fine local beaches. The inn's restaurant, Chef Michael (see "Where to Dine" below) serves the best food on Vieques.

Rte. 996 (P.O. Box 1556), Vieques, PR 00765. ✆ **787/741-3318.** Fax 787/741-0522. www.innontheblue horizon.com. 9 units (some with shower only). Winter $214–$270 double; $370 suite. Off-season $175–$203 double; $227 suite. AE, MC, V. **Amenities:** Restaurant, cafe/bar; pool; gym. *In room:* A/C, hair dryer, no phone.

MODERATE

Hacienda Tamarindo ✫   Established in the late 1990s on the site of an expanded nightclub, less than a mile west of Esperanza, this inn has lots of flair, style, and pizzazz. Vermont-born owners Burr and Linda Vail transformed a thick-walled, rather unimaginative-looking concrete building into a replica of a Spanish colonial hacienda, thanks to Linda's skills as a decorator. The inn was built around a massive 200-year-old tamarind tree, whose branches rise majestically through the hotel's atrium. Its production of fruit (between Feb and Mar) is heralded with much excitement. Rooms are stylish, tiled, and spacious. Each contains an appealing mishmash of art and antiques, some of which were brought from Vermont. Bathrooms are modern, clean, and well designed; some contain a tub, others a shower. Although the inn is set about one-eighth mile from the sea, there's access to a beach via a footpath, and there's a pool. The restaurant and cafe at the Inn on the Blue Horizon lie within a 5-minute walk.

Rte. 996, km 4.5 Barrio Puerto Real (P.O. Box 1569), Vieques, PR 00765. ✆ **787/741-8525.** Fax 787/741-3215. hactam@aol.com. 16 units (some with shower only, some with tub only). Winter $155–$180 double; $225 suite. Off-season $125–$150 double; $185 suite. Rates include breakfast. AE, MC, V. **Amenities:** Bar; pool; babysitting; laundry/dry cleaning. *In room:* A/C, coffeemaker, hair dryer, iron, no phone.

La Casa del Francés   This inn, just north of the center of Esperanza, is set in a field near the southern coastline. Built in 1905 by a retired French general as the headquarters for his working sugar plantation, it has an imposing column-fronted facade that rises from the lush surrounding landscape. The present owner has installed a pool and transformed the high-ceilinged bedrooms into old-fashioned hotel accommodations, which are both quirky and cozy. The shower-only bathrooms are in good working order, although not particularly plush. Many units enjoy access to the sweeping two-story verandas ringing the white facade.

Scattered throughout the dozen acres surrounding the main house are century-old trees. The estate's architectural highlight is the two-story interior courtyard, whose center is lush with bamboo, palms, philodendron, and Haitian art.

The fixed-price dinners attract many island residents, who partake of Italian, barbecue, or Puerto Rican buffets, which the staff spreads out beneath a 200-year-old mahogany tree.

Barrio Esperanza (P.O. Box 458), Vieques, PR 00765. © 787/741-3751. Fax 787/741-2330. greenblath@yahoo.com. 19 units (shower only). Winter $177.50 double; off-season $75 double. Rates include breakfast. AE, MC, V. **Amenities:** Restaurant, bar; pool; room service; laundry/dry cleaning. *In room:* A/C (in 7 units), no phone.

INEXPENSIVE

Bananas Guesthouse   On the island's south shore, on the main tourist strip of Esperanza and best known for its bar and restaurant (see "Where to Dine" below), this guesthouse has eight simple rooms, some recently renovated. Each has a ceiling fan; and some rooms are air-conditioned and have screened-in porches. We urge you to consider one of the air-conditioned rooms rather than those without, as a means of cutting down on heat and noise from the outside. Each unit has a bathroom with a tub. The units are unadorned cubicles with little architectural interest; they provide shelter and calm and a basic level of comfort. The ambience is convivial, the staff friendly and accommodating.

Barrio Esperanza (P.O. Box 1300), Vieques, PR 00765. © 787/741-8700. Fax 787/741-0790. www.bananas guesthouse.com. 8 units. Year-round $45–$70 double. AE, MC, V. **Amenities:** Restaurant/bar; room service; laundry/dry cleaning. *In room:* A/C (in 3 units), no phone.

Crow's Nest   Set high on 5 acres of forested hillside, about 1½ miles (2.5km) west/southwest of Isabel Segunda, this inn enjoys northward-facing views over the Atlantic and a cozy, responsive setting that's favored by many repeat guests. Each of the units has some kind of cooking facilities, and all but two offer air-conditioning. Rooms are more upscale-looking than those at either Bananas (which is very basic) or Trade Winds, but they're less elegant and charming than those at Inn on the Blue Horizon. Each unit has a neatly tiled, shower-only bathroom. Like most of the other hotels on the island, this one requires a car ride of around 10 minutes for access to the nearest worthwhile beach.

Rte. 201, km 1.6, Barrio Florida, Box 1521, Vieques, PR 00765. © 787/741-0033. Fax 787/741-1294. 16 units (shower only). Winter $75–$95 double; off-season $65–$85 double. AE, MC, V. **Amenities:** Bar; pool; babysitting; laundry/dry cleaning. *In room:* A/C (in 14 units), kitchen (7 units), coffeemaker, iron, microwave.

La Finca Caribe Guest House & Cottages   This bare-bones, eco-sensitive establishment caters to budget-conscious travelers and youthful adventurers. The present owners, the Merwin family, named it *Finca*, which means "rustic estate" in Spanish. The centerpiece of the property is a guesthouse with a spacious porch, outfitted with hammocks and swinging chairs. An admirably maintained garden wraps itself around the scattered components of the compound. The rustic-looking outbuildings include a bathhouse, a communal kitchen, and two self-contained cottages suitable for up to three ("The Casita") or four ("The Cabana") occupants. Both cottages have private decks and kitchens. There's a relatively new nonchlorinated pool on the premises (it stays clean through frequent recirculation of water from a mountain stream) and a crew of entrepreneurs that takes clients on bike tours to obscure parts of Vieques (see "Beaches, Diving & Other Outdoor Pursuits" above). La Finca is situated on a forested hillside 3 miles (5km) from Sun Bay.

Rte. 995, km 1.2 (P.O. Box 1332), Vieques, PR 00765. ☎ 787/741-0495. Fax 787/741-3584. www. lafinca.com. 6 units (none with bathroom), 2 cottages. Winter $80 double; off-season $60 double. 1-week cottage rental for 2–4 occupants, winter $700–$1,000; off-season $525–$650. MC, V. Closed Sept. **Amenities:** Pool; communal kitchen. *In room:* Kitchen (in cottages).

Trade Winds Guesthouse Along the shore on the south side of the island, in the fishing village of Esperanza, this oceanside guesthouse offers 11 units, 4 of which are air-conditioned and have terraces. The others have ceiling fans, and some open onto terraces. Bedrooms are white-walled and durable, with absolutely no imagination in terms of decor; the units might remind you of a barracks. They're almost equivalent to the rooms at Bananas, a few buildings away, but they're just a bit better. Each unit has a small, tiled, shower-only bathroom. Because of their low rates, they're usually booked solid, often with divers from the United States or residents of the Puerto Rican mainland who want low rates. This place is well known for its hospitable ambience and its open-air restaurant overlooking the ocean (see "Where to Dine" below).

Calle Flamboyan 107C, Barrio Esperanza (P.O. Box 1012), Vieques, PR 00765. ☎ 787/741-8666. Fax 787/741-2964. tradewns@coqui.net. 11 units (shower only). Winter $63–$73 double; off-season $53–63 double. AE, MC, V. **Amenities:** Restaurant/bar; laundry/dry cleaning. *In room:* A/C (in 4 units), coffeemaker, no phone.

Vieques Ocean View Hotel Situated in the heart of Isabel Segunda, directly on the coast and a block from the wharf where the ferry lands, this three-story building is one of the tallest on Vieques. Built in the early 1980s, it offers simple rooms with uncomplicated furniture and balconies overlooking either the sea or the town. Most of the rooms are air-conditioned, and each has a small shower-only bathroom. The hotel restaurant serves Chinese food daily from 11am to 11pm.

Isabel Segunda (P.O. Box 124), Vieques, PR 00765. ☎ 787/741-3696. Fax 787/741-1793. 30 units (shower only). Year-round $82 double. AE, MC, V. **Amenities:** Restaurant, bar; pool. *In room:* A/C (in 25 units), TV, no phone.

WHERE TO DINE
EXPENSIVE

Café Media Luna ★ *Finds* NUEVO LATINO/ASIAN This laid-back joint grew out of a dumpy building in Isabel Segunda. Today a charming little eatery, it is the domain of Ricardo Betancourt, a photographer turned restaurateur, and his wife, Monica, born in Bombay. Ricardo spent some 15 years in New York, photographing jazz musicians (sometimes for their record covers). Thanks to all the contacts he made, he invites many musicians to Vieques for jazz evenings. You are likely to catch the action on Saturday evenings. The kitchen turns out a terrific medley of New Latin cuisine with Asian fusion dishes. It's good and healthy. The appetizers are freshly made concoctions, based on the best shopping on any given day. We like to arrive here with a party, order several appetizers, and share the goodies. The fresh fish and well-flavored meats round out the main dishes. Ask what is good on any given day; the staff gives good advice.

Calle Antonio G. Mellado 351, Isabel Segunda. ☎ 787/741-2594. Reservations required. Main courses $24–$27. AE, MC, V. Wed–Sun 6:30–10pm.

Chef Michel ★★ INTERNATIONAL In the premises of the Inn on the Blue Horizon (see "Where to Stay" above), this restaurant serves the best food on Vieques. Also on-site is a bar that a team of journalists declared as one of their favorites in the world, so consider starting your evening with a drink or two in the octagonal Blue Bar. Meals are served within the inn's main building or beneath an awning on a seafront terrace lined with plants. Menu items include pan-blackened tuna; tenderloin of Black Angus beef; filet of rainbow trout with saffron-flavored butter sauce; and tenderloin of pork, pan-seared, and served with dark rum and sweet spices, with a sauce of caramelized red onions. Expect a crowd of fashion-industry folk, temporarily absent from New York and Los Angeles, and local residents, all mixing in ways that are gregarious, stylish, and usually a lot of fun.

In the Inn on the Blue Horizon, Rte. 996, 1 mile (1.5km) west of Esperanza. ℂ **787/741-3318.** Reservations recommended. Main courses $10–$30. AE, MC, V. Winter Thurs–Mon 6–10pm. Off-season Thurs–Sun 6–10pm. Closed Sept.

La Campesina ★ INTERNATIONAL/PUERTO RICAN   Designed to reflect indigenous dwellings, this restaurant was built a few steps from one of the richest archaeological deposits of Taíno artifacts in the Caribbean. It's located on a hillside about a quarter-mile (.5km) inland from the sea (follow the coast road from Esperanza), in the untrammeled fishing village of La Hueca. In a room lined with baskets and weavings amid trailing vines of jasmine and flickering candles, you can enjoy a cuisine with distinctly tropical or uniquely Puerto Rican flair. The food here features fresh herbs such as cilantro, tasty varieties of local vegetables, and fruits such as papaya, mango, and tamarind served in relishes and pastries. Nightly specials might include avocado rémoulade, conch fritters, lobster ravioli, local fish, and great steak.

La Hueca. ℂ **787/741-1239.** Reservations recommended. Main courses $16–$25. MC, V. Tues–Sat 6–10pm. Closed Oct.

INEXPENSIVE

Bananas Restaurant ★ *Value* INTERNATIONAL   This place serves some of the best food on the island, including familiar fare such as charbroiled New York sirloin, barbecued baby back ribs, and marinated boneless breast of chicken. Slightly more exotic main dishes might include grilled Jamaican-style jerk chicken or lemon chicken sautéed in butter and wine. You might opt instead for the grilled fresh catch of the day. You can also order pizzas with a wide array of toppings and baked potatoes in four different versions, including one with broccoli and chili. Sandwiches are available at lunch, including grilled chicken and fresh fish.

In Bananas Guesthouse, Barrio Esperanza. ℂ **787/741-8700.** Main courses $12.25–$15.50; sandwiches at lunch $5.25–$8. AE, MC, V (tab must exceed $15 to use a credit card). Daily 11am–10pm.

Chez Shack INTERNATIONAL   Chez Shack wins, almost without competition, as the most bohemian and countercultural restaurant on Vieques. The setting is exactly what the name implies—a battered wood-sided utility building that evolved from a virtual ruin after it was acquired by a grizzled and outspoken entrepreneur, Hugh Duffy, who was instrumental in the career of the Mamas and the Papas. This group, when still getting its act together, worked at Duffy's Love Shack in St. Thomas, where Mama Cass was said to have been the world's worst waitress. Today, replete with naughty anecdotes that are among the most valuable currency-in-trade on the island, the site is defined as a local monument. Chez Shack opens for business on summer nights even when other restaurants are closed. Menu items include tried-and-true favorites, many of which attract repeat diners who memorized the menu long ago. Examples include baked crab, seafood cocktail, steaks, fish filets, and barbecued ribs. You'll find the place near the edge of the highway, within the closest thing on Vieques to a tropical rain forest.

Hwy. 995 (Airport Rd.), north of Esperanza. ✆ **787/741-2175.** Reservations recommended. Main courses $14–$20. No credit cards. Mid-Nov–May Wed–Mon 6–11pm; June–Aug Thurs–Sat 6:30–11pm. Closed Sept–mid-Nov.

Trade Winds Restaurant STEAK/SEAFOOD   This restaurant is often recommended by hotel owners across the island and therefore manages to feed the residents of a large cross-section of island hotels. It lies beside the oceanfront esplanade in the fishing village of Esperanza. A dining experience here often begins with a drink at the open-air Topside Bar. For dinner, the chef's specialties revolve around steak, fish, and lobster, which is often served with butter-flavored rum sauce. The best steak is an 8-ounce filet, cooked just right over the charbroiler and served with a baked potato and a house or Caesar salad; also available is herb-marinated pork loin with mashed potatoes. The fresh fish special varies and is usually a good item to order, as is the jumbo shrimp sautéed with garlic and lemon, or served with curry sauce. Black-bean soup is a good opener.

In Trade Winds Guesthouse, Calle Flamboyan, Barrio Esperanza. ✆ **787/741-8666.** Reservations recommended. Main courses $12–$19.50. AE, MC, V. Dec–May daily 7:30am–2pm and 6–9pm; June–Nov Fri–Sun 6–9:30pm.

SHOPPING

There aren't a lot of shopping possibilities in Vieques; however, you might want to visit **Siddhia Hutchinson Fine Art Studio & Gallery,** Calle 3, A15, Isabel Segunda (✆ **787/741-8780**), located between the lighthouse and the ferry dock. Here you can purchase prints of local seascapes and landscapes, native flowers, fish, and birds. There are also lovely bowls, mugs, and platters for sale.

2 Culebra ⟨★

52 miles (84km) E of San Juan, 18 miles (29km) E of Fajardo

A tranquil, inviting little island, Culebra lies in a mini-archipelago of 24 chunks of land, rocks, and cays, 18 miles (29km) east of Puerto Rico's main island and halfway to St. Thomas, U.S. Virgin Islands. It's just 7 miles (11km) long and 3 miles (5km) wide and has only 2,000 residents. The landscape is dotted with everything from scrub and cacti to poincianas, frangipanis, and coconut palms.

Today vacationers and boaters can explore the island's beauties, both on land and underwater. Culebra's white-sand beaches (especially Flamenco Beach), its clear waters, and its long coral reefs invite swimmers, snorkelers, and scuba divers.

Culebra, in what was once called the Spanish Virgin Islands, was settled as a Spanish colony in 1886, but like Puerto Rico and Vieques, it became part of the United States after the Spanish-American War in 1898. In fact, Culebra's only town, a fishing village called **Dewey,** was named for Admiral George Dewey, a U.S. hero of that war, although the locals defiantly call it **Puebla.**

Both illustrious and notorious characters visited Culebra in the past. It is believed that Columbus spotted the island on his second voyage to the New World in 1493. When the Spanish started colonizing Puerto Rico, many of the Taíno Indians fled to Culebra as a last refuge. It wasn't many decades later that the swashbuckling Sir Henry Morgan and other notorious pirates used Culebra as a hideout. The island supposedly still shelters their buried loot.

From 1909 to 1975, the U.S. Navy used Culebra as a gunnery range and as a practice bomb site in World War II. Today the four tracts of the **Culebra Wildlife Refuge,** plus 23 other offshore islands, are managed by the U.S. Fish and Wildlife Service. The refuge is one of the most important turtle-nesting sites in the Caribbean, and it also houses large seabird colonies, notably terns and boobies.

Culebrita, a mile (1.5km) long coral-isle satellite of Culebra, has a hilltop lighthouse and crescent beaches.

ESSENTIALS

GETTING THERE   Vieques Air-Link (© 787/723-9882) flies to Culebra five times daily from San Juan's Isla Grande Airport. One-way transit costs $43; round-trip is $80.

The **Puerto Rico Port Authority** operates one or two **ferries** per day (depending on the day of the week) from the mainland port of Fajardo to Culebra; the trip takes about an hour. The round-trip fare is $5 for adults, $2.25 for children 3 to 12 (free for 2 and under). For reservations, call © **787/863-4560.**

GETTING AROUND   With no public transportation, the only way to get to Culebra's beaches is by bike or rental car.

There are a number of little **rental-car** agencies on the island, although they seem to open and close when the spirit moves them. **Carlos Jeep Rental,** Parcela 2, Barriada Clark, Dewey (© 787/742-3514), lies a 3-minute ride from the airport. The outfitter rents Jeeps for $50 to $60 per day. If you give them notice, they will meet you at the airport. When you drop off your rental, the staff will also drive you back to the airport. Charging exactly the same prices is another reliable operator, **Coral Reef,** Carretera Pedro Marquez 3, Dewey (© 787/ 742-0055). A final option for vehicles is **Willie's Jeep Rental,** Calle Escudero, Barriada Clark, Dewey (© 787/742-3537), lying a 5-minute walk from the airport. Vehicles here begin at $45 per day.

Bike riding is a popular means of getting around the island's hills, dirt trails, and bad roads. You can rent mountain bikes at **Culebra Bike Shop,** Calle Castelar 58, Dewey (© 787/742-2209). The cost is $15 for 24 hours. For the same price, you can also rent bikes from **Dick and Cathy** (© 787/742-0062). To rent from them, call them, and one of them will come by your hotel with your bike.

BEACHES, DIVING & OTHER OUTDOOR PURSUITS

The island's most popular and best beach is **Flamenco Beach** ⋆, a mile (1.5km) long horseshoe-shaped cove on the northwestern edge. It's popular partly because of its nearness to Dewey, partly because of its soft sands. If you find Flamenco too crowded, all you need do is walk over the hill to **Playa Carlos Rosario** ⋆. The sands here aren't quite as good as those at Flamenco, but the snorkeling is even better in these clear waters. A barrier reef protects this beach, so you are almost guaranteed tranquil waters. Snorkelers can also walk south from Playa Carlos Rosario for a quarter mile (.5km) to a place called **"The Wall"** ⋆. There are 40-foot dropoffs into the water where you are likely to see schools of fish gliding by.

The isolated **Zoni Beach** is a 1-mile (1.5km) strip of sand flanked by large boulders and scrub. Located on the island's northeastern edge, about 7 miles (11km) from Dewey (Puebla), it's one of the most beautiful beaches on the island. Snorkelers, but not scuba divers, find it particularly intriguing, despite the surf that makes underwater visibility a bit murky during rough weather.

Known for its beautiful corals, unspoiled underwater vistas, and absence of other divers, Culebra is what the Caribbean used to be before crowds of divers began exploring the sea. At least 50 dive sites, all around the island, are worthwhile. **Culebra Dive Shop,** Calle Escobar 138 (© **787/742-0566;** fax 787/742-1953), offers a resort course for novice divers, including training in a sheltered cove and a tank dive in 15 to 20 feet of water ($90). Full PADI certification costs $450 and requires 5 days of participation in both classroom and ocean experience. Certified divers pay $85 for a two-tank open-water dive. The outfitter provides all the equipment you need for any of the dive experiences. It's rare that more than six divers go out in one of these boats on any day.

Steve Harding, who runs **Culebra Bike Shop** (see "Getting Around" above), rents mountain bikes and beach chairs (two for $5 per day).

Kayak trips are offered by **Jim Petersen's Oceans Safaris,** Calle Escudero 189, Dewey (© **787/379-1973**). Kayaks can be rented for $30 to $40 per half day, and Jim will tell you the best spots to enjoy this sport. He also offers a full-day tour for $75, taking you to such remote islets as Isla Culebrita or Cayo Luis Peña.

WHERE TO STAY

If you operate happily within a rented villa, preparing your own meals, consider making a call to **Pelican Enterprises Vacation Rentals** (© **787/742-0052**). Jim Galasso, the rental agent, knows what's happening with most of the island's rental villas and can probably come up with something that's appropriate for your needs.

MODERATE

Club Seabourne   About an 8-minute drive from the center of town, this concrete-and-wood structure is set in a garden of crotons and palms, at the mouth of one of the island's best harbors, Ensenada Bay. It offers scattered villas and four rooms inside the clubhouse. Each unit has a small, tiled, shower-only bathroom.

Overlooking Fulladosa Bay, the club's dining room serves some of the best food on Culebra, with fresh lobster, shrimp, snapper, grouper, and conch, as well as steaks. The hotel also has a patio bar with a nightly happy hour, plus one of two pools on the island. Dive packages and day sails can be arranged at the office.

Fulladosa Rd. (P.O. Box 357), Culebra, PR 00775. (From Dewey [Puebla], follow Fulladosa Rd. along the south side of the bay for 1½ miles/2.5km.) © **787/742-3169.** Fax 787/742-3176. 13 units (shower only). Winter $165 double; $195 villa. Off-season $135 double; $165 villa. Rates include continental breakfast. AE, MC, V. **Amenities:** Restaurant, bar; pool; gym. *In room:* A/C, fridge, no phone.

Tamarindo Estates *(Finds)*   On 60 lush acres beside a private bay, this is a small, intimate Puerto Rican beachfront resort of kitchen-equipped cottages. Living here is like occupying your second home, with laid-back island living. There is a simple, even pristine, aura here, but comfort nonetheless with panoramic views from the roofed verandas. Each unit has either one or two bedrooms, and when *Travel and Leisure* staffers visited, they named this property one of the 20 great and affordable gateways in the Caribbean. The mecca of this nicely secluded place is a swimming pool with an ocean view and a roofed deck. There is easy access to shoreline snorkeling in gin-clear waters. The resort lies a 10-minute drive from town, and all cottages are screened and have ceiling fans. Each cottage has a shower-only bath. Housekeeping is not provided.

Tamarindo Beach Rd., Culebra, PR 00775. ℭ **787/742-3343**. Fax 787/742-3342. www.tamarindo estates.com. 12 cottages (shower only). Winter $150–$175 double; $265–$285 quad. Off-season $115–$135 double; $195–$225 quad. AE, MC, V. **Amenities:** Pool; beach house. *In room:* A/C, TV, kitchen, coffeemaker.

INEXPENSIVE

Casa Ensenada Waterfront Guesthouse   This is a laid-back tropical-look-ing house with relatively humble but clean and comfortable bedrooms. Many guests begin their day by taking a kayak over to the Dinghy Dock restaurant (see "Where to Dine" below) for breakfast and later return to sunbathe on the patio. In the evening guests gather again on the patio for drinks and for barbecue—the catch of the day on the grill. Each unit is midsize and has a tiled, shower-only bathroom. You can rent the Pequeño unit, which sleeps two in a double bed, or the Grande unit, for four (two in a king-size bed in the master bedroom and two on a double futon in the living room). The on-site Estudio unit sleeps four, in twin beds and a double futon. These latter two units also contain kitchenettes.

Calle Escudero 142, Dewey, Culebra, PR 00775. ℭ **800/484-9659** or 787/742-3559. Fax 787/742-0278. censenada@aol.com. 3 units (shower only). Winter $90–$130; off-season $75–$115. MC, V. **Amenities:** Kayaking; scuba diving; snorkeling; bikes; laundry; library. *In room:* A/C, kitchenette (in 2 units), coffeemaker.

Harbour View Villas *Value*   Set on a 5-acre estate and offering one of the best values on the island, these villas and suites are private but not isolated. They were designed for tropical living, with 12-foot ceilings and big French doors, which open onto the main balcony, with its 180-degree view of the ocean. The bedrooms also have private balconies, which provide panoramic views of the ocean. The complex lies within walking distance of Melones Beach. Five of the units have kitchens, the other has a smaller kitchenette. Each unit has a master bedroom with a queen-size bed; two of the villas have a second bedroom that can accommodate two more guests. Each unit has a small, tiled, shower-only bathroom. Because this is a compound of villas, Harbour View doesn't have the usual hotel amenities, such as housekeeping and room service.

Melones Beach, west of Dewey (P.O. Box 216), Culebra, PR 00775. ℭ **800/440-0070** or 787/742-3855. www.culebrahotel.com. 6 units (shower only). Year-round $95 1-bedroom suite; $150 2-bedroom suite; $125 1-bedroom villa; $175 2-bedroom villa. Extra person $20. No credit cards. *In room:* A/C (in 3 units), kitch-enette, coffeemaker, hair dryer, no phone.

Villa Boheme   This modest guesthouse opens onto views of Ensenada Bay, and its hosts invite you to explore their little island in kayaks or bikes. Out back is a great terrace with hammocks that invite you to lead the life of leisure. The best units are a trio of large efficiencies; they are better equipped than the other units here. Each of another three rooms has a small kitchen with a large refrig-erator. Occupants of the rest of the rooms share a fully equipped modern kitchen that is located in the patio area. Beds range from queen size to twins to king size. Room nos. 2 and 12 can house up to six guests comfortably.

Calle Fulladoza 368, Dewey, Culebra, PR 00775. ℭ or fax **787/742-3508**. www.villaboheme.com. 11 units. Winter $94.83–$136.25 double. Off-season $81–$116 double. Year-round $15 per extra person. AE, MC, V. **Amenities:** Kayaks; bikes; communal kitchen, water taxi. *In room:* A/C, kitchen (in some), no phone.

WHERE TO DINE
MODERATE

Dinghy Dock AMERICAN/CARIBBEAN   For the best preview of laid-back tropical Culebra, head here. The hangout lies on the banks of Ensenada Honda, just south of the Dewey drawbridge, and it has a dock where dinghies and other boats anchor. Come here for the bar or the restaurant—or perhaps both—and meet the locals along with visiting boaters from the Puerto Rican mainland. We like to come here to enjoy margaritas or Puerto Rico's own Medalla beer and watch the sunsets. You can visit three times a day if you wish: tropical fruit-flavored waffles for breakfast, freshly grilled tuna for lunch, and a lobster and rice dish for dinner.

Punta del Soldado Rd., outside Dewey. *C* **787/742-0233.** Reservations not necessary. Breakfast $3–$8; main courses $4–$8 lunch, $11–$20 dinner. MC, V. Daily 7:30–11am, noon–3pm, and 6–9pm.

Mamacita's ★ *Value* CARIBBEAN/PUERTO RICAN   This is not only the island's best bar but one of the choice and affordable dining spots on Culebra. As for the patrons, a waiter confided to us, "We attract modern-day pirates." Locals come here nightly to sample the bartender's special, a Bushwhacker—a lethal concoction of vodka, rum, Bailey's, Kahlua, and coconut. You can also sit on the deck, sipping more conventional drinks, such as a piña colada made with passion fruit, listening to recorded calypso and reggae as the sun sets. The chicken wings deserve the praise they receive, as does the conch salad. The main dishes aren't of the standard of a top San Juan restaurant, but they are satisfying nonetheless, especially the *churrasco*, the fresh sea bass with perfect mashed potatoes, the filet mignon, and the roast loin of pork studded with garlic.

Calle Castelar, Dewey. *C* **787/742-0090.** Reservations not needed. Main courses $5–$10 breakfast, $7–$10 lunch, $13–$24 dinner. MC, V. Daily 8am–4pm and 6–9:30pm.

INEXPENSIVE

El Batey DELI   Across from the harbor and cooled by its breezes, this large, clean establishment maintains a full bar and prepares an array of deli-style sandwiches. They'll hand you a cold beer when the afternoon sun is out, and the pool tables make the place lively, especially on weekends, when many locals come here. Disco reigns on Saturday night. Weekdays, it's much calmer. The owners, Digna Feliciano and Tomás Ayala, have many fans on the island.

Parque de Pelota 250, Carretera. *C* **787/742-3828.** Sandwiches $2.75–$3.75. No credit cards. Sun–Thurs 9am–3pm; Fri 9am–midnight; Sat 9am–2am.

El Caobo PUERTO RICAN   Locals call this place Tina's and view it as one of their favorite food joints on the island. We were told that Tina cooks for the local taste, which means "lot of chickens or roasted garlic, pork, and plenty of rice and beans." Try her grilled chicken or grilled pork cutlet. Tina will also fry these cuts of meat. If the catch came in, she might even grill you some fresh fish.

Calle Luís Muñoz Marín, La Carriada Clark. *C* **787/742-3235.** Reservations not necessary. Main courses $7–$13. No credit cards. Mon–Sat 11am–10:30pm; Sun 11am–4:30pm.

Oasis Pizzeria PIZZA   This is the best place to go for pizza on the island. With its funky decor, it is a popular hangout for local expatriates. In addition to those piping-hot pies, the kitchen also turns out an array of freshly made salads, pastas, and well-stuffed sandwiches. The food here is quite good.

Calle Marques 14, Dewey. *C* **787/742-3175.** Reservations not necessary. Pizzas, sandwiches, and platters $5–$12. No credit cards. Thurs–Mon 6–11pm. Closed first 2 weeks of Oct.

Appendix:
Puerto Rico in Depth

"It's heaven and hell—all rolled into one tiny island," a Trenton, N.J., woman said to us about Puerto Rico on a flight from San Juan to Miami. "My husband loved it. I couldn't wait to get back home. But then he's a golfer and a fisherman, and while he was doing that, there were only so many crafts I could buy."

Ever since Castro in the early 1960s started chasing the gringos out of Havana, Puerto Rico has blossomed as a tourist destination, with its towering mountains, rain forests, long beaches, and vibrant Spanish culture.

The woman we talked to saw only the island's crime, unemployment, bad traffic, and what to her was "poor food." But in spite of its many critics, Puerto Rico must be doing something right. Of course, you can get bad food here, but in many places the island's cuisine, an adaptation of many cooking styles, is the finest in the Caribbean.

History buffs will get more ancient buildings and monuments here than anywhere else in the Caribbean, many of them dating back some 500 years, to the Spanish conquistadores. Add some of the best golf and tennis in the West Indies, posh beach resorts, tranquil and offbeat (though not luxurious) government *paradores* (country inns or guesthouses), and lots of Las Vegas–type gambling, glitter, and extravagant shows, and you've got a formidable attraction.

There are problems here. As in many major cities, you could be mugged or have your car stolen or even hijacked. Service personnel are often gruff and unhelpful. Although there are country retreats where you can escape the masses, San Juan and most of the rest of the island are simply overcrowded.

There is also some anti-United States sentiment here. Not all locals passionately embrace Uncle Sam. When we were seeking some real lowdown salsa joints away from the tourist hordes, a taxi driver told us, "I can take you to a club—maybe several clubs—but I'm not sure you'd get back in one piece."

Despite its drawbacks, we still rate Puerto Rico as one of the top Caribbean destinations, right up there with Aruba, St. Thomas, Jamaica, and Barbados.

1 The Natural Environment: Beaches, Mountains, the Rain Forest, Off-Island Islands & More

Roughly half the size of New Jersey, this U.S. commonwealth with 272 miles (438km) of Atlantic and Caribbean coastline sits strategically some 1,000 miles (1,610km) southeast of Florida at the hub of the Caribbean chain of islands. You'll probably fly in and out of San Juan at least once if you're doing much touring in the region. And with a 2-year, $2.8 million project that restored its waterfront, this oldest capital city under the U.S. flag is also the world's second-largest home port for cruise-ship passengers.

Puerto Rico has experienced many political changes since the days of its first Spanish governor, Juan Ponce de León, the conquistador who sailed with Columbus and who tried in vain to find a fountain of youth in Florida. With nearly 500 years reflected in its restored Spanish colonial architecture, Old San Juan is the Caribbean's greatest historic center.

Puerto Rico is the most easterly and the smallest of the four major islands that form the Greater Antilles. The other three are Cuba, Jamaica, and Hispaniola (which is home to two nations, Haiti and the Dominican Republic). Surrounded by the Atlantic Ocean to the north and the Caribbean Sea to the south, Puerto Rico is flanked by a trio of smaller islands—Vieques and Culebra to the east and Mona to the west—which are its political and geologic satellites.

The island's terrain ranges from palm-lined beaches on four coastlines to rugged mountain ranges, gently rolling hills, and dry desert-like areas. There are 20 designated forest reserves in Puerto Rico.

BEACHES

The island has dozens of miles of sandy beaches, some long and straight, others broken into coves by headlands. On the northern coast, the Atlantic waters are often more turbulent than those along the more tranquil southern coast. (For a more detailed discussion of Puerto Rican beaches, refer to "Beaches" under "The Active Vacation Planner" in chapter 2. For even more strips of sand, refer to the previews of beaches given in the individual chapters of this book.)

TOWERING MOUNTAINS

Besides the beaches, the island's most noteworthy geological feature is the **Cordillera**—the towering mountains that rise high above its central region. Geologists have identified the island's summits as the high parts of a chain of mountains whose mass is mostly submerged beneath the sea. These mountains are some of the oldest of the many landmasses in the West Indies.

What makes the mountain altitudes even more impressive is the existence, about 75 miles (121km) to the island's north, of one of the deepest depressions in the Atlantic, the Puerto Rico Trough. Running more or less parallel to the island's northern shoreline, it plunges to depths of up to 30,000 feet. Although not as obvious as this trench, the sea floor a few miles from the island's southern coast also drops off, to nearly 17,000 feet below sea level. Geologists have calculated that if the base of this mountain chain were at sea level, it would be one of the highest landmasses in the world. Puerto Rico's highest summit— Cerro de Punta, at 4,389 feet—would exceed in altitude Mount Everest, the world's tallest peak.

Most of Puerto Rico's geology, especially its mountain peaks, resulted from volcanic activity that deposited lava and igneous rock in consecutive layers. To a lesser degree, the island is also composed of quartz, diomites, and, along some of its edges, coral limestone.

EL YUNQUE & THE OTHER FOREST PRESERVES

The mountains are home to the island's greatest natural attraction, **El Yunque** (© **787/888-1810** or 787/888-5646 for information), a 45-minute drive east of San Juan. Given national-park status by President Theodore Roosevelt, this 28,000-acre preserve is the only tropical rain forest on U.S. soil and is protected by the U.S. Forest Service.

Today, El Yunque offers visitors close encounters of the natural kind, from picnics amid rare flora and fauna to hikes along scenic trails. Encompassing four distinct forest types, it is home to 240 species of tropical trees; flowers, including more than 20 kinds of orchids; and other wildlife, including millions of tiny tree frogs whose distinctive cry of *coquí* (pronounced "ko-*kee*") has given them their name. For details on touring this unique attraction, refer to chapter 7.

Puerto Rico also has 19 other forest preserves. Directly east of San Juan lies **Piñones Forest,** which contains the island's largest mangrove forest. West of Ponce, **Guánica Forest** borders several white-sand beaches and the historic bay where U.S. troops first landed in 1898 during the Spanish-American War. **Cambalache Forest,** east of Arecibo, contains plantations of eucalyptus, teak, and mahoe trees. The driest vegetation and expansive views to the west coast are found in **Maricao Forest.** Few visitors will have time for a forest preserve other than El Yunque. If you do, make it **Toro Negro Forest Reserve,** which straddles the peaks of the Cordillera in the center of the island and boasts the island's tallest peak, with stunning drops to the Caribbean and the Atlantic. For more details on exploring Toro Negro, refer to the "Ponce" section of chapter 8. All of these forests are open to visitors, and several have picnic areas and campsites.

THE KARST COUNTRY & RIO CAMUY CAVES

One of the most mysterious areas of Puerto Rico is the **Karst Country.** One of the world's strangest rock formations, *karst* is formed by the process of water sinking into limestone. As time goes by, large basins are eroded, forming sinkholes. *Mogotes,* or karstic hillocks, are peaks of earth where the land didn't sink into the erosion pits. The Karst Country lies along the island's north coast, northeast of Mayagüez, in the foothills between Quebradillas and Manatí. The region is filled with an extensive network of caves. One sinkhole contains the 20-acre dish of the world's largest radio/radar telescope at the Arecibo Observatory.

Reached by Route 446, the **Guajataca Forest Reserve** is found here, offering some 25 miles (40km) of trails that take you through some of the most rugged parts of this country.

Eons ago, one of the world's largest underground rivers carved the **Río Camuy Caves** in northwest Puerto Rico, which experts today consider to be among the most spectacular caves on earth. The Río Camuy Caves contain evidence of occupation long before the island was sighted by Columbus in 1493. The first professional explorers of the system were led to the site by local boys already familiar with some of the entrances.

For a journey through this foreboding landscape, refer to chapter 7.

OFF-ISLAND ISLANDS

Three offshore islands—Mona, Vieques, and Culebra—are well worth exploring.

Despite bad publicity generated by U.S. Naval bombing exercises, **Vieques** is the most developed of the offshore islands from a tourist prospective. Shaped like a long fish, its spine is a mountain range that separates it lengthwise from west to east. At 21 miles (34km) in length and 5 miles (8km) in width, Vieques is the largest landmass of the Spanish Virgin Islands.

Although the Spanish referred to both Vieques and Culebra as *las islas inútiles* (the useless islands) because there was no gold to be mined there, they are islands *bonito* for the visitor. Offering the lazy life, Vieques has top-notch inns and excellent and relatively undiscovered dining. Most visitors come here to escape and to enjoy the gorgeous beaches.

Even sleepier than Vieques is the smaller and less developed island of **Culebra.** It's a place where you have to drive carefully to let Mother Hen cross the road. At a distance of some 17 miles (27km) east of the Puerto Rican port of Fajardo, Culebra, from the geologist's point of view, is closer to the U.S. Virgin Islands than "mainland" Puerto Rico. St. Thomas lies only 12 miles (19km) to the east.

With its rugged peaks, sandy beaches, and offshore caves, Culebra can quickly bring out the beach bum in you. Many visitors, in fact, have settled there. As two *culebrenses* (the name of the islanders) confided to us, "If you come here with gringo uptightness, you'll lose it in a few days."

Much of Culebra is a national wildlife refuge—so much so that in summer many of the beaches are closed by the U.S. Fish and Wildlife Service because they are nesting grounds for endangered sea turtles.

For touring details on the Vieques and Culebra, refer to chapter 11.

A unique environment can be found on **Mona Island,** 50 miles (81km) west of Puerto Rico. Like the Galapagos Islands, this untouched island has species that are not found elsewhere. Mona is a protected island, under the management of the U.S. National Park Service and the Puerto Rican Natural Resources Department. Accessible by a sometimes difficult, long boat ride, the island is available for sport diving to those who are willing to rough it. See chapter 8.

2 Puerto Rico Today

As the commonwealth moves more deeply into the new millennium, Puerto Rico continues to make headlines in mainland newspapers. Sometimes the news is good; at other times, troubling.

First the good. Puerto Rico's tourism figures have been rising annually since the beginning of the 21st century; the island's aggressive hotel and marketing promotion seems to be paying off. Travelers from the United States are the major visitors, and their numbers rose steadily throughout the late 1990s. Canadian tourism is also on the rise, and the greatest increase is in Latin American visitors.

The island's 3.56 million people—1 million of whom live in the San Juan metropolitan area—have forged ahead economically and made rapid strides. Their annual income is now the highest in Latin America, and their average life expectancy has risen to 73.8 years. And with the island's economy evolving from agriculture to manufacturing and tourism, a demand for an educated workforce has resulted in the ordinary worker having at least 12 years of schooling.

Tourism represents about 6% of the gross national product. Puerto Rico's present governor, and its first woman governor, Sila M. Calderón, has challenged both the private and public sectors of the tourism industry to double that contribution to the GNP within the next decade. At once both labor intensive and environmentally friendly, tourism is seen as the island's best alternative to continued heavy industrialization in pursuit of new jobs for its people.

Even in the now-prosperous tourism industry, storm clouds loom. The unspoken fear among developers of megaresorts is the possible impact of Cuba reopening to the American tourism market. Before Fidel Castro took over Cuba in 1959, Americans by the thousands flocked to Havana, and Puerto Rico was a mere dot on the tourist map. The island's growth was fueled enormously by the embargo imposed on Castro's communist government.

Now the bad. As part of legislation raising the U.S. minimum wage in 1996, President Bill Clinton vetoed a set of tax breaks for U.S. companies operating on the island. That ended 75 years of federal incentives that attracted stateside industries and helped make Puerto Rico the industrial powerhouse in the West Indies. For example, it produces about half the prescription drugs sold in the United States.

Even with the tax breaks, Puerto Rico struggles with a 12.5% unemployment rate and a per capita income of $8,509, about half the level of the poorest U.S. state, Mississippi.

Mirroring the U.S. mainland, rising crime, drugs, AIDS, unemployment, overpopulation, and more troubles plague Puerto Rico. The island has America's third-highest AIDS rate and the dubious distinction of being a major gateway into the United States for drugs from Latin America. The violence and social ills associated with drugs have beset the island. Although the drug issue is of epidemic proportions, you can visit Puerto Rico and be completely unaware that all this criminal activity is going on around you, especially if you're heading to one of the big, self-sufficient resorts. And efforts are being made to solve the drug problem. Since the mid-1990s, the government has increased the number of police officers, enacted harsher prison sentences for drug dealers, and conducted arms and drug raids—part of a battle to stop the flow of illegal drugs into the United States.

The New Progressive Party wants to make Puerto Rico the 51st state, but the opposition is strong, both on the island and in Congress. A nonbinding reference in 1998 resulted in a defeat of statehood.

3 History 101

IN THE BEGINNING

Although the Spanish occupation was the decisive factor defining Puerto Rico's current culture, the island was settled many thousands of years ago by Amerindians. The oldest archaeological remains yet discovered were unearthed in 1948. Found in a limestone cave a few miles east of San Juan, in Loíza Aldea, the artifacts consisted of conch shells, stone implements, and crude hatchets deposited by tribal peoples during the first century of the Christian Era. These people belonged to an archaic, seminomadic, cave-dwelling culture that had not developed either agriculture or pottery. Some ethnologists suggest that these early inhabitants originated in Florida, immigrated to Cuba, and from there began a steady migration along the West Indian archipelago.

Around A.D. 300, a different group of Amerindians, the Arawaks, migrated to Puerto Rico from the Orinoco Basin in what is now Venezuela. Known by ethnologists as the Saladoids, they were the first of Puerto Rico's inhabitants to make and use pottery, which they decorated with exotic geometric designs in red and white. Subsisting on fish, crabs, and whatever else they could catch, they populated the big island as well as the offshore island of Vieques.

By about A.D. 600, this culture had disappeared, bringing to an end the island's historic era of pottery making. Ethnologists' opinions differ as to whether the tribes were eradicated by new invasions from South America, succumbed to starvation or plague, or simply evolved into the next culture that dominated Puerto Rico—the Ostionoids.

Much less skilled at making pottery than their predecessors but more accomplished at polishing and grinding stones for jewelry and tools, the Ostionoids were the ethnic predecessors of the tribe that became the Taínos. The Taínos inhabited Puerto Rico when it was explored and invaded by the Spanish beginning in 1493. The Taínos were spread throughout the West Indies but reached their greatest development in Puerto Rico and neighboring Hispaniola (the island shared by Haiti and the Dominican Republic).

Ponce de León: Man of Myth & Legend

For an explorer of such myth and legend, Juan Ponce de León still remains an enigma to many historians, his exploits subject to as much myth as fact.

It is known that he was born around 1460 in San Tervas de Campos, a province of Valladolid in Spain, to a noble Castilian family. The red-haired youth grew into an active, aggressive, and perhaps impulsive young man, similar in some respects to Sir Francis Drake in England. After taking part in Spain's Moorish wars, Ponce de León sailed to America with Columbus on his second voyage, in 1493.

In the New World, Ponce de León served as a soldier in the Spanish settlement of Hispaniola, now the island home of Haiti and the Dominican Republic. From 1502 to 1504, he led Spanish forces against Indians in the eastern part of the island, finally defeating them.

In 1508 he explored Puerto Rico, discovering gold on the island and conquering the native tribes within a year. A year later, he was named governor of Puerto Rico and soon rose to become one of the most powerful Europeans in the Americas. From most accounts, Ponce de León was a good governor of Puerto Rico before his political rivals forced him from office in 1512.

At that time he received permission from King Ferdinand to colonize the island of Bimini in the Bahamas. In searching for Bimini, he came upon the northeast coast of Florida, which he at first thought was an island, in the spring of 1513. He named it La Florida because he discovered it at the time of Pascua Florida or "Flowery Easter." He was the first explorer to claim some of the North American mainland for Spain.

The following year he sailed back to Spain, carrying with him 5,000 gold pesos. King Ferdinand ordered him back to Puerto Rico with instructions to colonize both Bimini and Florida. Back in Puerto Rico, Ponce de León ordered the building of the city of San Juan. In 1521 he sailed to Florida with 200 men and supplies to start a colony. This was to be his downfall. Wounded by a poison arrow in his thigh, he was taken back to Cuba in June of 1521 and died there from his wound.

Legend says Ponce de León searched in vain for the so-called Fountain of Youth, first in Bimini and later in Florida. He never once mentioned it in any of his private or official writings—at least those writings that still exist—and historians believe his goal was gold and other treasures (and perhaps to convert the natives to Catholicism).

His legacy lives on at the Casa Blanca in Old San Juan (see "Seeing the Sights" in chapter 6). Casa Blanca is the oldest continuously occupied residence in the Western Hemisphere and the oldest of about 800 Spanish colonial buildings in Old San Juan's National Historic Zone. In 1968 it became a historic national monument. Today the building is the site of the Juan Ponce de León Museum. The conquistador's carved coat of arms greets visitors at the entrance.

Taíno culture impressed the colonial Spanish and it continues to impress modern sociologists. This people's achievements included construction of ceremonial ballparks whose boundaries were marked by upright stone dolmens, development of a universal language, and creation of a complicated religious cosmology. They believed in a hierarchy of deities who inhabited the sky. The god Yocahu was the supreme creator. Another god, Jurancán, was perpetually angry and ruled the power of the hurricane. Myths and traditions were perpetuated through ceremonial dances (*areytos*), drumbeats, oral traditions, and a ceremonial ballgame played between opposing teams (of 10–30 players per team) with a rubber ball; winning this game was thought to bring a good harvest and strong, healthy children. Skilled at agriculture and hunting, the Taínos were also good sailors, canoe makers, and navigators.

About 100 years before the Spanish invasion, the Taínos were challenged by an invading South American tribe—the Caribs. Fierce, warlike, sadistic, and adept at using poison-tipped arrows, the Caribs raided Taíno settlements for slaves (especially female) and bodies for the completion of their rites of cannibalism. Some ethnologists argue that the preeminence of the Taínos, shaken by the attacks of the Caribs, was already jeopardized by the time of the Spanish occupation. In fact, it was the Caribs who fought most effectively against the Europeans; their behavior led the Europeans to unfairly attribute warlike tendencies to all of the island's tribes. A dynamic tension between the Taínos and the Caribs certainly existed when Christopher Columbus landed on Puerto Rico.

To understand Puerto Rico's prehistoric era, it is important to know that the Taínos, far more than the Caribs, contributed greatly to the everyday life and language that evolved during the Spanish occupation. Taíno place names are still used for such towns as Utuado, Mayagüez, Caguas, and Humacao. Many Taíno implements and techniques were copied directly by the Europeans, including the *bohío* (straw hut), the *hamaca* (hammock), the musical instrument known as the maracas, and the method of making bread from the starchy cassava root. Also, many Taíno superstitions and legends were adopted and adapted by the Spanish and still influence the Puerto Rican imagination.

SPAIN, SYPHILIS & SLAVERY

Christopher Columbus became the first European to land on the shores of Puerto Rico, on November 19, 1493, near what would become the town of Aguadilla, during his second voyage to the New World. Giving the island the name San Juan Bautista, he sailed on in search of shores with more obvious riches for the taking. A European foothold on the island was established in 1508, when Juan Ponce de León, the first governor of Puerto Rico, imported colonists from the nearby island of Hispaniola. They founded the town of Caparra, which lay close to the site of present-day San Juan. The town was almost immediately wracked with internal power struggles among the Spanish settlers, who pressed the native peoples into servitude, evangelized them, and frantically sought for gold, thus quickly changing the face of the island.

Meanwhile, the Amerindians began dying at an alarming rate, victims of imported diseases such as smallpox and whooping cough, against which they had no biologic immunity. The natives paid the Spanish back, giving them diseases such as syphilis against which they had little immunity. Both communities reeled, disoriented from their contact with one another. In 1511 the Amerindians rebelled against attempts by the Spanish to enslave them. The rebellion was brutally suppressed by the Spanish forces of Ponce de León, whose muskets and firearms were vastly superior to the hatchets and arrows of the native peoples. In desperation, the Taínos joined forces with their traditional enemies, the Caribs, but even that union did little to check the growth of European power.

Because the Indians languished in slavery, sometimes preferring mass suicide to imprisonment, their work in the fields and mines of Puerto Rico was soon taken over by Africans who were imported by Spanish, Danish, Portuguese, British, and American slavers.

By 1521 the island had been renamed Puerto Rico ("Rich Port") and was one of the most strategic islands in the Caribbean, which was increasingly viewed as a Spanish sea. Officials of the Spanish Crown dubbed the island "the strongest foothold of Spain in America" and hastened to strengthen the already impressive bulwarks surrounding the city of San Juan.

PIRATES & PILLAGING ENGLISHMEN

Within a century, Puerto Rico's position at the easternmost edge of what would become Spanish America helped it play a major part in the Spanish expansion toward Florida, the South American coast, and Mexico. It was usually the first port of call for Spanish ships arriving in the Americas; recognizing that the island was a strategic keystone, the Spanish decided to strengthen its defenses. By 1540, La Fortaleza, the first of three massive fortresses built in San Juan, was completed. By 1600, San Juan was completely enclosed by some of the most formidable ramparts in the Caribbean, whereas, ironically, the remainder of Puerto Rico was almost defenseless. In 1565 the king of Spain ordered the governor of Puerto Rico to provide men and materials to strengthen the city of St. Augustine, Florida.

By this time, the English (and to a lesser extent, the French) were seriously harassing Spanish shipping in the Caribbean and north Atlantic. At least part of the French and English aggression was in retaliation for the 1493 Papal Bull dividing the New World between Portugal and Spain—an arrangement that eliminated all other nations from the spoils and colonization of the New World.

Queen Elizabeth I's most effective weapon against Spanish expansion in the Caribbean wasn't the Royal Navy; rather, it was buccaneers such as John Hawkins and Sir Francis Drake. Their victories included the destruction of St. Augustine in Florida, Cartagena in Colombia, and Santo Domingo in what is now the Dominican Republic, and the general harassment and pillaging of many Spanish ships and treasure convoys sailing from the New World to Europe with gold and silver from the Aztec and Inca empires. The Royal Navy did play an important role, however, for its 1588 defeat of the Spanish Armada marked the rise of the English as a major maritime power. The Spanish then began to aggressively fortify such islands as Puerto Rico.

In 1595, Drake and Hawkins persuaded Queen Elizabeth to embark on a bold and daring plan to invade and conquer Puerto Rico. An English general, the Earl of Cumberland, urged his men to bravery by "assuring your selves you have the maydenhead of Puerto Rico and so possesse the keyes of all the Indies." Confident that the island was "the very key of the West Indies which locketh and shutteth all the gold and silver in the continent of America and Brasilia," he brought into battle an English force of 4,500 soldiers and eventually captured La Fortaleza.

Although the occupation lasted a full 65 days, the English eventually abandoned Puerto Rico when their armies were decimated by tropical diseases and the local population, which began to engage in a kind of guerrilla warfare against the English. After pillaging and destroying much of the Puerto Rican countryside, the English left. Their short but abortive victory compelled the Spanish king, Philip III, to continue construction of the island's defenses. Despite these efforts, Puerto Rico retained a less-than-invincible aspect as Spanish soldiers in the forts often deserted or succumbed to tropical diseases.

A DUTCH TREAT

In 1625 Puerto Rico was covetously eyed by Holland, whose traders and merchants desperately wanted a foothold in the West Indies. Spearheaded by the Dutch West India Company, which had received trading concessions from the Dutch Crown covering most of the West Indies, the Dutch armies besieged El Morro Fortress in San Juan in one of the bloodiest assaults the fortress ever sustained. When the commanding officer of El Morro refused to surrender, the Dutch burned San Juan to the ground, including all church and civil archives and the bishop's library, by then the most famous and complete collection of books in America. Fueled by rage, the Spanish rallied and soon defeated the Dutch.

In response to the destruction of the strongest link in the chain of Spanish defenses, Spain threw itself wholeheartedly into improving and reinforcing the defenses around San Juan. King Philip IV justified his expenditures by declaring Puerto Rico the "front and vanguard of the Western Indies and, consequently, the most important of them and most coveted by the enemies of Spain."

Within 150 years, after extravagant expenditures of time and money, San Juan's walls were considered almost impregnable. Military sophistication was added during the 1760s, when two Irishmen, Tomas O'Daly and Alejandro O'Reilly, surrounded the city with some of Europe's most up-to-date defenses. Despite the thick walls, however, the island's defenses remained precarious because of the frequent tropical epidemics that devastated the ranks of the soldiers; the chronically late pay, which weakened the soldiers' morale; and the belated and often wrong-minded priorities of the Spanish monarchy.

A CATHOLIC CRUSADE

From the earliest days of Spanish colonization, an army of priests and missionaries embarked on a vigorous crusade to convert Puerto Rico's Taínos to Roman Catholicism. King Ferdinand himself paid for the construction of a Franciscan monastery and a series of chapels, and he required specific support of the church from the aristocrats who had been awarded land grants in the new territories. They were required to build churches, provide Christian burials, and grant religious instruction to both Taíno and African slaves.

Among the church's most important activities were the Franciscan monks' efforts to teach the island's children how to read, write, and count. In 1688 Bishop Francisco Padilla, who is now included among the legends of Puerto Rico, established one of the island's most famous schools. When it became clear that local parents were too poor to provide their children with appropriate clothing, he succeeded in persuading the king of Spain to pay for their clothes.

Puerto Rico was declared by the pope as the first *see* (ecclesiastical headquarters) in the New World. In 1519 it became the general headquarters of the Inquisition in the New World. (About 70 years later, the Inquisition's headquarters was transferred to the well-defended city of Cartagena, Colombia.)

FROM SMUGGLING TO SUGAR

The island's early development was shackled by Spain's insistence on a centrist economy. All goods exported from or imported to Puerto Rico had to pass through Spain itself, usually through Seville. In effect, this policy prohibited any official trade between Puerto Rico and its island neighbors.

In response, a flourishing black market developed. Cities such as Ponce became smuggling centers. This black market was especially prevalent after the Spanish colonization of Mexico and Peru, when many Spanish goods, which once would have been sent to Puerto Rico, ended up in those more immediately lucrative colonies instead. Although smugglers were punished if caught, nothing could curb this illegal (and untaxed) trade. Some historians estimate that almost everyone on the island—including priests, citizens, and military and civic authorities—was actively involved in smuggling.

By the mid-1500s, the several hundred settlers who had immigrated to Puerto Rico from Spain heard and sometimes believed rumors of the fortunes to be made in the gold mines of Peru. When the island's population declined because of the ensuing mass exodus, the king enticed 500 families from the Canary Islands to settle on Puerto Rico between 1683 and 1691. Meanwhile, an active trade in slaves—imported as labor for fields that were increasingly used for sugarcane and tobacco production—swelled the island's ranks. This happened despite the Crown's imposition of strict controls on the number of slaves that could be brought in. Sugarcane earned profits for many islanders, but Spanish mismanagement, fraud within the government bureaucracy, and a lack of both labor and ships to transport the finished product to market discouraged the fledgling industry. Later, fortunes were made and lost in the production of ginger, an industry that died as soon as the Spanish government raised taxes on ginger imports to exorbitant levels. Despite the arrival of immigrants to Puerto Rico from many countries, diseases such as spotted fever, yellow fever, malaria, smallpox, and measles wiped out the population almost as fast as it grew.

MORE SMUGGLING

As the philosophical and political movement known as the Enlightenment swept both Europe and North America during the late 1700s and the 1800s, Spain moved to improve Puerto Rico's economy through its local government. The island's defenses were beefed up, roads and bridges were built, and a public education program was launched. The island remained a major Spanish naval stronghold in the New World. Immigration from Europe and other places more than tripled the population. It was during this era that Puerto Rico began to develop a unique identity of its own, a native pride, and a consciousness of its importance within the Caribbean.

The heavily fortified city of San Juan, the island's civic centerpiece, remained under Spain's rigid control. Although it was the victim of an occasional pirate raid, or an attack by English or French forces, the outlying countryside was generally left alone to develop its own local power centers. The city of Ponce, for example, flourished under the Spanish Crown's lax supervision and grew wealthy from the tons of contraband and the high-quality sugar that passed through its port. This trend was also encouraged by the unrealistic law that declared San Juan the island's only legal port. Contemporary sources, in fact, cite the fledgling United States as among the most active of Ponce's early contraband trading partners.

RISING POWER

During the 18th century, the number of towns on the island grew rapidly. There were five settlements in Puerto Rico in 1700; 100 years later, there were almost 40 settlements, and the island's population had grown to more than 150,000.

Meanwhile, the waters of the Caribbean increasingly reflected the diplomatic wars unfolding in Europe. In 1797 the British, after easily capturing Trinidad (which was poorly defended by the Spanish), failed in a spectacular effort to conquer Puerto Rico. The *criollos,* or native Puerto Ricans, played a major role in the island's defense and later retained a growing sense of their cultural identity.

The islanders were becoming aware that Spain could not enforce the hundreds of laws it had previously imposed to support its centrist trade policies. Thousands of merchants, farmers, and civil authorities traded profitably with privateers from various nations, thereby deepening the tendency to evade or ignore the laws imposed by Spain and its colonial governors. The attacks by privateers on British shipping were especially severe because pirates based in Puerto Rico ranged as far south as Trinidad, bringing dozens of captured British ships into Puerto Rican harbors. (Several decades earlier, British privateers operating out of Jamaica had endlessly harassed Spanish shipping; the tradition of government-sanctioned piracy was well established.)

It was during this period that coffee—which would later play an essential role in the island's economy—was introduced to the Puerto Rican highlands from the nearby Dominican Republic.

Despite the power of San Juan and its Spanish institutions, 18th-century Puerto Rico was predominantly rural. The report of a special emissary of the Spanish king, Marshal Alejandro O'Reilly, remains a remarkably complete analysis of 18th-century Puerto Rican society. It helped promote a more progressive series of fiscal and administrative policies that reflected the Enlightenment ideals found in many European countries.

Puerto Rico began to be viewed as a potential source of income for the Spanish Empire rather than a drain on income. One of O'Reilly's most visible legacies was his recommendation that people live in towns rather than be scattered about the countryside. Shortly after this, seven new towns were established.

As the island prospered and its bourgeoisie became more numerous and affluent, life became more refined. New public buildings were erected; concerts were introduced; and everyday aspects of life—such as furniture and social ritual—grew more ornate. Insights into Puerto Rico's changing life can be seen in the works of its most famous 18th-century painter, José Campeche.

THE LAST BASTION

Much of the politics of 19th-century Latin America cannot be understood without a review of Spain's problems at that time. Up until 1850, there was political and military turmoil in Spain, a combination that eventually led to the collapse of its empire. Since 1796, Spain had been a military satellite of postrevolutionary France, an alliance that brought it into conflict with England. In 1804 Admiral Horatio Lord Nelson's definitive victory for England over French and Spanish ships during the Battle of Trafalgar left England in supreme control of the international sea lanes and interrupted trade and communications between Spain and its colonies in the New World.

These events led to changes for Spanish-speaking America. The revolutionary fervor of Simón Bolívar and his South American compatriots spilled over to the entire continent, embroiling Spain in a desperate attempt to hold on to the tattered remains of its empire. Recognizing that Puerto Rico and Cuba were probably the last bastions of Spanish Royalist sympathy in the Americas, Spain liberalized its trade policies, decreeing that goods no longer had to pass through Seville.

The sheer weight and volume of illegal Puerto Rican trade with such countries as Denmark, France, and—most important—the United States, forced Spain's hand in establishing a realistic set of trade reforms. A bloody revolution in Haiti, which had produced more sugarcane than almost any other West Indies island, spurred sugarcane and coffee production in Puerto Rico. Also important was the introduction of a new and more prolific species of sugarcane, the Otahiti, which helped increase production even more.

By the 1820s the United States was providing ample supplies of such staples as lumber, salt, butter, fish, grain, and foodstuffs, and huge amounts of Puerto Rican sugar, molasses, coffee, and rum were consumed in the United States. Meanwhile, the United States was increasingly viewed as the keeper of the peace in the Caribbean, suppressing the piracy that flourished while Spain's navy was preoccupied with its European wars.

During Venezuela's separation from Spain, Venezuelans loyal to the Spanish Crown fled en masse to the remaining Royalist bastions in the Americas— Puerto Rico and, to a lesser extent, Cuba. Although many arrived penniless, having forfeited their properties in South America in exchange for their lives, their excellent understanding of agriculture and commerce probably catalyzed much of the era's economic development in Puerto Rico. Simultaneously, many historians argue, their unflinching loyalty to the Spanish Crown contributed to one of the most conservative and reactionary social structures anywhere in the Spanish-speaking Caribbean. In any event, dozens of Spanish naval expeditions that were intended to suppress the revolutions in Venezuela were outfitted in Puerto Rican harbors during this period.

A REVOLT SUPPRESSED & SLAVERY ABOLISHED

During the latter half of the 19th century, political divisions were drawn in Puerto Rico, reflecting both the political instability in Spain and the increasing demands of Puerto Ricans for some form of self-rule. As governments and regimes in Spain rose and fell, Spanish policies toward its colonies in the New World changed, too.

In 1865 representatives from Puerto Rico, Cuba, and the Philippines were invited to Madrid to air their grievances as part of a process of liberalizing Spanish colonial policy. Reforms, however, did not follow as promised, and a much-publicized and very visible minirevolt (during which the mountain city of Lares was occupied) was suppressed by the Spanish governors in 1868. Some of the funds and much of the publicity for this revolt came from expatriate Puerto Ricans living in Chile, St. Thomas, and New York.

Slavery was abolished in March 1873, about 40 years after it had been abolished throughout the British Empire. About 32,000 slaves were freed following years of liberal agitation. Abolition was viewed as a major victory for liberal forces throughout Puerto Rico, although cynics claim that slavery was much less entrenched in Puerto Rico than in neighboring Cuba, where the sugar economy was far more dependent on slave labor.

The 1895 revolution in Cuba increased the Puerto Rican demand for greater self-rule; during the ensuing intellectual ferment, many political parties emerged. The Cuban revolution provided part of the spark that led to the Spanish-American War, Cuban independence, and U.S. control of Puerto Rico, the Philippines, and the Pacific island of Guam.

THE YANKS ARE COMING, THE YANKS ARE COMING!

In 1897, faced with intense pressure from sources within Puerto Rico, a weakened Spain granted its colony a measure of autonomy, but it came too late. Other events were taking place between Spain and the United States that would forever change the future of Puerto Rico.

On February 15, 1898, the U.S. battleship *Maine* was blown up in the harbor of Havana, killing 266 men. The so-called yellow press in the United States, especially the papers owned by the tycoon William Randolph Hearst, aroused Americans' emotions into a fever pitch for war, with the rallying cry "Remember the *Maine.*"

On April 20 of that year, President William McKinley signed a resolution demanding Spanish withdrawal from Cuba. The president ordered a blockade of Cuba's ports, and on April 24, Spain, in retaliation, declared a state of war with the United States. On April 25, the U.S. Congress declared war on Spain. In Cuba, the naval battle of Santiago was won by American forces, and in another part of the world, the Spanish colony of the Philippines was also captured by U.S. troops.

On July 25, after their victory at Santiago, U.S. troops landed at Guánica, Puerto Rico, and several days later they took over Ponce. U.S. Navy Capt. Alfred T. Mahan later wrote that the United States viewed Puerto Rico, Spain's remaining colonial outpost in the Caribbean, as vital to American interests in the area. Puerto Rico could be used as a military base to help the United States maintain control of the Isthmus of Panama and to keep communications and traffic flowing between the Atlantic and the Pacific.

Spain offered to trade other territory for Puerto Rico, but the United States refused and demanded Spain's ouster from the island. Left with little choice against superior U.S. forces, Spain capitulated. The Spanish-American War ended on August 31, 1898, with the surrender of Spain and the virtual collapse of the once-powerful Spanish Empire. Puerto Rico, in the words of McKinley, was to "become a territory of the United States."

Although the entire war lasted just over 4 months, the invasion of Puerto Rico took only 2 weeks. "It wasn't much of a war," remarked Theodore Roosevelt, who had led the Rough Riders cavalry outfit in their charge up San Juan Hill, "but it was all the war there was." The United States had suffered only four casualties while acquiring Puerto Rico, the Philippines, and the island of Guam. The Treaty of Paris, signed on December 10, 1898, settled the terms of Spain's surrender.

A DUBIOUS PRIZE

Some Americans looked on Puerto Rico as a "dubious prize." One-third of the population consisted of mulattoes and blacks, descended from slaves, who had no money or land. Only about 12% of the population could read or write. About 8% were enrolled in school. It is estimated that a powerful landed gentry—only about 2% of the population—owned more than two-thirds of the land.

Washington set up a military government in Puerto Rico, headed by the War Department. A series of governors-general were appointed to rule the island, with almost the authority of dictators. Although ruling over a rather unhappy populace, these governors-general brought about much-needed change, including tax and public health reforms. But most Puerto Ricans wanted autonomy, and many leaders, including Luís Muñoz Rivera, tried to persuade Washington to compromise. However, their protests generally fell on deaf ears.

Tensions mounted between Puerto Ricans and their new American governors. In 1900, U.S. Secretary of War Elihu Root decided that military rule of the island was inadequate; he advocated a program of autonomy that won the endorsement of President McKinley.

The island's beleaguered economy was further devastated by an 1899 hurricane that caused millions of dollars' worth of property damage, killed 3,000 people, and left one out of four people homeless. Belatedly, Congress allocated the sum of $200,000, but this did little to relieve the suffering.

Thus began a nearly 50-year colonial protectorate relationship, as Puerto Rico was recognized as an unincorporated territory with its governor named by the president of the United States. Only the president had the right to override the veto of the island's governors. The legislative branch was composed of an 11-member executive committee appointed by the president, plus a 35-member chamber of delegates elected by popular vote. A resident commissioner, it was agreed, would represent Puerto Rico in Congress, "with voice but no vote."

As the United States prepared to enter World War I in 1917, Puerto Ricans were granted U.S. citizenship and, thus, were subject to military service. The people of Puerto Rico were allowed to elect their legislature, which had been reorganized into a Senate and a House of Representatives. The president of the United States continued to appoint the governor of the island and retained the power to veto any of the governor's actions.

FROM HARVARD TO REVOLUTION

Many Puerto Ricans continued, at times rather violently, to agitate for independence. Requests for a plebiscite were constantly turned down. Meanwhile, economic conditions improved, as the island's population began to grow dramatically. Government revenues increased as large corporations from the U.S. mainland found Puerto Rico a profitable place in which to do business. There was much labor unrest, and by 1909, a labor movement demanding better working conditions and higher wages was gaining momentum.

The emerging labor movement showed its strength by organizing a cigar workers' strike in 1914 and a sugarcane workers' strike the following year. The 1930s proved to be disastrous for Puerto Rico, which suffered greatly from the worldwide depression. To make matters worse, two devastating hurricanes—one in 1928 and another in 1932—destroyed millions of dollars' worth of crops and property. There was also an outbreak of disease that demoralized the population. Some relief came in the form of food shipments authorized by Congress.

As tension between Puerto Rico and the United States intensified, there emerged Pedro Albizu Campos, a graduate of Harvard Law School and a former U.S. Army officer. Leading a group of militant anti-American revolutionaries, he held that America's claim to Puerto Rico was illegal, since the island had already been granted autonomy by Spain. Terrorist acts by his followers, including assassinations, led to Albizu's imprisonment, but terrorist activities continued.

In 1935 President Franklin D. Roosevelt launched the Puerto Rican Reconstruction Administration, which provided for agricultural development, public works, and electrification. The following year, Sen. Millard E. Tidings of Maryland introduced a measure to grant independence to the island. His efforts were cheered by a local leader, Luís Muñoz Marín, son of the statesman Luís Muñoz Rivera. In 1938 the young Muñoz founded the Popular Democratic Party, which adopted the slogan "Bread, Land, and Liberty." By 1940 this party had gained control of more than 50% of the seats of both the upper and lower houses of government, and the young Muñoz was elected leader of the Senate.

Roosevelt appointed Rexford Guy Tugwell governor of Puerto Rico; Tugwell spoke Spanish and seemed to have genuine concern for the plight of the islanders. Muñoz met with Tugwell and convinced him that Puerto Rico was capable of electing its own governor. As a step in that direction, Roosevelt appointed Jesús Piñero as the first resident commissioner of the island. In 1944 the U.S. Congress approved a bill granting Puerto Rico the right to elect its own governor. This was the beginning of the famed Operation Bootstrap, a pump-priming fiscal and economic aid package designed to improve the island's standard of living.

SHOOTING AT HARRY

In 1946 President Harry S. Truman appointed native-born Jesús Piñero as governor of Puerto Rico, and the following year the U.S. Congress recognized the right of Puerto Ricans to elect their own governor. In 1948, Luís Muñoz Marín became the first elected governor and immediately recommended that Puerto Rico be transformed into an "associated free state." Endorsement of his plan was delayed by Washington, but President Truman approved the Puerto Rican Commonwealth Bill in 1950, providing for a plebiscite in which voters would decide whether they would remain a colony or become a U.S. commonwealth. In June 1951, Puerto Ricans voted three to one for commonwealth status, and on July 25, 1952, the Commonwealth of Puerto Rico was born.

This event was marred when a group of nationalists marched on the Governor's Mansion in San Juan, resulting in 27 deaths and hundreds of casualties. A month later, two Puerto Rican nationalists made an unsuccessful attempt on Truman's life in Washington, killing a police officer in the process. And in March 1954, four Puerto Rican nationalists wounded five U.S. Congressmen when they fired down into the House of Representatives from the visitors' gallery.

Despite this violence, during the 1950s Puerto Rico began to take pride in its culture and traditions. In 1955 the Institute of Puerto Rican Culture was established, and 1957 saw the inauguration of the Pablo Casals Festival, which launched a renaissance of classical music and a celebration of the arts. In 1959 a wealthy industrialist, Luís A. Ferré, donated his personal art collection toward the establishment of the Museo de Arte de Ponce.

GIVE ME LIBERTY OR GIVE ME STATEHOOD

Luís Muñoz Marín resigned from office in 1964, but his party continued to win subsequent elections. The Independent Party, which demanded complete autonomy, gradually lost power. An election on July 23, 1967, reconfirmed the desire of most Puerto Ricans to maintain commonwealth status. In 1968 Luís A. Ferré won a close race for governor, spearheading a pro-statehood party, the New Progressive Party. It staunchly advocated statehood as an alternative to the island's commonwealth status, but in 1972, the Partido Popular Democrático returned to power; by then, the island's economy was based largely on tourism, rum, and industry. Operation Bootstrap had been successful in creating thousands of new jobs, although more than 100,000 Puerto Ricans moved to the U.S. mainland during the 1950s, seeking a better life. The island's economy continued to improve, although perhaps not as quickly as anticipated by Operation Bootstrap.

Puerto Rico grabbed the world's attention in 1979 with the launching of the Pan-American Games. The island's culture received a boost in 1981 with the opening of the Center of the Performing Arts in San Juan, which attracted world-famous performers and virtuosos. The international spotlight again focused on Puerto Rico at the time of the first papal visit there in 1986. John Paul II (or Juan Pablo II, as he was called locally) kindled a renewed interest in religion, especially among the Catholic youth of the island.

In 1996, Puerto Rico lost its special tax-break status, which had originally lured U.S. industry to the island. Down the road, some dire consequences to the island's economy are predicted as a result of this loss.

A flare-up between the U.S. Navy and Puerto Ricans, especially the islanders of Vieques, burst into the headlines in 1999. Islanders vehemently protested the Navy's use of Vieques for the testing of bombardments.

In 2001, Sila M. Calderón was inaugurated as Puerto Rico's first female governor. The daughter of a rich entrepreneur whose holdings include ice-cream factories and hotels, she was raised to a life of privilege. As head of the Popular Democratic Party, she took office and immediately angered Washington by advocating that the U.S. Navy halt bombing on Vieques. She also opposes statehood for Puerto Rico. "When I was a little girl everybody who had power were men," the new governor told the press. "Now girls know that it is very normal for power to be shared by men and women."

Under a new president, George W. Bush, the administration in 2002 announced that it is planning to withdraw the Navy from Vieques and seek another spot to conduct the Atlantic fleet's bombing exercises. A Navy-appointed panel is searching for a new training site.

4 A Portrait of the Puerto Ricans

The people of Puerto Rico represent a mix of races, cultures, languages, and religions. They draw their heritage from the original native population, from Spanish royalists who sought refuge here, from African slaves imported to work the sugar plantations, and from other Caribbean islanders who have come here seeking jobs. The Spanish they speak is a mix, too, with many words borrowed from the pre-Columbian Amerindian tongue as well as English. Even the Catholicism they practice incorporates some Taíno and African traditions.

THE ISLANDERS

Some 3.56 million people inhabit the main island of Puerto Rico, making it one of the most densely populated islands in the world. It has an average of about 1,000 people per square mile, a ratio higher than that of any of the 50 states. It is estimated that if the 2 million Puerto Ricans who have migrated to the United States (more Puerto Ricans are said to live in New York City than in San Juan) were to return home, the island would be so crowded that there would be virtually no room for them to live.

When the United States acquired the island in 1898, most Puerto Ricans worked in agriculture; today most jobs are industrial. One-third of Puerto Rico's population is concentrated in the San Juan metropolitan area.

When the Spanish forced the Taíno peoples into slavery, virtually the entire indigenous population was decimated, except for a few Amerindians who escaped into the remote mountains. Eventually they intermarried with the poor Spanish farmers and became known as *jíbaros*. Because of industrialization and migration to the cities, few jíbaros remain.

Besides the slaves imported from Africa to work on the plantations, other ethnic groups joined the island's racial mix. Fleeing Simón Bolívar's independence movements in South America, Spanish loyalists headed to Puerto Rico—a fiercely conservative Spanish colony during the early 1800s. French families also flocked here from both Louisiana and Haiti, as changing governments or violent revolutions turned their worlds upside down. As word of the rich sugarcane economy reached economically depressed Scotland and Ireland, many farmers from those countries also journeyed to Puerto Rico in search of a better life.

During the mid-19th century, labor was needed to build roads. Initially, Chinese workers were imported for this task, followed by workers from countries such as Italy, France, Germany, and even Lebanon. American expatriates came to the island after 1898. Long after Spain had lost control of Puerto Rico, Spanish immigrants continued to arrive on the island. The most significant new immigrant population arrived in the 1960s, when thousands of Cubans fled from Fidel Castro's communist state. The latest arrivals in Puerto Rico have come from the economically depressed Dominican Republic.

THEIR LANGUAGES

Spanish is the language of Puerto Rico, although English is widely spoken, especially in hotels, restaurants, shops, and nightclubs that attract tourists. In the hinterlands, however, Spanish prevails.

If you plan to travel extensively in Puerto Rico but don't speak Spanish, pick up a Spanish-language phrase book. The most popular is *Berlitz Spanish for Travelers,* published by Collier Macmillan. The University of Chicago's *Pocketbook Dictionary* is equally helpful. If you have a basic knowledge of Spanish and want to improve your word usage and your sentence structure, consider purchasing a copy of *Spanish Now,* published by Barron's.

Many Amerindian words from pre-Columbian times have been retained in the language. For example, the Puerto Rican national anthem, titled "La Borinqueña," refers to the Arawak name for the island Borinquén, and Mayagüez, Yauco, Caguas, Guaynabo, and Arecibo are all pre-Columbian place names.

Many Amerindian words were borrowed to describe the phenomena of the New World. The natives slept in *hamacas,* and today Puerto Ricans still lounge in hammocks. The god Juracán was feared by the Arawaks just as much as contemporaries fear autumn hurricanes. African words were also added to the linguistic mix, and Castilian Spanish was significantly modified.

With the American takeover in 1898, English became the first Germanic language to be introduced into Puerto Rico. This linguistic marriage led to what some scholars call Spanglish, a colloquial dialect blending English and Spanish into forms not considered classically correct in either linguistic tradition.

The bilingual confusion was also greatly accelerated by the mass migration to the U.S. mainland of thousands of Puerto Ricans, who quickly altered their speech patterns to conform to the language used in the urban Puerto Rican communities of cities such as New York.

THEIR RELIGIONS

The majority of Puerto Ricans are Roman Catholic, but religious freedom for all faiths is guaranteed by the Commonwealth Constitution. There is a Jewish Community Center in Miramar, and there's a Jewish Reformed Congregation in Santurce. There are Protestant services for Baptists, Episcopalians, Lutherans, and Presbyterians, and there are other interdenominational services.

Although it is predominantly Catholic, Puerto Rico does not follow Catholic dogma and rituals as assiduously as do the churches of Spain and Italy. Because the church supported slavery, there was a long-lasting resentment against the all-Spanish clergy of colonial days. Island-born men were excluded from the priesthood. When Puerto Ricans eventually took over the Catholic churches on the island, they followed some guidelines from Spain and Italy but modified or ignored others.

Following the U.S. acquisition of the island in 1898, Protestantism grew in influence and popularity. There were Protestants on the island before the invasion, but their numbers increased after Puerto Rico became a U.S. colony. Many islanders liked the idea of separation of church and state, as provided for in the U.S. Constitution. In recent years, Pentecostal fundamentalism has swept across the island. There are some 1,500 Evangelical churches in Puerto Rico today.

As throughout Latin America, the practice of Catholicism in Puerto Rico blends native Taíno and African traditions with mainstream tenets of the faith. It has been said that the real religion of Puerto Rico is *espiritsmo* (spiritualism), a quasi-magical belief in occult forces. Spanish colonial rulers outlawed spiritualism, but under the U.S. occupation it flourished in dozens of isolated pockets of the island.

Students of religion trace spiritualism to the Taínos, and to their belief that *jípia* (the spirits of the dead—somewhat like the legendary vampire) slumbered by day and prowled the island by night. Instead of looking for bodies, the jípia were seeking wild fruit to eat. Thus arose the Puerto Rican tradition of putting out fruit on the kitchen table. Even in modern homes today, you'll often find a bowl of plastic, flamboyantly colored fruit resting atop a refrigerator.

Many islanders still believe in the "evil eye," or *mal de ojo*. To look on a person or a person's possessions covetously, according to believers, can lead to that individual's sickness or perhaps death. Children are given bead charm bracelets to guard against the evil eye. Spiritualism also extends into healing, folk medicine, and food. For example, some spiritualists believe that cold food should never be eaten with hot food. Some island plants, herbs, and oils are believed to have healing properties, and spiritualist literature is available throughout the island.

Index

See also Accommodations index, below.